A
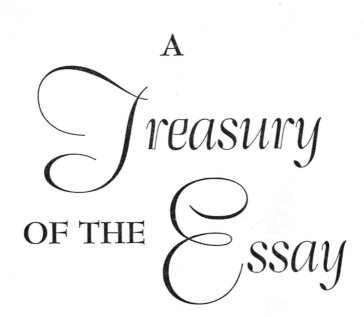

Treasury

OF THE Essay

FROM MONTAIGNE TO E. B. WHITE

Edited by

HOMER C. COMBS

Associate Professor of English
Washington University

Chicago
SPENCER PRESS, *Inc.*

Preface

This collection of essays is intended to provide readers, including students, with pleasing and profitable examples of the essay in English from its beginnings to the present. I have attempted to preserve enough familiar selections and to offer sufficient new materials to make the reader of English literature at once comfortable and stimulated.

The arrangement of these essays is chronological according to the birth dates of the authors—an arbitrary order, it is true, but one which is probably as logical as any other.

I wish to thank especially the following professors who have given me assistance and encouragement in the preparation of this book: Don Cameron Allen, of The Johns Hopkins University, to whom I am indebted for the use of his excellent text of Cornwallis; Alexander McIntosh Buchan, of Washington University; J. N. Douglas Bush, of Harvard University; Charles Carroll Camden, of The Rice Institute; H. L. Creek, of Purdue University; William B. Hunter, Jr., of Wofford College; William Roy Mackenzie, of Washington University; Ney MacMinn, of Northwestern University; James P. McCormick, of Wayne University; Richard Murphy, of the University of Illinois; and Louise Pound, of the University of Nebraska. My wife, Florence Palmer Combs, has helped greatly in the preparation of this volume— in the evaluation of hundreds of essays, in editing the text, and in typing the final manuscript.

Authors and publishers have been most generous in giving permission to reprint copyrighted material. The formal acknowledgments, appearing on the first page of each copyrighted selection, alone would be cold and insufficient recognition without this added word of thanks.

H. C. C.

WASHINGTON UNIVERSITY
ST. LOUIS, MISSOURI
October 29, 1949

Table of Contents

Introduction

Definitions of the essay abound, and yet no one has ever been able to confine it in a phrase. The best proof of the difficulty of assigning any final boundaries to the essay is found in the many terms used to describe it: personal, familiar, gnomic, aphoristic, formal, critical, biographical, and so on. The truth is that it cannot be limited as to either form or content. Charles Lamb, writing in the guise of a "friend of the late Elia," described his own kind of essay as "a sort of unlicked, incondite thing." However, one element in all definitions seems to be fairly constant—the personal point of view of the writer. It is this personal expression, more than anything else, that distinguishes the essay from the treatise or the article. Even in more formal or critical essays, the attitudes of the author are important. And individuality is quite as often revealed in the manner of writing as in the choice or treatment of subject.

Manner, or style, often takes first place in a thoughtful consideration of the essay. For example, Dr. Johnson gave it great emphasis in his essay on Addison: "Whoever wishes to attain an English style, familiar, but not coarse, and elegant, but not ostentatious, must give his days and nights to the volumes of Addison." Franklin and Stevenson both followed this advice in learning to write. Distinguished style is essential to the success of an essay, whether the subject is serious or slight. Some of the essays of Swift, Emerson, Arnold, and Huxley treat problems of the utmost gravity, and we choose to read the works of these men whose style lends pleasure and conviction to their themes rather than the earnest but sprawling efforts of other men who have written with less effectiveness. A lighter subject in the vein of Lamb or Irving or Thurber may be pleasing largely because of style; from less skillful writers the same themes often appear flat and trivial. Of course, it should be obvious that manner alone cannot be everything and that style without content is mere affectation.

The essay had its start during a time when there were no newspapers or magazines to fix the limits of prose writing. Three traditions soon developed—traditions which have influenced the English essay throughout its history. Montaigne's essays first appeared in France in 1580 and were probably rather widely read in England even before John Florio's translation was published in 1603. Montaigne, writing a first book made up of collections of maxims and lessons, developed in his second and third books an intensely personal kind of essay. In "The Author to the Reader," he makes a statement that many a later writer could support without change: "I have proposed unto myself no other than a familiar and private end: . . . for it is my self I portray."

In 1597, Francis Bacon brought out the first ten of his short essays, which were essentially collections of maxims or aphorisms related to general themes. Bacon's influence is more diffuse than that of Montaigne, for his style is hard to imitate even by those who might be inclined to follow him. Emerson's essays probably show more of the aphoristic tendency than do those of any other great writer.

In 1608, Joseph Hall published a little book of "characters"—sketches descriptive of types of people or abstract moral qualities. The "character" essays of Hall, Earle, and others exercised a diminishing influence after the seventeenth century, but they continue to appear even today as paragraphs in longer works. The "profiles" in *The New Yorker* frequently owe a debt to this type of essay.

By the time Steele began publication of *The Tatler*, in 1709, newspapers and journals were being circulated widely, and it was no longer necessary for a writer to publish his essays in book form. Steele and Addison, who are credited with establishing the popular periodical essay, made use of the traditions of Montaigne, Bacon, and the writers of "characters," but they enlarged the range of subjects and seemed to give more attention to society and less to themselves. The success of *The Tatler* and *The Spectator* led to the publication of scores of imitations, and by the end of the eighteenth century most literary men of prominence had engaged in publishing or writing for journals of this kind. Fielding, Johnson, and Goldsmith in England, and Franklin in America, all derived the basic patterns of their periodical essays from the works of Addison and Steele. A full century after Steele started *The Tatler*, Washington Irving wrote an introduction to the *Salmagundi* papers in which he only slightly exaggerated the aims of the typical periodical essayist: "Our intention is simply to instruct the young, reform the old, correct the town, and castigate the age."

In the early part of the nineteenth century, the periodical gave way to the more pretentious magazine. Improved methods of printing and the increasing use of illustrations made these publications more attractive than their predecessors. Public education was increasing the size of the reading public and widening their interests. Essayists no longer confined their attention to moral problems, to themes of interest to the city dwellers, and to gentle satire. One looks in vain in the essays of Lamb, Hazlitt, Hunt, and De Quincey for any uniformity of theme or attitude. Each man wrote according to his own tastes and abilities and appealed to that segment of the public that was sympathetic to his views. They all kept only one quality in common—their individuality. Each essayist asserted his bias, rode his hobby, or aired his prejudices with complete confidence in the worth of his opinions.

Since the days of Lamb and Hazlitt, the essay has changed little in form. However, today the essay no longer holds the place of prominence in the more popular magazines. Fiction, especially short stories, and factual articles attract more readers than do essays, and so the literary essay is found in such magazines as *Harper's* and *The Atlantic Monthly* rather than in *The Saturday Evening Post*. This change in emphasis does not mean that the essay has disappeared, for essays continue to be written and read in increasing numbers: in the editorial pages of newspapers and magazines, in syndicated columns, in featured departments of many magazines.

There is a vital difference between the essay and the article—one that needs to be pointed out because of a current tendency to confuse the two. The essay differs from the article in at least one important point: it is the work of an individual, a man, a person, while the article may be the product of any man, or combination of men, or even a whole editorial staff. The author of an essay is significant in his own right, and his views carry weight for this reason. The writer of an article is depersonalized; his material is the essential point of interest, not his own concepts of the material. The essay, as the work of a person, can be and often is a work of art, but the article rarely rises above the level of a craft. These distinctions could give rise to endless bickering between critics who fail to agree on some basic terms and principles, but they must be made. In an age when human values have been minimized for the glorification of the machine and the committee, when demand for efficiency has obscured the more vital need for the preservation of the dignity of the individual, it is most important to preserve awareness of the validity of the arts. In the arts, more than in any other products of human endeavor, the aspirations of individual men, the bright visions of the best of mankind reach their fullest expression. The essay is one form of art which is available to everyone who will take time to read and has the capacity for reflection. At its best, the essay can lead one to the contemplation of life from the vantage point of the highest truths. Even the average essay affords one a pleasure comparable to that produced by good conversation with a man whose rich experience, humorous outlook, or captivating eccentricities make him a good companion for an hour.

A Treasury of the Essay

Michel de Montaigne

1533 · 1592

Michel Eyquem de Montaigne, French gentleman and student of law, turned from the political and social confusion which surrounded him and sought peace in retirement and study. The essays reveal his constant search for answers to moral problems, his scepticism, and his intellectuality, which set the pattern for many later writers of essays. John Florio's translation of the Essais, *from which these two selections are taken, appeared in 1603.*

HOW THAT OUR SPIRIT HINDERETH IT SELFE

IT IS A PLEASANT IMAGINATION, to conceive a spirit justly ballanced betweene two equall desires. For, it is not to be doubted, that he shall never be resolved upon any match: Forsomuch as the application and choise brings an inequality of prise: And who should place us betweene a Bottle of wine, and a Gammon of Bacon, with an equall appetite to eat and drinke, doubtlesse there were noe remedy, but to die of thirst and of hunger. To provide against this inconvenient, when the Stoikes were demanded, whence the election of two indifferent things commeth into our soule (and which causeth, that from out a great number of Crownes or Angells we rather take one then another, when there is no reason to induce us to preferre any one before others) they answer, that this motion of the soule is extraordinarie and irregular, comming into us by a strange, accidentall and casuall impulsion. In my opinion, it might rather be said, that nothing is presented unto us, wherein there is not some difference, how light so ever it bee: And that either to the sight, or to the feeling, there is ever some choise, which tempteth and drawes us to it, though imperceptible and not to bee distinguished. In like manner, hee that shall presuppose a twine-thrid equally strong all-through, it is impossible by all impossibilitie that it breake, for, where would you have the flaw, or breaking to beginne? And at once to breake in all places together, it is not in nature. Who should also adde to this, the Geometricall propositions, which by the certainety of their demonstrations, conclude, the contained greater than the containing, and the centre as great as his circumference: And that finde two lines uncessantly approaching one unto another, and yet can never meete and joyne together: And the Philosophers stone, and quadrature of the circle, where the reason and the effects are so opposite: might peradventure draw thence some argument to salve and helpe this bold speech of *Plinie; Solum certum, nihil esse certi, et homine nihil miserius aut superbius* (PLIN. *nat. hist., ii. c.* 7). *This onely is sure, that there is nothing sure; and nothing more miserable, and yet more arrogant then man.*

OF THE INCOMMODITIE OF GREATNESSE

SINCE WE CANNOT ATTAINE UNTO IT, let us revenge ourselves with railing against it: yet is it not absolute railing, to finde fault with any thing: *There are defects found in all things, how faire soever in show, and desirable they be.* It hath generally this evident advantage, that when ever it pleaseth it will decline, and hath well-nigh the choise of one and other condition. For man doth not fall from all heights; divers there are, whence a man may descend without falling. Verily, me seemeth, that we value it at too high a rate: and prize over-deare the resolution of those, whom we have either seene or heard, to have contemned, or of their owne motion rejected the same. Her essence is not so evidently commodious, but a man may refuse it without wonder. Indeed I finde the labour very hard in suffering of evils; but in the contentment of a meane measure of fortune, and shunning of greatnesse, therein

I see no great difficulty. In my conceit, it is a vertue, where-unto my selfe, who am but a simple ninny, might easily attaine, and without great contention. What shall they doe, who would also bring into consideration, the glory, which ac-companieth this refusall, wherein may fall more ambition, then even in the desire and absolute enjoying of greatnesse? *For somuch as ambition is never better directed according to it selfe, then by a straying and unfrequented path.* I sharpen my courage toward patience, and weaken the same against desire. I have as much to wish for as another, and leave my wishes as much liberty and indiscretion: but yet, it never came into my minde, to wish for Empire, for Royalty or eminency of high and commanding fortunes. I aime not that way: I love my selfe too well. When I thinke to grow, It is but meanly: with a forced and coward advancement; fit for me: yea in resolution, in wisedome, in health, in beauty, and also in riches. But this credite, this aspiring reputation, this over-swaying authority, suppresseth my imagination. And cleane opposite to some other, I should peradventure love my selfe better, to be the second or third man in *Perigot*, then the first in *Paris:* At least, without faining, I had rather be the third man in *Paris*, then the first in charge. I will neither contend with an Usher of a doore, as a silly unknowen man; nor with gaping and adoration make a Lane through the throng as I passe. I am enured to a meane calling; mediocrity best fitteth me, as well by my fortune, as by mine owne humor. And have shewed by the conduct of my life and course of my enterprises, that I have rather sought to avoid, then otherwise to embrace beyond the degree of fortune that at my birth it pleased God to call me unto. *Each naturall constitution, is equally just and easie.* My minde is so dull and slowe, that I measure not good fortune according to her height, but rather according to her facility. And if my hart be not great enough, it is ratably free and open, and who biddeth me, bouldly to publish my weak-nesse. Should any will me, on the one part, to conferre and consider the life of *L. Thurius Balbus*, a worthy gallant man, wise, faire, goodly, healthy, of good understanding, richly-plentious in all manner of commodities and pleasures, leading a quiet easefull life, altogether his owne, with a minde armed, and well prepared against death, superstition, griefes, cares and other encombrances of humane necessity; dying in his old age, in an honourable battell, with his weapons in his hand, for the defence of his countrie; and on the other side the life of *M. Regulus* so high and great, as all men know, together with his admirable and glorious end: the one unmentioned and without dignity, the other exemplare and wonderfully renouned: truly I would say that *Cicero* saith of it, had I the gift of well-speaking as hee had. But if I were to sute them unto mine, I would also say, that the former is as much agreeing to my quality, and to the desire I endeavour to conforme my quality unto, as the second is farre beyond it. That to this I cannot attaine but by veneration; and to the other I would willingly attaine by custome. But returne we to our temporall greatnesse, whence we have digressed. I am distasted of all mastry, both active and pasive. *Otanes* one of the seaven that by right might chalenge the Crowne, or pretend the Kingdome of *Persia*, resolved upon such a resolution as I should easily have done the like: which was, that he utterly renounced all maner of claime he might in any sort pretend unto that crowne, to his fellow competitores, were it either by election or chance: alwayes provided that both himselfe and all his, might live in that Empire, free from all subjections, and exempted from all maner of commandement, except that of the ancient lawes: and might both challenge all liberty, and enjoy all immunities, that should not prejudice them: being as impacient to command, as to be commanded. *The sharpest and most dificile profession of the world*, is (in mine opinion) *worthily to act and play the King*. I excuse more of their faults, then commonly other men doe: and that in consideration of the downe-bearing waight of their immense charge, which much astonisheth me: *It is a very hard task to keep a due measure, in so unmeasurable a power*. Yet is it, that even with those, that are of a lesse excellent nature, it is a singular incitation to vertue, to be seated in such a place, where you shall doe no maner of good, that is not registred and recorded: And where the least wel-dooing extendeth to so many persons:

Of the Incommoditie of Greatnesse

And where your sufficiency (as that of Preachers) is principally directed to the people; a weake and partiall judge, easily to be beguiled, and easie to be pleased. *There are but few things, of which we may give a sincere judgement:* for there be very few, wherein in some sort or other, we are not particularly interested. Superiority and inferiority, maistry and subjection, are joyntly tied unto a naturall kinde of envy and contestation; they must perpetually enter-spoile one another. I beleeve neither the one nor the other, concerning hir companions rights: let us suffer reason to speake of it, which is inflexible and impassible, when or how we shall make an end. I was not long since reading of two Scottish bookes striving upon this subject. The popular makes the King to be of worse condition then a Carter: and he that extolleth Monarchy, placeth him both in power and soveraignty, many steps above the Gods. Now the incommodity of greatnesse, which here I have undertaken to note and speake of, (upon some occasion lately befalne mee) is this. There is peradventure nothing more pleasing to the commerce of men, then the *Essayes*, which we through jealousie of honour or valour, make one against another, be it in the exercise of the body or minde: wherein soveraigne greatnesse, hath no true or essentiall part. Verily, it hath often seemed unto me, that through over much respect, Princes are therein used disdainefully and treated injuriously: For, the thing whereat (in my youth) I was infinitely offended, was, that those which were trained and schooled with mee, should forbeare to doe it in good earnest, because they found me unworthy to bee withstood or to resist their endeavours. It is that we dayly see to happen unto them; every man finding himselfe unworthy to force himselfe against them. If one perceive them never so little affected to have the victory, there is none but will strive to yeeld it them, and that will not rather wrong his glory, then offend theirs: No man imployeth more diligence then needs he must to serve their honour. What share have Princes in the throng, where all are for them? Mee thinks I see those *Paladines* of former ages, presenting themselves in joustes, tiltings and combats, with bodies and armes enchanted. *Brisson* running against *Alexander*, counterfeited his course: *Alexander* chid him for it: but he should have caused him to be whipt. For this consideration, was *Carneades* wont to say, that *Princes children learn't nothing aright but to manage and ride horses; forsomuch as in all other exercises, every man yeeldeth, and giveth them the victory: but a horse who is neyther a flatterer nor a Courtier, will as soone throw the child of a King as the son of a base porter. Homer* hath beene forced to consent that *Venus* (so sweet a saint and delicate a Goddesse) should be hurt at the siege of *Troy*, thereby to ascribe courage and hardinesse unto her qualities never seen in those that are exempted from danger. The Gods themselves are fained to be angry, to feare, to be jealous, to grieve, to shew passion, and be subject to mortall sense, thereby to honour them with the vertues which the Poets and Philosophers invent amongst us: Nay, they are supposed to runne away, and to have a feeling of all our imperfections. *Who doth not participate both hazard and difficulties, cannot justly pretend interest in the honor, or challenge share in the pleasure, that followeth dangerous actions or hazardous attempts.* It is pitty a man should be so powerfull, that all things must yeeld and give place unto him. Such as are in so high eminency of greatnesse, their fortune rejects society and conversation too farre from them; she placeth them in over remote and uncouth places. This easefull life and plausible facility to bring all under, and subject mens mindes, is an enemy to all manner of pleasure. It is a kinde of sliding, and not a going: It is to sleepe, and not to live. Conceive man accompanied with omnipotency, you overwhelme him: he must in begging manner crave some empeachment and resistance of you. His being and his good, is in want and indigence. Their good qualities are dead and lost: for, they are not heard but by comparison, and they are excluded: they have little knowledge of true praise, being beaten with so continuall and uniforme an approbation. Have they to doe with the simplest of their subjects? they have no meane to take advantage of him, if he but say; It is because he is my King, he supposeth to have sufficiently expressed, and you must understand, that in so saying, he hath lent a helping hand to overthrow himselfe. This quality suppresseth and consumeth all other true and essential qualities: they are even drowned in the Royalty; which gives them no leave, to make the offices of their charge to prevaile, except in such actions as directly concerne and stead the same. *To be a King, is a matter of that consequence, that onely by it he is so.* That strange glimmering and eye-dazeling light, which round about environeth, over-casteth and hideth from us: our weake sight is thereby bleared and dissipated, as beeing filled and obscured by that greater and further-spredding brightnesse. The Senate allotted the honor and prise of eloquence unto *Tiberius;* he refused it, supposing that if it hath beene true, he could not revenge himselfe of so limited and partiall judgement. As we yeeld Princes all advantages of honor, so we aucthorize their defects and sooth-up their vices: not onely by approbation, but also by imitation. All *Alexanders* followers bare their heads sideling, as he did. And such as flattered *Dionysius*, in his owne presence did run and justle one another, and either stumbled at, or over-threw what ever stood before their feete, to inferre; that they were as shortsighted or spur-blinde, as he was. Naturall imperfections have sometimes served for commendation and favour. Nay I have seene deafnesse affected. And because the maister hated his wife, *Plutarke* hath seen courtiers to sue a divorce of theirs, whom they loved very well. And which is more, paillardise and all maner of dissolution hath there by beene held in credit; as also disloyalty, blasphemy, cruelty, heresie, superstition, irreligion, wantonnesse and worse, if worse may be. Yea by an example more dangerous, then that of *Mithridates* his flatterers, who for somuch as their master pretended to have skill in phisick and aspired to the honor of a good Physitian, came to him to have their members incized and cauterized. For these others suffer to have their soules cauterized; a much more precious and nobler part then the body. But to end where I began: *Adrian* the Emperor debating with *Favorinus* the Philosopher about the interpretation of some word; *Favorinus* did soone yeeld the victory unto him, his friends finding fault with him for it; you but jest, my masters (quoth he) *would you not have him to be much wiser then I, who hath the absolute command over thirty legions? Augustus* writ some verses against *Asinius Pollio*, which *Pollio* hearing, he said, I will hould my peace; for, *it is no wisedome to contend in writing with him, who may proscribe.* And they had reason: For *Dionysius*, because he could not equall *Philoxenus* in Poesie, nor match *Plato* in discourse, condemned the one to the stone-quarries, and sent the other to bee sold as a slave in the Ile of Ægina.

Sir Francis Bacon

1561 · 1626

Sir Francis Bacon, English essayist, philosopher, scientist, and statesman, displayed great ambition for himself and for his country. He rose rapidly through a succession of public offices and titles to become Lord Keeper of the Great Seal and Lord Chancellor. Meanwhile he was busy with his philosophical writings, which were intended to form a great work entitled Magna Instauratio. *In 1621 he was charged with bribery and corruption, fined, and imprisoned; however, the fine was remitted and he spent only a few days in the Tower. His death came as a result of experimenting with the effect of snow in preserving the flesh of a fowl, for he contracted a chill which brought on a fatal illness.*

OF TRUTH

W*hat is truth?* SAID JESTING PILATE, and would not stay for an answer. Certainly there be that delight in giddiness, and count it a bondage to fix a belief; affecting free-will in thinking, as well as in acting. And though the sects of philosophers of that kind be gone, yet there remain certain discoursing wits which are of the same veins, though there be not so much blood in them as was in those of the ancients. But it is not only the difficulty and labor which men take in finding out of truth, nor again that when it is found it imposeth upon men's thoughts, that doth bring lies in favor; but a natural though corrupt love of the lie itself. One of the later schools of the Grecians examineth the matter, and is at a stand to think what should be in it, that men should love lies, where neither they make for pleasure, as with poets, nor for advantage, as with the merchant; but for the lie's sake. But I cannot tell: this same truth is a naked and open daylight, that doth not show the masques and mummeries and triumphs of the world, half so stately and daintily as candlelights. Truth may perhaps come to the price of a pearl, that showeth best by day; but it will not rise to the price of a diamond or carbuncle, that showeth best in varied lights. A mixture of a lie doth ever add pleasure. Doth any man doubt, that if there were taken out of men's minds vain opinions, flattering hopes, false valuations, imaginations as one would, and the like, but it would leave the minds of a number of men poor shrunken things, full of melancholy and indisposition, and unpleasing to themselves? One of the fathers, in great severity, called poesy *vinum dæmonum*, because it filleth the imagination; and yet it is but with the shadow of a lie. But it is not the lie that passeth through the mind, but the lie that sinketh in and settleth in it, that doth the hurt, such as we spake of before. But howsoever these things are thus in men's depraved judgments and affections, yet truth, which only doth judge itself, teacheth that the inquiry of truth, which is the love-making or wooing of it, the knowledge of truth, which is the presence of it, and the belief of truth, which is the enjoying of it, is the sovereign good of human nature. The first creature of God, in the works of the days, was the light of the sense; the last was the light of reason; and his sabbath work ever since, is the illumination of his Spirit. First he breathed light upon the face of the matter or chaos; then he breathed light into the face of man; and still he breatheth and inspireth light into the face of his chosen. The poet that beautified the sect that was otherwise inferior to the rest, saith yet excellently well: *It is a pleasure to stand upon the shore, and to see ships tossed upon the sea; a pleasure to stand in the window of a castle, and to see a battle and the adventures thereof below: but no pleasure is comparable to the standing upon the vantage ground of truth* (a hill not to be commanded, and where the air is always clear and serene), *and to see the errors, and wanderings, and mists, and tempests, in the vale below;* so always that this prospect be with pity, and not with swelling or pride. Certainly, it is heaven upon earth, to have a man's mind move in charity, rest in providence, and turn upon the poles of truth.

To pass from theological and philosophical truth to the truth of civil business: it will be acknowledged, even by those that practice it not, that clear and round dealing is the honor of man's nature; and that mixture of falsehood is like allay in coin of gold and silver, which may make the metal work the better, but it embaseth it. For these winding and crooked courses are the goings of the serpent; which goeth basely upon the belly, and not upon the feet. There is no vice that doth so cover a man with shame as to be found false and perfidious. And therefore Montaigne saith prettily, when he inquired the reason why the word of the lie should be such a disgrace and such an odious charge; saith he, *If it be well weighed, to say that a man lieth is as much to say as that he is brave towards God and a coward towards men.* For a lie faces God, and shrinks from man. Surely the wickedness of falsehood and breach of faith cannot possibly be so highly expressed, as in that it shall be the last peal to call the judgments of God upon the generations of men; it being foretold that, when Christ cometh, *he shall not find faith upon the earth.*

OF TRAVEL

Travel, in the younger sort, is a part of education; in the elder, a part of experience. He that traveleth into a country before he hath some entrance into the language, goeth to school, and not to travel. That young men travel under some tutor, or grave servant, I allow well; so that he be such a one that hath the language and hath been in the country before; whereby he may be able to tell them what things are worthy to be seen in the country where they go; what acquaintances they are to seek; what exercises or discipline the place yieldeth. For else young men shall go hooded, and look abroad little. It is a strange thing, that in sea-voyages, where there is nothing to be seen but sky and sea, men should make diaries; but in land-travel, wherein so much is to be observed, for the most part they omit it; as if chance were fitter to be registered than observation. Let diaries therefore be brought in use. The things to be seen and observed are: the courts of princes, especially when they give audience to ambassadors; the courts of justice, while they sit and hear causes; and so of consistories ecclesiastic; the churches and monasteries, with the monuments which are therein extant; the walls and fortifications of cities and towns, and so the havens and harbors; antiquities and ruins; libraries; colleges, disputations, and lectures, where any are; shipping and navies; houses and gardens of state and pleasure, near great cities; armories; arsenals; magazines; exchanges; burses; warehouses; exercises of horsemanship, fencing, training of soldiers, and the like; comedies, such whereunto the better sort of persons do resort; treasuries of jewels and robes; cabinets and rarities; and, to conclude, whatsoever is memorable in the places where they go. After all which the tutors or servants ought to make diligent inquiry. As for triumphs, masks, feasts, weddings, funerals, capital executions, and such shows, men need not to be put in mind of them; yet are they not to be neglected. If you will have a young man to put his travel into a little room, and in short time to gather much, this you must do. First, as was said, he must have some entrance into the language before he goeth. Then he must have such a servant or tutor as knoweth the country, as was likewise said. Let him carry with him also some card or book describing the country where he traveleth; which will be a good key to his inquiry. Let him keep also a diary. Let him not stay long in one city or town; more or less as the place deserveth, but not long; nay, when he stayeth in one city or town, let him change his lodging from one end and part of the town to another; which is a great adamant of acquaintance. Let him sequester himself from the company of his countrymen, and diet in such places where there is good company of the nation where he traveleth. Let him, upon his removes from one place to another, procure recommendation to some person of quality residing in the place whither he removeth; that he may use his favor in those things he desireth to see or know. Thus he may abridge his travel with much profit. As for the

28

acquaintance which is to be sought in travel; that which is most of all profitable is acquaintance with the secretaries and employed men of ambassadors; for so in traveling in one country he shall suck the experience of many. Let him also see and visit eminent persons in all kinds, which are of great name abroad; that he may be able to tell how the life agreeth with the fame. For quarrels, they are with care and discretion to be avoided; they are commonly for mistresses, healths, place, and words. And let a man beware how he keepeth company with choleric and quarrelsome persons; for they will engage him into their own quarrels. When a traveler returneth home, let him not leave the countries where he hath traveled altogether behind him, but maintain a correspondence by letters with those of his acquaintance which are of most worth. And let his travel appear rather in his discourse than in his apparel or gesture; and in his discourse let him be rather advised in his answers than forwards to tell stories; and let it appear that he doth not change his country manners for those of foreign parts, but only prick in some flowers of that he hath learned abroad into the customs of his own country.

OF GARDENS

G OD ALMIGHTY FIRST PLANTED A GARDEN. And indeed it is the purest of human pleasures. It is the greatest refreshment to the spirits of man; without which buildings and palaces are but gross handiworks: and a man shall ever see that when ages grow to civility and elegancy, men come to build stately sooner than to garden finely; as if gardening were the greater perfection. I do hold it, in the royal ordering of gardens, there ought to be gardens for all the months in the year; in which severally things of beauty may be then in season. For December and January, and the latter part of November, you must take such things as are green all winter: holly; ivy; bays; juniper; cypress-trees; yew; pine-apple-trees; fir-trees; rosemary; lavender; periwinkle, the white, the purple, and the blue; germander; flags; orange-trees; lemon-trees; and myrtles, if they be stoved; and sweet marjoram, warm set. There follow-eth, for the latter part of January and February, the mezereon-tree, which then blossoms; crocus vernus, both the yellow and the grey; primroses; anemones; the early tulippa; hyacinthus orientalis; chamaïris; fritellaria. For March, there come vio-lets, specially the single blue, which are the earliest; the yellow daffodil; the daisy; the almond-tree in blossom; the peach-tree in blossom; the cornelian-tree in blossom; sweet-briar. In April follow the double white violet; the wall-flower; the stock-gilliflower; the cowslip; flower-de-lices, and lilies of all na-tures; rosemary-flowers; the tulippa; the double peony; the pale daffodil; the French honeysuckle; the cherry-tree in blossom; the damson and plum-trees in blossom; the white thorn in leaf; the lilac-tree. In May and June come pinks of all sorts, specially the blush-pink; roses of all kinds, except the musk, which comes later; honeysuckles; strawberries; bugloss; columbine; the French marigold, flos Africanus; cherry-tree in fruit; ribes; figs in fruit; rasps; vine-flowers; lavender in flowers; the sweet satyrian, with the white flower; herba muscaria; lilium convallium; the apple-tree in blossom. In July come gilliflowers of all varieties; musk-roses; the lime-tree in blossom; early pears and plums in fruit; jennetings; codlins. In August come plums of all sorts in fruit; pears; apricocks; berberries; filberds; musk-melons; monks-hoods, of all colors. In September come grapes; apples; poppies of all colors; peaches; melocotones; nectarines; cornelians; wardens; quinces. In October and the beginning of November come services; medlars; bullaces; roses cut or removed to come late; holly-hocks; and such like. These particulars are for the cli-mate of London; but my meaning is perceived, that you may have *ver perpetuum* [perpetual spring], as the place affords.

And because the breath of flowers is far sweeter in the air (where it comes and goes like the warbling of music) than in the hand, therefore nothing is more fit for that delight, than to know what be the flowers and plants that do best perfume the air. Roses, damask and red, are fast flowers of their smells; so that you may walk by a whole row of them, and find noth-ing of their sweetness; yea though it be in a morning's dew.

Bays likewise yield no smell as they grow. Rosemary little; nor sweet marjoram. That which above all others yields the sweetest smell in the air is the violet, specially the white double violet, which comes twice a year; about the middle of April, and about Bartholomew-tide. Next to that is the musk-rose. Then the strawberry-leaves dying, which [yield] a most excellent cordial smell. Then the flower of the vines; it is a little dust, like the dust of a bent, which grows upon the cluster in the first coming forth. Then sweet-briar. Then wall-flowers, which are very delightful to be set under a parlor or lower chamber window. Then pinks and gilliflowers, specially the matted pink and clove gilliflower. Then the flowers of the lime-tree. Then the honeysuckles, so they be somewhat afar off. Of bean-flowers I speak not, because they are field flowers. But those which perfume the air most delightfully, not passed by as the rest, but being trodden upon and crushed, are three; that is, burnet, wild-thyme, and water-mints. Therefore you are to set whole alleys of them, to have the pleasure when you walk or tread.

For gardens (speaking of those which are indeed prince-like, as we have done of buildings), the contents ought not well to be under thirty acres of ground, and to be divided into three parts: a green in the entrance; a heath or desert in the going forth; and the main garden in the midst; besides alleys on both sides. And I like well that four acres of ground be assigned to the green; six to the heath; four and four to either side; and twelve to the main garden. The green hath two pleasures: the one, because nothing is more pleasant to the eye than green grass kept finely shorn; the other, because it will give you a fair alley in the midst, by which you may go in front upon a stately hedge, which is to enclose the garden. But because the alley will be long, and, in great heat of the year or day, you ought not to buy the shade in the garden by going in the sun through the green, therefore you are, of either side the green, to plant a covert alley upon carpenter's work, about twelve foot in height, by which you may go in shade into the garden. As for the making of knots or figures with divers colored earths, that they may lie under the windows of the house on that side which the garden stands, they be but toys; you may see as good sights many times in tarts. The garden is best to be square, encompassed on all the four sides with a stately arched hedge. The arches to be upon pillars of carpenter's work, of some ten foot high, and six foot broad; and the spaces between of the same dimension with the breadth of the arch. Over the arches let there be an entire hedge of some four foot high, framed also upon carpenter's work; and upon the upper hedge, over every arch, a little turret, with a belly, enough to receive a cage of birds; and over every space between the arches some other little figure, with broad plates of round colored glass, gilt, for the sun to play upon. But this hedge I intend to be raised upon a bank, not steep, but gently slope, of some six foot, set all with flowers. Also I understand that this square of the garden should not be the whole breadth of the ground, but to leave on either side ground enough for diversity of side alleys; unto which the two covert alleys of the green may deliver you. But there must be no alleys with hedges at either end of this great enclosure; not at the hither end, for letting your prospect upon this fair hedge from the green; nor at the further end, for letting your prospect from the hedge through the arches upon the heath.

For the ordering of the ground within the great hedge, I leave it to variety of device; advising nevertheless that whatsoever form you cast it into, first, it be not too busy, or full of work. Wherein I, for my part, do not like images cut out in juniper or other garden stuff; they be for children. Little low hedges, round, like welts, with some pretty pyramids, I like well; and in some places, fair columns upon frames of carpenter's work. I would have the alleys spacious and fair. You may have closer alleys upon the side grounds, but none in the main garden. I wish also, in the very middle, a fair mount, with three ascents, and alleys, enough for four to walk abreast; which I would have to be perfect circles, without any bulwarks or embossments; and the whole mount to be thirty foot high; and some fine banqueting-house, with some chimneys neatly cast, and without too much glass.

For fountains, they are a great beauty and refreshment; but pools mar all, and make the garden unwholesome, and full of flies and frogs. Fountains I intend to be of two natures: the one that sprinkleth or spouteth water; the other a fair receipt of water, of some thirty or forty foot square, but without fish, or slime, or mud. For the first, the ornaments of images gilt, or of marble, which are in use, do well: but the main matter is so to convey the water, as it never stay, either in the bowls or in the cistern; that the water be never by rest discolored, green or red or the like, or gather any mossiness or putrefaction. Besides that, it is to be cleansed every day by the hand. Also some steps up to it, and some fine pavement about it, doth well. As for the other kind of fountain, which we may call a bathing pool, it may admit much curiosity and beauty, wherewith we will not trouble ourselves: as, that the bottom be finely paved, and with images; the sides likewise; and withal embellished with colored glass, and such things of lustre; encompassed also with fine rails of low statuas. But the main point is the same which we mentioned in the former kind of fountain; which is, that the water be in perpetual motion, fed by a water higher than the pool, and delivered into it by fair spouts, and then discharged away under ground by some equality of bores, that it stay little. And for fine devices, of arching water without spilling, and making it rise in several forms (of feathers, drinking glasses, canopies, and the like), they be pretty things to look on, but nothing to health and sweetness.

For the heath, which was the third part of our plot, I wish it to be framed, as much as may be, to a natural wildness. Trees I would have none in it, but some thickets made only of sweet-briar and honeysuckle, and some wild vine amongst; and the ground set with violets, strawberries, and primroses. For these are sweet, and prosper in the shade. And these to be in the heath, here and there, not in any order. I like also little heaps, in the nature of molehills (such as are in wild heaths), to be set, some with wild thyme, some with pinks, some with germander, that gives a good flower to the eye, some with periwinkle, some with violets, some with strawberries, some with cow-slips, some with daisies, some with red roses, some with lilium convallium, some with sweet-williams red, some with bear's-foot, and the like low flowers, being withal sweet and sightly. Part of which heaps are to be with standards of little bushes pricked upon their top, and part without. The standards to be roses, juniper, holly, berberries (but here and there, because of the smell of their blossom), red currants, gooseberries, rosemary, bays, sweet-briar, and such like. But these standards to be kept with cutting, that they grow not out of course.

For the side grounds, you are to fill them with variety of alleys, private, to give a full shade, some of them, wheresoever the sun be. You are to frame some of them likewise for shelter, that when the wind blows sharp you may walk as in a gallery. And those alleys must be likewise hedged at both ends, to keep out the wind; and these closer alleys must be ever finely gravelled, and no grass, because of going wet. In many of these alleys, likewise, you are to set fruit-trees of all sorts; as well upon the walls as in ranges. And this would be generally observed, that the borders wherein you plant your fruit-trees be fair and large, and low, and not steep; and set with fine flowers, but thin and sparingly, lest they deceive the trees. At the end of both the side grounds, I would have a mount of some pretty height, leaving the wall of the enclosure breast high, to look abroad into the fields.

For the main garden, I do not deny but there should be some fair alleys ranged on both sides, with fruit-trees; and some pretty tufts of fruit-trees, and arbors with seats, set in some decent order; but these to be by no means set too thick; but to leave the main garden so as it be not close, but the air open and free. For as for shade, I would have you rest upon the alleys of the side grounds, there to walk, if you be disposed, in the heat of the year or day; but to make account that the main garden is for the more temperate parts of the year; and in the heat of summer, for the morning and the evening, or over-cast days.

For aviaries, I like them not, except they be of that largeness as they may be turfed, and have living plants and bushes set in them; that the birds may have more scope and natural nestling, and that no foulness appear in the floor of the aviary. So I have made a platform of a princely garden, partly by precept, partly by drawing, not a model, but some general lines of it; and in this I have spared for no cost. But it is nothing for great princes, that for the most part taking advice with workmen, with no less cost set their things together; and sometimes add statuas and such things for state and magnificence, but nothing to the true pleasure of a garden.

OF STUDIES

STUDIES SERVE FOR DELIGHT, for ornament, and for ability. Their chief use for delight is in privateness and retiring; for ornament, is in discourse; and for ability, is in the judgment and disposition of business. For expert men can execute, and perhaps judge of particulars, one by one; but the general counsels, and the plots and marshalling of affairs, come best from those that are learned. To spend too much time in studies is sloth; to use them too much for ornament is affectation; to make judgment wholly by their rules is the humour of a scholar. They perfect nature, and are perfected by experience: for natural abilities are like natural plants, that need pruning by study; and studies themselves do give forth directions too much at large, except they be bounded in by experience. Crafty men contemn studies, simple men admire them, and wise men use them: for they teach not their own use; but that is a wisdom without them, and above them, won by observation. Read not to contradict and confute; nor to believe and take for granted; nor to find talk and discourse; but to weigh and consider. Some books are to be tasted, others to be swallowed, and some few to be chewed and digested; that is, some books are to be read only in parts; others to be read, but not curiously; and some few to be read wholly, and with diligence and attention. Some books also may be read by deputy, and extracts made of them by others; but that would be only in the less important arguments, and the meaner sort of books; else distilled books are like common distilled waters, flashy things. Reading maketh a full man; conference a ready man; and writing an exact man. And therefore, if a man write little, he had need have a great memory; if he confer little, he had need have a present wit; and if he read little, he had need have much cunning, to seem to know that he doth not. Histories make men wise; poets witty; the mathematics subtile; natural philosophy deep; moral grave; logic and rhetoric able to contend. *Abeunt studia in mores*. Nay, there is no stond or impediment in the wit but may be wrought out by fit studies; like as diseases of the body may have appropriate exercises. Bowling is good for the stone and reins; shooting for the lungs and breast; gentle walking for the stomach; riding for the head; and the like. So if a man's wit be wandering, let him study the mathematics; for in demonstrations, if his wit be called away never so little, he must begin again. If his wit be not apt to distinguish or find differences, let him study the schoolmen; for they are *cymini sectores*. If he be not apt to beat over matters, and to call up one thing to prove and illustrate another, let him study the lawyers' cases. So every defect of the mind may have a special receipt.

Henry Peacham

1576? · 1643?

*Henry Peacham was a man of great versatility in
all the arts suitable to a gentleman. At Cambridge he
was known as a poet and historian; later he
displayed in his writings a considerable knowledge
of the arts of war, painting, engraving, and music,
and an interest in antiquities. His most famous
work,* The Compleat Gentleman *(1622), a courtesy
book, was very popular. Peacham's wide experience
and varied learning show to advantage in*
The Truth of Our Times *(1638), from which
the two essays are taken.*

OF LIBERTY

THERE IS NOTHING SO SWEETE and agreeable to
the nature of Man, next unto his health, as
his *liberty*, which, according to *Tullie's* definition hereof, is
an *Arbitrium vivendi ut velis, The choice of living as a man
list himselfe.* Wherefore, *Paracelsus* (that glory of *Germany*,
for his depth of knowledge in the nature of Minerals) to shew
his true happinesse herein, when hee travelled by the way, and
came to his Inne at night, the first thing hee did, he would lay
his sword upon the Table, professing hee would not give the
same to bee Emperour of *Germany:* it was a long broad sword,
and had engraven upon the blade this: *Alterius non sit qui
suus esse potest.* As being the Embleme of his Liberty: In the
pommell (which was hollow, and to bee opened with a skrew)
were all his chiefe *Quintessencies*, and spirits of Metalls and
Hearbs, wherewith hee cured the most desperate Diseases,
gaining hereby infinite treasure and summes of money.

And the old *Burgundians* possessing that part of *Germany*

37

which belongeth at this time to the *Lantgrave* of *Hessen*, to expresse their hatred to bondage, and their love of Liberty, gave in their warlicke Ensigne a Cat, because no creature in the world is more impatient of bondage than it; for put her into a cage or grate, shee never will bee quiet, but rather beate her selfe to death there, than want her liberty. Hence that Prince is called *Princeps Catorum*, and in the *Germane, Die Lantgraffe von Hessen: Hesse* as well in the high as low Dutch signifying a *Cat*; for as wee call heere *Pusse*, so they there *Hesse:* yet in Gelderland they call her *Pous* as we doe.

Servitude was as a curse pronounced to them who had offended *God*, and transgressed his Law; as *Noah* cursed *Canaan*, saying, *A servant of servants shall he be unto his brethren (Gen.* 9. 25): and we find indeed bondage to be but an effect of *vice*, as in unthrifty idle persons, and offenders of the Law, withall intemperate persons, who by their ill living fall into many long and loathsome diseases, are as it were in bonds bound to their beds, and imprisoned within their chambers, and set in the stocks by the Gout.

There is also the want of halfe a mans Liberty in Marriage; for he is not absolutely himselfe, though many beleeve, when they are going to Church upon their Wedding-day, they are going into the Land of Liberty: But *Salomon* telleth them, *The foole laugheth when he is going to the stocks*. For my part, I am not married; if I were, I should finde my wings clipt, and the collar too streight for my neck.

The *Low countries* having tasted the sweetnesse of their liberty, when they had shaken off the yoake of *Spaine*, gave for their Embleme a *Lyon*, who having slipt his collar, look't behind him to the same, with this *Liber Leo revinciri nescit:* An absolute man cannot be he who wanteth his liberty.

Who enjoy their liberty, commonly are longer lived than others who want it; they are more able in wit and judgement, they are more usefull to the Common-wealth, when the rest are but *Vmbratiles*, but shadows of men; they have done the best workes either of *wit*, or *expence;* they are the fastest & truest friends: lastly, they have beene the fairest presidents of *Piety* and *Goodnesse*.

But you tell me, every man cannot enjoy that condition, but some (yea, the most) must serve, and obey: It is true; I onely speake of the ingenuous, and those as may, if it please them, be *fabri fati sui*, shape out their owne fortune, yet rather choose a servile condition, before Liberty and Freedome: as if a Master of Arts should turne Gentleman Usher to an ordinary Lady; or a Lieutenant in the warres leave his honourable profession to become a Lords Porter; or like a foolish Vicar in *Lincolnshire* who would suffer his wife to raise him in cold winter mornings to make her a fire. Some againe are by nature so base and obsequious, that being overcome with the presence of those who were greater or braver then themselves, they sooth him up, and foolishly applaud and admire whatsoever hee sayes; and if hee speakes in his owne opinion any thing wisely, or like a Statist, and looketh about him for applause, they reply, Your Honor or Worship is in the right, the best Counsellor the King hath, could not have spoken to better purpose, God maintaine your life, if some would be rul'd by you it would bee better for all *England;* with the like grosse and palpable flattery. And if happely he utter any thing savouring of a jest, they feigne a *Sardonian* smile by way of allowance of his facetious conceipt. And indeed many there are so stately, & affecting greatnesse after so foolish a manner, that they become ridiculous, in suffering men ofttimes as good as themselves to stand bare before them three or foure houres together, and therefore many times they hold them in talk for the purpose, in expecting the title of Honor or Worship at every word that is spoken, as if they were the Constables of the next Wapentake. Sometimes they will bee bold to commaund you as their menial servant, which also you must take as a favour. In briefe, I will ever commend that gentile freedome of the French nation, who affect servility least of all other, especially that of standing bare, yea even in waiting at the table, were it before the greatest Lord in *France*, (they usually bringing up the dishes with their hats on their heads) as also in freedome of speech, whereof none save slaves are debarred. For mine owne part I affect freedome so much, and I have found such happinesse therein, that I had rather dine even at a three peny

Ordinary, where I may be free and merry, then to bee a dumbe tenant for two houres at a Lords table, preferring health and liberty, *bono corporis*, before those of Fortune, and all the wealth the greatest Usurer hath in the world, and will ever say, *O bona libertas pretio, pretiosior omni*.

OF QUIETNESSE AND HEALTH

WE DOE FINDE BY DAILY EXPERIENCE, that the Age of man very much declineth, and that men now, for the most part, are not halfe so strong & vigorous as they were in the memory of our fathers, as we may easily perceive by those arrowes of a yard or an ell long, which hang by the wals in many places of the North and west part of *England*, which the owners grandfather or great grandfather left behinde him for a monument of his loyall affection to one of the Roses, under whose conduct he served an Archer; the shooting-Buts in Countrey Townes have lost much of their length since the beginning of *Q. Elizabeths* reigne. Who can wield that launce which *Charles Brandon* D. of *Suffolke* tilted withall, yet to be seene in the Tower? neither can so heavy armes be borne, as were not many years [since]; our Pikes and Muskets are made farre lesse, because our lesser bodies finde them rather for burthen than use: Now if wee looke into the cause and true reason hereof, wee shall finde first the world declining, and like a mother in her age, to bring forth but weake and short-lived children; neither is this all, but we living in the last age of the world, wherein all iniquity and vice doth abound, men shorten their lives by over-eating and drinking, ease and want of exercise, luxury and incontinence, *Temperance* and *Continencie* being the maine and onely supporters of our health, as incomparable *Fernelius* affirmeth: there are two things more (as these to our health) which conduce to our happinesse in this world, which are, Liberty and tranquillity or quiet of minde; these I confesse fall not to every mans share, most men living being involved in so many affaires: variety of cares and businesse which attend us in this our earthly pilgrimage, that this quiet of minde is as rare as *Homers Nepen-the*, many men not out of necessity, but of selfe-wilfulnesse, vexing and disquieting themselves without cause or reason. As how many rich, and men of great estates bee there in this Kingdome, of whose care of getting & purchasing there is no end; they never in all their lives (like the Asse that carried Venison, Pheasants, Capons, bottles of Wine, and other dainties upon his backe) tasting the sweetnes of what they had about them, but fedde upon the Thornes and Thistles of Vexation, griefe, and needlesse carefulnesse, to enrich some unthrifty sonne or kinse-man; or scrape up thousands for some dainty thing troubled with the green sicknesse, who within a year or two is stolen and marryed by a Tailor or Hostler.

Others againe are by nature cholericke, fretfull, quarrelsome, and evermore enemies to their owne rest, delighting to be meddlers and brokers in other mens businesse, as Eeles in troubled waters and mudde. Some out of curiosity, or the scarch of some deepe, and uncouth invention, as firing shippes under water, making traps for the monstrous Beare of *Nova, Zemla &c.*, or secret in Nature, as setting the Load-stone and Iet at enmity about Iron and strawes: Others draw misery and vexation as with cords unto them, through weaknesse of judgment, when they marry disadvantagiously to themselves either for estate, or their owne dispositions, I meane, when themselves being gentle, and addicted to peace, match with errant scolds; honest of life, meete with whoores, and the like.

So since we cannot make our selves Master of this so sweete a benefit *Tranquillity* of minde, let us (which is in our own power) looke unto our health, whereof the most men are carelesse and negligent. To the conservation whereof, let us first consider the quality of the aire in that place where we live, which is not only an Element, but an Aliment; for by it, if it be pure and good, our spirits are clarified and quickned, our blood rarified, and our hearts recomforted; for the whole body fareth the better for the goodnes of a pure & sweet aire: so that we find by experience, that men are more sprightly, lively, and merry in an upland perfumed, and fanned with the flower-sented aire of the Countrey, and of better complexions, then in close lanes and noysome allies about the City, where the aire in such places is not good, but raw and cold: you may better it (especially in infectious & dangerous times) by burning of severall sorts of sweete Wood, as *Cipres, Iuniper, Bay, Rosemarie, Pine,* the *Turpentine,* and *Rosin-tree:* if it bee too hot, open your windowes, and place your bedde toward the North, strewing the flowre with rushes, water-Lillies, Nenuphar, Lettuce, Endive, Sorrell, and ever and anon sprinkle cold water with a little vinegar of Roses. If any in *Rome* were troubled with Vlcers of the Lungs, or fell into consumptions, *Galen* would presently send them to mount Tabian, a most sweet Aire neare unto *Naples,* where, through the drynes of the place, and drinking the milke of goates & kine, which fed upon many medicinable hearbes (and proper to those diseases growing in that place) they recovered in a short time: having perhaps learned out of *Hippocrites,* that in long & languishing diseases, there is nothing better then Aire, and place of our dwelling.

The next thing for our health we must have especiall care of our eating and drinking: our meate wherewith our bodies are nourished, proceedeth either from living creatures, or vegetables, that is plants: & of these there must bee a choyse had, that of Plants nourisheth farre lesse than the flesh of living creatures, excepting that grain whereof wee make our bread, as Wheat, Rie, Barly, Oates, &c. Wheat being the chiefe: fruits nourish very little; of fruits, Cheries and Grapes are the best. Melon, Cow-cumbers, and Citrulls are good for cholericke stomackes, they breed grosse blood, are very cold, and hard of digestion: *Platina* tels us in the life of Pope *Paul* the second, how the said Pope two houres before night was taken suddenly with an *Apoplexie,* being a little before very well, and complaining of no disease or paine, which came through eating of 2 whole *Muskmellons. An.* 1471.

And how many in these our times kill themselves with overmuch drinking, the cause of many long and deadly diseases; as *Apoplexies, Dropsies, Palsies,* the *Gout,* & many other; and I know not whether any of the colder Northern Nation herein excell us, drunkennesse now a dayes being growne into that request, that it is almost esteemed a vertue, at least a gentleman like quality to carouse, sit up whole dayes & nights at it.

> *. . . Donec vertigine tectum*
> *Ambulet & geminis exurgat mensa lucernis.*

Keeping neither Method nor measure in their eating and drinking, which the ancient *Grecians*, and other nations were so precise in it: England formerly having beene accounted the most sober and temperate nation in the world: neither were we ever noted for this vice, till (as Mr. *Camden* saith) wee had to do with the *Netherlands* in their warres. Also being from all antiquity our English drinke: *Britanni* (saith *Pliny*) *habent potus genus quod Alicam vocant:* which doubtlesse was our Ale, Beere, and Base-viols, came into England in one yeare, in the time of King *Henry* the seaventh. But that I may conclude concerning those things whereon ours doth principally depend, which are, the Aire, eating, drinking, sleepe, & waking, mooving, and exercise, rest, evacuation of excrements, venerall recreation, and passions of the minde; that wee may live to serve God, to doe our King and Country service, to bee a comfort to our friends, and helpfull to our Children, and others that depend upon us, let us follow Sobriety and Temperance, and have (as *Tully* saith) a diligent care of our health, which we shall bee sure to doe, if we will observe and keepe that one short (but true) rule of *Hippocritas, All things moderately, and in measure.*

Sir William Cornwallis

1579 · 1614

*Sir William Cornwallis has some claim to the title
of first English essayist, for his Essayes appeared in
1600, twelve years before Bacon expanded his
first attempts (1597) into more fully developed
essays. He took his inspiration for the essays from
Montaigne but did not borrow extensively from
the French author. His Stoic attitude toward
misfortunes and poverty and his philosophical and
literary interests appear throughout the essays,
together with his regrets for habits of extravagance,
which as a father of eleven children and an
unsuccessful courtier he could ill afford.*

OF ENTERTAINMENT

THERE ARE BUT TWO CAUSES that pull on
Ghests: Loue and Businesse. I must in good
nature make much of the former, and the latter necessitie in-
forceth me to entertaine. But I like not to dwell vpon these.
A short time may satisfie visitation, and busines not hindered
by complement cannot last long.

Mee thinks, I should haue done now. It is tedious to meete
with a fellow that will stay to day & to morrow and the next
day on purpose to say he loueth. If he feare my memory that
he thus reiterateth Loue, let him giue me some token of remembrance. This tarriing perswades me rather the contrary;
hee is my enemy that thus eats vp my meate and Time without
any cause that perswadeth his stay. Truly, the name of a good
fellow is so deare a title that I had rather traffick with courser
stuffe and be called parsimonious, yea, miserable, if they will;
it smarts not halfe so ill as the phrase, *Euery bodies friend but
his owne.* I know some whome modesty restraineth from tell-

ing Impudency their faults. Alas, good Vertue, that thou art growne a coward and darest not discouer thy selfe. Well, I haue a medicine for these people; I will not be consumed liuing by these wormes. "What's your pleasure?" This is my answere, "Farewell."

These wordes haue an excellent vertue in thē; they deliuer you to Solitarinesse, the mother of Contemplation; they keepe your house sweete; and at dinner if you like a dish, it is your owne fault if you haue it not cold. When my occasions grow so desperately mad as, in despight of me, they will hale me abroad into throngs & great assemblies, he that entertains me, I will him speak to all, reserue a straunge familiaritie for the best, and my good word & courtesie generally. I haue knowne some affecting Courtesie ouerthrow their labours with not hauing choyse of Cōplements, but confounding a Gentleman and a Peasant with the likenesse of salutation and farewell. They were too blame to set vp shop so ill furnished. As men differ, so must their vsages and respectes; not to all, *I am the seruant of your seruant's seruant.* In truth, I am naturally kind and pittiful and would gladly giue euery man a testimonie that I neither hate nor contemne them. I will speake and pittie and lament with all; and to some giue my time without a fee, but not destroy my selfe for their sakes. They are no Gods; I need not sacrifice my selfe. There is crueltie in this courtesie; I must not do thus. Marry, any kindnes that shortens not in the spēding, that makes not the purse emptie, and the household-booke rich in *Items.* I am readie to be their Host and to entertaine all, but to keepe open house, vntill I shall be compelled to shut vp my doores, must be pardoned me. I haue a purse and a life, and all that I am for some fewe; but they are, indeed, but a fewe. *Non omnibus Dormio.*

OF HUMANE CONTENTMENT

BEHOLD THE GODS OF THE WORLD, the soule of action, the motion of the inhabitants of the earth, the point, the conclusion whereunto all thoughts are reflected; this is the master of al trades, Artes, Sciences, and Professions; for this, the husbandman findes a sweetnesse in labour, the Artizan in following his trade, the Artist in the inquisition of knowledge, souldiers in pursuing danger, polititians in the working of the minde, in plotting and fetching in strange conclusions to vphold practises. This is the garland that makes euery one loue victory. This is the reconciling object of the dissenting constitution and courses of men, for they all agree that contentment is the place where they desire to end their iournies. But that the world should haue still the right vse and not bee desolated with man's neglect of inquiring and vttering her secrets, this contentment is fashioned like our loues; what I call fayre, another thinkes ill fauored; another out of deformities pickes beauties; thus contentment, which according to the minds of men is drawne out of a numberlesse number of courses, which mystery of Nature's doth make all agree. That contentment is to be sought (and to disseuer them in the manner of their search, ioyned with the other of making all formes louely in some eyes) vpholdes the world, for by this last the world is peopled. By the first, her people made industrious, and the great volume of the world in no corner left vnnoted but stirres and flourisheth as the chiefe and master peece of Nature. Thus doe we propound a cause & reason of our life and make euery day beget vs occasion either of following or learning to follow our quest. When we do not goe forward our selues, we behold others, which like a map layes out the course of our trauaile. But when, according to the excellency or grosnesse of our choise, the determined contentment approcheth, we flie from, not the enjoying, but the opinion we had. Another contentment is set vp; that obtained, another. So doth our humane liues runne after contentment, but neuer ouertake her—wee cannot, for contentment is diuine, our bodies earthly. Our mindes, we feele, ouertakes her, for the propounded cōtentment pleaseth her. She embraceth it and is already in possession. But whē it comes, so short doth it fall of her expectation as she erects another—a plaine argument of her diuinity and a true signe that reall contentment is not of this world nor to be grasped within our earthly armes.

John Earle

1600? · 1665

*John Earle composed his little book of "characters"
while he was an undergraduate at Oxford. It was
immediately popular on its first appearance, in
1628, and was republished nine or ten times before
the author's death. Earle rose rapidly in the
Anglican church, and during the exile of the court
he served as personal chaplain to Prince Charles.
After the Restoration, he was rewarded by being
made Bishop, first of Worcester and later of Salisbury. In 1665, he went with the king to Oxford to
escape the Plague but was stricken and died there.
He is remembered as a man of wit and good sense,
of understanding and great kindness of heart.*

A CHILD

IS A MAN IN A SMALL LETTER, yet the best copy
of Adam before he tasted of Eve or the apple;
and he is happy whose small practice in the world can only
write his character. He is nature's fresh picture newly drawn
in oil, which time, and much handling, dims and defaces.
His soul is yet a white paper unscribbled with observations
of the world, wherewith, at length, it becomes a blurred
notebook. He is purely happy, because he knows no evil, nor
hath made means by sin to be acquainted with misery. He
arrives not at the mischief of being wise, nor endures evils to
come, by forseeing them. He kisses and loves all, and, when
the smart of the rod is past, smiles on his beater. Nature and
his parents alike dandle him, and tice him on with a bait of
sugar to a draught of wormwood. He plays yet, like a young
'prentice the first day, and is not come to his task of melan-

choly. All the language he speaks yet is tears, and they serve him well enough to express his necessity. His hardest labor is his tongue, as if he were loth to use so deceitful an organ; and he is best company with it when he can but prattle. We laugh at his foolish sports, but his game is our earnest; and his drums, rattles, and hobby-horses, but the emblems and mocking of man's business. His father hath writ him as his own little story, wherein he reads those days of his life that he cannot remember, and sighs to see what innocence he has out-lived. The older he grows, he is a stair lower from God; and, like his first father, much worse in his breeches. He is the Christian's example, and the old man's relapse; the one imitates his pureness. and the other falls into his simplicity. Could he put off his body with his little coat, he had got eternity without a burden, and exchanged but one heaven for another.

A YOUNG GENTLEMAN OF THE UNIVERSITY

IS ONE THAT COMES THERE TO WEAR A GOWN, and to say hereafter, he has been at the university. His father sent him thither because he heard there were the best fencing and dancing schools; from these he has his education, from his tutor the oversight. The first element of his knowledge is to be shown the colleges, and initiated in a tavern by the way, which hereafter he will learn of himself. The two marks of his seniority is the bare velvet of his gown, and his proficiency at tennis, where when he can once play a set, he is a freshman no more. His study has commonly handsome shelves, his books neat silk strings, which he shows to his father's man, and is loth to untie or take down for fear of misplacing. Upon foul days for recreation he retires thither, and looks over the pretty book his tutor reads to him, which is commonly some short history, or a piece of *Euphormio;* for which his tutor gives him money to spend next day. His main loitering is at the library, where he studies arms and books of honor, and turns a gentleman critic in pedigrees. Of all things he endures not to be mistaken for a scholar, and hates a black suit though it be made of satin. His companion is ordinarily some stale fellow, that has been notorious for an ingle to gold hatbands, whom he admires at first, afterwards scorns. If he have spirit or wit he may light of better company, and may learn some flashes of wit, which may do him knight's service in the country hereafter. But he is now gone to the inns-of-court, where he studies to forget what he learned before, his acquaintance and the fashion.

A DETRACTOR

Is ONE OF A MORE CUNNING AND ACTIVE ENVY, wherewith he gnaws not foolishly himself but throws it abroad and would have it blister others. He is commonly some weak-parted fellow, and worse minded, yet is strangely ambitious to match others, not by mounting to their worth but by bringing them down with his tongue to his own poorness. He is indeed like the red dragon that pursued the woman, for when he cannot over-reach another, he opens his mouth and throws a flood after to drown him. You cannot anger him worse than to do well, and he hates you more bitterly for this than if you had cheated him of his patrimony with your own discredit. He is always slighting the general opinion and wondering why such and such men should be applauded. Commend a good divine, he cries postilling; a philologer, pedantry; a poet, riming; a schoolman, dull wrangling; a sharp conceit, boyishness; an honest man, plausibility. He comes to public things not to learn but to catch, and if there be but one solecism, that's all he carries away. He looks on all things with a prepared sourness, and is still furnished with a "pish" beforehand or some musty proverb that disrelishes all things whatsoever. If fear of the company make him second a commendation, it is like a law-writ, always with a clause and exception, or to smooth his way to some greater scandal. He will grant you something and abate more; and this abatement shall in conclusion take away all he granted. His speech concludes still with an "Oh but" and "I could wish one thing amended;" and this one thing shall be enough to deface all his former commendations. He will be very inward with a man to fish some bad out of him and make his slanders hereafter more authentic, when it is said a friend reported it. He will inveigle you to naughtiness to get your good name into his clutches, and make you drunk to show you reeling. He passes the more plausibly because all men have a smack of his humor and that is thought freeness which is malice. If he can say nothing of a man, he will seem to speak riddles, as if he could tell strange stories if he would, and when he has racked his invention to the utmost, he ends, "But I wish him well, and therefore must hold my peace." He is always listening and enquiring after men and suffers not a cloak to pass by him unexamined. In brief, he is one that has lost all good himself and is loth to find it in another.

Abraham Cowley

1618 · 1667

*Abraham Cowley, English poet and physician, was
famous in his own day for his poetry and a
play, "The Guardian." His sympathies with the
Royalist cause led him to follow the exiled court to
France, where he remained for twelve years in
the service of the queen. His inept speech
alienated many of his Royalist friends after his
return to England in 1656, and subsequently he
failed in gaining the preferment to which his
faithful service should have entitled him.
His Essays were published in the folio
edition of his works in 1668.*

THE DANGERS OF AN HONEST MAN
IN MUCH COMPANY

IF TWENTY THOUSAND NAKED AMERICANS were
not able to resist the assaults of but twenty
well-armed Spaniards, I see little possibility for one honest
man to defend himself against twenty thousand knaves who
are all furnished *cap-a-pie* with the defensive arms of worldly
prudence, and the offensive, too, of craft and malice. He will
find no less odds than this against him, if he have much to do
in human affairs. The only advice, therefore, which I can
give him is to be sure not to venture his person any longer in
the open campaign, to retreat and entrench himself, to stop
up all avenues, and draw up all bridges against so numerous an
enemy.

The truth of it is that a man in much business must either
make himself a knave, or else the world will make him a fool;
and, if the injury went no farther than the being laughed at, a

wise man would content himself with the revenge of retalia-
tion; but the case is much worse, for these civil cannibals, too,
as well as the wild ones, not only dance about such a taken
stranger, but at last devour him. A sober man cannot get too
soon out of drunken company, though they be never so kind
and merry among themselves; 'tis not unpleasant only, but
dangerous to him.

Do ye wonder that a virtuous man should love to be alone?
It is hard for him to be otherwise; he is so when he is among
ten thousand: neither is the solitude so uncomfortable to be
alone without any other creature, as it is to be alone in the
midst of wild beasts. Man is to man all kind of beasts: a fawn-
ing dog, a roaring lion, a thieving fox, a robbing wolf, a dis-
sembling crocodile, a treacherous decoy, and a rapacious
vulture. The civilest, methinks, of all nations, are those whom
we account the most barbarous; there is some moderation and
good-nature in the Toupinambaltians, who eat no men but
their enemies, whilst we learned and polite and Christian
Europeans, like so many pikes and sharks, prey upon everything that we can swallow. It is the great boast of eloquence
and philosophy that they first congregated men dispersed,
united them into societies, and built up the houses and the
walls of cities. I wish they could unravel all they had woven,
that we might have our woods and our innocence again instead of our castles and our policies. They have assembled
many thousands of scattered people into one body: 'tis true,
they have done so; they have brought them into cities to
cozen, and into armies to murder one another; they found
them hunters and fishers of wild creatures; they have made
them hunters and fishers of their brethren; they boast to have
reduced them to a state of peace, when the truth is, they have
only taught them an art of war; they have framed, I must
confess, wholesome laws for the restraint of vice, but they
raised first that devil which now they conjure and cannot bind;
though there were before no punishments for wickedness,
yet there was less committed, because there were no rewards
for it.

But the men who praise philosophy from this topic are

much deceived; let oratory answer for itself, the tinkling perhaps of that may unite a swarm: it never was the work of philosophy to assemble multitudes, but to regulate only, and govern them when they were assembled; to make the best of an evil, and bring them, as much as is possible, to unity again. Avarice and ambition only were the first builders of towns and founders of empire; they said, *Go to, let us build us a city and a tower whose top may reach unto heaven, and let us make us a name, lest we be scattered abroad upon the face of the earth.* What was the beginning of Rome, the metropolis of all the world? What was it but a concourse of thieves and a sanctuary of criminals? It was justly named by the augury of no less than twelve vultures, and the founder cemented his walls with the blood of his brother. Not unlike to this was the beginning even of the first town, too, in the world, and such is the original sin of most cities: their actual increase daily with their age and growth; the more people, the more wicked all of them; every one brings in his part to inflame the contagion, which becomes at last so universal and so strong that no precepts can be sufficient preservatives, nor anything secure our safety but flight from among the infected.

We ought, in the choice of a situation, to regard above all things the healthfulness of the place, and the healthfulness of it for the mind rather than for the body. But suppose (which is hardly to be supposed) we had antidote enough against this poison; nay, suppose further, we were always and at all pieces armed and provided both against the assaults of hostility and the mines of treachery, 'twill yet be but an uncomfortable life to be ever in alarms; though we were compassed round with fire, to defend ourselves from wild beasts, the lodging would be unpleasant, because we must always be obliged to watch that fire, and to fear no less the defects of our guard than the diligence of our enemy. The sum of this is, that a virtuous man is in danger to be trod upon and destroyed in the crowd of his contraries, nay, which is worse, to be changed and corrupted by them; and that 'tis impossible to escape both these inconveniences without so much caution as will take away the whole quiet, that is, the happiness, of his life.

Ye see, then, what he may lose; but, I pray, what can he get there?

Quid Romae faciam? Mentiri nescio.

What should a man of truth and honesty do at Rome? He can neither understand nor speak the language of the place; a naked man may swim in the sea, but 'tis not the way to catch fish there; they are likelier to devour him than he them, if he bring no nets and use no deceits. I think, therefore, it was wise and friendly advice which Martial gave to Fabian when he met him newly arrived at Rome:

> Honest and poor, faithful in word and thought;
> What has thee, Fabian, to the city brought?
> Thou neither the buffoon nor bawd canst play,
> Nor with false whispers th' innocent betray;
> Nor corrupt wives, nor from rich beldames get
> A living by thy industry and sweat;
> Nor with vain promises and projects cheat,
> Nor bribe or flatter any of the great.
> But you're a man of learning, prudent, just;
> A man of courage, firm, and fit for trust.
> Why, you may stay, and live unenvied here;
> But (faith) go back, and keep you where you were.

Nay, if nothing of all this were in the case, yet the very sight of uncleanness is loathsome to the cleanly; the sight of folly and impiety, vexatious to the wise and pious.

Lucretius, by his favour, though a good poet, was but an ill-natured man when he said, "It was delightful to see other men in a great storm." And no less ill-natured should I think Democritus, who laughed at all the world, but that he retired himself so much out of it, that we may perceive he took no great pleasure in that kind of mirth. I have been drawn twice or thrice by company to go to Bedlam, and have seen others very much delighted with the fantastical extravagency of so many various madnesses, which upon me wrought so contrary an effect that I always returned, not only melancholy, but even sick with the sight. My comparison there was perhaps too tender, for I meet a thousand madmen abroad without any perturbation; though to weigh the matter justly, the total loss of reason is less deplorable than the total depravation of it. An exact judge of human blessings, of riches, honours, beauty, even of wit itself, should pity the abuse of them more than the want.

Briefly, though a wise man could pass never so securely through the great roads of human life, yet he will meet perpetually with so many objects and occasions of compassion, grief, shame, anger, hatred, indignation, and all passions but envy (for he will find nothing to deserve that) that he had better strike into some private path; nay, go so far, if he could, out of the common way, *ut nec facta audiat Pelopidarum*, that he might not so much as hear of the actions of the sons of Adam. But whither shall we fly then? Into the deserts, like the ancient hermits?

—*Qua terra patet, fera regnat Erinnys,*
In facinus iurasse putes.

One would think that all mankind had bound themselves by an oath to do all the wickedness they can, that they had all (as the Scripture speaks) *sold themselves to sin*. The difference only is, that some are a little more crafty (and but a little, God knows) in making of the bargain. I thought, when I went first to dwell in the country, that without doubt I should have met there with the simplicity of the old poetical golden age; I thought to have found no inhabitants there but such as the shepherds of Sir Philip Sidney in Arcadia, or of Monsieur d'Urfe upon the banks of Lignon, and began to consider with myself which way I might recommend no less to posterity the happiness and innocence of the men of Chertsea: but to confess the truth, I perceived quickly by infallible demonstrations that I was still in Old England, and not in Arcadia or La Forrest; that, if I could not content myself with any thing less than exact fidelity in human conversation, I had almost as good go back and seek for it in the Court, or the Exchange, or Westminster Hall. I ask again then, whither shall we fly, or what shall we do? The world may so come in a man's way that he cannot choose but salute it; he must take heed, though, not to go a-whoring after it. If by any lawful vocation or just necessity men happen to be married to it, I can only give them St. Paul's advice: *Brethren, the time is short; it remains that they that have wives be as though they had none. But I would that all men were even as I myself.*

In all cases they must be sure that they do *mundum ducere*, and not *mundo nubere*. They must retain the superiority and headship over it; happy are they, who can get out of the sight of this deceitful beauty, that they may not be led so much as into temptation, who have not only quitted the metropolis, but can abstain from ever seeing the next market town of their country.

Jonathan Swift

1667 · 1745

Jonathan Swift was an Irish-born Englishman who entered the church after being disappointed in a political career. Even in the church he failed to achieve his aim and spent his most productive period as Dean of St. Patrick's in Dublin. His rare gift for satire showed itself early in The Battle of the Books *and* A Tale of a Tub *and reached its fullest expression in* Gulliver's Travels *(1726). His later life was darkened by loneliness and despair for the human race and, finally, madness.*

A MODEST PROPOSAL

FOR PREVENTING THE CHILDREN OF POOR PEOPLE IN IRELAND
FROM BEING A BURDEN TO THEIR PARENTS OR COUNTRY,
AND FOR MAKING THEM BENEFICIAL TO THE PUBLIC

IT IS A MELANCHOLY OBJECT to those who walk through this great town [Dublin] or travel in the country, when they see the streets, the roads, and cabin doors crowded with beggars of the female sex, followed by three, four, or six children, all in rags and importuning every passenger for an alms. These mothers, instead of being able to work for their honest livelihood, are forced to employ all their time in strolling to beg sustenance for their helpless infants, who, as they grow up, either turn thieves for want of work, or leave their dear native country to fight for the Pretender in Spain, or sell themselves to the Barbadoes.

I think it is agreed by all parties that this prodigious number of children in the arms, or on the backs, or at the heels of their mothers, and frequently of their fathers, is in the present deplorable state of the kingdom a very great additional grievance; and, therefore, whoever could find out a fair, cheap, and easy method of making these children sound, useful members of the commonwealth, would deserve so well of the public as to have his statue set up for a preserver of the nation.

But my intention is very far from being confined to provide only for the children of professed beggars; it is of a much greater extent, and shall take in the whole number of infants at a certain age who are born of parents in effect as little able to support them as those who demand our charity in the streets.

As to my own part, having turned my thoughts for many years upon this important subject, and maturely weighed the several schemes of our projectors, I have always found them grossly mistaken in their computation. It is true, a child just dropped from its dam may be supported by her milk for a solar year with little other nourishment, at most not above the value of two shillings, which the mother may certainly get, or the value in scraps, by her lawful occupation of begging; and it is exactly at one year old that I propose to provide for them in such a manner as instead of being a charge upon their parents or the parish, or wanting food and raiment for the rest of their lives, they shall, on the contrary, contribute to the feeding and partly to the clothing of many thousands.

There is likewise another great advantage in my scheme, that it will prevent those voluntary abortions, and that horrid practice of women murdering their bastard children, alas! too frequent among us! sacrificing the poor innocent babes, I doubt, more to avoid the expense than the shame, which would move tears and pity in the most savage and inhuman breast.

The number of souls in this kingdom being usually reckoned one million and a half, of these, I calculate there may be about two hundred thousand couples whose wives are breeders; from which number I subtract thirty thousand couples, who are able to maintain their own children (although I apprehend there cannot be so many, under the present distresses of the kingdom); but this being granted, there will remain one hundred and seventy thousand breeders. I again subtract fifty thousand for those women who miscarry, or whose children die by accident or disease within the year. There only remain an hundred and twenty thousand children of poor parents annually born. The question therefore is, how this number shall be reared and provided for? which, as I have already said, under the present situation of affairs, is utterly impossible by all the methods hitherto proposed. For we can neither employ them in handicraft or agriculture; we neither build houses (I mean in the country) nor cultivate land; they can very seldom pick up a livelihood by stealing till they arrive at six years old, except where they are of towardly parts, although I confess they learn the rudiments much earlier, during which time, they can, however, be properly looked upon only as probationers, as I have been informed by a principal gentleman in the county of Cavan, who protested to me that he never knew above one or two instances under the age of six, even in a part of the kingdom so renowned for the quickest proficiency in that art.

I am assured by our merchants that a boy or girl before twelve years old is no saleable commodity, and even when they come to this age they will not yield above three pounds or three pounds and half-a-crown at most on the exchange; which cannot turn to account either to the parents or the kingdom, the charge of nutriment and rags having been at least four times that value.

I shall now therefore humbly propose my own thoughts, which I hope will not be liable to the least objection.

I have been assured by a very knowing American of my acquaintance in London, that a young healthy child well nursed is at a year old a most delicious, nourishing, and wholesome food, whether stewed, roasted, baked, or boiled; and I make no doubt that it will equally serve in a fricassee or a ragout.

I do therefore humbly offer it to public consideration that of the hundred and twenty thousand children already computed, twenty thousand may be reserved for breed, whereof only one-fourth part to be males, which is more than we allow to sheep, black cattle or swine; and my reason is that these children are seldom the fruits of marriage, a circumstance not much regarded by our savages; therefore one male will be sufficient to serve four females. That the remaining hundred thousand may, at a year old, be offered in sale to the persons of quality and fortune through the kingdom, always advising the mother to let them suck plentifully in the last month, so as to render them plump and fat for a good table. A child will make two dishes at an entertainment for friends, and when the family dines alone, the fore or hind quarter will make a reasonable dish, and seasoned with a little pepper or salt will be very good boiled on the fourth day, especially in winter.

I have reckoned upon a medium that a child just born will weigh twelve pounds, and in a solar year, if tolerably nursed, will increase to twenty-eight pounds.

I grant this food will be somewhat dear, and therefore very proper for landlords, who, as they have already devoured most of the parents, seem to have the best title to the children.

Infants' flesh will be in season throughout the year, but more plentiful in March, and a little before and after; for we are told by a grave author, an eminent French physician, that fish being a prolific diet, there are more children born in Roman Catholic countries about nine months after Lent than at any other season; therefore, reckoning a year after Lent, the markets will be more glutted than usual, because the number of popish infants is at least three to one in this kingdom, and therefore it will have one other collateral advantage, by lessening the number of papists among us.

I have already computed the charge of nursing a beggar's child (in which list I reckon all cottagers, laborers, and four-fifths of the farmers) to be about two shillings per annum, rags included; and I believe no gentleman would repine to give ten shillings for the carcass of a good fat child, which, as I have said, will make four dishes of excellent nutritive meat, when he has only some particular friend or his own family to dine with him. Thus the squire will learn to be a good landlord, and grow popular among his tenants; the mother will have eight shillings net profit, and be fit for work till she produces another child.

Those who are more thrifty (as I must confess the times require) may flay the carcass, the skin of which artificially dressed will make admirable gloves for ladies, and summer boots for fine gentlemen.

As to our city of Dublin, shambles may be appointed for this purpose in the most convenient parts of it, and butchers, we may be assured, will not be wanting, although I rather recommend buying the children alive, and dressing them hot from the knife as we do roasting pigs.

A very worthy person, a true lover of his country, and whose virtues I highly esteem, was lately pleased, in discoursing on this matter, to offer a refinement upon my scheme. He said that many gentlemen of this kingdom, having of late destroyed their deer, he conceived that the want of venison might be well supplied by the bodies of young lads and maidens, not exceeding fourteen years of age nor under twelve, so great a number of both sexes in every country being now ready to starve for want of work and service, and these to be disposed of by their parents, if alive, or otherwise by their nearest relations. But with due deference to so excellent a friend and so deserving a patriot, I cannot be altogether in his sentiments; for as to the males, my American acquaintance assured me from frequent experience that their flesh was generally tough and lean, like that of our school-boys, by continual exercise, and their taste disagreeable; and to fatten them would not answer the charge. Then as to the females, it would, I think, with humble submission, be a loss to the public, because they soon would become breeders themselves; and besides, it is not improbable that some scrupulous people might be apt to censure such a practice (although indeed very unjustly) as a little bordering upon cruelty, which, I confess, has always been with me the strongest objection against any project, however so well intended.

But in order to justify my friend, he confessed that this expedient was put into his head by the famous Psalmanazar, a native of the island Formosa, who came from thence to London above twenty years ago, and in conversation told my friend, that in his country when any young person happened to be put to death, the executioner sold the carcass to persons of quality as a prime dainty, and that in his time the body of a plump girl of fifteen, who was crucified for an attempt to poison the emperor, was sold to his imperial majesty's prime minister of state and other great mandarins of the court, in joints from the gibbet, at four hundred crowns. Neither indeed can I deny that if the same use were made of several plump young girls in this town, who, without one single groat to their fortunes, cannot stir abroad without a chair, and appear at the playhouse and assemblies in foreign fineries which they never will pay for, the kingdom would not be the worse.

Some persons of a desponding spirit are in great concern about that vast number of poor people, who are aged, diseased, or maimed, and I have been desired to employ my thoughts what course may be taken to ease the nation of so grievous an encumbrance. But I am not in the least pain upon that matter, because it is very well known that they are every day dying and rotting by cold, and famine, and filth, and vermin, as fast as can be reasonably expected. And as to the younger laborers, they are now in as hopeful a condition; they cannot get work, and consequently pine away for want of nourishment, to a degree that if at any time they are accidentally hired to common labor, they have not strength to perform it; and thus the country and themselves are happily delivered from the evils to come.

I have too long digressed, and therefore shall return to my subject. I think the advantages by the proposal which I have made are obvious, and many, as well as of the highest importance.

For first, as I have already observed, it would greatly lessen the number of papists, with whom we are yearly overrun, being the principal breeders of the nation as well as our most dangerous enemies; and who stay at home on purpose with a design to deliver the kingdom to the Pretender, hoping to take their advantage by the absence of so many good protestants, who have chosen rather to leave their country than stay at home and pay tithes against their conscience to an episcopal curate.

Secondly, The poorer tenants will have something valuable of their own, which by law may be made liable to distress, and help to pay their landlord's rent, their corn and cattle being already seized, and money a thing unknown.

Thirdly, Whereas the maintenance of an hundred thousand children, from two years old and upward, cannot be computed at less than ten shillings a-piece per annum, the nation's stock will be thereby increased fifty thousand pounds per annum, besides the profit of a new dish introduced to the tables of all gentlemen of fortune in the kingdom who have any refinement in taste. And the money will circulate among ourselves, the goods being entirely of our own growth and manufacture.

Fourthly, The constant breeders, beside the gain of eight shillings sterling per annum by the sale of their children, will be rid of the charge of maintaining them after the first year.

Fifthly, This food would likewise bring great custom to taverns, where the vintners will certainly be so prudent as to procure the best receipts for dressing it to perfection, and consequently have their houses frequented by all the fine gentlemen, who justly value themselves upon their knowledge in good eating; and a skilful cook, who understands how to oblige his guests, will contrive to make it as expensive as they please.

Sixthly, This would be a great inducement to marriage, which all wise nations have either encouraged by rewards or enforced by laws and penalties. It would increase the care and tenderness of mothers toward their children, when they were sure of a settlement for life to the poor babes, provided in some sort by the public, to their annual profit instead of expense. We should see an honest emulation among the married women, which of them could bring the fattest child to the market. Men would become as fond of their wives during the time of their pregnancy as they are now of their mares in foal, their cows in calf, or sows when they are ready to farrow; nor offer to beat or kick them (as is too frequent a practice) for fear of a miscarriage.

Many other advantages might be enumerated. For instance, the addition of some thousand carcasses in our exportation of barreled beef, the propagation of swine's flesh, and improvement in the art of making good bacon, so much wanted among us by the great destruction of pigs, too frequent at our tables; which are in no way comparable in taste or magnificence to a well-grown, fat yearling child, which roasted whole will make a considerable figure at a lord mayor's feast, or any other public entertainment. But this and many others I omit, being studious of brevity.

Supposing that one thousand families in this city would be constant customers for infants' flesh, beside others who might have it at merry-meetings, particularly weddings and christenings, I compute that Dublin would take off annually about twenty thousand carcasses, and the rest of the kingdom (where probably they will be sold somewhat cheaper) the remaining eighty thousand.

I can think of no one objection that will possibly be raised against this proposal, unless it should be urged that the number of people will be thereby much lessened in the kingdom. This I freely own, and it was indeed one principal design in offering it to the world. I desire the reader will observe that I calculate my remedy for this one individual kingdom of Ireland, and for no other that ever was, is, or, I think, ever can be upon earth. Therefore let no man talk to me of other expedients: of taxing our absentees at five shillings a pound; of using neither clothes nor household furniture, except what is of our own growth and manufacture; of utterly rejecting the materials and instruments that promote foreign luxury; of curing the expensiveness of pride, vanity, idleness, and gaming in our women; of introducing a vein of parsimony, prudence, and temperance; of learning to love our country, in the want of which we differ even from Laplanders and the inhabitants of Topinamboo; of quitting our animosities and factions, nor act any longer like the Jews, who were murdering one another at the very moment their city was taken; of being a little cautious not to sell our country and consciences for nothing; of teaching landlords to have at least one degree of mercy toward their tenants; lastly, of putting a spirit of honesty, industry, and skill into our shop-keepers, who, if a resolution could now be taken to buy only our native goods, would immediately unite to cheat and exact upon us in the price, the measure, and the goodness, nor could ever yet be brought to make one fair proposal of just dealing, though often and earnestly invited to it.

Therefore, I repeat, let no man talk to me of these and the like expedients, till he has at least some glimpse of hope that there will be ever some hearty and sincere attempt to put them in practice.

But as to myself, having been wearied out for many years with offering vain, idle, visionary thoughts, and at length utterly despairing of success, I fortunately fell upon this proposal, which, as it is wholly new, so it has something solid and real, of no expense and little trouble, full in our own power, and whereby we can incur no danger in disobliging England. For this kind of commodity will not bear exportation, the flesh being of too tender a consistence to admit a long continuance in salt, although perhaps I could name a country which would be glad to eat up our whole nation without it.

After all, I am not so violently bent upon my own opinion as to reject any offer proposed by wise men, which shall be found equally innocent, cheap, easy, and effectual. But before something of that kind shall be advanced in contradiction to my scheme, and offering a better, I desire the author or authors will be pleased maturely to consider two points. First, as things now stand, how they will be able to find food and raiment for an hundred thousand useless mouths and backs. And secondly, there being a round million of creatures in human figure throughout this kingdom, whose whole subsistence put into a common stock would leave them in debt two millions of pounds sterling, adding those who are beggars by profession to the bulk of farmers, cottagers, and laborers, with their wives and children, who are beggars in effect; I desire those politicians, who dislike my overture, and may perhaps be so bold as to attempt an answer, that they will first ask the parents of these mortals, whether they would not at this day think it a great happiness to have been sold for food at a year old in the manner I prescribe, and thereby have avoided such a perpetual scene of misfortunes as they have since gone through by the oppression of landlords, the impossibility of paying rent without money or trade, the want of common sustenance, with neither house nor clothes to cover them from the inclemencies of the weather, and the most inevitable prospect of entailing the like or greater miseries upon their breed for ever.

I profess, in the sincerity of my heart, that I have not the least personal interest in endeavoring to promote this necessary work, having no other motive than the public good of my country, by advancing our trade, providing for infants, relieving the poor, and giving some pleasure to the rich. I have no children by which I can propose to get a single penny; the youngest being nine years old, and my wife past child-bearing

HINTS TOWARD AN
ESSAY ON CONVERSATION

I HAVE OBSERVED FEW OBVIOUS SUBJECTS to have been so seldom, or at least so slightly, handled as this; and indeed I know few so difficult to be treated as it ought, nor yet, upon which there seems so much to be said.

Most things pursued by men for the happiness of public or private life, our wit or folly have so refined that they seldom subsist but in idea; a true friend, a good marriage, a perfect form of government, with some others, require so many ingredients, so good in their several kinds, and so much niceness in mixing them, that for some thousands of years men have despaired of reducing their schemes to perfection; but in conversation it is or might be otherwise; for here we are only to avoid a multitude of errors, which, although a matter of some difficulty, may be in every man's power, for want of which it remains as mere an idea as the other. Therefore, it seems to me that the truest way to understand conversation is to know the faults and errors to which it is subject, and from thence every man to form maxims to himself whereby it may be regulated, because it requires few talents to which most men are not born, or at least may not acquire without any great genius or study. For nature has left every man a capacity of being agreeable, though not of shining in company; and there are a hundred men sufficiently qualified for both, who, by a very few faults, that they might correct in half an hour, are not so much as tolerable.

I was prompted to write my thoughts upon this subject by mere indignation, to reflect that so useful and innocent a pleasure, so fitted for every period and condition of life, and so much in all men's power, should be so much neglected and abused.

And in this discourse it will be necessary to note those errors that are obvious, as well as others which are seldomer observed, since there are few so obvious or acknowledged into which most men, some time or other, are not apt to run.

For instance, nothing is more generally exploded than the folly of talking too much; yet I rarely remember to have seen five people together, where some one among them has not been predominant in that kind, to the great constraint and disgust of all the rest. But among such as deal in multitudes of words, none are comparable to the sober, deliberate talker, who proceeds with much thought and caution, makes his preface, branches out into several digressions, finds a hint that puts him in mind of another story, which he promises to tell you when this is done; comes back regularly to his subject, cannot readily call to mind some person's name, holding his head, complains of his memory; the whole company all this while in suspense; at length says it is no matter, and so goes on. And, to crown the business, it perhaps proves at last a story the company has heard fifty times before; or, at best, some insipid adventure of the relater.

Another general fault in conversation is that of those who affect to talk of themselves; some, without any ceremony, will run over the history of their lives; will relate the annals of their diseases, with the several symptoms and circumstances of them; will enumerate the hardships and injustice they have suffered in court, in parliament, in love, or in law. Others are more dexterous, and with great art will lie on the watch to hook in their own praise; they will call a witness to remember they always foretold what would happen in such a case, but none would believe them; they advised such a man from the beginning, and told him the consequences, just as they happened, but he would have his own way. Others make a vanity of telling their faults; they are the strangest men in the world; they cannot dissemble; they own it is a folly; they have lost abundance of advantages by it; but, if you would give them the world, they cannot help it; there is something in their nature that abhors insincerity and constraint—with many other insufferable topics of the same altitude.

Of such mighty importance every man is to himself, and ready to think he is so to others, without once making this easy and obvious reflection, that his affairs can have no more weight with other men than theirs have with him; and how little that is, he is sensible enough.

Where a company has met, I often have observed two persons discover, by some accident, that they were bred together at the same school or university; after which the rest are condemned to silence, and to listen while these two are refreshing each other's memory with the arch tricks and passages of themselves and their comrades.

I know a great officer of the army who will sit for some time with a supercilious and impatient silence, full of anger and contempt for those who are talking; at length, of a sudden, demand audience, decide the matter in a short, dogmatical way; then withdraw within himself again, and vouchsafe to talk no more until his spirits circulate again to the same point.

There are some faults in conversation which none are so subject to as the men of wit, nor ever so much as when they are with each other. If they have opened their mouths without endeavouring to say a witty thing, they think it is so many words lost: it is a torment to the hearers, as much as to themselves, to see them upon the rack for invention, and in perpetual constraint, with so little success. They must do something extraordinary in order to acquit themselves and answer their character, else the standers-by may be disappointed, and be apt to think them only like the rest of mortals. I have known two men of wit industriously brought together, in order to entertain the company, where they have made a very ridiculous figure and provided all the mirth at their own expense.

I know a man of wit who is never easy but where he can be allowed to dictate and preside; he neither expects to be informed or entertained, but to display his own talents. His business is to be good company, and not good conversation; and therefore he chooses to frequent those who are content to listen and profess themselves his admirers. And, indeed, the worst conversation I ever remember to have heard in my life was that at Will's coffee-house, where the wits (as they were called) used formerly to assemble; that is to say, five or six men who had writ plays, or at least prologues, or had a share in a miscellany, came thither and entertained one another with their trifling composures, in so important an air as if they had been the noblest efforts of human nature, or that the fate of kingdoms depended on them; and they were usually attended with an humble audience of young students from the inns of court or the universities, who at due distance listened to these oracles, and returned home with great contempt for their law and philosophy, their heads filled with trash under the name of politeness, criticism, and *belles-lettres*.

By these means, the poets, for many years past, were all overrun with pedantry. For, as I take it, the word is not properly used, because pedantry is the too frequent or unseasonable obtruding our own knowledge in common discourse, and placing too great a value upon it; by which definition, men of the court or the army may be as guilty of pedantry as a philosopher or a divine; and it is the same vice in women, when they are over copious upon the subject of their petticoats, or their fans, or their china. For which reason, although it be a piece of prudence as well as good manners to put men upon talking on subjects they are best versed in, yet that is a liberty a wise man could hardly take, because, beside the imputation of pedantry, it is what he would never improve by.

The great town is usually provided with some player, mimic, or buffoon, who has a general reception at the good tables; familiar and domestic with persons of the first quality, and usually sent for at every meeting to divert the company—against which I have no objection. You go there as to a farce or a puppetshow; your business is only to laugh in season, either out of inclination or civility, while this merry companion is acting his part. It is a business he has undertaken, and we are to suppose he is paid for his day's work. I only quarrel when, in select and private meetings, where men of wit and learning are invited to pass an evening, this jester should be admitted to run over his circle of tricks and make the whole company unfit for any other conversation, beside the indignity of confounding men's talents at so shameful a rate.

Raillery is the finest part of conversation; but, as it is our usual custom to counterfeit and adulterate whatever is too dear for us, so we have done with this, and turned it all into what is generally called repartee, or being smart; just as when an expensive fashion comes up, those who are not able to reach it, content themselves with some paltry imitation. It now passes for raillery to run a man down in discourse, to put him out of countenance and make him ridiculous; sometimes to expose the defects of his person or understanding; on all which occasions he is obliged not to be angry, to avoid the imputation of not being able to take a jest. It is admirable to observe one who is dexterous at this art of singling out a weak adversary, getting the laugh on his side, and then carrying all before him. The French, from whence we borrow the word, have a quite different idea of the thing, and so had we in the politer age of our fathers. Raillery was to say something that at first appeared a reproach or reflection, but by some turn of wit, unexpected and surprising, ended always in a compliment, and to the advantage of the person it was addressed to. And surely one of the best rules in conversation is, never say a thing which any of the company can reasonably wish we had rather left unsaid; nor can there anything be well more contrary to the ends for which people meet together than to part unsatisfied with each other or themselves.

There are two faults in conversation which appear very different, yet arise from the same root and are equally blameable; I mean an impatience to interrupt others, and the uneasiness of being interrupted ourselves. The two chief ends of conversation are to entertain and improve those we are among, or to receive those benefits ourselves; which whoever will consider, cannot easily run into either of these two errors; because, when any man speaks in company, it is to be supposed he does it for his hearers' sake, and not his own; so that common discretion will teach us not to force their attention, if they are not willing to lend it; nor, on the other side, to interrupt him who is in possession, because that is in the grossest manner to give the preference to our own good sense.

There are some people whose good manners will not suffer them to interrupt you, but, what is almost as bad, will discover abundance of impatience and lie upon the watch until you have done, because they have started something in their own thoughts which they long to be delivered of. Meantime, they are so far from regarding what passes that their imaginations are wholly turned upon what they have in reserve, for fear it should slip out of their memory; and thus they confine their invention, which might otherwise range over a hundred things full as good, and that might be much more naturally introduced.

There is a sort of rude familiarity which some people, by practicing among their intimates, have introduced into their general conversation, and would have it pass for innocent freedom or humour; which is a dangerous experiment in our northern climate, where all the little decorum and politeness we have are purely forced by art, and are so ready to lapse into barbarity. This, among the Romans, was the raillery of slaves, of which we have many instances in Plautus. It seems to have been introduced among us by Cromwell, who by preferring the scum of the people made it a court entertainment, of which I have heard many particulars; and, considering all things were turned upside down, it was reasonable and judicious; although it was a piece of policy found out to ridicule a point of honour in the other extreme, when the smallest word misplaced among gentlemen ended in a duel.

There are some men excellent at telling a story, and provided with a plentiful stock of them, which they can draw out upon occasion in all companies; and, considering how low conversation runs now among us, it is not altogether a contemptible talent; however, it is subject to two unavoidable defects, frequent repetition, and being soon exhausted; so that whoever values this gift in himself has need of a good memory, and ought frequently to shift his company, that he may not discover the weakness of his fund; for those who are thus endowed have seldom any other revenue, but live upon the main stock.

Great speakers in public are seldom agreeable in private conversation, whether their faculty be natural, or acquired by practice and often venturing. Natural elocution, although it may seem a paradox, usually springs from a barrenness of invention and of words; by which men who have only one stock of notions upon every subject and one set of phrases to express them in, they swim upon the superficies and offer themselves on every occasion; therefore, men of much learning, and who know the compass of a language, are generally the worst talkers on a sudden, until much practice has inured and emboldened them; because they are confounded with plenty of matter, variety of notions and of words, which they cannot readily choose, but are perplexed and entangled by too great a choice; which is no disadvantage in private conversation, where, on the other side, the talent of haranguing is, of all others, most unsupportable.

Nothing has spoiled men more for conversation than the character of being wits; to support which, they never fail of encouraging a number of followers and admirers, who list themselves in their service, wherein they find their accounts on both sides by pleasing their mutual vanity. This has given the former such an air of superiority, and made the latter so pragmatical, that neither of them arc well to be endured. I say nothing here of the itch of dispute and contradiction, telling of lies, or of those who are troubled with the disease called the wandering of the thoughts, that they are never present in mind at what passes in discourse; for whoever labours under any of these possessions is as unfit for conversation as a madman in Bedlam.

I think I have gone over most of the errors in conversation that have fallen under my notice or memory, except some that are merely personal, and others too gross to need exploding, such as lewd or profane talk; but I pretend only to treat the errors of conversation in general, and not the several subjects of discourse, which would be infinite. Thus we see how human nature is most debased by the abuse of that faculty which is held the greatest distinction between men and brutes, and how little advantage we make of that which might be the greatest, the most lasting, and the most innocent as well as useful pleasure of life; in default of which we are forced to take up with those poor amusements of dress and visiting, or the more pernicious ones of play, drink, and vicious amours; whereby the nobility and gentry of both sexes are entirely corrupted both in body and mind, and have lost all notions of love, honour, friendship, generosity; which, under the name of fopperies, have been for some time laughed out of doors.

This degeneracy of conversation, with the pernicious consequences thereof upon our humours and dispositions, has been owing, among other causes, to the custom arisen, for some time past, of excluding women from any share in our society, farther than in parties at play, or dancing, or in the pursuit of an amour. I take the highest period of politeness in England (and it is of the same date in France) to have been the peaceable part of King Charles the First's reign; and from what we read of those times, as well as from the accounts I have formerly met with from some who lived in that court, the methods then used for raising and cultivating conversation were altogether different from ours: several ladies, whom we find celebrated by the poets of that age, had assemblies at their houses, where persons of the best understanding, and of both sexes, met to pass the evenings in discoursing upon whatever agreeable subjects were occasionally started; and although we are apt to ridicule the sublime platonic notions they had, or personated, in love and friendship, I conceive their refinements were grounded upon reason, and that a little grain of the romance is no ill ingredient to preserve and exalt the dignity of human nature, without which it is apt to degenerate into everything that is sordid, vicious, and low. If there were no other use in the conversation of ladies, it is sufficient that it would lay a restraint upon those odious topics of immodesty and indecencies into which the rudeness of our northern genius is so apt to fall. And, therefore, it is observable in those sprightly gentlemen about the town who are so very dexterous at entertaining a vizard mask in the park or the playhouse, that in the company of ladies of virtue and honour, they are silent and disconcerted, and out of their element.

There are some people who think they sufficiently acquit themselves, and entertain their company with relating facts of no consequence, nor at all out of the road of such common incidents as happen every day; and this I have observed more frequently among the Scots than any other nation, who are very careful not to omit the minutest circumstances of time or place; which kind of discourse, if it were not a little relieved by the uncouth terms and phrases, as well as accent and gesture, peculiar to that country, would be hardly tolerable. It is not a fault in company to talk much, but to continue it long is certainly one; for if the majority of those who are got together be naturally silent or cautious, the conversation will flag unless it be often renewed by one among them who can start new subjects, provided he does not dwell upon them, that leave room for answers and replies.

Joseph Addison

1672 · 1719

*Joseph Addison made a name as a classical scholar
and as a poet while he was an undergraduate at
Oxford and was elected a fellow of Magdalen
College. His early promise of literary ability and an
interest in politics made him attractive to the Whig
party as a political writer. In 1717 he became
Secretary of State. As a frequent contributor to The
Tatler and as associate with Steele in The Spectator,
he helped to establish high standards for literary
journalism. Among the prose writers of the period,
Addison remains supreme as a master of style,
and his gentle, urbane treatment of manners,
morals, and taste has drawn the highest praise
of scholars and 'mere readers' alike.*

TOM FOLIO

Faciunt næ intelligendo, ut nihil intelligant.—TER.

TOM FOLIO IS A BROKER IN LEARNING, employed to get together good editions, and stock the libraries of great men.
There is not a sale of books begins until Tom Folio is seen
at the door. There is not an auction where his name is not
heard, and that too in the very nick of time, in the critical
moment, before the last decisive stroke of the hammer.
There is not a subscription goes forward in which Tom
is not privy to the first rough draught of the proposals; nor
a catalogue printed, that doth not come to him wet from
the press. He is an universal scholar, so far as the title-page of
all authors; knows the manuscripts in which they were discovered, the editions through which they have passed, with
the praises or censures which they have received from the

several members of the learned world. He has a greater esteem for Aldus and Elzevir, than for Virgil and Horace. If you talk of Herodotus, he breaks out into a panegyric upon Harry Stephens. He thinks he gives you an account of an author, when he tells you the subject he treats of, the name of the editor, and the year in which it was printed. Or if you draw him into farther particulars, he cries up the goodness of the paper, extols the diligence of the corrector, and is transported with the beauty of the letter. This he looks upon to be sound learning, and substantial criticism. As for those who talk of the fineness of style, and the justness of thought, or describe the brightness of any particular passages; nay, though they themselves write in the genius and spirit of the author they admire, Tom looks upon them as men of superficial learning and flashy parts.

I had yesterday morning a visit from this learned ideot (for that is the light in which I consider every pedant), when I discovered in him some little touches of the coxcomb which I had not before observed. Being very full of the figure which he makes in the republic of letters, and wonderfully satisfied with his great stock of knowledge, he gave me broad intimations that he did not "believe" in all points as his forefathers had done. He then communicated to me a thought of a certain author upon a passage of Virgil's account of the dead, which I made the subject of a late paper. This thought hath taken very much among men of Tom's pitch and understanding, though universally exploded by all that know how to construe Virgil, or have any relish of antiquity. Not to trouble my reader with it, I found, upon the whole, that Tom did not believe a future state of rewards and punishments, because Æneas, at his leaving the empire of the dead, passed through the gate of ivory, and not through that of horn. Knowing that Tom had not sense enough to give up an opinion which he had once received, that I might avoid wrangling, I told him that Virgil possibly had his oversights as well as another author. "Ah! Mr. Bickerstaff," says he, "you would have another opinion of him, if you would read him in Daniel Heinsius's edition. I have perused him myself several times in that edition," continued he; "and after the strictest and most malicious examination, could find but two faults in him: one of them is in the *Æneids*, where there are two commas instead of a parenthesis; and another in the third *Georgic*, where you may find a semicolon turned upside down." "Perhaps," said I, "these were not Virgil's faults, but those of the transcriber." "I do not design it," says Tom, "as a reflection on Virgil: on the contrary, I know that all the manuscripts declaim against such a punctuation. Oh! Mr. Bickerstaff," says he, "what would a man give to see one simile of Virgil writ in his own hand?" I asked him which was the simile he meant, but was answered, "any simile in Virgil." He then told me all the secret history in the commonwealth of learning: of modern pieces that had the names of ancient authors annexed to them; of all the books that were now writing or printing in the several parts of Europe; of many amendments which are made, and not yet published; and a thousand other particulars, which I would not have my memory burdened with for a Vatican.

At length, being fully persuaded that I thoroughly admired him and looked upon him as a prodigy of learning, he took his leave. I know several of Tom's class who are professed admirers of Tasso without understanding a word of Italian, and one in particular, that carries a *Pastor Fido* in his pocket, in which, I am sure, he is acquainted with no other beauty but the clearness of the character.

There is another kind of pedant who, with all Tom Folio's impertinences, hath greater superstructures and embellishments of Greek and Latin, and is still more insupportable than the other, in the same degree as he is more learned. Of this kind very often are editors, commentators, interpreters, scholiasts, and critics; and, in short, all men of deep learning without common sense. These persons set a greater value on themselves for having found out the meaning of a passage in Greek, than upon the author for having written it; nay, will allow the passage itself not to have any beauty in it, at the same time that they would be considered as the greatest men of the age for having interpreted it. They will look with contempt on the most beautiful poems that have been composed by any of their contemporaries; but will lock themselves up in their studies for a twelve-month together, to correct, publish, and expound such trifles of antiquity, as a modern author would be contemned for. Men of the strictest morals, severest lives, and the gravest professions will write volumes upon an idle sonnet that is originally in Greek or Latin, give editions of the most immoral authors, and spin out whole pages upon the various readings of a lewd expression. All that can be said in excuse for them is that their works sufficiently shew they have no taste of their authors, and that what they do in this kind is out of their great learning and not out of any levity or lasciviousness of temper.

A pedant of this nature is wonderfully well described in six lines of Boileau, with which I shall conclude his character:

Un Pédant enyvré de sa vaine science,
Tout herissé de Grec, tout bouffi d'arrogance,
Et qui de mille auteurs retenus mot pour mot,
Dans sa tête entassez n'a souvent fait qu'un sot,
Croit qu'un livre fait tout, & que sans Aristote,
La raison ne voit goute, & le bon sens radote.

THE SPECTATOR

Non fumum ex fulgore, sed ex fumo dare lucem
Cogitat, ut speciosa dehinc miracula promat.—HOR.

I HAVE OBSERVED THAT A READER seldom peruses a book with pleasure till he knows whether the writer of it be a black or a fair man, of a mild or choleric disposition, married or a bachelor, with other particulars of the like nature, that conduce very much to the right understanding of an author. To gratify this curiosity, which is so natural to a reader, I design this paper and my next as prefatory discourses to my following writings, and shall give some account in them of the several persons that are engaged in this work. As the chief trouble of compiling, digesting and correcting will fall to my share, I must do myself the justice to open the work with my own history.

I was born to a small hereditary estate, which, according to the tradition of the village where it lies, was bounded by the same hedges and ditches in William the Conqueror's time that it is at present, and has been delivered down from father to son, whole and entire, without the loss or acquisition of a single field or meadow, during the space of six hundred years. There runs a story in the family, that, when my mother was gone with child of me about three months, she dreamed that she was brought to bed of a judge. Whether this might proceed from a lawsuit which was then depending in the family, or my father's being a justice of the peace, I cannot determine; for I am not so vain as to think it presaged any dignity that I should arrive at in my future life, though that was the interpretation which the neighborhood put upon it. The gravity of my behavior at my very first appearance in the world, and all the time that I sucked, seemed to favor my mother's dream; for, as she has often told me, I threw away my rattle before I was two months old, and would not make use of my coral till they had taken away the bells from it.

As for the rest of my infancy, there being nothing in it remarkable, I shall pass it over in silence. I find that during my nonage, I had the reputation of a very sullen youth, but was always a favorite of my schoolmaster, who used to say "that my parts were solid, and would wear well." I had not been long at the University before I distinguished myself by a most profound silence; for during the space of eight years, excepting in the public exercises of the college, I scarce uttered the quantity of a hundred words; and indeed do not remember that I ever spoke three sentences together in my whole life. Whilst I was in this learned body, I applied myself with so much diligence to my studies that there are very few celebrated books, either in the learned or the modern tongues, which I am not acquainted with.

Upon the death of my father, I was resolved to travel into foreign countries, and therefore left the University with the character of an odd, unaccountable fellow, that had a great deal of learning, if I would but show it. An insatiable thirst after knowledge carried me into all the countries of Europe, in which there was anything new or strange to be seen; nay, to such a degree was my curiosity raised, that having read the controversies of some great men concerning the antiquities of Egypt, I made a voyage to Grand Cairo on purpose to take the measure of a pyramid; and as soon as I had set myself right in that particular, returned to my native country with great satisfaction.

I have passed my latter years in this city, where I am frequently seen in most public places, though there are not above half a dozen of my select friends that know me; of whom my next paper shall give a more particular account. There is no place of general resort wherein I do not often make my appearance. Sometimes I am seen thrusting my head into a round of politicians at Will's, and listening with great attention to the narratives that are made in those little circular audiences. Sometimes I smoke a pipe at Child's, and whilst I seem attentive to nothing but the *Postman*, overhear the conversation of every table in the room. I appear on Sunday nights at St. James's coffee-house, and sometimes join the little committee of politics in the inner room, as one who comes there to hear and improve. My face is likewise very well known at the Grecian, the Cocoa Tree, and in the theatres, both of Drury Lane and the Hay Market. I have been taken for a merchant upon the Exchange for above these ten years, and sometimes pass for a Jew in the assembly of stock-jobbers at Jonathan's. In short, wherever I see a cluster of people, I always mix with them, though I never open my lips but in my own club.

Thus I live in the world rather as a Spectator of mankind, than as one of the species, by which means I have made myself a speculative statesman, soldier, merchant, and artisan, without ever meddling with any practical part in life. I am very well versed in the theory of a husband, or a father, and can discern the errors in the economy, business, and diversion of others, better than those who are engaged in them; as standers-by discover blots which are apt to escape those who are in the game. I never espoused any party with violence, and am resolved to observe an exact neutrality between the Whigs and Tories, unless I shall be forced to declare myself by the hostilities of either side. In short, I have acted in all the parts of my life as a looker-on, which is the character I intend to preserve in this paper.

I have given the reader just so much of my history and character as to let him see I am not altogether unqualified for the business I have undertaken. As for other particulars in my life and adventures, I shall insert them in following papers as I shall see occasion. In the mean time, when I consider how much I have seen, read, and heard, I begin to blame my own taciturnity; and since I have neither time nor inclination to communicate the fulness of my heart in speech, I am resolved to do it in writing, and to print myself out, if possible, before I die. I have been often told by my friends that it is pity so many useful discoveries which I have made should be in the possession of a silent man. For this reason, therefore, I shall publish a sheetful of thoughts every morning for the benefit of my contemporaries; and if I can any way contribute to the diversion or improvement of the country in which I live, I shall leave it, when I am summoned out of it, with the secret satisfaction of thinking that I have not lived in vain.

There are three very material points which I have not spoken to in this paper, and which, for several important reasons, I must keep to myself, at least for some time: I mean, an account of my name, my age, and my lodgings. I must confess, I would gratify my reader in anything that is reasonable; but as for these three particulars, though I am sensible they might tend very much to the embellishment of my paper, I cannot yet come to a resolution of communicating them to the public. They would indeed draw me out of that obscurity which I have enjoyed for many years, and expose me in public places to several salutes and civilities, which have been always very disagreeable to me; for the greatest pain I can suffer is the being talked to and being stared at. It is for this reason, likewise, that I keep my complexion and dress as very great secrets; though it is not impossible but I may make discoveries of both in the progress of the work I have undertaken.

After having been thus particular upon myself, I shall in to-morrow's paper give an account of those gentlemen who are concerned with me in this work. For, as I have before intimated, a plan of it is laid and concerted (as all other matters of importance are) in a club. However, as my friends have engaged me to stand in the front, those who have a mind to correspond with me, may direct their letters to the *Spectator*, at Mr. Buckley's, in Little Britain. For I must further acquaint the reader, that though our club meets only on Tuesdays and Thursdays, we have appointed a committee to sit every night for the inspection of all such papers as may contribute to the advancement of the public weal.

POPULAR SUPERSTITIONS

Somnia, terrores magicos, miracula, sagas,
Nocturnos lemures portentaque Thessala rides?—HOR.

GOING YESTERDAY TO DINE with an old acquaintance, I had the misfortune to find his whole family very much dejected. Upon asking him the occasion of it, he told me that his wife had dreamt a very strange dream the night before, which they were afraid portended some misfortune to themselves or to their children. At her coming into the room I observed a settled melancholy in her countenance, which I should have been troubled for, had I not heard from whence it proceeded. We were no sooner sat down but, after having looked upon me a little while, "My Dear," says she, turning to her husband, "you may now see the stranger that was in the candle last night." Soon after this, as they began to talk of family affairs, a little boy at the lower end of the table told her that he was to go into joinhand on Thursday. "Thursday?" says she; "No, child, if it please God, you shall not begin upon Childermas-day; tell your writing-master that Friday will be soon enough." I was reflecting with myself on the oddness of her fancy, and wondering that anybody would establish it as a rule to lose a day in every week. In the midst of these my musings, she desired me to reach her a little salt upon the point of my knife, which I did in such a trepidation and hurry of obedience that I let it drop by the way; at which she immediately startled, and said it fell towards her. Upon this I looked very blank; and, observing the concern of the whole table, began to consider myself, with some confusion, as a person that had brought a disaster upon the family. The lady, however, recovering herself after a little space, said to her husband with a sigh, "My Dear, misfortunes never come single." My friend, I found, acted but an underpart at his table, and, being a man of more good-nature than understanding, thinks himself obliged to fall in with all the passions and humors of his yokefellow. "Do not you remember, child," says she, "that the pigeon house fell the very afternoon that our careless wench spilt the salt upon the table?" "Yes," says he, "my dear, and the next post brought us an account of the Battle of Almanza." The reader may guess at the figure I made, after having done all this mischief. I dispatched my dinner as soon as I could, with my usual taciturnity; when, to my utter confusion, the lady seeing me quitting my knife and fork, and laying them across one another upon my plate, desired me that I would humor her so far as to take them out of that figure, and place them side by side. What the absurdity was which I had committed I did not know, but I suppose there was some traditionary superstition in it; and, therefore, in obedience to the lady of the house, I disposed of my knife and fork in two parallel lines, which is the figure I shall always lay them in for the future, though I do not know any reason for it.

It is not difficult for a man to see that a person has conceived an aversion to him. For my own part, I quickly found, by the lady's looks, that she regarded me as a very odd kind of fellow, with an unfortunate aspect; for which reason I took my leave immediately after dinner, and withdrew to my own lodgings. Upon my return home, I fell into a profound contemplation on the evils that attend these superstitious follies of mankind; how they subject us to imaginary afflictions and additional sorrows that do not properly come within our lot. As if the natural calamities of life were not sufficient for it, we turn the most indifferent circumstances into misfortunes, and suffer as much from trifling accidents as from real evils. I have known the shooting of a star spoil a night's rest; and have seen a man in love grow pale and lose his appetite upon the plucking of a merrythought. A screech owl at midnight has alarmed a family more than a band of robbers; nay, the voice of a cricket hath struck more terror than the roaring of a lion. There is nothing so inconsiderable, which may not appear dreadful to an imagination that is filled with omens and prognostics. A rusty nail or a crooked pin shoot up into prodigies.

I remember I was once in a mixed assembly that was full of noise and mirth, when on a sudden an old woman unluckily observed there were thirteen of us in company. This remark struck a panic terror into several who were present, insomuch that one or two of the ladies were going to leave the room; but a friend of mine, taking notice that one of our female companions was big with child, affirmed there were fourteen in the room, and, that instead of portending one of the company should die, it plainly foretold one of them should be born. Had not my friend found out this expedient to break the omen, I question not but half the women in the company would have fallen sick that very night.

An old maid that is troubled with the vapors produces infinite disturbances of this kind among her friends and neighbors. I know a maiden aunt of a great family who is one of these antiquated sibyls that forbodes and prophesies from one end of the year to the other. She is always seeing apparitions and hearing deathwatches, and was the other day almost frighted out of her wits by the great house dog that howled in the stable at a time when she lay ill of the toothache. Such an extravagant cast of mind engages multitudes of people, not only in impertinent terrors, but in supernumerary duties of life, and arises from that fear and ignorance which are natural to the soul of man. The horror with which we entertain the thoughts of death (or indeed of any future evil) and the uncertainty of its approach, fill a melancholy mind with innumerable apprehensions and suspicions, and consequently dispose it to the observation of such groundless prodigies and predictions. For as it is the chief concern of wise men to retrench the evils of life by the reasonings of philosophy, it is the employment of fools to multiply them by the sentiments of superstition.

For my own part, I should be very much troubled were I endowed with this divining quality, though it should inform me truly of everything that can befall me. I would not anticipate the relish of any happiness, nor feel the weight of any misery, before it actually arrives.

I know but one way of fortifying my soul against these gloomy presages and terrors of mind, and that is by securing to myself the friendship and protection of that Being who disposes of events and governs futurity. He sees, at one view, the whole thread of my existence, not only that part of it which I have already passed through, but that which runs forward into all the depths of eternity. When I lay me down to sleep, I recommend myself to his care; when I awake, I give myself up to his direction. Amidst all the evils that threaten me I will look up to him for help, and question not but he will either avert them or turn them to my advantage. Though I know neither the time nor the manner of the death I am to die, I am not at all solicitous about it, because I am sure that he knows them both, and that he will not fail to comfort and support me under them.

WESTMINSTER ABBEY

Pallida mors aequo pulsat pede pauperum tabernas
Regumque turres, O beate Sexti.
Vitae summa brevis spem nos vetat incohare longam,
Jam te premet nox, fabulaeque manes,
Et domus exilis Plutonia.—HOR.

WHEN I AM IN A SERIOUS HUMOR I very often walk by myself in Westminster Abbey, where the gloominess of the place, and the use to which it is applied, with the solemnity of the building, and the condition of the people who lie in it are apt to fill the mind with a kind of melancholy, or rather thoughtfulness, that is not disagreeable. I yesterday passed a whole afternoon in the churchyard, the cloisters, and the church, amusing myself with the tombstones and inscriptions that I met with in those several regions of the dead. Most of them recorded nothing else of the buried person but that he was born upon one day and died upon another; the whole history of his life being comprehended in those two circumstances that are common to all mankind. I could not but look upon these registers of existence, whether of brass or marble, as a kind of satire upon the departed persons, who left no other memorial of them but that they were born and that they died. They put me in mind of several persons mentioned in the battles of heroic poems, who have sounding names given them for no other reason but that they may be killed, and are celebrated for nothing but being knocked on the head.

"Γλαῦχόν τε Μεδόντα τε Θερσιλοχόν τε."—HOM.
Glaucumque, Medontaque, Thersilochumque.—VIRG.

The life of these men is finely described in Holy Writ by "the path of an arrow," which is immediately closed up and lost.

Upon my going into the church, I entertained myself with the digging of a grave, and saw in every shovelful of it that was thrown up the fragment of a bone or skull intermixed with a kind of fresh moldering earth that some time or other had a place in the composition of an human body. Upon this I began to consider with myself what innumerable multitudes of people lay confused together under the pavement of that ancient cathedral; how men and women, friends and enemies, priests and soldiers, monks and prebendaries, were crumbled amongst one another, and blended together in the same common mass; how beauty, strength, and youth, with old age, weakness, and deformity, lay undistinguished in the same promiscuous heap of matter.

After having thus surveyed this great magazine of mortality, as it were in the lump, I examined it more particularly by the accounts which I found on several of the monuments which are raised in every quarter of that ancient fabric. Some of them were covered with such extravagant epitaphs that if it were possible for the dead person to be acquainted with them, he would blush at the praises which his friends have bestowed upon him. There are others so excessively modest that they deliver the character of the person departed in Greek or Hebrew, and by that means are not understood once in a twelvemonth. In the poetical quarter, I found there were poets who had no monuments, and monuments which had no poets. I observed, indeed, that the present war had filled the church with many of these uninhabited monuments, which had been erected to the memory of persons whose bodies were, perhaps, buried in the plains of Blenheim, or in the bosom of the ocean.

I could not but be very much delighted with several modern epitaphs, which are written with great elegance of expression and justness of thought, and therefore do honor to the living as well as to the dead. As a foreigner is very apt to conceive an idea of the ignorance or politeness of a nation from the turn of their public monuments and inscriptions, they should be submitted to the perusal of men of learning and genius before they are put in execution. Sir Cloudesley Shovel's monument has very often given me great offense. Instead of the brave, rough, English admiral, which was the distinguishing character of that plain, gallant man, he is represented on his tomb by the figure of a beau, dressed in a long periwig, and reposing himself upon velvet cushions under a canopy of state. The inscription is answerable to the monument, for, instead of celebrating the many remarkable actions he had performed in the service of his country, it acquaints us only with the manner of his death, in which it was impossible for him to reap any honor. The Dutch, whom we are apt to despise for want of genius, show an infinitely greater taste of antiquity and politeness in their buildings and works of this nature than what we meet with in those of our own country. The monuments of their admirals, which have been erected at the public expense, represent them like themselves, and are adorned with rostral crowns and naval ornaments, with beautiful festoons of seaweed, shells, and coral.

But to return to our subject. I have left the repository of our English kings for the contemplation of another day, when I shall find my mind disposed for so serious an amusement. I know that entertainments of this nature are apt to raise dark and dismal thoughts in timorous minds and gloomy imaginations; but for my own part, though I am always serious, I do not know what it is to be melancholy, and can therefore take a view of nature in her deep and solemn scenes with the same pleasure as in her most gay and delightful ones. By this means I can improve myself with those objects which others consider with terror. When I look upon the tombs of the great, every emotion of envy dies in me; when I read the epitaphs of the beautiful, every inordinate desire goes out; when I meet with the grief of parents upon a tombstone, my heart melts with compassion; when I see the tomb of the parents themselves, I consider the vanity of grieving for those whom we must quickly follow. When I see kings lying by those who deposed them, when I considered rival wits placed side by side, or the holy men that divided the world with their contests and disputes, I reflect with sorrow and astonishment on the little competitions, factions, and debates of mankind. When I read the several dates of the tombs, of some that died yesterday and some six hundred years ago, I consider that great day when we shall all of us be contemporaries, and make our appearance together.

COVERLEY HALL

—Hinc tibi copia manabit ad plenum benigno
*Ruris honorum opulenta cornu.—*HOR.

HAVING OFTEN RECEIVED AN INVITATION from my friend, Sir Roger de Coverley, to pass away a month with him in the country, I last week accompanied him thither, and am settled with him for some time at his country-house, where I intend to form several of my ensuing speculations. Sir Roger, who is very well acquainted with my humor, lets me rise and go to bed when I please, dine at his own table or in my chamber, as I think fit, sit still and say nothing, without bidding me be merry. When the gentlemen of the country come to see him, he only shows me at a distance. As I have been walking in his fields I have observed them stealing a sight of me over a hedge, and have heard the knight desiring them not to let me see them, for that I hated to be stared at.

I am the more at ease in Sir Roger's family because it consists of sober and staid persons; for, as the knight is the best master in the world, he seldom changes his servants; and as he is beloved by all about him, his servants never care for leaving him; by this means his domestics are all in years, and grown old with their master. You would take his *valet de chambre* for his brother, his butler is gray-headed, his groom is one of the gravest men that I have ever seen, and his coachman has the looks of a privy-counsellor. You see the goodness of the master even in the old house-dog, and in a gray pad that is kept in the stable with great care and tenderness, out of regard to his past services, though he has been useless for several years.

I could not but observe with a great deal of pleasure the joy that appeared in the countenances of these ancient domestics upon my friend's arrival at his country-seat. Some of them could not refrain from tears at the sight of their old master; every one of them pressed forward to do something for him, and seemed discouraged if they were not employed. At the same time the good old knight, with a mixture of the father and the master of the family, tempered the inquiries after his own affairs with several kind questions relating to themselves. This humanity and good-nature engages everybody to him, so that when he is pleasant upon any of them, all his family are in good humor, and none so much as the person whom he diverts himself with; on the contrary, if he coughs, or betrays any infirmity of old age, it is easy for a stander-by to observe a secret concern in the looks of all his servants.

My worthy friend has put me under the particular care of his butler, who is a very prudent man, and, as well as the rest of his fellow-servants, wonderfully desirous of pleasing me, because they have often heard their master talk of me as of his particular friend.

My chief companion, when Sir Roger is diverting himself in the woods or the fields, is a very venerable man who is ever with Sir Roger, and has lived at his house in the nature of a chaplain above thirty years. This gentleman is a person of good sense and some learning, of a very regular life and obliging conversation; he heartily loves Sir Roger, and knows that he is very much in the old knight's esteem, so that he lives in the family rather as a relation than a dependant.

I have observed in several of my papers that my friend Sir Roger, amidst all his good qualities, is something of a humorist; and that his virtues as well as imperfections are, as it were, tinged by a certain extravagance which makes them particularly his, and distinguishes them from those of other men. This cast of mind, as it is generally very innocent in itself, so it renders his conversation highly agreeable, and more delightful than the same degree of sense and virtue would appear in their common and ordinary colors. As I was walking with him last night, he asked me how I liked the good man whom I have just now mentioned, and without staying for my answer, told me that he was afraid of being insulted with Latin and Greek at his own table; for which reason he desired a particular friend of his at the University to find him out a clergyman rather of plain sense than much learning, of a good aspect, a clear voice, a sociable temper, and, if possible, a man that understood a little of backgammon. "My friend," says Sir Roger, "found me out this gentleman, who, beside the endowments required of him, is, they tell me, a good scholar, though he does not show it. I have given him the parsonage of the parish; and, because I know his value, have settled upon him a good annuity for life. If he outlives me, he shall find that he was higher in my esteem than perhaps he thinks he is. He has now been with me thirty years; and though he does not know I have taken notice of it, has never in all that time asked anything of me for himself, though he is every day soliciting me for something in behalf of one or other of my tenants, his parishioners. There has not been a lawsuit in the parish since he has lived among them; if any dispute arises they apply themselves to him for the decision; if they do not acquiesce in his judgment, which I think never happened above once, or twice at most, they appeal to me. At his first settling with me, I made him a present of all the good sermons which have been printed in English, and only begged of him that every Sunday he would pronounce one of them in the pulpit. Accordingly, he has digested them into such a series that they follow one another naturally, and make a continued system of practical divinity."

As Sir Roger was going on in his story, the gentleman we were talking of came up to us; and upon the knight's asking him who preached to-morrow (for it was Saturday night), told us the Bishop of St. Asaph in the morning, and Doctor South in the afternoon. He then showed us his list of preachers for the whole year, where I saw with a great deal of pleasure Archbishop Tillotson, Bishop Saunderson, Doctor Barrow, Doctor Calamy, with several living authors who have published discourses of practical divinity. I no sooner saw this venerable man in the pulpit but I very much approved of my friend's insisting upon the qualifications of a good aspect and a clear voice; for I was so charmed with the gracefulness of his figure and delivery, as well as with the discourses he pronounced, that I think I never passed any time more to my satisfaction. A sermon repeated after this manner is like the composition of a poet in the mouth of a graceful actor.

I could heartily wish that more of our country clergy would follow this example; and, instead of wasting their spirits in laborious compositions of their own, would endeavor after a handsome elocution, and all those other talents that are proper to enforce what has been penned by greater masters. This would not only be more easy to themselves, but more edifying to the people.

THE DEATH OF SIR ROGER

Heu pietas! heu prisca fides!—VIRGIL.

WE LAST NIGHT RECEIVED a Piece of ill News at our Club, which very sensibly afflicted every one of us. I question not but my Readers themselves will be troubled at the hearing of it. To keep them no longer in Suspence, Sir ROGER DE COVERLEY *is dead.* He departed this Life at his House in the Country, after a few Weeks Sickness. Sir ANDREW FREEPORT has a Letter from one of his Correspondents in those Parts, that informs him the old Man caught a Cold at the County-Sessions, as he was very warmly promoting an Address of his own penning, in which he succeeded according to his Wishes. But this Particular comes from a Whig-Justice of Peace, who was always Sir ROGER's Enemy and Antagonist. I have Letters both from the Chaplain and Captain *Sentry* which mention nothing of it, but are filled with many Particulars to the Honour of the good old Man. I have likewise a Letter from the Butler, who took so much care of me last Summer when I was at the Knight's House. As my Friend the Butler mentions, in the Simplicity of his Heart, several Circumstances the others have passed over in Silence, I shall give my Reader a Copy of his Letter, without any Alteration or Diminution.

"*Honoured Sir,*

"Knowing that you was my old Master's good Friend, I could not forbear sending you the melancholy News of his Death, which has afflicted the whole Country, as well as his poor Servants, who loved him, I may say, better than we did our Lives. I am afraid he caught his Death the last County Sessions, where he would go to see Justice done to a poor Widow Woman, and her Fatherless Children, that had been wronged by a neighbouring Gentleman; for you know, Sir, my good Master was always the poor Man's Friend. Upon his coming home, the first Complaint he made was, that he had lost his Roast-Beef Stomach, not being able to touch a Sirloin, which was served up according to Custom; and you know he used to take great Delight in it. From that time forward he grew worse and worse, but still kept a good Heart to the last. Indeed, we were once in great Hope of his Recovery, upon a kind Message that was sent from the Widow Lady whom he had made love to the Forty last Years of his Life; but this only proved a Light'ning before Death. He has bequeathed to this Lady, as a token of his Love, a great Pearl Necklace, and a Couple of Silver Bracelets set with Jewels, which belonged to my good old Lady his Mother: He has bequeathed the fine white Gelding, that he used to ride a hunting upon, to his Chaplain, because he thought he would be kind to him, and has left you all his Books. He has, moreover, bequeathed to the Chaplain a very pretty Tenement with good Lands about it. It being a very cold Day when he made his Will, he left for Mourning, to every Man in the Parish, a great Frize-Coat, and to every Woman a black Riding-hood. It was a most moving Sight to see him take leave of his poor Servants, commending us all for our Fidelity, whilst we were not able to speak a Word for weeping. As we most of us are grown Gray-headed in our Dear Master's Service, he has left us Pensions and Legacies, which we may live very comfortably upon, the remaining part of our Days. He has bequeath'd a great deal more in Charity, which is not yet come to my Knowledge, and it is peremptorily said in the Parish, that he has left Mony to build a Steeple to the Church; for he was heard to say some time ago, that if he lived two Years longer, *Coverly* Church should have a Steeple to it. The Chaplain tells everybody that he made a very good End, and never speaks of him without Tears. He was buried according to his own Directions, among the Family of the *Coverly's*, on the Left Hand of his Father, Sir *Arthur*. The Coffin was carried by Six of his Tenants, and the Pall held up by Six of the *Quorum:* The whole Parish follow'd the Corps with heavy Hearts, and in their Mourning Suits, the Men in Frize, and the Women in Riding-Hoods. Captain SENTRY, my Master's Nephew, has taken Possession of the Hall-House, and the whole Estate.

When my old Master saw him a little before his Death, he shook him by the Hand, and wished him Joy of the Estate which was falling to him, desiring him only to make good Use of it, and to pay the several Legacies, and the Gifts of Charity which he told him he had left as Quitrents upon the Estate. The Captain truly seems a courteous Man, though he says but little. He makes much of those whom my Master loved, and shews great Kindness to the old House-dog, that you know my poor Master was so fond of. It would have gone to your Heart to have heard the Moans the dumb Creature made on the Day of my Master's Death. He has ne'er joyed himself since; no more has any of us. 'Twas the melancholiest Day for the poor People that ever happened in *Worcestershire*. This being all from,

> "*Honoured Sir,*
> > "*Your most Sorrowful Servant,*
> > > "Edward Biscuit."

"*P. S.* My Master desired, some Weeks before he died, that a Book which comes up to you by the Carrier should be given to Sir *Andrew Freeport*, in his Name."

This Letter, notwithstanding the poor Butler's Manner of writing it, gave us such an Idea of our good old Friend, that upon the reading of it there was not a dry Eye in the Club. Sir *Andrew* opening the Book, found it to be a Collection of Acts of Parliament. There was in particular the Act of Uniformity, with some Passages in it marked by Sir *Roger's* own Hand. Sir *Andrew* found that they related to two or three Points, which he had disputed with Sir *Roger* the last time he appeared at the Club. Sir *Andrew*, who would have been merry at such an Incident on another Occasion, at the sight of the old Man's Handwriting burst into Tears, and put the Book into his Pocket. Captain *Sentry* informs me, that the Knight has left Rings and Mourning for every one in the Club.

Sir Richard Steele

1672 · 1729

*Sir Richard Steele was born in Dublin and educated
in England, at Charterhouse School and Oxford,
where he and Addison became friends. He left the
university without a degree and entered the army,
in which he remained long enough to become
a captain. Plays, especially* The Conscious Lovers
*(1722), brought him fame in his own day, but now
he is remembered chiefly for his essays in* The
Gazette, The Tatler, The Spectator, The Guardian,
*and other periodicals which he edited. Steele
was a vigorous and impulsive man and a somewhat
less polished writer than Addison; however, his
warmer sympathies make him at times a more pleasing essayist than his reserved, intellectual friend.*

DUELLING

Quicquid agunt homines—
   —nostri est farrago libelli.—JUV. SAT. i. 85, 86.

Whate'er men do, or say, or think, or dream,
Our motley paper seizes for its theme.—POPE.

White's Chocolate-House, June 6.

A LETTER FROM A YOUNG LADY, written in the most passionate terms, wherein she laments the misfortune of a gentleman, her lover, who was lately wounded in a duel, has turned
my thoughts to that subject, and inclined me to examine
into the causes which precipitate men into so fatal a folly.
And as it has been proposed to treat of subjects of gallantry
in the article from hence, and no one point in nature is more
proper to be considered by the company who frequent this

place than that of duels, it is worth our consideration to examine into this chimerical groundless humor, and to lay every other thought aside, till we have stripped it of all its false pretences to credit and reputation amongst men.

But I must confess, when I consider what I am going about, and run over in my imagination all the endless crowd of men of honor who will be offended at such a discourse, I am undertaking, methinks, a work worthy an invulnerable hero in romance, rather than a private gentleman with a single rapier. But as I am pretty well acquainted by great opportunities with the nature of man, and know of a truth that all men fight against their will, the danger vanishes, and resolution rises upon this subject. For this reason I shall talk very freely on a custom which all men wish exploded, though no man has courage enough to resist it.

But there is one unintelligible word, which I fear will extremely perplex my dissertation, and I confess to you I find very hard to explain, which is the term "satisfaction." An honest country gentleman had the misfortune to fall into company with two or three modern men of honor, where he happened to be very ill-treated; and one of the company, being conscious of his offense, sends a note to him in the morning, and tells him he was ready to give him satisfaction. "This is fine doing," says the plain fellow. "Last night he sent me away cursedly out of humor, and this morning he fancies it would be a satisfaction to be run throught the body."

As the matter at present stands, it is not to do handsome actions denominates a man of honor; it is enough if he dares to defend ill ones. Thus you often see a common sharper in competition with a gentleman of the first rank; though all mankind is convinced that a fighting gamester is only a pickpocket with the courage of a highwayman. One cannot with any patience reflect on the unaccountable jumble of persons and things in this town and nation, which occasions very frequently that a brave man falls by a hand below that of the common hangman, and yet his executioner escapes the clutches of the hangman for doing it. I shall therefore hereafter consider how the bravest men in other ages and nations have behaved themselves upon such incidents as we decide by combat, and show, from their practice, that this resentment neither has its foundation from true reason or solid fame, but is an imposture, made up of cowardice, falsehood, and want of understanding. For this work, a good history of quarrels would be very edifying to the public, and I apply myself to the town for particulars and circumstances within their knowledge, which may serve to embellish the dissertation with proper cuts. Most of the quarrels I have ever known have proceeded from some valiant coxcomb's persisting in the wrong, to defend some prevailing folly, and preserve himself from the ingenuity of owning a mistake.

By this means it is called "giving a man satisfaction" to urge your offense against him with your sword; which puts me in mind of Peter's order to the keeper in *The Tale of a Tub:* "If you neglect to do all this, damn you and your generation for ever; and so we bid you heartily farewell." If the contradiction in the very terms of one of our challengers were as well explained and turned into plain English, would it not run after this manner?

> "*Sir:*
>
> Your extraordinary behavior last night, and the liberty you were pleased to take with me, makes me this morning give you this, to tell you, because you are an ill-bred puppy, I will meet you in Hyde Park an hour hence; and because you want both breeding and humanity, I desire you would come with a pistol in your hand, on horseback, and endeavor to shoot me through the head, to teach you more manners. If you fail of doing me this pleasure, I shall say you are a rascal on every post in town. And so, sir, if you will not injure me more, I shall never forgive what you have done already. Pray, sir, do not fail of getting everything ready; and you will infinitely oblige, sir, your most obedient, humble servant, etc." . . .

HAPPY MARRIAGE

Interea dulces pendent circum oscula nati;
Casta pudicitiam servat domus.—VIRG., *Georg.* ii, 523.

From my own apartment.

THERE ARE SEVERAL PERSONS who have many pleasures and entertainments in their possession which they do not enjoy. It is therefore a kind and good office to acquaint them with their own happiness, and turn their attention to such instances of their good fortune which they are apt to overlook. Persons in the married state often want such a monitor, and pine away their days by looking upon the same condition in anguish and murmur which carries with it, in the opinion of others, a complication of all the pleasures of life, and a retreat from its inquietudes.

I am led into this thought by a visit I made an old friend who was formerly my school-fellow. He came to town last week with his family for the winter, and yesterday morning sent me word his wife expected me to dinner. I am, as it were, at home at that house, and every member of it knows me for their well-wisher. I cannot indeed express the pleasure it is, to be met by the children with so much joy as I am when I go thither; the boys and girls strive who shall come first, when they think it is I that am knocking at the door; and that child which loses the race to me, runs back again to tell the father it is Mr. Bickerstaff. This day I was led in by a pretty girl, that we all thought must have forgot me; for the family has been out of town these two years. Her knowing me again was a mighty subject with us, and took up our discourse at the first entrance. After which they began to rally me upon a thousand little stories they heard in the country about my marriage to one of my neighbor's daughters; upon which the gentleman my friend said: "Nay, if Mr. Bickerstaff marries a child of any of his old companions, I hope mine shall have the preference. There's Mrs. Mary is now sixteen, and would make him as fine a widow as the best of them. But I know him too well; he is so enamored with the very memory of those who flourished in our youth, that he will not so much as look upon the modern beauties. I remember, old gentleman, how often you went home in a day to refresh your countenance and dress, when Teraminta reigned in your heart. As we came up in the coach, I repeated to my wife some of your verses on her."

With such reflections on little passages which happened long ago, we passed our time during a cheerful and elegant meal. After dinner his lady left the room, as did also the children. As soon as we were alone, he took me by the hand. "Well, my good friend," says he, "I am heartily glad to see thee; I was afraid you would never have seen all the company that dined with you to-day again. Do not you think the good woman of the house a little altered, since you followed her from the playhouse, to find out who she was, for me?" I perceived a tear fall down his cheek as he spoke, which moved me not a little. But to turn the discourse, said I, "She is not, indeed, quite the creature she was when she returned me the letter I carried from you, and told me she hoped, as I was a gentleman, I would be employed no more to trouble her who had never offended me, but would be so much the gentleman's friend as to dissuade him from a pursuit which he could never succeed in. You may remember I thought her in earnest, and you were forced to employ your cousin Will, who made his sister get acquainted with her for you. You cannot expect her to be forever fifteen."

"Fifteen?" replied my good friend. "Ah! you little understand, you that have lived a bachelor, how great, how exquisite a pleasure there is in being really beloved! It is impossible that the most beauteous face in nature should raise in me such pleasing ideas as when I look upon that excellent woman. That fading in her countenance is chiefly caused by her watching with me in my fever. This was followed by a fit of sickness, which had like to have carried her off last winter. I tell you sincerely, I have so many obligations to her that I cannot with any sort of moderation think of her present state of health. But as to what you say of fifteen, she gives me every day pleasures beyond what I ever knew in the possession of her beauty when I was in the vigor of youth. Every moment of her life brings me fresh instances of her complacency to my inclinations, and her prudence in regard to my fortune. Her face is to me much more beautiful than when I first saw it; there is no decay in any feature which I cannot trace from the very instant it was occasioned by some anxious concern for my welfare and interests. Thus at the same time, methinks, the love I conceived towards her for what she was, is heightened by my gratitude for what she is. The love of a wife is as much above the idle passion commonly called by that name, as the loud laughter of buffoons is inferior to the elegant mirth of gentlemen. Oh! she is an inestimable jewel. In her examination of her household affairs, she shows a certain fearfulness to find a fault, which makes her servants obey her like children; and the meanest we have has an ingenuous shame for an offense, not always to be seen in children in other families. I speak freely to you, my old friend; ever since her sickness, things that gave me the quickest joy before, turn now to a certain anxiety. As the children play in the next room, I know the poor things by their steps, and am considering what they must do, should they lose their mother in their tender years. The pleasure I used to take in telling my boy stories of the battles, and asking my girl questions about the disposal of her baby, and the gossiping of it, is turned into inward reflection and melancholy."

He would have gone on in this tender way, when the good lady entered, and, with an inexpressible sweetness in her countenance, told us she had been searching her closet for something very good to treat such an old friend as I was. Her husband's eyes sparkled with pleasure at the cheerfulness of her countenance, and I saw all his fears vanish in an instant. The lady, observing something in our looks which showed we had been more serious than ordinary, and seeing her husband receive her with great concern under a forced cheerfulness, immediately guessed at what we had been talking of; and, applying herself to me, said, with a smile, "Mr. Bickerstaff, don't believe a word of what he tells you. I shall still live to have you for my second, as I have often promised you, unless he takes more care of himself than he has done since his coming to town. You must know, he tells me that he finds London a much more healthy place than the country; for he sees several of his old acquaintances and school-fellows are here, young fellows, with fair full-bottomed periwigs. I could scarce keep him this morning from going out open-breasted."

My friend, who is always extremely delighted with her agreeable humor, made her sit down with us. She did it with that easiness which is peculiar to women of sense; and, to keep up the good humor she had brought in with her, turned her raillery upon me. "Mr. Bickerstaff, you remember you followed me one night from the playhouse; supposing you should carry me thither to-morrow night, and lead me into the front box."

This put us into a long field of discourse about the beauties who were mothers to the present, and shone in the boxes twenty years ago. I told her I was glad she had transferred so many of her charms, and I did not question but her eldest daughter was within half a year of being a toast. We were pleasing ourselves with this fantastical preferment of the young lady, when on a sudden we were alarmed with the noise of a drum, and immediately entered my little godson, to give me a point of war. His mother, between laughing and chiding, would have put him out of the room; but I would not part with him so. I found, upon conversation with him, though he was a little noisy in his mirth, that the child had excellent parts, and was a great master of all the learning on the other side eight years old. I perceived him a very great historian in Æsop's fables; but he frankly declared to me his mind that he did not delight in that learning, because he did not believe they were true. For which reason I found he had very much turned his studies, for about a twelvemonth past, into the lives and adventures of Don Bellianis of Greece, Guy of Warwick, the Seven Champions, and other historians of that age. I could not but observe the satisfaction the father took in the forwardness of his son; and that these diversions might turn to some profit, I found the boy had made remarks which might be of service to him during the course of his whole life. He would tell you the mismanagements of John Hickathrift, find fault with the passionate temper in Bevis of Southampton, and loved St. George for being the champion of England; and by this means had his thoughts insensibly moulded into the notions of discretion, virtue, and honor.

I was extolling his accomplishments, when the mother told me that the little girl who led me in this morning was in her way a better scholar than he. "Betty," says she, "deals chiefly in fairies and sprites; and sometimes, in a winter night, will terrify the maids with her accounts, till they are afraid to go up to bed."

I sat with them till it was very late, sometimes in merry, sometimes in serious discourse, with this particular pleasure, which gives the only true relish to all conversation,—a sense that every one of us liked each other. I went home considering the different conditions of a married life and that of a bachelor; and I must confess it struck me with a secret concern to reflect that, whenever I shall go off, I shall leave no traces behind me. In this pensive mood I returned to my family,—that is to say, to my maid, my dog, and my cat, who only can be the better or worse for what happens to me.

THE SPECTATOR CLUB

—Ast alii sex,
*Et plures, uno conclamant ore.—*JUV.

THE FIRST OF OUR SOCIETY is a gentleman of Worcestershire, of ancient descent, a baronet, his name Sir Roger de Coverley. His great grandfather was inventor of that famous country-dance which is called after him. All who know that shire are very well acquainted with the parts and merits of Sir Roger. He is a gentleman that is very singular in his behavior, but his singularities proceed from his good sense, and are contradictions to the manners of the world only as he thinks the world is in the wrong. However, this humor creates him no enemies, for he does nothing with sourness or obstinacy; and his being unconfined to modes and forms makes him but the readier and more capable to please and oblige all who know him. When he is in town, he lives in Soho Square. It is said he keeps himself a bachelor by reason he was crossed in love by a perverse, beautiful widow of the next county to him. Before this disappointment, Sir Roger was what you call a fine gentleman, had often supped with my Lord Rochester and Sir George Etherege, fought a duel upon his first coming to town, and kicked Bully Dawson in a public coffee-house for calling him "youngster." But being ill-used by the above-mentioned widow, he was very serious for a year and a half; and though, his temper being naturally jovial, he at last got over it, he grew careless of himself, and never dressed afterwards. He continues to wear a coat and doublet of the same cut that were in fashion at the time of his repulse, which, in his merry humors, he tells us, has been in and out twelve times since he first wore it. * * * * He is now in his fifty-sixth year, cheerful, gay, and hearty; keeps a good house both in town and country; a great lover of mankind; but there is such a mirthful cast in his behavior that he is rather beloved than esteemed. His tenants grow rich, his servants look satisfied, all the young women profess love to him, and the young men are glad of his company. When he comes into a house he calls the servants by their names, and talks all the way up stairs to a visit. I must not omit that Sir Roger is a justice of the quorum; that he fills the chair at a quarter-session with great abilities, and, three months ago, gained universal applause by explaining a passage in the Game Act.

The gentleman next in esteem and authority among us is another bachelor, who is a member of the Inner Temple; a man of great probity, wit, and understanding; but he has chosen his place of residence rather to obey the direction of an old humorsome father, than in pursuit of his own inclinations. He was placed there to study the laws of the land, and is the most learned of any of the house in those of the stage. Aristotle and Longinus are much better understood by him than Littleton or Coke. The father sends up, every post, questions relating to marriage-articles, leases, and tenures, in the neighborhood; all which questions he agrees with an attorney to answer and take care of in the lump. He is studying the passions themselves, when he should be inquiring into the debates among men which arise from them. He knows the argument of each of the orations of Demosthenes and Tully, but not one case in the reports of our own courts. No one ever took him for a fool; but none, except his intimate friends, know he has a great deal of wit. This turn makes him at once both disinterested and agreeable: As few of his thoughts are drawn from business, they are most of them fit for conversation. His taste of books is a little too just for the age he lives in; he has read all, but approves of very few. His familiarity with the customs, manners, actions, and writings of the ancients, makes him a very delicate observer of what occurs to him in the present world. He is an excellent critic, and the time of the play is his hour of business; exactly at five he passes through New Inn, crosses through Russell Court, and takes a turn at Will's till the play begins; he has his shoes rubbed and his periwig powdered at the barber's as you go into the Rose. It is for the good of the audience when he is at a play, for the actors have an ambition to please him.

The person of next consideration is Sir Andrew Freeport, a merchant of great eminence in the city of London, a person of indefatigable industry, strong reason, and great experience. His notions of trade are noble and generous, and (as every rich man has usually some sly way of jesting, which would make no great figure were he not a rich man) he calls the sea the British Common. He is acquainted with commerce in all its parts, and will tell you that it is a stupid and barbarous way to extend dominion by arms: for true power is to be got by arts and industry. He will often argue, that if this part of our trade were well cultivated, we should gain from one nation; and if another, from another. I have heard him prove that diligence makes more lasting acquisitions than valor, and that sloth has ruined more nations than the sword. He abounds in several frugal maxims, among which the greatest favorite is, "A penny saved is a penny got." A general trader of good sense is pleasanter company than a general scholar; and Sir Andrew having a natural, unaffected eloquence, the perspicuity of his discourse gives the same pleasure that wit would in another man. He has made his fortunes himself; and says that England may be richer than other kingdoms, by as plain methods as he himself is richer than other men; though at the same time I can say this of him, that there is not a point in the compass, but blows home a ship in which he is an owner.

Next to Sir Andrew in the club-room sits Captain Sentry, a gentleman of great courage, good understanding, but invincible modesty. He is one of those that deserve very well, but are very awkward at putting their talents within the observation of such as should take notice of them. He was some years a captain, and behaved himself with great gallantry in several engagements and at several sieges; but having a small estate of his own, and being next heir to Sir Roger, he has quitted a way of life in which no man can rise suitably to his merit, who is not something of a courtier as well as a soldier. I have heard him often lament that in a profession where merit is placed in so conspicuous a view, impudence should get the better of modesty. When he had talked to this purpose, I never heard him make a sour expression, but frankly confess that he left the world because he was not fit for it. A strict honesty, and an even regular behavior, are in themselves obstacles to him that must press through crowds, who endeavor at the same end with himself, the favor of a commander. He will, however, in this way of talk excuse generals for not disposing according to men's desert, or inquiring into it; "For," says he, "that great man who has a mind to help me, has as many to break through to come at me as I have to come at him": therefore he will conclude, that the man who would make a figure, especially in a military way, must get over all false modesty, and assist his patron against the importunity of other pretenders, by a proper assurance in his own vindication. He says it is a civil cowardice to be backward in asserting what you ought to expect, as it is a military fear to be slow in attacking when it is your duty. With this candor does the gentleman speak of himself and others. The same frankness runs through all his conversation. The military part of his life has furnished him with many adventures, in the relation of which he is very agreeable to the company; for he is never overbearing, though accustomed to command men in the utmost degree below him; nor ever too obsequious from a habit of obeying men highly above him.

But that our society may not appear a set of humorists, unacquainted with the gallantries and pleasures of the age, we have among us the gallant Will Honeycomb, a gentleman who, according to his years, should be in the decline of his life, but having ever been very careful of his person, and always had a very easy fortune, time has made but very little impression either by wrinkles on his forehead, or traces in his brain. His person is well turned, of a good height. He is very ready at that sort of discourse with which men usually entertain women. He has all his life dressed very well, and remembers habits as others do men. He can smile when one speaks to him, and laughs easily. He knows the history of every mode, and can inform you from which of the French king's wenches our wives and daughters had this manner of curling their hair, that way of placing their hoods; whose frailty was covered by such a sort of petticoat, and whose vanity to show her foot made that part of the dress so short in such a year. In a word, all his conversation and knowledge has been in the female world. As other men of his age will take notice to you what such a minister said upon such and such an occasion, he will tell you, when the Duke of Monmouth danced at court, such a woman was then smitten—another was taken with him at the head of his troop in the Park. In all these important relations, he has ever about the same time received a kind glance, or a blow of a fan from some celebrated beauty, mother of the present Lord Such-a-one. If you speak of a young commoner that said a lively thing in the House, he starts up: "He has good blood in his veins, Tom Mirabell begot him; the rogue cheated me in that affair; that young fellow's mother used me more like a dog than any woman I ever made advances to." This way of talking of his very much enlivens the conversation among us of a more sedate turn; and I find there is not one of the company, but myself, who rarely speak at all, but speaks of him as of that sort of man, who is usually called a well-bred fine gentleman. To conclude his character, where women are not concerned, he is an honest, worthy man.

I cannot tell whether I am to account him whom I am next to speak of as one of our company, for he visits us but seldom; but when he does, it adds to every man else a new enjoyment of himself. He is a clergyman, a very philosophic man, of general learning, great sanctity of life, and the most exact good breeding. He has the misfortune to be of a very weak constitution, and consequently cannot accept of such cares and business as preferments in his function would oblige him to; he is therefore among divines what a chamber-counsellor is among lawyers. The probity of his mind and the integrity of his life, create him followers, as being eloquent or loud advances others. He seldom introduces the subject he speaks upon; but we are so far gone in years that he observes, when he is among us, an earnestness to have him fall on some divine topic, which he always treats with much authority, as one who has no interests in this world, as one who is hastening to the object of all his wishes, and conceives hope from his decays and infirmities. These are my ordinary companions.

COFFEE HOUSES

Hominem pagina nostra sapit.—MART.

IT IS VERY NATURAL FOR A MAN who is not turned for mirthful meetings of men, or assemblies of the fair sex, to delight in that sort of conversation which we find in coffeehouses. Here a man of my temper is in his element; for if he cannot talk, he can still be more agreeable to his company, as well as pleased in himself, in being only a hearer. It is a secret known but to few, yet of no small use in the conduct of life, that when you fall into a man's conversation, the first thing you should consider is, whether he has a greater inclination to hear you or that you should hear him. The latter is the more general desire, and I know very able flatterers that never speak a word in praise of the persons from whom they obtain daily favors, but still practice a skillful attention to whatever is uttered by those with whom they converse. We are very curious to observe the behavior of great men and their clients, but the same passions and interests move men in lower spheres; and I (that have nothing else to do but make observations) see in every parish, street, lane, and alley of this populous city, a little potentate that has his court and his flatterers, who lay snares for his affection and favor by the same arts that are practiced upon men in higher stations.

In the place I most usually frequent, men differ rather in the time of day in which they make a figure, than in any real greatness above one another. I, who am at the coffee-house at six in the morning, know that my friend Beaver, the haberdasher, has a levee of more undissembled friends and admirers than most of the courtiers or generals of Great Britain. Every man about him has, perhaps, a newspaper in his hand; but none can pretend to guess what step will be taken in any one court of Europe, till Mr. Beaver has thrown down his pipe, and declares what measures the Allies must enter into, upon this new posture of affairs. Our coffee-house is near one of the Inns of Court, and Beaver has the audience and admiration of his neighbors from six till within a quarter of eight, at which time he is interrupted by the students of the house, some of whom are ready dressed for Westminster at eight in a morning, with faces as busy as if they were retained in every cause there; and others come in their night-gowns to saunter away their time, as if they never designed to go thither. I do not know that I meet in any of my walks objects which move both my spleen and laughter so effectually, as those young fellows at the Grecian, Squire's, Searle's, and all other coffee-houses adjacent to the law, who rise early for no other purpose but to publish their laziness. One would think these young virtuosos take a gay cap and slippers, with a scarf and parti-colored gown, to be the ensigns of dignity; for the vain things approach each other with an air which shows they regard one another for their vestments. I have observed that the superiority among these proceeds from an opinion of gallantry and fashion. The gentleman in the strawberry sash, who presides so much over the rest, has, it seems, subscribed to every opera this last winter, and is supposed to receive favors from one of the actresses.

When the day grows too busy for these gentlemen to enjoy any longer the pleasures of their dishabille with any manner of confidence, they give place to men who have business or good sense in their faces, and come to the coffee-house either to transact affairs or enjoy conversation. The persons to whose behavior and discourse I have most regard, are such as are between these two sorts of men; such as have not spirits too active to be happy and well pleased in a private condition, nor complexions too warm to make them neglect the duties and relations of life. Of these sort of men consist the worthier part of mankind; of these are all good fathers, generous brothers, sincere friends, and faithful subjects. Their entertainments are derived rather from reason than imagination, which is the cause that there is no impatience or instability in their speech or action. You see in their countenances they are at home, and in quiet possession of the present instant as it passes, without desiring to quicken it by gratifying any passion, or prosecuting any new design. These are the men formed for society, and those little communities which we express by the word neighborhood.

The coffee-house is the place of rendezvous to all that live near it, who are thus turned to relish calm and ordinary life. Eubulus presides over the middle hours of the day, when this assembly of men meet together. He enjoys a great fortune handsomely, without launching into expense; and exerts many noble and useful qualities, without appearing in any public employment. His wisdom and knowledge are serviceable to all that think fit to make use of them; and he does the office of a counsel, a judge, an executor, and a friend, to all his acquaintance, not only without the profits which attend such offices, but also without the deference and homage which are usually paid to them. The giving of thanks is displeasing to him. The greatest gratitude you can show him is to let him see that you are a better man for his services, and that you are as ready to oblige others as he is to oblige you.

In the private exigencies of his friends, he lends at legal

value considerable sums which he might highly increase by rolling in the public stocks. He does not consider in whose hands his money will improve most, but where it will do most good.

Eubulus has so great an authority in his little diurnal audience, that when he shakes his head at any piece of public news, they all of them appear dejected; and on the contrary, go home to their dinners with a good stomach and cheerful aspect, when Eubulus seems to intimate that things go well. Nay, their veneration towards him is so great that when they are in other company they speak and act after him, are wise in his sentences, and are no sooner sat down at their own tables, but they hope or fear, rejoice or despond, as they saw him do at the coffee-house. In a word, every man is Eubulus as soon as his back is turned.

Having here given an account of the several reigns that succeed each other from daybreak till dinner-time, I shall mention the monarchs of the afternoon on another occasion, and shut up the whole series of them with the history of Tom the Tyrant, who, as the first minister of the coffee-house, takes the government upon him between the hours of eleven and twelve at night, and gives his orders in the most arbitrary manner to the servants below him, as to the disposition of liquors, coal, and cinders.

THE COVERLEY FAMILY PORTRAITS

Abnormis sapiens.—HOR.

I WAS THIS MORNING WALKING in the gallery, when Sir Roger entered at the end opposite to me, and, advancing towards me, said he was glad to meet me among his relations, the de Coverleys, and hoped I liked the conversation of so much good company, who were as silent as myself. I knew he alluded to the pictures, and, as he is a gentleman who does not a little value himself upon his ancient descent, I expected he would give me some account of them. We were now arrived at the upper end of the gallery, when the knight faced towards one of the pictures, and, as we stood before it, he entered into the matter, after his blunt way of saying things as they occur to his imagination, without regular introduction or care to preserve the appearance of chain of thought.

"It is," said he, "worth while to consider the force of dress, and how the persons of one age differ from those of another merely by that only. One may observe also, that the general fashion of one age has been followed by one particular set of people in another, and by them preserved from one generation to another. Thus, the vast jetting coat and small bonnet, which was the habit in Harry the Seventh's time, is kept on in the yeomen of the guard; not without a good and politic view, because they look a foot taller, and a foot and a half broader—besides that the cap leaves the face expanded, and consequently more terrible and fitter to stand at the entrance of palaces.

"This predecessor of ours, you see, is dressed after this manner, and his cheeks would be no larger than mine, were he in a hat as I am. He was the last man that won a prize in the Tilt Yard (which is now a common street before White-hall). You see the broken lance that lies there by his right foot: he shivered that lance of his adversary all to pieces; and, bearing himself, look you, Sir, in this manner, at the same time he came within the target of the gentleman who rode against him, and taking him with incredible force before him on the pommel of his saddle, he in that manner rid the tournament over, with an air that showed he did it rather to perform the rules of the lists than expose his enemy: however, it appeared he knew how to make use of a victory, and, with a gentle trot, he marched up to a gallery where their mistress sat (for they were rivals) and let him down with laudable courtesy and pardonable insolence. I don't know but it might be exactly where the coffee-house is now.

"You are to know this my ancestor was not only of a military genius, but fit also for the arts of peace, for he played on the bass-viol as well as any gentleman at court; you see where his viol hangs by his basket-hilt sword. The action at the Tilt Yard you may be sure won the fair lady, who was a maid of honor and the greatest beauty of her time; here she stands, the next picture. You see, Sir, my great-great-great-grandmother has on the new-fashioned petticoat, except that the modern is gathered at the waist; my grandmother appears as if she stood in a large drum, whereas the ladies now walk as if they were in a go-cart. For all this lady was bred at court, she became an excellent country wife; she brought ten children, and, when I show you the library, you shall see, in her own hand (allowing for the difference of the language), the best receipt now in England both for an hasty-pudding and a white-pot.

"If you please to fall back a little, because it is necessary to look at the three next pictures at one view; these are three sisters. She on the right hand, who is so very beautiful, died a maid; the next to her, still handsomer, had the same fate, against her will; this homely thing in the middle had both their portions added to her own, and was stolen by a neighboring gentleman, a man of stratagem and resolution, for he poisoned three mastiffs to come at her, and knocked down two deer-stealers in carrying her off. Misfortunes happen in all families. The theft of this romp and so much money was no great matter to our estate. But the next heir that possessed it was this soft gentleman, whom you see there. Observe the small buttons, the little boots, the laces, the slashes about his clothes, and, above all, the posture he is drawn in (which to be sure was his own choosing); you see he sits with one hand on a desk, writing and looking, as it were, another way, like an easy writer or a sonneteer. He was one of those that had too much wit to know how to live in the world; he was a man of no justice, but great good manners; he ruined every body that had any thing to do with him, but never said a rude thing in his life; the most indolent person in the world, he would sign a deed that passed away half his estate, with his gloves on, but would not put on his hat before a lady if it were to save his country. He is said to be the first that made love by squeezing the hand. He left the estate with ten thousand pound's debt upon it; but, however, by all hands I have been informed that he was every way the finest gentleman in the world. That debt lay heavy on our house for one generation; but it was retrieved by a gift from that honest man you see there, a citizen of our name, but nothing at all akin to us. I know Sir Andrew Freeport has said behind my back that this man was descended from one of the ten children of the maid of honor I showed you above; but it was never made out. We winked at the thing, indeed, because money was wanting at that time."

Here I saw my friend a little embarrassed, and turned my face to the next portraiture.

Sir Roger went on with his account of the gallery in the following manner: "This man" (pointing to him I looked at) "I take to be the honor of our house, Sir Humphrey de Coverley; he was, in his dealings, as punctual as a tradesman and as generous as a gentleman. He would have thought himself as much undone by breaking his word as if it were to be followed by bankruptcy. He served his country as knight of this shire to his dying day. He found it no easy matter to maintain an integrity in his words and actions, even in things that regarded the offices which were incumbent upon him, in the care of his own affairs and relations of life, and therefore dreaded (though he had great talents) to go into employments of state, where he must be exposed to the snares of ambition. Innocence of life and great ability were the distinguishing parts of his character; the latter, he had often observed, had led to the destruction of the former, and used frequently to lament that *great* and *good* had not the same signification. He was an excellent husbandman, but had resolved not to exceed such a degree of wealth; all above it he bestowed in secret bounties many years after the sum he aimed at for his own use was attained. Yet he did not slacken his industry, but to a decent old age spent the life and fortune which was superfluous to himself, in the service of his friends and neighbors."

Here we were called to dinner, and Sir Roger ended the discourse of this gentleman by telling me, as we followed the servant, that this his ancestor was a brave man, and narrowly escaped being killed in the Civil Wars; "for," said he, "he was sent out of the field upon a private message the day before the battle of Worcester."

The whim of narrowly escaping by having been within a day of danger, with other matters above mentioned, mixed with good sense, left me at a loss whether I was more delighted with my friend's wisdom or simplicity.

Benjamin Franklin

1706 · 1790

*Benjamin Franklin was a printer, publisher, founder
of libraries, hospitals, and schools, scientist, and
statesman. Much of his writing was directed
toward furthering the causes which interested him
and so was primarily practical. He wrote
simply, wittily, and always to the point. The*
Autobiography *which he wrote late in life shows
his style to best advantage, and its humor, wisdom,
and grace have delighted readers ever since it first
appeared in 1817. Many of Franklin's most charming
essays remain in the form of letters, of which
"The Ephemera" is a good example.*

THE EPHEMERA:
AN EMBLEM OF HUMAN LIFE

A Letter to Madam Brillon de Jouy, 1778

YOU MAY REMEMBER, my dear friend, that when we lately
spent that happy day in the delightful garden and sweet
society of the Moulin Joly, I stopt a little in one of our walks,
and staid some time behind the company. We had been shown
numberless skeletons of a kind of little fly, called an ephemera,
whose successive generations, we were told, were bred and
expired within the day. I happened to see a living company of
them on a leaf, who appeared to be engaged in conversation.
You know I understand all the inferior animal tongues: my
too great application to the study of them is the best excuse I
can give for the little progress I have made in your charming
language. I listened through curiosity to the discourse of these
little creatures; but as they, in their national vivacity, spoke

three or four together, I could make but little of their conversation. I found, however, by some broken expressions that I heard now and then, they were disputing warmly on the merit of two foreign musicians, one a *cousin*, the other a *moscheto;* in which dispute they spent their time, seemingly as regardless of the shortness of life as if they had been sure of living a month. Happy people! thought I, you live certainly under a wise, just, and mild government, since you have no public grievances to complain of, nor any subject of contention but the perfections and imperfections of foreign music. I turned my head from them to an old grey-headed one, who was single on another leaf, and talking to himself. Being amused with his soliloquy, I put it down in writing, in hopes it will likewise amuse her to whom I am so much indebted for the most pleasing of all amusements, her delicious company and heavenly harmony.

"It was," said he, "the opinion of learned philosophers of our race, who lived and flourished long before my time, that this vast world, the Moulin Joly, could not itself subsist more than eighteen hours; and I think there was some foundation for that opinion, since, by the apparent motion of the great luminary that gives life to all nature, and which in my time has evidently declined considerably towards the ocean at the end of our earth, it must then finish its course, be extinguished in the waters that surround us, and leave the world in cold and darkness, necessarily producing universal death and destruction. I have lived seven of those hours, a great age, being no less than four hundred and twenty minutes of time. How very few of us continue so long! I have seen generations born, flourish, and expire. My present friends are the children and grandchildren of the friends of my youth, who are now, alas, no more! And I must soon follow them; for, by the course of nature, though still in health, I cannot expect to live above seven or eight minutes longer. What now avails all my toil and labor, in amassing honey-dew on this leaf, which I cannot live to enjoy! What the political struggles I have been engaged in, for the good of my compatriot inhabitants of this bush, or my philosophical studies for the benefit of our race in general! for, in politics, what can laws do without morals? Our present race of ephemeræ will in a course of minutes become corrupt, like those of other and older bushes, and consequently as wretched. And in philosophy how small our progress! Alas! art is long, and life is short! My friends would comfort me with the idea of a name, they say, I shall leave behind me; and they tell me I have lived long enough to nature and to glory. But what will fame be to an ephemera who no longer exists? And what will become of all history in the eighteenth hour, when the world itself, even the whole Moulin Joly, shall come to its end, and be buried in universal ruin?"

To me, after all my eager pursuits, no solid pleasures now remain, but the reflection of a long life spent in meaning well, the sensible conversation of a few good lady ephemeræ, and now and then a kind smile and a tune from the ever amiable *Brillante*.

B. FRANKLIN.

Henry Fielding

1707 · 1754

Henry Fielding, English novelist, essayist, and playwright, went to Eton, studied law for a time at Leyden, and then gave his attention to the theater. In his farce, Tom Thumb *(1730), he burlesqued most of the popular playwrights among his contemporaries. Misfortunes, financial and legal, brought an end to his theatrical career, and he began the practice of law in 1740. Two years later he began a career as novelist with the publication of* Joseph Andrews, *which he started as a parody of Richardson's* Pamela. Tom Jones *(1749), a rambling novel full of digressions and essays on subjects not related to the story, was his other major success in this form.*

A COMPARISON BETWEEN THE WORLD AND THE STAGE

THE WORLD HATH BEEN often compared to the theatre; and many grave writers, as well as the poets, have considered human life as a great drama, resembling, in almost every particular, those scenical representations which Thespis is first reported to have invented, and which have been since received with so much approbation and delight in all polite countries.

This thought hath been carried so far, and is become so general, that some words proper to the theatre, and which were at first metaphorically applied to the world, are now indiscriminately and literally spoken of both; thus stage and scene are by common use grown as familiar to us, when we speak of life in general, as when we confine ourselves to dramatic performances: and when transactions behind the curtain are mentioned, St. James's is more likely to occur to our thoughts than Drury Lane.

It may seem easy enough to account for all this, by reflecting that the theatrical stage is nothing more than a representation, or, as Aristotle calls it, an imitation of what really exists; and hence, perhaps, we might fairly pay a very high compliment to those who by their writings or actions have been so capable of imitating life, as to have their pictures in a manner confounded with, or mistaken for, the originals.

But, in reality, we are not so fond of paying compliments to these people, whom we use as children frequently do the instruments of their amusement; and have much more pleasure in hissing and buffeting them, than in admiring their excellence. There are many other reasons which have induced us to see this analogy between the world and the stage.

Some have considered the larger part of mankind in the light of actors, as personating characters no more their own, and to which, in fact, they have no better title than the player hath to be in earnest thought the king or emperor whom he represents. Thus the hypocrite may be said to be a player; and indeed the Greeks called them both by one and the same name.

The brevity of life hath likewise given occasion to this comparison. So the immortal Shakespeare—

> ————Life's a poor player,
> That struts and frets his hour upon the stage,
> And then is heard no more.

For which hackneyed quotation I will make the reader amends by a very noble one, which few, I believe, have read. It is taken from a poem called the Deity, published about nine years ago, and long since buried in oblivion; a proof that good books, no more than good men, do always survive the bad.

> From Thee all human actions take their springs,
> The rise of empires and the fall of kings!
> See the vast Theatre of Time display'd,

While o'er the scene succeeding heroes tread!
With pomp the shining images succeed,
What leaders triumph, and what monarchs bleed!
Perform the parts Thy providence assign'd,
Their pride, their passions, to Thy ends inclin'd:
Awhile they glitter in the face of day,
Then at Thy nod the phantoms pass away;
No traces left of all the busy scene,
But that remembrance says—*The things have been!*

In all these, however, and in every other similitude of life to the theatre, the resemblance hath been always taken from the stage only. None, as I remember, have at all considered the audience at this great drama.

But as Nature often exhibits some of her best performances to a very full house, so will the behaviour of her spectators no less admit the above-mentioned comparison than that of her actors. In this vast theatre of time are seated the friend and the critic; here are claps and shouts, hisses and groans; in short, everything which was ever seen or heard at the Theatre-Royal.

Let us examine this in one example; for instance, in the behaviour of the great audience on that scene which Nature was pleased to exhibit in the twelfth chapter of the preceding book, where she introduced Black George running away with the £500 from his friend and benefactor.

Those who sat in the world's upper gallery treated that incident, I am well convinced, with their usual vociferation; and every term of scurrilous reproach was most probably vented on that occasion.

If we had descended to the next order of spectators, we should have found an equal degree of abhorrence, though less of noise and scurrility; yet here the good women gave Black George to the devil, and many of them expected every minute that the cloven-footed gentleman would fetch his own.

The pit, as usual, was no doubt divided; those who delight in heroic virtue and perfect character objected to the producing such instances of villainy, without punishing them very severely for the sake of example. Some of the author's friends cried, 'Look'e, gentlemen, the man is a villain, but it is nature for all that.' And all the young critics of the age, the clerks, apprentices, etc., called it low, and fell a-groaning.

As for the boxes, they behaved with their accustomed politeness. Most of them were attending to something else. Some of those few who regarded the scene at all declared he was a bad kind of man; while others refused to give their opinion till they had heard that of the best judges.

Now we, who are admitted behind the scenes of this great theatre of Nature (and no author ought to write anything besides dictionaries and spelling-books who hath not this privilege), can censure the action, without conceiving any absolute detestation of the person, whom perhaps Nature may not have designed to act an ill part in all her dramas; for in this instance life most exactly resembles the stage, since it is often the same person who represents the villain and the hero; and he who engages your admiration to-day will probably attract your contempt to-morrow. As Garrick, whom I regard in tragedy to be the greatest genius the world hath ever produced, sometimes condescends to play the fool; so did Scipio the Great, and Lælius the Wise, according to Horace, many years ago; nay, Cicero reports them to have been 'incredibly childish.' These, it is true, played the fool, like my friend Garrick, in jest only; but several eminent characters have, in numberless instances of their lives, played the fool egregiously in earnest; so far as to render it a matter of some doubt whether their wisdom or folly was predominant; or whether they were better entitled to the applause or censure, the admiration or contempt, the love or hatred of mankind.

Those persons, indeed, who have passed any time behind the scenes of this great theatre, and are thoroughly acquainted not only with the several disguises which are there put on, but also with the fantastic and capricious behaviour of the Passions, who are the managers and directors of this theatre (for as to Reason, the patentee, he is known to be a very idle fellow and seldom to exert himself), may most probably have learned to understand the famous *nil admirari* of Horace, or in the English phrase, to stare at nothing.

A single bad act no more constitutes a villain in life than a single bad part on the stage. The passions, like the managers of a playhouse, often force men upon parts without consulting their judgment, and sometimes without any regard to their talents. Thus the man, as well as the player, may condemn what he himself acts; nay, it is common to see vice sit as awkwardly on some men, as the character of Iago would on the honest face of Mr. William Mills.

Upon the whole, then, the man of candour and of true understanding is never hasty to condemn. He can censure an imperfection, or even a vice, without rage against the guilty party. In a word, they are the same folly, the same childishness, the same ill-breeding, and the same ill-nature, which raise all the clamours and uproars both in life and on the stage. The worst of men generally have the words rogue and villain most in their mouths, as the lowest of all wretches are the aptest to cry out low in the pit.

ON TASTE IN BOOKS

THE PRESENT AGE seems pretty well agreed in an opinion that the utmost scope and end of reading is amusement only; and such, indeed, are now the fashionable books that a reader can propose no more than mere entertainment, and it is sometimes very well for him if he finds even this in his studies.

Letters, however, were surely intended for a much more noble and profitable purpose than this. Writers are not, I presume, to be considered as mere jack-puddings, whose business it is only to excite laughter; this, indeed, may sometimes be intermixed and served up with graver matters, in order to titillate the palate and to recommend wholsesome food to the mind; and for this purpose it hath been used by many excellent authors. *"For why,"* as Horace says, *"should not any one promulgate truth with a smile on his countenance?"* Ridicule, indeed, as he again intimates, is commonly a stronger and better method of attacking vice than the severer kind of satire.

When wit and humor are introduced for such good pur-poses, when the agreeable is blended with the useful, then is the writer said to have succeeded in every point. Pleasantry (as the ingenious author of *Clarissa* says of a story) should be made only the vehicle of instruction; and thus romances them-selves, as well as epic poems, may become worthy the perusal of the greatest of men. But when no moral, no lesson, no in-struction is conveyed to the reader, where the whole design of the composition is no more than to make us laugh, the writer comes very near to the character of a buffoon; and his admir-ers, if an old Latin proverb be true, deserve no great compli-ments to be paid to their wisdom.

After what I have here advanced, I cannot fairly, I think, be represented as an enemy to laughter, or to all those kinds of writing that are apt to promote it. On the contrary, few men, I believe, do more admire the works of those great mas-ters who have sent their satire (if I may use the expression) laughing into the world. Such are the great triumvirate, Lucian, Cervantes, and Swift. These authors I shall ever hold in the highest degree of esteem; not indeed for that wit and humor alone which they all so eminently possessed, but be-cause they all endeavored, with the utmost force of their wit and humor, to expose and extirpate those follies and vices which chiefly prevailed in their several countries. I would not be thought to confine wit and humor to these writers. Shakespeare, Moliere, and some other authors have been blessed with the same talents and have employed them to the same purposes. There are some, however, who, though not void of these talents, have made so wretched a use of them that, had the consecration of their labors been committed to the hands of the hangman, no good man would have regretted their loss; nor am I afraid to mention Rabelais and Aristophanes himself in this number. For, if I may speak my opinion freely of these two last writers and of their works, their design ap-pears to me very plainly to have been to ridicule all sobriety, modesty, decency, virtue, and religion out of the world. Now whoever reads over the five great writers first mentioned in this paragraph must either have a very bad head or a very bad heart if he doth not become both a wiser and a better man.

In the exercise of the mind, as well as in the exercise of the body, diversion is a secondary consideration, and designed only to make that agreeable which is at the same time useful to such noble purposes as health and wisdom. But what should we say to a man who mounted his chamber-hobby or fought with his own shadow for his amusement only? How much more absurd and weak would he appear who swallowed poison because it was sweet?

How differently did Horace think of study from our modern readers!

Quid verum atque decens curo et rogo, et omnis in hoc sum:
Condo et compono, quae mox depromere possim.

"*Truth and decency are my whole care and inquiry. In this study I am entirely occupied; these I am always laying up, and so disposing, that I can at any time draw forth my stores for my immediate use.*" The whole epistle, indeed, from which I have paraphrased this passage, is a comment upon it, and affords many useful lessons of philosophy.

When we are employed in reading a great and good author, we ought to consider ourselves as searching after treasures, which, if well and regularly laid up in the mind, will be of use to us on sundry occasions in our lives. If a man, for instance, should be overloaded with prosperity or adversity (both of which cases are liable to happen to us), who is there so very wise or so very foolish that, if he was a master of Seneca and Plutarch, could not find great matter of comfort and utility from their doctrines? I mention these rather than Plato and Aristotle, as the works of the latter are not, I think, yet completely made English, and, consequently, are less within the reach of most of my countrymen.

But perhaps it may be asked, will Seneca or Plutarch make us laugh? Perhaps not; but if you are not a fool, my worthy friend, which I can hardly with civility suspect, they will both (the latter especially) please you more than if they did. For my own part, I declare I have not read even Lucian himself with more delight than I have Plutarch, but surely it is astonishing that such scribblers as Tom Brown, Tom D'Urfey, and the wits of our age should find readers, while the writings of so excellent, so entertaining, and so voluminous an author as Plutarch remain in the world, and, as I apprehend, are very little known.

The truth, I am afraid, is that real taste is a quality with which human nature is very slenderly gifted. It is indeed so very rare and so little known that scarce two authors have agreed in their notions of it, and those who have endeavored to explain it to others seem to have succeeded only in showing us that they know it not themselves. If I might be allowed to give my own sentiments, I should derive it from a nice harmony between the imagination and the judgment; and hence perhaps it is that so few have ever possessed this talent in any eminent degree. Neither of these will alone bestow it; nothing is indeed more common than to see men of very bright imaginations and of very accurate learning (which can hardly be acquired without judgment) who are entirely devoid of taste; and Longinus, who of all men seems most exquisitely to have possessed it, will puzzle his reader very much if he should attempt to decide whether imagination or judgment shine the brighter in that inimitable critic.

But as for the bulk of mankind, they are clearly void of any degree of taste. It is a quality in which they advance very little beyond a state of infancy. The first thing a child is fond of in a book is a picture, the second is a story, and the third a jest. Here then is the true *Pons Asinorum* which very few readers ever get over.

From what I have said, it may perhaps be thought to appear that true taste is the real gift of nature only; and if so, some may ask to what purpose have I endeavored to show men that they are without a blessing which it is impossible for them to attain?

Now, though it is certain that to the highest consummation of taste, as well as of every other excellence, nature must lend much assistance; yet great is the power of art, almost of itself, or at best with only slender aids from nature; and, to say the truth, there are very few who have not in their minds some small seeds of taste. *"All men,"* says Cicero, *"have a sort of tacit sense of what is right or wrong in arts and sciences, even without the help of arts."* This surely it is in the power of art very greatly to improve. That most men, therefore, proceed no farther than as I have above declared, is owing either to the want of any, or (which is perhaps yet worse) to an improper education.

I shall probably, therefore, in a future paper endeavor to lay down some rules by which all men may acquire at least some degree of taste. In the meanwhile, I shall (according to the method observed in inoculation) recommend to my readers, as a preparative for their receiving my instructions, a total abstinence from all bad books; I do therefore most earnestly entreat all my young readers that they would cautiously avoid the perusal of any modern book till it hath first had the sanction of some wise and learned man, and the same caution I propose to all fathers, mothers, and guardians.

"Evil communications corrupt good manners" is a quotation of St. Paul from Menander. *Evil books corrupt at once both our manners and our taste.*

Samuel Johnson

1709 · 1784

*Samuel Johnson overcame the obstacles of poverty
and ill health to become the most distinguished
literary figure in England in the eighteenth century.
The famous* Dictionary, Rasselas, *and* Lives of the
English Poets *are his chief contributions to English
letters, but his essays from* The Rambler *(1750–52)
and* The Idler *(1758–60) display his tastes and
interests to advantage. These publications,
however, lacked the light touch of Addison and
Steele, and so they were only mildly successful.
His personal influence was even greater than his
fame as a writer, for he drew to himself such
men as Reynolds, Gibbon, Burke, Goldsmith,
and others, who constituted the most famous
literary association of its time—The Club.*

BIOGRAPHY

ALL JOY OR SORROW for the happiness or calamities of others is produced by an act of the
imagination that realizes the event, however fictitious, or approximates it, however remote, by placing us for a time in
the condition of him whose fortune we contemplate; so that
we feel, while the deception lasts, whatever motions would be
excited by the same good or evil happening to ourselves.

Our passions are therefore more strongly moved, in proportion as we can more readily adopt the pains or pleasure proposed to our minds, by recognizing them as once our own or
considering them as naturally incident to our state of life. It
is not easy for the most artful writer to give us an interest in
happiness or misery, which we think ourselves never likely to

feel, and with which we have never yet been made acquainted. Histories of the downfall of kingdoms and revolutions of empires are read with great tranquillity; the imperial tragedy pleases common auditors only by its pomp of ornament and grandeur of ideas; and the man whose faculties have been engrossed by business, and whose heart never fluttered but at the rise or fall of the stocks, wonders how the attention can be seized or the affection agitated by a tale of love.

Those parallel circumstances and kindred images to which we readily conform our minds are, above all other writings, to be found in narritives of the lives of particular persons; and therefore no species of writing seems more worthy of cultivation than biography, since none can be more delightful or more useful, none can more certainly enchain the heart by irresistible interest, or more widely diffuse instruction to every diversity of condition.

The general and rapid narratives of history, which involve a thousand fortunes in the business of a day and complicate innumerable incidents in one great transaction, afford few lessons applicable to private life, which derives its comforts and its wretchedness from the right or wrong management of things which nothing but their frequency makes considerable, *Parva si non fiunt quotidie*, says Pliny, and which can have no place in those relations which never descend below the consultation of senates, the motions of armies, and the schemes of conspirators.

I have often thought that there has rarely passed a life of which a judicious and faithful narrative would not be useful. For, not only every man has, in the mighty mass of the world, great numbers in the same condition with himself, to whom his mistakes and miscarriages, escapes and expedients, would be of immediate and apparent use; but there is such an uniformity in the state of man, considered apart from adventitious and separable decorations and disguises, that there is scarce any possibility of good or ill but is common to human kind. A great part of the time of those who are placed at the greatest distance by fortune, or by temper, must unavoidably pass in the same manner; and though, when the claims of nature are satisfied, caprice and vanity and accident begin to produce discriminations and peculiarities, yet the eye is not very heedful or quick which cannot discover the same causes still terminating their influence in the same effects, though sometimes accelerated, sometimes retarded, or perplexed by multiplied combinations. We are all prompted by the same motives, all deceived by the same fallacies, all animated by hope, obstructed by danger, entangled by desire, and seduced by pleasure.

It is frequently objected to relations of particular lives that they are not distinguished by any striking or wonderful vicissitudes. The scholar who passed his life among his books, the merchant who conducted only his own affairs, the priest whose sphere of action was not extended beyond that of his duty, are considered as no proper objects of public regard, however they might have excelled in their several stations, whatever might have been their learning, integrity, and piety. But this notion arises from false measures of excellence and dignity, and must be eradicated by considering that in the esteem of uncorrupted reason what is of most use is of most value.

It is, indeed, not improper to take honest advantages of prejudice and to gain attention by a celebrated name; but the business of the biographer is often to pass slightly over those performances and incidents which produce vulgar greatness, to lead the thoughts into domestic privacies and display the minute details of daily life where exterior appendages are cast aside and men excel each other only by prudence and by virtue. The account of Thuanus is, with great propriety, said by its author to have been written that it might lay open to posterity the private and familiar character of that man, *cuius ingenium et candorem ex ipsius scriptis sunt olim semper miraturi*, whose candor and genius will to the end of time be by his writings preserved in admiration.

There are many invisible circumstances which, whether we read as enquirers after natural or moral knowledge, whether we intend to enlarge our science or increase our virtue, are more important than public occurrences. Thus Sallust, the great master of nature, has not forgot, in his account of Catiline, to remark that "his walk was now quick, and again slow," as an indication of a mind revolving something with violent commotion. Thus the story of Melanchthon affords a striking lecture on the value of time by informing us that when he made an appointment he expected not only the hour but the minute to be fixed, that the day might not run out in the idleness of suspense; and all the plans and enterprises of De Witt are now of less importance to the world than that part of his personal character which represents him as "careful of his health and negligent of his life."

But biography has often been allotted to writers who seem very little acquainted with the nature of their task, or very negligent about the performance. They rarely afford any other account than might be collected from public papers, but imagine themselves writing a life when they exhibit a chronological series of actions or preferments; and so little regard the manners or behavior of their heroes that more knowledge may be gained of a man's real character by a short conversation with one of his servants than from a formal and studied narrative begun with his pedigree and ended with his funeral.

If now and then they condescend to inform the world of particular facts, they are not always so happy as to select the most important. I know not well what advantage posterity can receive from the only circumstance by which Tickell has distinguished Addison from the rest of mankind, "the irregularity of his pulse"; nor can I think myself overpaid for the time spent in reading the life of Malherb by being enabled to relate, after the learned biographer, that Malherb had two predominant opinions: one, that the looseness of a single woman might destroy all her boast of ancient descent; the other, that the French beggars made use very improperly and barbarously of the phrase "noble Gentleman," because either word included the sense of both.

There are, indeed, some natural reasons why these narratives are often written by such as were not likely to give much instruction or delight, and why most accounts of particular persons are barren and useless. If a life be delayed till interest and envy are at an end, we may hope for impartiality, but must expect little intelligence; for the incidents which give excellence to biography are of a volatile and evanescent kind, such as soon escape the memory and are rarely transmitted by tradition. We know how few can portray a living acquaintance, except by his most prominent and observable particularities and the grosser features of his mind; and it may be easily imagined how much of this little knowledge may be lost in imparting it, and how soon a succession of copies will lose all resemblance of the original.

If the biographer writes from personal knowledge, and makes haste to gratify the public curiosity, there is danger lest his interest, his fear, his gratitude, or his tenderness, overpower his fidelity and tempt him to conceal if not to invent. There are many who think it an act of piety to hide the faults or failings of their friends, even when they can no longer suffer by their detection; we therefore see whole ranks of characters adorned with uniform panegyric, and not to be known from one another but by extrinsic and casual circumstances. "Let me remember," says Hale, "when I find myself inclined to pity a criminal, that there is likewise a pity due to the country." If we owe regard to the memory of the dead, there is yet more respect to be paid to knowledge, to virtue, and to truth.

THE THEORY OF A GARRET

Οσσαν ἐπ' Οὐλύμπῳ μήμασαν θέμεν· αὐτὰρ' επ' ῞Οσση.
Πήλιον εἰνοσ ἰφυλλον, ἵυ' οὐρανὸς ἀμβατὸς εἴπ.—HOMER.

The gods they challenge, and affect the skies:
Heav'd on Olympus tott'ring Ossa stood;
On Ossa, Pelion nods with all his wood.—POPE.

To the Rambler. Sir:
Nothing has more retarded the advancement of learning than the disposition of vulgar minds to ridicule and vilify what they cannot comprehend. All industry must be excited

by hope; and as the student often proposes no other reward to himself than praise, he is easily discouraged by contempt and insult. He who brings with him into a clamorous multitude the timidity of recluse speculation, and has never hardened his front in public life, or accustomed his passions to the vicissitudes and accidents, the triumphs and defeats of mixed conversation, will blush at the stare of petulant incredulity, and suffer himself to be driven by a burst of laughter from the fortresses of demonstration. The mechanist will be afraid to assert, before hardy contradiction, the possibility of tearing down bulwarks with a silkworm's thread; and the astronomer of relating the rapidity of light, the distance of the fixed stars, and the height of the lunar mountains.

If I could by any efforts have shaken off this cowardice, I had not sheltered myself under a borrowed name, nor applied to you for the means of communicating to the public the theory of a garret; a subject which, except some slight and transient strictures, has been hitherto neglected by those who were best qualified to adorn it, either for want of leisure to prosecute the various researches in which a nice discussion must engage them, or because it requires such diversity of knowledge, and such extent of curiosity, as is scarcely to be found in any single intellect; or perhaps others foresaw the tumults which would be raised against them, and confined their knowledge to their own breasts, and abandoned prejudice and folly to the direction of chance.

That the professors of literature generally reside in the highest stories, has been immemorially observed. The wisdom of the ancients was well acquainted with the intellectual advantages of an elevated situation; why else were the Muses stationed on Olympus or Parnassus by those who could with equal right have raised them bowers in the vale of Tempe, or erected their altars among the flexures of Meander? Why was Jove himself nursed upon a mountain? Or why did the goddesses, when the prize of beauty was contested, try the cause upon the top of Ida? Such were the fictions by which the great masters of the earlier ages endeavored to inculcate to posterity the importance of a garret, which, though they had

been long obscured by the negligence and ignorance of succeeding times, were well enforced by the celebrated symbol
of Pythagoras, ἀνεμῶν πνεόντων τὴν ἠχῶ προσκύνει, "when the
wind blows, worship its echo." This could not but be understood by his disciples as an inviolable injunction to live in
a garret, which I have found frequently visited by the echo
and the wind. Nor was the tradition wholly obliterated in the
age of Augustus, for Tibullus evidently congratulates himself upon his garret, not without some allusion to the Pytha-
gorean precept:—

> *Quam juvat immites ventos audire cubantem—*
> *Aut, gelidas hybernus aquas cum fuderit auster,*
> *Securum somnos, imbre juvante, sequi!*

> How sweet in sleep to pass the careless hours,
> Lull'd by the beating winds and dashing show'rs!

And it is impossible not to discover the fondness of Lucretius, an earlier writer, for a garret, in his description of the
lofty towers of serene learning, and of the pleasure with
which a wise man looks down upon the confused and erratic
state of the world moving below him:—

> *Sed nil dulcius est, bene quam munita tenere*
> *Edita doctrina sapientum templa serena;*
> *Despicere unde queas alios, passimque videre*
> *Errare, atque viam palantis quaerere vitae.*

> ——'Tis sweet thy lab'ring steps to guide
> To virtue's heights, with wisdom well supplied.
> And all the magazines of learning fortified;
> From thence to look below on human kind,
> Bewilder'd in the maze of life, and blind.—DRYDEN.

The institution has, indeed, continued to our own time;
the garret is still the usual receptacle of the philosopher and
poet; but this, like many ancient customs, is perpetuated only
by an accidental imitation, without knowledge of the original
reason for which it was established.

Causa latet; res est notissima.
The cause is secret, but th' effect is known—

Conjectures have, indeed, been advanced concerning these habitations of literature, but without much satisfaction to the judicious inquirer. Some have imagined that the garret is generally chosen by the wits as most easily rented, and concluded that no man rejoices in his aërial abode, but on the days of payment. Others suspect that a garret is chiefly convenient, as it is remoter than any other part of the house from the outer door, which is often observed to be infested by visitants, who talk incessantly of beer, or linen, or a coat, and repeat the same sounds every morning, and sometimes again in the afternoon, without any variation, except that they grow daily more importunate and clamorous, and raise their voices in time from mournful murmurs to raging vociferations. This eternal monotony is always detestable to a man whose chief pleasure is to enlarge his knowledge and vary his ideas. Others talk of freedom from noise, and abstraction from common business or amusements; and some, yet more visionary, tell us that the faculties are enlarged by open prospects, and that the fancy is more at liberty when the eye ranges without confinement.

These conveniences may perhaps all be found in a well-chosen garret; but surely they cannot be supposed sufficiently important to have operated unvariably upon different climates, distant ages, and separate nations. Of an universal practice, there must still be presumed an universal cause, which, however recondite and abstruse, may be perhaps reserved to make me illustrious by its discovery, and you by its promulgation.

It is universally known that the faculties of the mind are invigorated or weakened by the state of the body, and that the body is in a great measure regulated by the various compressions of the ambient element. The effects of the air in the production or cure of corporeal maladies have been acknowledged from the time of Hippocrates; but no man has yet sufficiently considered how far it may influence the operations of the genius, though every day affords instances of local understanding, of wits and reasoners, whose faculties are adapted to some single spot, and who, when they are removed to any other place, sink at once into silence and stupidity. I have discovered, by a long series of observations, that invention and elocution suffer great impediments from dense and impure vapors, and that the tenuity of a defecated air, at a proper distance from the surface of the earth, accelerates the fancy and sets at liberty those intellectual powers which were before shackled by too strong attraction, and unable to expand themselves under the pressure of a gross atmosphere. I have found dullness to quicken into sentiment in a thin ether, as water, though not very hot, boils in a receiver partly exhausted; and heads, in appearance empty, have teemed with notions upon rising ground, as the flaccid sides of a football would have swelled out into stiffness and extension.

For this reason I never think myself qualified to judge decisively of any man's faculties whom I have only known in one degree of elevation, but take some opportunity of attending him from the cellar to the garret, and try upon him all the various degrees of rarefaction and condensation, tension and laxity. If he is neither vivacious aloft, nor serious below, I then consider him as hopeless; but as it seldom happens that I do not find the temper to which the texture of his brain is fitted, I accommodate him in time with a tube of mercury, first marking the points most favorable to his intellects, according to rules which I have long studied, and which I may, perhaps, reveal to mankind in a complete treatise of barometrical pneumatology.

Another cause of the gayety and sprightliness of the dwellers in garrets is probably the increase in that vertiginous motion with which we are carried round by the diurnal revolution of the earth. The power of agitation upon the spirits is well known; every man has felt his heart lightened in a rapid vehicle, or on a galloping horse; and nothing is plainer than that he who towers to the fifth story is whirled through more space by every circumrotation, than another that grovels upon the ground-floor. The nations between the tropics are known to be fiery, inconstant, inventive, and fanciful; because, living at the utmost length of the earth's diameter, they are carried about with more swiftness than those whom nature has placed nearer to the poles; and therefore, as it becomes a wise man to struggle with the inconveniences of his country, whenever celerity and acuteness are requisite, we must actuate our languor by taking a few turns round the centre in a garret.

If you imagine that I ascribe to air and motion effects which they cannot produce, I desire you to consult your own memory, and consider whether you have never known a man acquire reputation in his garret, which, when fortune or a patron had placed him upon the first floor, he was unable to maintain; and who never recovered his former vigor of understanding, till he was restored to his original situation. That a garret will make every man a wit, I am very far from supposing; I know there are some who would continue blockheads even on the summit of the Andes, or on the peak of Teneriffe. But let not any man be considered as unimprovable till this potent remedy has been tried; for perhaps he was formed to be great only in a garret, as the joiner of Aretaeus was rational in no other place but his own shop.

I think a frequent removal to various distances from the centre so necessary to a just estimate of intellectual abilities, and consequently of so great use in education, that, if I hoped that the public could be persuaded to so expensive an experiment, I would propose that there should be a cavern dug, and a tower erected, like those which Bacon describes in Solomon's house, for the expansion and concentration of understanding, according to the exigence of different employments or constitutions. Perhaps some that fume away in meditations upon time and space in the tower, might compose tables of interest at a certain depth; and he that upon level ground stagnates in silence, or creeps in narrative, might, at the height of half a mile, ferment into merriment, sparkle with repartee, and froth with declamation.

Addison observes that we may find the heat of Virgil's climate in some lines of his *Georgic;* so, when I read a composition, I immediately determine the height of the author's habitation. As an elaborate performance is commonly said to smell of the lamp, my commendation of a noble thought, a sprightly sally, or a bold figure, is to pronounce it fresh from the garret,—an expression which would break from me upon the perusal of most of your papers, did I not believe that you sometimes quit the garret, and ascend into the cockloft.

HYPERTATUS.

JACK WHIRLER

SOME OF THOSE ANCIENT SAGES that have exercised their abilities in the inquiry after the *supreme good*, have been of opinion that the highest degree of earthly happiness is quiet; a calm repose both of mind and body, undisturbed by the sight of folly or the noise of business, the tumults of public commotion, or the agitations of private interests; a state in which the mind has no other employment, but to observe and regulate her own motions, to trace thought from thought, combine one image with another, raise systems of science and form theories of virtue.

To the scheme of these solitary speculatists, it has been justly objected that if they are happy, they are happy only by being useless. That mankind is one vast republic, where every individual receives many benefits from the labors of others, which, by laboring in his turn for others, he is obliged to repay; and that where the united efforts of all are not able to exempt all from misery, none have a right to withdraw from their task of vigilance or to be indulged in idle wisdom or solitary pleasures.

It is common for controvertists, in the heat of disputation, to add one position to another till they reach the extremities of knowledge, where truth and falsehood lose their distinction. Their admirers follow them to the brink of absurdity, and then start back from each side towards the middle point. So it has happened in this great disquisition. Many perceive alike the force of the contrary arguments, find quiet shameful and business dangerous, and therefore pass their lives between them, in bustle without business and negligence without quiet.

Among the principal names of this moderate set is that great philosopher Jack Whirler, whose business keeps him in perpetual motion and whose motion always eludes his business; who is always to do what he never does, who cannot stand still because he is wanted in another place, and who is wanted in many places because he stays in none.

Jack has more business than he can conveniently transact in one house; he has therefore one habitation near Bow-church, and another about a mile distant. By this ingenious distribution of himself between two houses, Jack has contrived to be found at neither. Jack's trade is extensive, and he has many dealers; his conversation is sprightly, and he has many companions; his disposition is kind, and he has many friends. Jack neither forbears pleasures for business, nor omits business for pleasure, but is equally invisible to his friends and his customers; to him that comes with an invitation to a club, and to him that waits to settle an account.

When you call at his house, his clerk tells you that Mr. Whirler has just stepped out, but will be at home exactly at two; you wait at a coffee-house till two, and then find that he has been at home and is gone out again, but left word that he should be at the Half-moon tavern at seven where he hopes to meet you. At seven you go to the tavern. At eight in comes Mr. Whirler to tell you that he is glad to see you, and only begs leave to run for a few minutes to a gentleman that lives near the Exchange, from whom he will return before supper can be ready. Away he runs to the Exchange, to tell those who are waiting for him that he must beg them to defer the business till to-morrow, because his time is come at the Half-moon.

Jack's cheerfulness and civility rank him among those whose presence never gives pain and whom all receive with fondness and caresses. He calls often on his friends, to tell them that he will come again to-morrow; on the morrow he comes again, to tell them how an unexpected summons hurries him away. When he enters a house, his first declaration is, that he cannot sit down; and so short are his visits that he seldom appears to have come for any other reason but to say he must go.

The dogs of Egypt, when thirst brings them to the Nile, are said to run as they drink for fear of the crocodiles. Jack Whirler always dines at full speed. He enters, finds the family at table, sits familiarly down, and fills his plate; but while the first morsel is in his mouth, hears the clock strike, and rises; then goes to another house, sits down again, recollects another engagement, has only time to taste the soup, makes a short excuse to the company, and continues through another street his desultory dinner.

But, overwhelmed as he is with business, his chief desire is to have still more. Every new proposal takes possession of his thoughts; he soon balances probabilities, engages in the project, brings it almost to completion, and then forsakes it for another, which he catches with the same alacrity, urges with the same vehemence, and abandons with the same coldness.

Every man may be observed to have a certain strain of lamentation, some peculiar theme of complaint, on which he dwells in his moments of dejection. Jack's topic of sorrow is the want of time. Many an excellent design languishes in empty theory for want of time. For the omission of any civilities, want of time is his plea to others; for the neglect of any affairs, want of time is his excuse to himself. That he wants time, he sincerely believes, for he once pined away many months with a lingering distemper, for want of time to attend to his health.

Thus Jack Whirler lives in perpetual fatigue without proportionate advantage, because he does not consider that no man can see all with his own eyes or do all with his own hands, that whoever is engaged in multiplicity of business must transact much by substitution and leave something to hazard, and that he who attempts to do all will waste his life in doing little.

David Hume

1711 · 1776

David Hume, English philosopher and historian, is better remembered today for his History of England *than for his essays. As a young man he studied law and then went to France to live for three years. His essays, treatises, and historical writings brought him fame and censure together, for he was severely attacked for his sceptical views. His interests were wide, and he served as librarian, diplomat, and legal adviser. For some time he was secretary to the embassy in Paris, where he became a friend—as much as one could—of Rousseau.*

ON TRAGEDY

IT SEEMS AN UNACCOUNTABLE PLEASURE which the spectators of a well-written tragedy receive from sorrow, terror, anxiety, and other passions that are in themselves disagreeable and uneasy. The more they are touched and affected, the more are they delighted with the spectacle; and as soon as the uneasy passions cease to operate, the piece is at an end. One scene of full joy and contentment and security is the utmost that any composition of this kind can bear; and it is sure always to be the concluding one. If in the texture of the piece there be interwoven any scenes of satisfaction, they afford only faint gleams of pleasure, which are thrown in by way of variety, and in order to plunge the actors into deeper distress by means of that contrast and disappointment. The whole art of the poet is employed in rousing and supporting the compassion and indignation, the anxiety and resentment, of his audience. They are pleased in proportion as they are afflicted, and never are so happy as when they employ tears, sobs, and cries, to give vent to their sorrow, and relieve their heart, swoln with the tenderest sympathy and compassion.

The few critics who have had some tincture of philosophy have remarked this singular phenomenon, and have endeavoured to account for it.

L'Abbé Dubos, in his *Reflections on Poetry and Painting*, asserts, that nothing is in general so disagreeable to the mind as the languid, listless state of indolence into which it falls upon the removal of all passion and occupation. To get rid of this painful situation, it seeks every amusement and pursuit; business, gaming, shows, executions; whatever will rouse the passions and take its attention from itself. No matter what the passion is; let it be disagreeable, afflicting, melancholy, disordered; it is still better than that insipid languor which arises from perfect tranquillity and repose.

It is impossible not to admit this account as being, at least in part, satisfactory. You may observe, when there are several tables of gaming, that all the company run to those where the deepest play is, even though they find not there the best players. The view, or, at least, imagination of high passions, arising from great loss or gain, affects the spectator by sympathy, gives him some touches of the same passions, and serves him for a momentary entertainment. It makes the time pass the easier with him, and is some relief to that oppression under which men commonly labour when left entirely to their own thoughts and meditations.

We find that common liars always magnify, in their narrations, all kinds of danger, pain, distress, sickness, deaths, murders, and cruelties, as well as joy, beauty, mirth, and magnificence. It is an absurd secret which they have for pleasing their company, fixing their attention, and attaching them to such marvellous relation by the passions and emotions which they excite.

There is, however, a difficulty in applying to the present subject, in its full extent, this solution, however ingenious and satisfactory it may appear. It is certain that the same object of distress, which pleases in a tragedy, were it really set before us, would give the most unfeigned uneasiness, though it be then the most effectual cure to languor and indolence. Monsieur Fontenelle seems to have been sensible of this difficulty, and accordingly attempts another solution of the phenomenon, at least makes some addition to the theory above mentioned [1]:

'Pleasure and pain,' says he, 'which are two sentiments so different in themselves, differ not so much in their cause. From the instance of tickling it appears, that the movement of pleasure, pushed a little too far, becomes pain, and that the movement of pain, a little moderate, becomes pleasure. Hence it proceeds, that there is such a thing as a sorrow, soft and agreeable: it is a pain weakened and diminished. The heart likes naturally to be moved and affected. Melancholy objects suit it, and even disastrous and sorrowful, provided they are softened by some circumstance. It is certain, that, on the theatre, the representation has almost the effect of reality; yet it has not altogether that effect. However we may be hurried away by the spectacle, whatever dominion the senses and imagination may usurp over the reason, there still lurks at the bottom a certain idea of falsehood in the whole of what we see. This idea, though weak and disguised, suffices to diminish the pain which we suffer from the misfortunes of those whom we love, and to reduce that affliction to such a pitch as converts it into a pleasure. We weep for the misfortune of a hero to whom we are attached. In the same instant we comfort ourselves by reflecting, that it is nothing but a fiction: and it is precisely that mixture of sentiments which composes an agreeable sorrow, and tears that delight us. But as that affliction which is caused by exterior and sensible objects is stronger than the consolation which arises from an internal reflection, they are the effects and symptoms of sorrow that ought to predominate in the composition.'

This solution seems just and convincing: but perhaps it wants still some new addition, in order to make it answer fully the phenomenon which we here examine. All the passions, excited by eloquence, are agreeable in the highest

[1] *Reflections sur la Poëtique*, §36.

degree, as well as those which are moved by painting and the theatre. The Epilogues of Cicero are, on this account chiefly, the delight of every reader of taste; and it is difficult to read some of them without the deepest sympathy and sorrow. His merit as an orator, no doubt, depends much on his success in this particular. When he had raised tears in his judges and all his audience, they were then the most highly delighted, and expressed the greatest satisfaction with the pleader. The pathetic description of the butchery made by Verres of the Sicilian captains, is a masterpiece of this kind; but I believe none will affirm, that the being present at a melancholy scene of that nature would afford any entertainment. Neither is the sorrow here softened by fiction; for the audience were convinced of the reality of every circumstance. What is it then which in this case raises a pleasure from the bosom of uneasiness, so to speak, and a pleasure which still retains all the features and outward symptoms of distress and sorrow?

I answer: this extraordinary effect proceeds from that very eloquence with which the melancholy scene is represented. The genius required to paint objects in a lively manner, the art employed in collecting all the pathetic circumstances, the judgment displayed in disposing them; the exercise, I say, of these noble talents, together with the force of expression, and beauty of oratorial numbers, diffuse the highest satisfaction on the audience, and excite the most delightful movements. By this means, the uneasiness of the melancholy passions is not only overpowered and effaced by something stronger of an opposite kind, but the whole impulse of those passions is converted into pleasure, and swells the delight which the eloquence raises in us. The same force of oratory, employed on an uninteresting subject, would not please half so much, or rather would appear altogether ridiculous; and the mind, being left in absolute calmness and indifference, would relish none of those beauties of imagination or expression, which, if joined to passion, give it such exquisite entertainment. The impulse or vehemence arising from sorrow, compassion, indignation, receives a new direction from the sentiments of beauty. The latter, being the predominant emotion, seize the whole mind, and convert the former into themselves, at least tincture them so strongly as totally to alter their nature. And the soul being at the same time roused by passion and charmed by eloquence, feels on the whole a strong movement, which is altogether delightful.

The same principle takes place in tragedy; with this addition, that tragedy is an imitation, and imitation is always of itself agreeable. This circumstance serves still further to smooth the motions of passion, and convert the whole feeling into one uniform and strong enjoyment. Objects of the greatest terror and distress please in painting, and please more than the most beautiful objects that appear calm and indifferent.[1] The affection, rousing the mind, excites a large stock of spirit and vehemence; which is all transformed into pleasure by the force of the prevailing movement. It is thus the fiction of tragedy softens the passion, by an infusion of a new feeling, not merely by weakening or diminishing the sorrow. You may by degrees weaken a real sorrow, till it totally disappears; yet in none of its gradations will it ever give pleasure; except, perhaps, by accident, to a man sunk under lethargic indolence, whom it rouses from that languid state.

To confirm this theory, it will be sufficient to produce other instances, where the subordinate movement is converted into the predominant, and gives force to it, though of a different, and even sometimes though of a contrary nature.

Novelty naturally rouses the mind, and attracts our attention; and the movements which it causes are always converted into any passion belonging to the object, and join their force to it. Whether an event excite joy or sorrow, pride or shame, anger or good-will, it is sure to produce a stronger affection, when new or unusual. And though novelty of itself

---

[1] *Painters make no scruple of representing distress and sorrow, as well as any other passion; but they seem not to dwell so much on these melancholy affections as the poets, who, though they copy every motion of the human breast, yet pass quickly over the agreeable sentiments. A painter represents only one instant; and if that be passionate enough, it is sure to affect and delight the spectator; but nothing can furnish to the poet a variety of scenes, and incidents, and sentiments, except distress, terror, or anxiety. Complete joy and satisfaction is attended with security, and leaves no further room for action.* [*Author's note.*]

be agreeable, it fortifies the painful, as well as agreeable passions.

Had you any intention to move a person extremely by the narration of any event, the best method of increasing its effect would be artfully to delay informing him of it, and first to excite his curiosity and impatience before you let him into the secret. This is the artifice practised by Iago in the famous scene of Shakespeare; and every spectator is sensible that Othello's jealousy acquires additional force from his preceding impatience, and that the subordinate passion is here readily transformed into the predominant one.

Difficulties increase passions of every kind; and by rousing our attention and exciting our active powers, they produce an emotion which nourishes the prevailing affection.

Parents commonly love that child most whose sickly infirm frame of body has occasioned them the greatest pains, trouble, and anxiety, in rearing him. The agreeable sentiment of affection here acquires force from sentiments of uneasiness.

Nothing endears so much a friend as sorrow for his death. The pleasure of his company has not so powerful an influence.

Jealousy is a painful passion; yet without some share of it, the agreeable affection of love has difficulty to subsist in its full force and violence. Absence is also a great source of complaint among lovers, and gives them the greatest uneasiness: yet nothing is more favourable to their mutual passion than short intervals of that kind. And if long intervals often prove fatal, it is only because, through time, men are accustomed to them, and they cease to give uneasiness. Jealousy and absence in love compose the *dolce peccante* of the Italians, which they suppose so essential to all pleasure.

There is a fine observation of the elder Pliny, which illustrates the principle here insisted on: 'It is very remarkable,' says he, 'that the last works of celebrated artists, which they left imperfect, are always the most prized, such as the IRIS of Aristides, the TYNDARIDES of Nicomachus, the MEDEA of Timomachus, and the VENUS of Apelles. These are valued even above their finished productions. The broken lineaments of the piece, and the half-formed idea of the painter, are carefully studied; and our very grief for that curious hand, which had been stopped by death, is an additional increase to our pleasure.'

These instances (and many more might be collected) are sufficient to afford us some insight into the analogy of nature, and to show us, that the pleasure which poets, orators, and musicians give us, by exciting grief, sorrow, indignation, compassion, is not so extraordinary or paradoxical as it may at first sight appear. The force of imagination, the energy of expression, the power of numbers, the charms of imitation; all these are naturally, of themselves, delightful to the mind: and when the object presented lays also hold of some affection, the pleasure still rises upon us, by the conversion of this subordinate movement into that which is predominant. The passion, though perhaps naturally, and when excited by the simple appearance of a real object, it may be painful; yet is so smoothed, and softened, and mollified, when raised by the finer arts, that it affords the highest entertainment.

To confirm this reasoning, we may observe, that if the movements of the imagination be not predominant above those of the passion, a contrary effect follows; and the former, being now subordinate, is converted into the latter, and still further increases the pain and affliction of the sufferer.

Who could ever think of it as a good expedient for comforting an afflicted parent, to exaggerate, with all the force of elocution, the irreparable loss which he has met with by the death of a favourite child? The more power of imagination and expression you here employ, the more you increase his despair and affliction.

The shame, confusion, and terror of Verres, no doubt, rose in proportion to the noble eloquence and vehemence of Cicero: so also did his pain and uneasiness. These former passions were too strong for the pleasure arising from the beauties of elocution; and operated, though from the same principle, yet in a contrary manner, to the sympathy, compassion, and indignation of the audience.

Lord Clarendon, when he approaches towards the catastrophe of the royal party, supposes that his narration must then become infinitely disagreeable; and he hurries over the king's death without giving us one circumstance of it. He considers it as too horrid a scene to be contemplated with any satisfaction, or even without the utmost pain and aversion. He himself, as well as the readers of that age, were too deeply concerned in the events, and felt a pain from subjects which an historian and a reader of another age would regard as the most pathetic and most interesting, and, by consequence, the most agreeable.

An action, represented in tragedy, may be too bloody and atrocious. It may excite such movements of horror as will not soften into pleasure; and the greatest energy of expression, bestowed on descriptions of that nature, serves only to augment our uneasiness. Such is that action represented in the *Ambitious Step-mother*, where a venerable old man, raised to the height of fury and despair, rushes against a pillar, and striking his head upon it, besmears it all over with mingled brains and gore. The English theatre abounds too much with such shocking images.

Even the common sentiments of compassion require to be softened by some agreeable affection, in order to give a thorough satisfaction to the audience. The mere suffering of plaintive virtue, under the triumphant tyranny and oppression of vice, forms a disagreeable spectacle, and is carefully avoided by all masters of the drama. In order to dismiss the audience with entire satisfaction and contentment, the virtue must either convert itself into a noble courageous despair, or the vice receive its proper punishment.

Most painters appear in this light to have been very unhappy in their subjects. As they wrought much for churches and convents, they have chiefly represented such horrible subjects as crucifixions and martyrdoms, where nothing appears but tortures, wounds, executions, and passive suffering, without any action or affection. When they turned their pencil from this ghastly mythology, they had commonly recourse to Ovid, whose fictions, though passionate and agreeable, are scarcely natural or probable enough for painting.

The same inversion of that principle which is here insisted on, displays itself in common life, as in the effects of oratory and poetry. Raise so the subordinate passion that it becomes the predominant, it swallows up that affection which it before nourished and increased. Too much jealousy extinguishes love; too much difficulty renders us indifferent; too much sickness and infirmity disgusts a selfish and unkind parent.

What so disagreeable as the dismal, gloomy, disastrous stories, with which melancholy people entertain their companions? The uneasy passion being there raised alone, unaccompanied with any spirit, genius, or eloquence, conveys a pure uneasiness, and is attended with nothing that can soften it into pleasure or satisfaction.

Oliver Goldsmith

1728 · 1774

Oliver Goldsmith, son of an Irish clergyman, led an unsettled and irresponsible life but charmed most people who knew him. He is said to have taken a medical degree at Padua or Louvain. Upon his return to England after some years on the Continent, he undertook to divide his time between medicine and journalism. He failed at first one and then the other until he gained a kind of security as a writer in 1759. His plays and one novel, The Vicar of Wakefield, *relieved him from poverty from time to time, but only temporarily. Hack-writing enabled him to pay some of his debts, but overwork and anxiety exhausted him. Dr. Johnson, Burke, Reynolds, and other members of The Club regarded Goldsmith with affection, with respect for his genius, and with dismay for his follies.*

A SERVICE AT ST. PAUL'S

SOME TIME SINCE I SENT THEE, O holy disciple of Confucius, an account of the grand abbey, or mausoleum, of the kings and heroes of this nation: I have since been introduced to a temple, not so ancient, but far superior in beauty and magnificence. In this, which is the most considerable of the empire, there are no pompous inscriptions, no flattery paid the dead, but all is elegant and awfully simple. There are, however, a few rags hung round the walls, which have, at a vast expense, been taken from the enemy in the present war. The silk of which they are composed, when new, might be valued at half a string of copper money in China; yet this wise people fitted out a fleet and an army in order to

seize them, though now grown old, and scarcely capable of
being patched up into a handkerchief. By this conquest the
English are said to have gained, and the French to have lost,
much honor. Is the honor of European nations placed only in
tattered silk?

In this temple I was permitted to remain during the whole
service; and were you not already acquainted with the religion
of the English, you might from my description be inclined to
believe them as grossly idolatrous as the disciples of Lao. The
idol which they seem to address strides like a colossus over
the door of the inner temple, which here, as with the Jews,
is esteemed the most sacred part of the building. Its oracles
are delivered in a hundred various tones, which seem to inspire the worshipers with enthusiasm and awe: an old woman,
who appeared to be the priestess, was employed in various
attitudes as she felt the inspiration. When it began to speak,
all the people remained fixed in silent attention, nodding
assent, looking approbation, appearing highly edified by those
sounds which to a stranger might seem inarticulate and unmeaning.

When the idol had done speaking, and the priestess had
locked up its lungs with a key, observing almost all the company leaving the temple, I concluded the service was over, and,
taking my hat, was going to walk away with the crowd, when
I was stopped by the Man in Black, who assured me that the
ceremony had scarcely yet begun.

"What!" cried I, "do I not see almost the whole body of
the worshipers leaving the church? Would you persuade me
that such numbers who profess religion and morality would,
in this shameless manner, quit the temple before the service
was concluded? You surely mistake: not even the Kalmucks
would be guilty of such an indecency, though all the object
of their worship was but a joint-stool." My friend seemed to
blush for his countrymen, assuring me that those whom I saw
running away were only a parcel of musical blockheads, whose
passion was merely for sounds, and whose heads were as
empty as a fiddle-case. "Those who remain behind," says he,
"are the true religious; they make use of music to warm their

hearts, and to lift them to a proper pitch of rapture. Examine their behavior, and you will confess there are some among us who practice true devotion."

I now looked round me as he directed, but saw nothing of that fervent devotion which he had promised: one of the worshipers appeared to be ogling the company through a glass; another was fervent, not in addresses to heaven, but to his mistress; a third whispered; a fourth took snuff; and the priest himself, in a drowsy tone, read over the *duties* of the day.

"Bless my eyes!" cried I, as I happened to look towards the door, "what do I see? one of the worshipers fallen fast asleep, and actually sunk down on his cushion! He is now enjoying the benefit of a trance, or does he receive the influence of some mysterious vision?"

"Alas! alas!" replied my companion, "no such thing; he has only had the misfortune of eating too hearty a dinner, and finds it impossible to keep his eyes open."

Turning to another part of the temple, I perceived a young lady just in the same circumstances and attitude. "Strange," cried I. "Can she too have over-eaten herself?"

"Oh, fie!" replied my friend, "you now grow censorious. She grow drowsy from eating too much! That would be profanation. She only sleeps now from having sat up all night at a brag party."

"Turn me where I will, then," says I, "I can perceive no single symptom of devotion among the worshipers, except from that old woman in the corner, who sits groaning behind the long sticks of a mourning fan; she indeed seems greatly edified with what she hears."

"Ay," replied my friend, "I knew we should find some to catch you. I know her; that is the deaf lady who lives in the cloisters."

In short, the remissness of behavior in almost all the worshipers, and some even of the guardians, struck me with surprise. I had been taught to believe that none were ever promoted to offices in the temple but men remarkable for their superior sanctity, learning, and rectitude; that there was no such thing heard of as persons being introduced into the church merely to oblige a senator, or provide for the younger branch of a noble family. I expected, as their minds were continually set upon heavenly things, to see their eyes directed there also, and hoped from their behavior to perceive their inclinations corresponding with their duty. But I am since informed that some are appointed to preside over temples they never visit; and, while they receive all the money, are contented with letting others do all the good.—Adieu.

NATIONAL PREJUDICES

A S I AM ONE of that sauntering tribe of mortals who spend the greatest part of their time in taverns, coffee-houses, and other places of public resort, I have thereby an opportunity of observing an infinite variety of characters, which to a person of a contemplative turn is a much higher entertainment than a view of all the curiosities of art or nature. In one of these my late rambles I accidentally fell into a company of half a dozen gentlemen, who were engaged in a warm dispute about some political affair, the decision of which, as they were equally divided in their sentiments, they thought proper to refer to me, which naturally drew me in for a share of the conversation.

Amongst a multiplicity of other topics, we took occasion to talk of the different characters of the several nations of Europe; when one of the gentlemen, cocking his hat, and assuming such an air of importance as if he had possessed all the merit of the English nation in his own person, declared that the Dutch were a parcel of avaricious wretches; the French a set of flattering sycophants; that the Germans were drunken sots, and beastly gluttons; and the Spaniards proud, haughty, and surly tyrants; but that in bravery, generosity, clemency, and in every other virtue, the English excelled all the world.

This very learned and judicious remark was received with a general smile of approbation by all the company—all, I mean, but your humble servant, who, endeavouring to keep my gravity as well as I could, and reclining my head upon my arm, continued for some time in a posture of affected thoughtfulness, as if I had been musing on something else, and did not seem to attend to the subject of conversation; hoping by this means to avoid the disagreeable necessity of explaining myself, and thereby depriving the gentleman of his imaginary happiness.

But my pseudo-patriot had no mind to let me escape so easily. Not satisfied that his opinion should pass without contradiction, he was determined to have it ratified by the suffrage of every one in the company; for which purpose, addressing himself to me with an air of inexpressible confidence, he asked me if I was not of the same way of thinking. As I am never forward in giving my opinion, especially when I have reason to believe that it will not be agreeable; so, when I am obliged to give it, I always hold it for a maxim to speak my real sentiments. I therefore told him that, for my own part, I should not have ventured to talk in such a peremptory strain unless I had made the tour of Europe, and examined the manners of these several nations with great care and accuracy: that perhaps a more impartial judge would not scruple to affirm, that the Dutch were more frugal and industrious, the French more temperate and polite, the Germans more hardy and patient of labour and fatigue, and the Spaniards more staid and sedate, than the English; who, though undoubtedly brave and generous, were at the same time rash, headstrong, and impetuous; too apt to be elated with prosperity, and to despond in adversity.

I could easily perceive, that all the company began to regard me with a jealous eye before I had finished my answer, which I had no sooner done, than the patriotic gentleman observed, with a contemptuous sneer, that he was greatly surprised how some people could have the conscience to live in a country which they did not love, and to enjoy the protection of a government to which in their hearts they were inveterate enemies. Finding that by this modest declaration of my sentiments I had forfeited the good opinion of my companions, and given them occasion to call my political principles in question and well knowing that it was in vain to argue with men who were so very full of themselves, I threw down my reckoning and retired to my own lodgings, reflecting on the absurd and ridiculous nature of national prejudice and prepossession.

Among all the famous sayings of antiquity, there is none that does greater honour to the author, or affords greater pleasure to the reader, (at least if he be a person of a generous and benevolent heart,) than that of the philosopher who, being asked what countryman he was, replied, that he was "a citizen of the world." How few are there to be found in modern times who can say the same, or whose conduct is consistent with such a profession! We are now become so much Englishmen, Frenchmen, Dutchmen, Spaniards, or Germans, that we are no longer citizens of the world; so much the natives of one particular spot, or members of one petty society, that we no longer consider ourselves as the general inhabitants of the globe, or members of that grand society which comprehends the whole human kind.

Did these prejudices prevail only among the meanest and lowest of the people, perhaps they might be excused, as they have few, if any, opportunities of correcting them by reading, travelling, or conversing with foreigners: but the misfortune is, that they infect the minds, and influence the conduct, even of our gentlemen; of those, I mean, who have every title to this appellation but an exemption from prejudice, which, however, in my opinion, ought to be regarded as the characteristical mark of a gentleman; for let a man's birth be ever so high, his station ever so exalted, or his fortune ever so large, yet if he is not free from national and other prejudices, I should make bold to tell him, that he had a low and vulgar mind, and had no just claim to the character of a gentleman. And, in fact, you will always find that those are most apt to boast of national merit, who have little or no merit of their own to depend on; than which, to be sure, nothing is more natural: the slender vine twists around the sturdy oak, for no other reason in the world but because it has not strength sufficient to support itself.

Should it be alleged in defence of national prejudice, that it is the natural and necessary growth of love to our country, and that therefore the former cannot be destroyed without hurting the latter, I answer that this is a gross fallacy and delusion. That it is the growth of love to our country, I will allow; but that it is the natural and necessary growth of it, I absolutely deny. Superstition and enthusiasm, too, are the growth of religion; but who ever took it in his head to affirm, that they are the necessary growth of this noble principle? They are, if you will, the bastard sprouts of this heavenly plant, but not its natural and genuine branches, and may safely enough be lopped off, without doing any harm to the parent stock: nay, perhaps, till once they are lopped off, this goodly tree can never flourish in perfect health and vigour.

Is it not very possible that I may love my own country, without hating the natives of other countries? that I may exert the most heroic bravery, the most undaunted resolution, in defending its laws and liberty, without despising all the rest of the world as cowards and poltroons? Most certainly it is; and if it were not—But why need I suppose what is absolutely impossible?—But if it were not, I must own I should prefer the title of the ancient philosopher, viz., a citizen of the world, to that of an Englishman, a Frenchman, a European, or to any other appellation whatever.

ON EDUCATION

A S FEW SUBJECTS ARE MORE INTERESTING to society, so few have been more frequently written upon, than the education of youth. Yet is it not a little surprising, that it should have been treated almost by all in a declamatory manner? They have insisted largely on the advantages that result from it, both to the individual and to society, and have expatiated in the praise of what no one has ever been so hardy as to call in question.

Instead of giving us fine but empty harangues upon this subject, instead of indulging each his particular and whimsical system, it had been much better if the writers on this subject had treated it in a more scientific manner, repressed all the sallies of imagination, and given us the result of their observations with didactic simplicity. Upon this subject the smallest errors are of the most dangerous consequence; and the author should venture the imputation of stupidity upon a topic, where his slightest deviations may tend to injure the rising generation.

I shall, therefore, throw out a few thoughts upon this subject, which have not been attended to by others, and shall dismiss all attempts to please, while I study only instruction.

The manner in which our youth of London are at present educated is, some in free schools in the city, but the far greater number in boarding schools about town. The parent justly consults the health of his child, and finds that an education in the country tends to promote this much more than a continuance in the town. Thus far they are right: if there were a possibility of having even our free schools kept a little out of town, it would certainly conduce to the health and vigour of perhaps the mind as well as of the body. It may be thought whimsical, but it is truth,—I have found by experience, that they who have spent all their lives in cities contract not only an effeminacy of habit, but even of thinking.

But when I have said that the boarding schools are preferable to free schools, as being in the country, this is certainly the only advantage I can allow them; otherwise it is impossible to conceive the ignorance of those who take upon them the important trust of education. Is any man unfit for any of the professions? he finds his last resource in setting up school. Do any become bankrupts in trade? they still set up a boarding school, and drive a trade this way, when all others fail: nay, I have been told of butchers and barbers who have turned schoolmasters; and, more surprising still, made fortunes in their new professions.

Could we think ourselves in a country of civilized people— could it be conceived that we have any regard for posterity— when such are permitted to take the charge of the morals, genius, and health of those dear little pledges, who may one day be the guardians of the liberties of Europe, and who may serve as the honour and bulwark of their aged parents? The care of our children, is it below the state? is it fit to indulge the caprice of the ignorant with the disposal of their children in this particular? For the state to take the charge of all its children, as in Persia or Sparta, might at present be inconvenient; but surely with great ease it might cast an eye to their instructors. Of all members of society, I do not know a more useful or a more honourable one than a schoolmaster; at the same time that I do not see any more generally despised, or whose talents are so ill rewarded.

Were the salaries of schoolmasters to be augmented from a diminution of useless sinecures, how might it turn to the advantage of this people—a people whom, without flattery, I may in other respects term the wisest and greatest upon earth! But, while I would reward the deserving, I would dismiss those utterly unqualified for their employment: in short, I would make the business of a schoolmaster every way more respectable, by increasing their salaries, and admitting only men of proper abilities.

There are already schoolmasters appointed, and they have some small salaries; but where at present there is but one schoolmaster appointed, there should at least be two; and wherever the salary is at present twenty pounds, it should be an hundred. Do we give immoderate benefices to those who instruct ourselves, and shall we deny even subsistence to those who instruct our children? Every member of society should be paid in proportion as he is necessary: and I will be bold enough to say, that schoolmasters in a state are more necessary than clergymen, as children stand in more need of instruction than their parents.

But instead of this, as I have already observed, we send them to board in the country to the most ignorant set of men that can be imagined. But lest the ignorance of the master be not sufficent, the child is generally consigned to the usher. This is generally some poor needy animal, little superior to a footman either in learning or spirit, invited to his place by an advertisement, and kept there merely from his being of a complying disposition, and making the children fond of him. "You give your child to be educated to a slave," says a philosopher to a rich man: "instead of one slave, you will then have two."

It were well, however, if parents, upon fixing their children in one of these houses, would examine the abilities of the usher as well as of the master; for, whatever they are told to the contrary, the usher is generally the person most employed in their education. If, then, a gentleman upon putting out his son to one of these houses, sees the usher disregarded by the master, he may depend upon it, that he is equally disregarded by the boys; the truth is, in spite of all their endeavours to please, they are generally the laughing-stock of the school. Every trick is played upon the usher; the oddity of his manners, his dress, or his language, is a fund of eternal ridicule; the master himself now and then cannot avoid joining in the laugh, and the poor wretch, eternally resenting this ill usage, seems to live in a state of war with all the family. This is a very proper person, is it not, to give children a relish for learning? They must esteem learning very much when they see its professors used with such ceremony. If the usher be despised, the father may be assured his child will never be properly instructed.

But let me suppose that there are some schools without these inconveniences,—where the master and ushers are men of learning, reputation, and assiduity. If there are to be found such, they cannot be prized in a state sufficiently. A boy will learn more true wisdom in a public school in a year, than by private education in five. It is not from masters, but from their equals, youth learn a knowledge of the world: the little tricks they play each other, the punishment that frequently attends the commission, is a just picture of the great world, and all the ways of men are practised in a public school in miniature. It is true a child is early made acquainted with some vices in a school; but it is better to know these when a boy, than be first taught them when a man, for their novelty then may have irresistible charms.

In a public education boys early learn temperance; and if the parents and friends would give them less money upon their usual visits, it would be much to their advantage, since it may justly be said, that a great part of their disorders arise from surfeit,—*plus occidit gula quam gladius.* And now I am come to the article of health, it may not be amiss to observe, that Mr. Locke and some others have advised, that children should be inured to cold, to fatigue, and hardship, from their youth; but Mr. Locke was but an indifferent physician. Habit, I grant, has great influence over our constitutions; but we have not precise ideas upon this subject.

We know that among savages, and even among our peasants, there are found children born with such constitutions, that they cross rivers by swimming, endure cold, thirst, hunger, and want of sleep, to a surprising degree; that when they happen to fall sick, they are cured, without the help of medicine, by nature alone. Such examples are adduced, to persuade us to imitate their manner of education, and accustom ourselves betimes to support the same fatigues. But had these gentlemen considered, first, that those savages and peasants are generally not so long lived as they who have led a more indolent life; secondly, that the more laborious the life is, the less populous is the country: had they considered that what physicians call the *stamina vitae* by fatigue and labour become rigid, and thus anticipate old age; that the number who survive those rude trials bears no proportion to those who die in the experiment: had these things been properly considered, they would not have thus extolled an education begun in fatigue and hardships. Peter the Great, willing to inure the children of his seamen to a life of hardship, ordered that they should drink only sea-water; but they unfortunately all died under the experiment.

But while I would exclude all unnecessary labours, yet still I would recommend temperance in the highest degree. No luxurious dishes with high seasoning, nothing given children to force an appetite, as little sugared or salted provisions as possible, though never so pleasing; but milk, morning and night, should be their constant food. This diet would make them more healthy than any of those slops that are usually cooked by the mistress of a boarding school; besides, it corrects any consumptive habits, not unfrequently found amongst the children of city parents.

As boys should be educated with temperance, so the first, greatest lesson that should be taught them is, to admire frugality. It is by the exercise of this virtue alone they can ever expect to be useful members of society. It is true lectures continually repeated upon this subject may make some boys, when they grow up, run into an extreme, and become misers; but it were well had we more misers than we have among us. I know few characters more useful in society; for a man's having a larger or smaller share of money lying useless by him no way injures the commonwealth: since, should every miser now exhaust his stores, this might make gold more plenty, but it would not increase the commodities or pleasures of life; they would still remain as they are at present: it matters not, therefore, whether men are misers or not, if they be only frugal, laborious, and fill the station they have chosen. If they deny themselves the necessaries of life, society is no way injured by their folly.

Instead, therefore, of romances, which praise young men of spirit, who go through a variety of adventures, and, at last, conclude a life of dissipation, folly, and extravagance, in riches and matrimony, there should be some men of wit employed to compose books that might equally interest the passions of our youth; where such an one might be praised for having resisted allurements when young, and how he, at last, became lord mayor—how he was married to a lady of great sense, fortune, and beauty: to be as explicit as possible, the old story of Whittington, were his cat left out, might be more serviceable to the tender mind than either Tom Jones, Joseph Andrews, or an hundred others, where frugality is the only good quality the hero is not possessed of. Were our schoolmasters, if any of them had sense enough to draw up such a work, thus employed, it would be much more serviceable to their pupils than all the grammars and dictionaries they may publish these ten years.

Children should early be instructed in the arts from which they would afterwards draw the greatest advantages. When the wonders of nature are never exposed to our view, we have no great desire to become acquainted with those parts of learning which pretend to account for the phenomena. One of the ancients complains, that as soon as young men have left school, and are obliged to converse in the world, they fancy themselves transported into a new region: "Ut cum in forum venerint existiment se in aliam terrarum orbem delatos." We should early, therefore, instruct them in the experiments, if I may so express it, of knowledge, and leave to maturer age the accounting for the causes. But instead of that, when boys begin natural philosophy in colleges, they have not the least curiosity for those parts of the science which are proposed for their instruction; they have never before seen the phenomena, and consequently have no curiosity to learn the reasons. Might natural philosophy, therefore, be made their pastime in school, by this means it would in college become their amusement.

In several of the machines now in use there would be ample field both for instruction and amusement: the different sorts of the phosphorus, the artificial pyrites, magnetism, electricity, the experiments upon the rarefaction and weight of the air, and those upon elastic bodies, might employ their idle hours, and none should be called from play to see such experiments but such as thought proper. At first, then, it would be sufficient if the instruments, and the effects of their combination, were only shown; the causes should be deferred to a maturer age, or to those times when natural curiosity prompts us to discover the wonders of nature. Man is placed in this world as a spectator; when he is tired with wondering at all the novelties about him, and not till then, does he desire to be made acquainted with the causes that create those wonders.

What I have observed with regard to natural philosophy, I would extend to every other science whatsoever. We should teach them as many of the facts as were possible, and defer the causes until they seemed of themselves desirous of knowing them. A mind thus leaving school stored with all the simple experiences of science, would be the fittest in the world for the college course; and though such a youth might not appear so bright, or so talkative, as those who had learned the real principles and causes of some of the sciences, yet he would make a wiser man, and would retain a more lasting passion for letters, than he who was early burdened with the disagreeable institution of effect and cause.

In history, such stories alone should be laid before them as might catch the imagination: instead of this, they are too frequently obliged to toil through the four empires, as they are called, where their memories are burdened by a number of disgusting names, that destroy all their future relish for our best historians, who may be termed the truest teachers of wisdom.

Every species of flattery should be carefully avoided: a boy who happens to say a sprightly thing is generally applauded so much, that he happens to continue a coxcomb sometimes all his life after. He is reputed a wit at fourteen, and becomes a blockhead at twenty. Nurses, footmen, and such, should therefore be driven away as much as possible. I was even going to add, that the mother herself should stifle her pleasure or her vanity, when little master happens to say a good or smart thing. Those modest lubberly boys who seem to want spirit generally go through their business with more ease to themselves and more satisfaction to their instructors.

There has of late a gentleman appeared, who thinks the study of rhetoric essential to a perfect education. That bold male eloquence, which often without pleasing convinces, is generally destroyed by such institutions. Convincing eloquence, however, is infinitely more serviceable to its possessor than the most florid harangue or the most pathetic tones that can be imagined; and the man who is thoroughly convinced himself, who understands his subject and the language he speaks in, will be more apt to silence opposition, than he who studies the force of his periods, and fills our ears with sounds, while our minds are destitute of conviction.

It was reckoned the fault of the orators at the decline of the Roman empire, when they had been long instructed by rhetoricians, that their periods were so harmonious, as that they could be sung as well as spoken. What a ridiculous figure must one of these gentlemen cut, thus measuring syllables, and weighing words, when he should plead the cause of his client! Two architects were once candidates for the building a certain temple at Athens: the first harangued the crowd very learnedly upon the different orders of architecture, and showed them in what manner the temple should be built; the other, who got up to speak after him, only observed, that what his brother had spoken he could do; and thus he at once gained his cause.

To teach men to be orators, is little less than to teach them to be poets; and for my part, I should have too great a regard for my child, to wish him a manor only in a bookseller's shop.

Another passion which the present age is apt to run into is to make children learn all things,—the languages, the sciences, music, the exercises, and painting. Thus the child soon becomes a *talker* in all, but a *master* in none. He thus acquires a superficial fondness for everything, and only shows his ignorance when he attempts to exhibit his skill.

As I deliver my thoughts without method or connexion, so the reader must not be surprised to find me once more addressing schoolmasters on the present method of teaching the learned languages, which is commonly by literal translations. I would ask such, if they were to travel a journey, whether those parts of the road in which they found the greatest difficulties would not be most strongly remembered? Boys who, if I may continue the allusion, gallop through one of the ancients with the assistance of a translation can have but a very slight acquaintance either with the author or his language. It is by the exercise of the mind alone that a language is learned; but a literal translation, on the opposite page, leaves no exercise for the memory at all. The boy will not be at the fatigue of remembering, when his doubts are at once satisfied by a glance of the eye; whereas, were every word to be sought from a dictionary, the learner would attempt to remember, in order to save him the trouble of looking out for it for the future.

To continue in the same pedantic strain, though no schoolmaster, of all the various grammars now taught in schools about town I would recommend only the old common one; I have forgot whether Lilly's or an emendation of him. The others may be improvements; but such improvements seem to me only mere grammatical niceties, no way influencing the learner, but perhaps loading him with trifling subtleties, which at a proper age he must be at some pains to forget.

Whatever pains a master may take to make the learning of the languages agreeable to his pupil, he may depend upon it, it will be at first extremely unpleasant. The rudiments of every language, therefore, must be given as a task, not as an amusement. Attempting to deceive children into instruction of this kind is only deceiving ourselves; and I know no passion capable of conquering a child's natural laziness but fear. Solomon has said it before me; nor is there any more certain, though perhaps more disagreeable truth, than the proverb in verse, too well known to repeat on the present occasion. It is very probable that parents are told of some masters who never use the rod, and consequently are thought the properest instructors for their children; but though tenderness is a requisite quality in an instructor, yet there is too often the truest tenderness in well-timed correction.

Some have justly observed, that all passion should be banished on this terrible occasion; but, I know not how, there is a frailty attending human nature, that few masters are able to keep their temper whilst they correct. I knew a good-natured man, who was sensible of his own weakness in this respect, and consequently had recourse to the following expedient to prevent his passions from being engaged, yet at the same time administer justice with impartiality:—Whenever any of his pupils committed a fault, he summoned a jury of his peers,—I mean of the boys of his own or the next classes to him; his accusers stood forth; he had a liberty of pleading in his own defence, and one or two more had a liberty of pleading against him: when found guilty by the panel, he was consigned to the footman who attended in the house, who had previous orders to punish, but with lenity. By this means the master took off the odium of punishment from himself; and the footman, between whom and the boys there could not be even the slightest intimacy, was placed in such a light as to be shunned by every boy in the school.

And now I have gone thus far, perhaps you will think me some pedagogue, willing, by a well-timed puff, to increase the reputation of his own school; but such is not the case. The regard I have for society, for those tender minds who are the objects of the present essay, is the only motive I have for offering those thoughts, calculated not to surprise by their novelty or the elegance of composition, but merely to remedy some defects which have crept into the present system of school education. If this letter should be inserted, perhaps I may trouble you in my next with some thoughts upon a university education, not with an intent to exhaust the subject, but to amend some few abuses.

William Cobbett
1762 · 1835

William Cobbett was a self-educated writer and editor who dabbled in politics and agriculture. He had little sympathy with the arts, institutions of higher learning, and all of the more polite social accomplishments. His style was his own—vigorous, rough, and idiomatic—without literary borrowings or influence. As editor of the Political Register, *he supported radical interests and the causes of common men and for more than thirty years commanded a large following. The two essays in this collection are taken from his* Advice to Young Men *and (Incidentally) to Young Women (1829).*

ADVICE ON MONEY

I SHALL CONFINE MYSELF PRINCIPALLY to the conduct of a young man with regard to the management of his means, or money.

Be you in what line of life you may, it will be amongst your misfortunes if you have not time properly to attend to this matter; for it very frequently happens, it has happened to thousands upon thousands, not only to be ruined, according to the common acceptation of the word; not only to be made poor, and to suffer from poverty, in consequence of want of attention to pecuniary matters; but it has frequently, and even generally, happened, that a want of attention to these matters has impeded the progress of science, and of genius itself. A man, oppressed with pecuniary cares and dangers, must be next to a miracle, if he have his mind in a state fit for intellectual labours; to say nothing of the temptations, arising from such distress, to abandon good principles, to suppress useful opinions, and useful facts; and, in short, to become a disgrace to his kindred, and an evil to his country, instead of being an honour to the former and a blessing to the latter. To be poor and independent, is very nearly an impossibility.

But, then, poverty is not a positive, but a relative term. BURKE observed, and very truly, that a labourer who earned a sufficiency to maintain him as a labourer, and to maintain him in a suitable manner; to give him a sufficiency of good food, of clothing, of lodging, and of fuel, ought not to be called *a poor man*; for that, though he had little riches, though his, *compared* with that of a lord, was a state of poverty, it was not a state of poverty in itself. When, therefore, I say that poverty is the cause of a depression of spirit, of inactivity and of servility in men of literary talent, I must say, at the same time, that the evil arises from their own fault; from their having created for themselves imaginary wants; from their having indulged in unnecessary enjoyments, and from their having caused that to be poverty, which would not have been poverty, if they had been moderate in their enjoyments.

As it may be your lot (such has been mine) to live by your literary talent, I will here, before I proceed to matter more applicable to persons in other states of life, observe, that I cannot form an idea of a mortal more wretched than a man of real talent, compelled to curb his genius, and to submit himself in the exercise of that genius, to those whom he knows to be far inferior to himself, and whom he must despise from the bottom of his soul. The late MR. WILLIAM GIFFORD, who was the son of a shoemaker at ASHBURTON in Devonshire; who was put to school and sent to the university at the expense of a generous and good clergyman of the name of COOKSON, and who died, the other day, a sort of whipper-in of MURRAY'S QUARTERLY REVIEW; this was a man of real genius; and, to my certain personal knowledge, he detested, from the bottom of his soul, the whole of the paper-money and Boroughmongering system, and despised those by whom the system was carried on. But, he had imaginary wants; he had been bred up in company with the rich and the extravagant; expensive indulgences had been made necessary to him by habit; and, when in the year 1798, or thereabouts, he had to choose between a bit of bacon, a scrag of mutton, and a lodging at ten shillings a week, on the one side, and made-dishes, wine, a fine house and a footman on the other side, he chose the latter. He became the servile Editor of CAN-NING'S Anti-jacobin newspaper; and he, who had more wit and learning than all the rest of the writers put together, became the miserable tool in circulating their attacks upon everything that was hostile to a system which he deplored and detested. But he secured the made-dishes, the wine, the foot-man and the coachman. A sinecure as '*clerk of the Foreign Estreats*,' gave him 329£. a year, a double commissionership of the lottery gave him 600£. or 700£. more; and, at a later period, his Editorship of the Quarterly Review gave him perhaps as much more. He rolled in his carriage for several years; he fared sumptuously; he was buried at *Westminster Abbey*, of which his friend and formerly his brother pamphleteer in de-fense of PITT was the *Dean*; and never is he to be heard of more! MR. GIFFORD would have been full as happy; his health would have been better, his life longer, and his name would have lived for ages, if he could have turned to the bit of bacon and scrag of mutton in 1798; for his learning and talents were such, his reasonings so clear and conclusive, and his wit so pointed and keen, that his writings must have been generally read, must have been of long duration! and, indeed, must have enabled him (he being always a single man) to live in his latter days in as good style as that which he procured by becoming a sinecurist, a pensioner and a *hack*, all which he was from the moment he lent himself to the Quarterly Re-view. Think of the mortification of such a man, when he was called upon to justify the power-of-imprisonment bill in 1817! But to go into particulars would be tedious: his life was a life of luxurious misery, than which a worse is not to be imagined.

So that poverty is, except where there is an actual want of food and raiment, a thing much more imaginary than real. *The shame of poverty*, the shame of being thought poor, is a great and fatal weakness, though arising, in this country, from the fashion of the times themselves. When a *good man*, as in the phraseology of the city, means a *rich man*, we are not to wonder that every one wishes to be thought richer than he is. When adulation is sure to follow wealth, and when contempt would be awarded to many if they were not wealthy, who are spoken of with deference, and even lauded to the skies, because their riches are great and notorious; when this is the case, we are not to be surprised that men are ashamed to be thought to be poor. This is one of the greatest of all the dangers at the outset of life: it has brought thousands and hundreds of thousands to ruin, even to *pecuniary* ruin. One of the most amiable features in the character of American society is this; that men never boast of their riches, and never disguise their poverty; but they talk of both as of any other matter fit for public conversation. No man shuns another because he is poor: no man is preferred to another because he is rich. In hundreds and hundreds of instances, men, not worth a shilling, have been chosen by the people and entrusted with their rights and interests, in preference to men who ride in their carriages.

This shame of being thought poor, is not only dishonourable in itself, and fatally injurious to men of talent; but it is ruinous even in a *pecuniary* point of view, and equally destructive to farmers, traders, and even gentlemen of landed estate. It leads to everlasting efforts to *disguise one's poverty:* the carriage, the servants, the wine, (oh, that fatal wine!) the spirits, the decanters, the glasses, all the table apparatus, the dress, the horses, the dinners, the parties, all must be kept up; not so much because he or she who keeps or gives them, has any pleasure arising therefrom, as because not to keep and give them, would give rise to a suspicion *of the want of means* so to give and keep; and thus thousands upon thousands are yearly brought into a state of real poverty by their great *anxiety not to be thought poor.* Look round you, mark well what you behold, and say if this be not the case. In how many instances have you seen most amiable and even most industrious families brought to ruin by nothing but this! Mark it well; resolve to set this false shame at defiance, and when you have done that, you have laid the first stone of the surest foundation of your future tranquillity of mind. There are thousands of families, at this very moment, who are thus struggling to keep up appearances. The farmers accommodate themselves to circumstances more easily than tradesmen and professional men. They live at a greater distance from their neighbours: they can change their style of living unperceived: they can banish the decanter, change the dishes for a bit of bacon, make a treat out of a rasher and eggs, and the world is none the wiser all the while. But the tradesman, the doctor, the attorney, and the trader, cannot make the change so quietly, and unseen. The accursed wine, which is a sort of criterion of the style of living, a sort of *scale* to the *plan*, a sort of *key* to the *tune;* this is the thing to banish first of all; because all the rest follow, and come down to their proper level in a short time. The accursed decanter cries footman or waiting maid, puts bells to the side of the wall, screams aloud for carpets; and when I am asked, 'Lord, *what* is a glass of wine?' my answer is, that, in this country, it is *everything;* it is the pitcher of the key; it demands all the other unnecessary expenses; it is injurious to health, and must be injurious, every bottle of wine that is drunk containing a certain portion of ardent spirits, besides other drugs deleterious in their nature; and, of all the friends to the doctors, this fashionable beverage is the greatest. And, which adds greatly to the folly, or, I should say, the real vice of using it, is, that the parties themselves, nine times out of ten, do not drink it by *choice;* do not like it; do not relish it; but use it from mere ostentation, being ashamed to be seen even by their own servants, not to drink wine. At the very moment I am writing this, there are thousands of families in and near London, who daily have wine upon their tables, and who *drink* it too, merely because their own servants should not suspect them to be poor, and not deem them to be genteel; and thus families by thousands are ruined, only because they are ashamed to be thought poor.

ADVICE ON READING AND WRITING

I HOPE THAT YOUR TASTE would keep you aloof from the writings of those detestable villains, who employ the powers of their mind in debauching the minds of others, or in endeavours to do it. They present their poison in such captivating forms, that it requires great virtue and resolution to withstand their temptations; and, they have, perhaps, done a thousand times as much mischief in the world as all the infidels and atheists put together. These men ought to be called *literary pimps:* they ought to be held in universal abhorrence, and never spoken of but with execration. Any appeal to bad passions is to be despised; any appeal to ignorance and prejudice; but here is an appeal to the frailties of human nature, and an endeavour to make the mind corrupt, just as it is beginning to possess its powers. I never have known any but bad men, worthless men, men unworthy of any portion of respect, who took delight in, or even kept in their possession, writings of the description to which I here allude. The writings of SWIFT have this blemish; and, though he is not a teacher of *lewdness*, but rather the contrary, there are certain parts of his poems which are much too filthy for any decent person to read. It was beneath him to stoop to such means of setting forth that wit which would have been far more brilliant without them. I have heard, that, in the library of what is called an *'illustrious* person,' sold some time ago, there was an immense collection of books of this infamous description; and from this circumstance, if from no other, I should have formed my judgment of the character of that person.

Besides reading, a young man ought to write, if he have the capacity and the leisure. If you wish to remember a thing well, put it into writing, even if you burn the paper immediately after you have done; for the eye greatly assists the mind. Memory consists of a concatenation of ideas, the place, the time, and other circumstances, lead to the recollection of facts; and no circumstance more effectually than stating the facts upon paper. A JOURNAL should be kept by every young man. Put down something against every day in the year, if it be merely a description of the weather. You will not have done this for one year without finding the benefit of it. It disburthens the mind of many things to be recollected; it is amusing and useful, and ought by no means to be neglected. How often does it happen that we cannot make a statement of facts, sometimes very interesting to ourselves and our friends, for the want of a record of the places where we were, and of things that occurred on such and such a day! How often does it happen that we get into disagreeable disputes about things that have passed, and about the time and other circumstances attending them! As a thing of mere curiosity, it is of some value, and may frequently prove of very great utility. It demands not more than a minute in the twenty-four hours; and that minute is most agreeably and advantageously employed. It tends greatly to produce regularity in the conducting of affairs: it is a thing demanding a small portion of attention *once in every day;* I myself have found it to be attended with great and numerous benefits, and I therefore strongly recommend it to the practice of every reader.

Charles Lamb

1775 · 1834

*Charles Lamb was born in London and educated
at Christ's Hospital, where he became a friend of
Coleridge. He left school to work, first in the South
Sea House, and later in the India House, where he
spent most of his career. A strain of insanity in his
family prevented his marrying and cast a blight on
his life and that of his sister, who killed their
mother in a fit of madness. With Mary he wrote the
famous* Tales from Shakespeare. *He turned to
writing essays and built for himself a world of the
mind to take the place of the unhappy conditions
which surrounded his life, and as "Elia" he became
the best-loved familiar essayist in English literature.*

THE TWO RACES OF MEN

THE HUMAN SPECIES, according to the best
theory I can form of it, is composed of two
distinct races, *the men who borrow*, and *the men who lend*.
To these two original diversities may be reduced all those
impertinent classifications of Gothic and Celtic tribes, white
men, black men, red men. All the dwellers upon earth,
"Parthians, and Medes, and Elamites," flock hither, and do
naturally fall in with one or other of these primary distinctions. The infinite superiority of the former, which I choose
to designate as the *great race*, is discernible in their figure, port,
and a certain instinctive sovereignty. The latter are born
degraded. "He shall serve his brethren." There is something
in the air of one of this cast, lean and suspicious; contrasting
with the open, trusting, generous manner of the other.
Observe who have been the greatest borrowers of all ages—

Alcibiades—Falstaff—Sir Richard Steele—our late incomparable Brinsley—what a family likeness in all four!

What a careless, even deportment hath your borrower! what rosy gills! what a beautiful reliance on Providence doth he manifest,—taking no more thought than lilies! What contempt for money,—accounting it (yours and mine especially) no better than dross! What a liberal confounding of those pedantic distinctions of *meum* and *tuum!* or rather, what a noble simplification of language (beyond Tooke), resolving these supposed opposites into one clear, intelligible pronoun adjective!—What near approaches doth he make to the primitive *community*,—to the extent of one-half of the principle at least!——

He is the true taxer who "calleth all the world up to be taxed"; and the distance is as vast between him and *one of us*, as subsisted betwixt the Augustan Majesty and the poorest obolary Jew that paid it tribute-pittance at Jerusalem!—His exactions, too, have such a cheerful, voluntary air! So far removed from your sour parochial or state-gatherers,—those ink-horn varlets who carry their want of welcome in their faces! He cometh to you with a smile, and troubleth you with no receipt; confining himself to no set season. Every day is his Candlemas, or his Feast of Holy Michael. He applieth the *lene tormentum* of a pleasant look to your purse,—which to that gentle warmth expands her silken leaves, as naturally as the cloak of the traveller, for which sun and wind contended! He is the true Propontic which never ebbeth! The sea which taketh handsomely at each man's hand. In vain the victim, whom he delighteth to honour, struggles with destiny; he is in the net. Lend therefore cheerfully, O man ordained to lend—that thou lose not in the end, with thy worldly penny, the reversion promised. Combine not preposterously in thine own person the penalties of Lazarus and of Dives!—but, when thou seest the proper authority coming, meet it smilingly, as it were half-way. Come, a handsome sacrifice! See how light *he* makes of it! Strain not courtesies with a noble enemy.

Reflections like the foregoing were forced upon my mind

by the death of my old friend, Ralph Bigod, Esq., who departed this life on Wednesday evening; dying, as he had lived, without much trouble. He boasted himself a descendant from mighty ancestors of that name, who heretofore held ducal dignities in this realm. In his actions and sentiments he belied not the stock to which he pretended. Early in life he found himself invested with ample revenues; which, with that noble disinterestedness which I have noticed as inherent in men of the *great race*, he took almost immediate measures entirely to dissipate and bring to nothing: for there is something revolting in the idea of a king holding a private purse; and the thoughts of Bigod were all regal. Thus furnished, by the very act of disfurnishment; getting rid of the cumbersome luggage of riches, more apt (as one sings)

> To slacken virtue, and abate her edge,
> Than prompt her to do aught may merit praise,

he set forth, like some Alexander, upon his great enterprise, "borrowing and to borrow!"

In his periegesis, or triumphant progress throughout this island, it has been calculated that he laid a tithe part of the inhabitants under contribution. I reject this estimate as greatly exaggerated:—but having had the honour of accompanying my friend, divers times, in his perambulations about this vast city, I own I was greatly struck at first with the prodigious number of faces we met, who claimed a sort of respectful acquaintance with us. He was one day so obliging as to explain the phenomenon. It seems, these were his tributaries; feeders of his exchequer; gentlemen, his good friends (as he was pleased to express himself), to whom he had occasionally been beholden for a loan. Their multitudes did no way disconcert him. He rather took a pride in numbering them; and, with Comus, seemed pleased to be "stocked with so fair a herd."

With such sources, it was a wonder how he contrived to keep his treasury always empty. He did it by force of an aphorism, which he had often in his mouth, that "money kept longer than three days stinks." So he made use of it while it was fresh. A good part he drank away (for he was an excellent toss-pot), some he gave away, the rest he threw away, literally tossing and hurling it violently from him—as boys do burrs, or as if it had been infectious,—into ponds or ditches, or deep holes,—inscrutable cavities of the earth;—or he would bury it (where he would never seek it again) by a river's side under some bank, which (he would facetiously observe) paid no interest—but out away from him it must go peremptorily, as Hagar's offspring into the wilderness, while it was sweet. He never missed it. The streams were perennial which fed his fisc. When new supplies became necessary, the first person that had the felicity to fall in with him, friend or stranger, was sure to contribute to the deficiency. For Bigod had an *undeniable* way with him. He had a cheerful, open exterior, a quick jovial eye, a bald forehead, just touched with grey (*cana fides*). He anticipated no excuse, and found none. And, waiving for a while my theory as to the *great race*, I would put it to the most untheorising reader, who may at times have disposable coin in his pocket, whether it is not more repugnant to the kindliness of his nature to refuse such a one as I am describing, than to say *no* to a poor petitionary rogue (your bastard borrower), who, by his mumping visnomy, tells you that he expects nothing better; and, there-fore, whose preconceived notions and expectations you do in reality so much less shock in the refusal.

When I think of this man; his fiery glow of heart; his swell of feeling; how magnificent, how *ideal* he was; how great at the midnight hour; and when I compare with him the companions with whom I have associated since, I grudge the saving of a few idle ducats, and think that I am fallen into the society of *lenders*, and *little men*.

To one like Elia, whose treasures are rather cased in leather covers than closed in iron coffers, there is a class of alienators more formidable than that which I have touched upon; I mean your *borrowers of books*—those mutilators of collec-tions, spoilers of the symmetry of shelves, and creators of odd volumes. There is Comberbatch, matchless in his depre-dations!

That foul gap in the bottom shelf facing you, like a great eye-tooth knocked out—(you are now with me in my little back study in Bloomsbury, reader!)—with the huge Switzer-like tomes on each side (like the Guildhall giants, in their reformed posture, guardant of nothing) once held the tallest of my folios, *Opera Bonaventuræ*, choice and massy divinity, to which its two supporters (school divinity also, but of a lesser calibre,—Bellarmine, and Holy Thomas), showed but as dwarfs,—itself an Ascapart!—*that* Comberbatch abstracted upon the faith of a theory he holds, which is more easy, I confess, for me to suffer by than to refute, namely, that "the title to property in a book (my Bonaventure, for instance), is in exact ratio to the claimant's powers of understanding and appreciating the same." Should he go on acting upon this theory, which of our shelves is safe?

The slight vacuum in the left hand case—two shelves from the ceiling—scarcely distinguishable but by the quick eye of a loser—was whilom the commodious resting-place of Brown on Urn Burial. C. will hardly allege that he knows more about that treatise than I do, who introduced it to him, and was indeed the first (of the moderns) to discover its beauties—but so have I known a foolish lover to praise his mistress in the presence of a rival more qualified to carry her off than himself.—Just below, Dodsley's dramas want their fourth volume, where *Vittoria Corombona* is! The remainder nine are as distasteful as Priam's refuse sons, when the Fates *borrowed* Hector. Here stood the *Anatomy of Melancholy*, in sober state.—There loitered *The Complete Angler*; quiet as in life, by some stream side.—In yonder nook *John Buncle*, a widower-volume, with "eyes closed," mourns his ravished mate.

One justice I must do my friend, that if he sometimes, like the sea, sweeps away a treasure, at another time, sea-like, he throws up as rich an equivalent to match it. I have a small under-collection of this nature (my friend's gatherings in his various calls), picked up, he has forgotten at what odd places, and deposited with as little memory at mine. I take in these orphans, the twice-deserted. These proselytes of the gate are welcome as the true Hebrews. There they stand in conjunction; natives, and naturalised. The latter seemed as little disposed to inquire out their true lineage as I am.—I charge no warehouse-room for these deodands, nor shall ever put myself to the ungentlemanly trouble of advertising a sale of them to pay expenses.

To lose a volume to C. carries some sense and meaning in it. You are sure that he will make one hearty meal on your viands, if he can give no account of the platter after it. But what moved thee, wayward, spiteful K., to be so importunate to carry off with thee, in spite of tears and adjurations to thee to forbear, the *Letters* of that princely woman, the thrice noble Margaret Newcastle?—knowing at the time, and knowing that I knew also, that thou most assuredly wouldst never turn over one leaf of the illustrious folio:—what but the mere spirit of contradiction, and childish love of getting the better of they friend?—Then, worst cut of all! to transport it with thee to the Gallican land—

> Unworthy land to harbour such a sweetness,
> A virtue in which all ennobling thoughts dwelt,
> Pure thoughts, kind thoughts, high thoughts,
>   her sex's wonder!

—hadst thou not thy play-books, and books of jests and fancies, about thee, to keep thee merry, even as thou keepest all companies with thy quips and mirthful tales?—Child of the Greenroom, it was unkindly done of thee. Thy wife, too, that part-French, better-part Englishwoman!—that *she* could fix upon no other treatise to bear away in kindly token of remembering us, than the works of Fulke Greville, Lord Brook—of which no Frenchman, nor woman of France, Italy, or England, was ever by nature constituted to comprehend a tittle! *Was there not Zimmerman on Solitude?*

Reader, if haply thou art blessed with a moderate collection, be shy of showing it; or if thy heart overfloweth to lend them, lend thy books; but let it be to such a one as S. T. C.—he will return them (generally anticipating the time appointed) with usury; enriched with annotations, tripling their value. I have had experience. Many are these precious MSS. of his—(in *matter* oftentimes, and almost in *quantity* not infrequently, vying with the originals)—in no very clerkly hand—legible in my Daniel; in old Burton; in Sir Thomas Browne; and those abstruser cogitations of the Greville, now, alas! wandering in Pagan lands—I counsel thee, shut not thy heart, nor thy library, against S. T. C.

MRS. BATTLE'S OPINIONS ON WHIST

A CLEAR FIRE, A CLEAN HEARTH, AND THE RIGOUR OF THE GAME." This was the celebrated *wish* of old Sarah Battle (now with God), who, next to her devotions, loved a good game of whist. She was none of your lukewarm gamesters, your half-and-half players, who have no objection to take a hand, if you want one to make up a rubber; who affirm that they have no pleasure in winning; that they like to win one game and lose another; that they can while away an hour very agreeably at a card-table, but are indifferent whether they play or no; and will desire an adversary, who has slipped a wrong card, to take it up and play another. These insufferable triflers are the curse of a table. One of these flies will spoil a whole pot. Of such it may be said that they do not play at cards, but only play at playing at them.

Sarah Battle was none of that breed. She detested them, as I do, from her heart and soul, and would not, save upon a striking emergency, willingly seat herself at the same table with them. She loved a thorough-paced partner, a determined enemy. She took, and gave, no concessions. She hated favours. She never made a revoke, nor ever passed it over in her adversary without exacting the utmost forfeiture. She fought a good fight: cut and thrust. She held not her good sword (her cards) "like a dancer." She sate bolt upright; and neither showed you her cards, nor desired to see yours. All people have their blind side—their superstitions; and I have heard her declare, under the rose, that Hearts was her favourite suit.

I never in my life—and I knew Sarah Battle many of the best

years of it—saw her take out her snuff-box when it was her turn to play; or snuff a candle in the middle of a game; or ring for a servant, till it was fairly over. She never introduced, or connived at, miscellaneous conversation during its process. As she emphatically observed, cards were cards; and if I ever saw unmingled distaste in her fine last-century countenance, it was at the airs of a young gentleman of a literary turn, who had been with difficulty persuaded to take a hand; and who, in his excess of candour, declared, that he thought there was no harm in unbending the mind now and then, after serious studies, in recreation of that kind! She could not bear to have her noble occupation, to which she wound up her faculties, considered in that light. It was her business, her duty, the thing she came into the world to do—and she did it. She unbent her mind afterwards—over a book.

Pope was her favourite author: his *Rape of the Lock* her favourite work. She once did me the favour to play over with me (with the cards) his celebrated game of Ombre in that poem; and to explain to me how far it agreed with, and in what points it would be found to differ from, tradrille. Her illustrations were apposite and poignant; and I had the pleasure of sending the substance of them to Mr. Bowles; but I suppose they came too late to be inserted among his ingenious notes upon that author.

Quadrille, she has often told me, was her first love; but whist had engaged her maturer esteem. The former, she said, was showy and specious, and likely to allure young persons. The uncertainty and quick shifting of partners—a thing which the constancy of whist abhors; the dazzling supremacy and regal investiture of Spadille—absurd, as she justly observed, in the pure aristocracy of whist, where his crown and garter give him no proper power above his brother-nobility of the Aces;—the giddy vanity, so taking to the inexperienced, of playing alone; above all, the overpowering attractions of a *Sans Prendre Vole*,—to the triumph of which there is certainly nothing parallel or approaching in the contingencies of whist;—all these, she would say, make quadrille a game of captivation to the young and enthusiastic. But whist was the *solider* game:

that was her word. It was a long meal; not like quadrille, a feast of snatches. One or two rubbers might co-extend in duration with an evening. They gave time to form rooted friendships, to cultivate steady enmities. She despised the chance-started, capricious, and ever fluctuating alliances of the other. The skirmishes of quadrille, she would say, reminded her of the petty ephemeral embroilments of the little Italian states, depicted by Machiavel: perpetually changing postures and connections; bitter foes to-day, sugared darlings to-morrow; kissing and scratching in a breath;—but the wars of whist were comparable to the long, steady, deep-rooted, rational antipathies of the great French and English nations.

A grave simplicity was what she chiefly admired in her favourite game. There was nothing silly in it, like the nob in cribbage—nothing superfluous. No *flushes*—that most irrational of all pleas that a reasonable being can set up:—that anyone should claim four by virtue of holding cards of the same mark and colour, without reference to the playing of the game, or the individual worth or pretensions of the cards themselves! She held this to be a solecism; as pitiful an ambition at cards as alliteration is in authorship. She despised superficiality, and looked deeper than the colours of things. Suits were soldiers, she would say, and must have a uniformity of array to distinguish them: but what should we say to a foolish squire, who should claim a merit from dressing up his tenantry in red jackets, that never were to be marshalled—never to take the field?—She even wished that whist were more simple than it is; and, in my mind, would have stripped it of some appendages, which, in the state of human frailty, may be venially, and even commendably, allowed of. She saw no reason for the deciding of the trump by the turn of the card. Why not one suit always trumps?—Why two colours, when the mark of the suit would have sufficiently distinguished them without it?

"But the eye, my dear madam, is agreeably refreshed with the variety. Man is not a creature of pure reason—he must have his senses delightfully appealed to. We see it in Roman Catholic countries, where the music and the paintings draw in many to worship, whom your Quaker spirit of unsensualizing would have kept out.—You yourself have a pretty collection of paintings—but confess to me, whether, walking in your gallery at Sandham, among those clear Vandykes, or among the Paul Potters in the ante-room, you ever felt your bosom glow with an elegant delight, at all comparable to *that* you have it in your power to experience most evenings over a well-arranged assortment of the court-cards?—the pretty antic habits, like heralds in a procession—the gay triumph-assuring scarlets—the contrasting deadly-killing sables—the 'hoary majesty of spades'—Pam in all his glory!——

"All these might be dispensed with; and with their naked names upon the drab pasteboard, the game might go on very well, pictureless; but the *beauty* of cards would be extinguished for ever. Stripped of all that is imaginative in them, they must degenerate into mere gambling. Imagine a dull deal board, or drum head, to spread them on, instead of that nice verdant carpet (next to nature's), fittest arena for those courtly combatants to play their gallant jousts and tourneys in!—Exchange those delicately-turned ivory markers—(work of Chinese artist, unconscious of their symbol,—or as profanely slighting their true application as the arrantest Ephesian journeyman that turned out those little shrines for the goddess)—exchange them for little bits of leather (our ancestors' money), or chalk and a slate!"——

The old lady, with a smile, confessed the soundness of my logic; and to her approbation of my arguments on her favourite topic that evening, I have always fancied myself indebted for the legacy of a curious cribbage-board, made of the finest Sienna marble, which her maternal uncle (old Walter Plumer, whom I have elsewhere celebrated) brought with him from Florence:—this, and a trifle of five hundred pounds, came to me at her death.

The former bequest (which I do not least value) I have kept with religious care; though she herself, to confess a truth, was never greatly taken with cribbage. It was an essentially vulgar game, I have heard her say,—disputing with her uncle, who was very partial to it. She could never heartily bring her mouth to pronounce "*Go*," or "*That's a go*." She called it an

ungrammatical game. The pegging teased her. I once knew her
to forfeit a rubber (a five-dollar stake) because she would
not take advantage of the turn-up knave, which would have
given it her, but which she must have claimed by the dis-
graceful tenure of declaring *"two for his heels."* There is
something extremely genteel in this sort of self-denial. Sarah
Battle was a gentlewoman born.

Piquet she held the best game at the cards for two persons,
though she would ridicule the pedantry of the terms—such
as pique—repique—the capot—they savoured (she thought) of
affectation. But games for two, or even three, she never greatly
cared for. She loved the quadrate or square. She would argue
thus:—Cards are warfare: the ends are gain, with glory. But
cards are war, in disguise of a sport: when single adversaries
encounter, the ends proposed are too palpable. By themselves,
it is too close a fight; with spectators, it is not much bettered.
No looker-on can be interested, except for a bet, and then it
is a mere affair of money; he cares not for your luck *sympa-
thetically*, or for your play.—Three are still worse; a mere
naked war of every man against every man, as in cribbage,
without league or alliance; or a rotation of petty and contra-
dictory interests, a succession of heartless leagues, and not
much more hearty infractions of them, as in tradrille.—But in
square games (*she meant whist*), all that is possible to be attained in card-playing is accomplished. There are the incen-
tives of profit with honour, common to every species—though
the *latter* can be but very imperfectly enjoyed in those other
games, where the spectator is only feebly a participator. But
the parties in whist are spectators and principals too. They
are a theatre to themselves, and a looker-on is not wanted. He
is rather worse than nothing, and an impertinence. Whist
abhors neutrality, or interests beyond its sphere. You glory in
some surprising stroke of skill or fortune, not because a cold—
or even an interested—bystander witnesses it, but because your
partner sympathizes in the contingency. You win for two. You
triumph for two. Two are exalted. Two again are mortified;
which divides their disgrace, as the conjunction doubles (by
taking off the invidiousness) your glories. Two losing to two

are better reconciled, than one to one in that close butchery. The hostile feeling is weakened by multiplying the channels. War becomes a civil game. By such reasonings as these the old lady was accustomed to defend her favourite pastime.

No inducement could ever prevail upon her to play at any game, where chance entered into the composition, *for nothing*. Chance, she would argue—and here again, admire the subtlety of her conclusion;—chance is nothing, but where something else depends upon it. It is obvious that cannot be *glory*. What rational cause of exultation could it give to a man to turn up size ace a hundred times together by himself? or before spectators, where no stake was depending?—Make a lottery of a hundred thousand tickets with but one fortunate number—and what possible principle of our nature, except stupid wonderment, could it gratify to gain that number as many times successively without a prize? Therefore she disliked the mixture of chance in backgammon, where it was not played for money. She called it foolish, and those people idiots, who were taken with a lucky hit under such circumstances. Games of pure skill were as little to her fancy. Played for a stake, they were a mere system of over-reaching. Played for glory, they were a mere setting of one man's wit,—his memory, or combination-faculty rather—against another's; like a mock-engagement at a review, bloodless and profitless. She could not conceive a *game* wanting the spritely infusion of chance, the handsome excuses of good fortune. Two people playing at chess in a corner of a room, whilst whist was stirring in the centre, would inspire her with insufferable horror and ennui. Those well-cut similitudes of Castles and Knights, the *imagery* of the board, she would argue (and I think in this case justly), were entirely misplaced and senseless. Those hard-head contests can in no instance ally with the fancy. They reject form and colour. A pencil and dry slate (she used to say) were the proper arena for such combatants.

To those puny objectors against cards, as nurturing the bad passions, she would retort, that man is a gaming animal. He must be always trying to get the better in something or other: —that this passion can scarcely be more safely expended than upon a game at cards: that cards are a temporary illusion; in truth, a mere drama; for we do but *play* at being mightily concerned, where a few idle shillings are at stake, yet, during the illusion, we *are* as mightily concerned as those whose stake is crowns and kingdoms. They are a sort of dream-fighting; much ado; great battling, and little bloodshed; mighty means for disproportioned ends: quite as diverting, and a great deal more innoxious, than many of those more serious *games* of life, which men play without esteeming them to be such.

With great deference to the old lady's judgment in these matters, I think I have experienced some moments in my life, when playing at cards *for nothing* has even been agreeable. When I am in sickness, or not in the best spirits, I sometimes call for the cards, and play a game at piquet *for love* with my cousin Bridget—Bridget Elia.

I grant there is something sneaking in it; but with a tooth-ache, or a sprained ankle,—when you are subdued and humble, —you are glad to put up with an inferior spring of action.

There is such a thing in nature, I am convinced, as *sick whist*.

I grant it is not the highest style of man—I deprecate the manes of Sarah Battle—she lives not, alas! to whom I should apologize.

At such times, those *terms* which my old friend objected to, come in as something admissible. I love to get a tierce or a quatorze, though they mean nothing. I am subdued to an inferior interest. Those shadows of winning amuse me.

That last game I had with my sweet cousin (I capotted her)—(dare I tell thee, how foolish I am?)—I wished it might have lasted for ever, though we gained nothing, and lost nothing, though it was a mere shade of play: I would be content to go on in that idle folly for ever. The pipkin should be ever boiling, that was to prepare the gentle lenitive to my foot, which Bridget was doomed to apply after the game was over: and, as I do not much relish appliances, there it should ever bubble. Bridget and I should be ever playing.

THE PRAISE OF CHIMNEY-SWEEPERS

I LIKE TO MEET A SWEEP—understand me—not a grown
sweeper—old chimney-sweepers are by no means attractive—but one of those tender novices, blooming through
their first nigritude, the maternal washings not quite effaced
from the cheek—such as come forth with the dawn, or somewhat earlier, with their little professional notes sounding like
the *peep peep* of a young sparrow; or liker to the matin lark
should I pronounce them, in their aerial ascents not seldom
anticipating the sun-rise?

I have a kindly yearning toward these dim specks—poor
blots—innocent blacknesses—

I reverence these young Africans of our own growth—these
almost clergy imps, who sport their cloth without assumption;
and from their little pulpits (the tops of chimneys), in the
nipping air of a December morning, preach a lesson of patience
to mankind.

When a child, what a mysterious pleasure it was to witness
their operation! to see a chit no bigger than one's-self enter,
one knew not by what process, into what seemed the *fauces
Averni*—to pursue him in imagination, as he went sounding on
through so many dark stifling caverns, horrid shades!—to
shudder with the idea that "now, surely, he must be lost for
ever!"—to revive at hearing his feeble shout of discovered
day-light—and then (O fulness of delight) running out of
doors, to come just in time to see the sable phenomenon
emerge in safety, the brandished weapon of his art victorious
like some flag waved over a conquered citadel! I seem to
remember having been told that a bad sweep was once left
in a stack with his brush, to indicate which way the wind
blew. It was an awful spectacle certainly; not much unlike
the old stage direction in *Macbeth*, where the "Apparition of
a child crowned, with a tree in his hand, rises."

Reader, if thou meetest one of these small gentry in thy
early rambles, it is good to give him a penny. It is better to
give him two-pence. If it be starving weather, and to the

proper troubles of his hard occupation, a pair of kibed heels (no unusual accompaniment) be superadded, the demand on thy humanity will surely rise to a tester.

There is a composition, the ground-work of which I have understood to be the sweet wood 'yclept sassafras. This wood boiled down to a kind of tea, and tempered with an infusion of milk and sugar, hath to some tastes a delicacy beyond the China luxury. I know not how thy palate may relish it; for myself, with every deference to the judicious Mr. Read, who hath time out of mind kept open a shop (the only one he avers in London) for the vending of this "wholesome and pleasant beverage," on the south side of Fleet Street, as thou approachest Bridge Street—*the only Salopian house*,—I have never yet ventured to dip my own particular lip in a basin of his commended ingredients—a cautious premonition to the olfactories constantly whispering to me that my stomach must infallibly, with all due courtesy, decline it. Yet I have seen palates, otherwise not uninstructed in dietetical elegancies, sup it up with avidity.

I know not by what particular conformation of the organ it happens, but I have always found that this composition is surprisingly gratifying to the palate of a young chimney-sweeper—whether the oily particles (sassafras is slightly oleaginous) do attenuate and soften the fuliginous concretions, which are sometimes found (in dissections) to adhere to the roof of the mouth in these unfledged practitioners; or whether Nature, sensible that she had mingled too much of bitter wood in the lot of these raw victims, caused to grow out of the earth her sassafras for a sweet lenitive—but so it is, that no possible taste or odour to the senses of a young chimney-sweeper can convey a delicate excitement comparable to this mixture. Being penniless, they will yet hang their black heads over the ascending steam, to gratify one sense if possible, seemingly no less pleased than those domestic animals—cats—when they purr over a new-found sprig of valerian. There is something more in these sympathies than philosophy can inculcate.

Now albeit Mr. Read boasteth, not without reason, that

his is the *only Salopian house*; yet be it known to thee, reader—
if thou art one who keepest what are called good hours, thou
art haply ignorant of the fact—he hath a race of industrious
imitators, who from stalls, and under open sky, dispense the
same savoury mess to humbler customers, at that dead time of
the dawn, when (as extremes meet) the rake, reeling home
from his midnight cups, and the hard-handed artisan leaving
his bed to resume the premature labours of the day, jostle, not
unfrequently to the manifest disconcerting of the former, for
the honours of the pavement. It is the time when, in summer,
between the expired and the not yet relumined kitchen-fires,
the kennels of our fair metropolis give forth their least satisfactory odours. The rake, who wisheth to dissipate his o'er-
night vapours in more grateful coffee, curses the ungenial
fume, as he passeth; but the artisan stops to taste, and blesses
the fragrant breakfast.

This is *saloop*—the precious herb-woman's darling—the
delight of the early gardener, who transports his smoking
cabbages by break of day from Hammersmith to Covent
Garden's famed piazzas—the delight, and, oh I fear, too
often the envy, of the unpennied sweep. Him shouldest thou
haply encounter, with his dim visage pendent over the grateful steam, regale him with a sumptuous basin (it will cost
thee but three half-pennies) and a slice of delicate bread and
butter (an added halfpenny)—so may thy culinary fires,
eased of the o'er-charged secretions from thy worse-placed
hospitalities, curl up a lighter volume to the welkin—so may
the descending soot never taint thy costly well-ingredienced
soups—nor the odious cry, quick-reaching from street to
street, of the *fired chimney*, invite the rattling engines from
ten adjacent parishes, to disturb for a casual scintillation thy
peace and pocket!

I am by nature extremely susceptible of street affronts;
the jeers and taunts of the populace; the low-bred triumph
they display over the casual trip, or splashed stocking, of
a gentleman. Yet can I endure the jocularity of a young
sweep with something more than forgiveness.—In the last
winter but one, pacing along Cheapside with my accustomed

precipitation when I walk westward, a treacherous slide brought me upon my back in an instant. I scrambled up with pain and shame enough—yet outwardly trying to face it down, as if nothing had happened—when the roguish grin of one of these young wits encountered me. There he stood, pointing me out with his dusky finger to the mob, and to a poor woman (I suppose his mother) in particular, till the tears for the exquisiteness of the fun (so he thought it) worked themselves out at the corners of his poor red eyes, red from many a previous weeping, and soot-inflamed, yet twinkling through all with such a joy, snatched out of desolation, that Hogarth—but Hogarth has got him already (how could he miss him?) in the *March to Finchley*, grinning at the pie-man —there he stood, as he stands in the picture, irremovable, as if the jest was to last for ever—with such a maximum of glee, and minimum of mischief, in his mirth—for the grin of a genuine sweep hath absolutely no malice in it—that I could have been content, if the honour of a gentleman might endure it, to have remained his butt and his mockery till midnight.

I am by theory obdurate to the seductiveness of what are called a fine set of teeth. Every pair of rosy lips (the ladies must pardon me) is a casket, presumably holding such jewels; but, methinks, they should take leave to "air" them as frugally as possible. The fine lady, or fine gentleman, who show me their teeth, show me bones. Yet must I confess, that from the mouth of a true sweep a display (even to ostentation) of those white and shining ossifications strikes me as an agreeable anomaly in manners, and an allowable piece of foppery. It is, as when

> A sable cloud
> Turns forth her silver lining on the night.

It is like some remnant of gentry not quite extinct; a badge of better days; a hint of nobility:—and, doubtless, under the obscuring darkness and double night of their forlorn disguisement, oftentimes lurketh good blood, and gentle conditions, derived from lost ancestry, and a lapsed pedigree. The premature apprenticements of these tender victims give but too much encouragement, I fear, to clandestine, and almost infantile abductions; the seeds of civility and true courtesy, so often discernible in these young grafts (not otherwise to be accounted for) plainly hint at some forced adoptions; many noble Rachels mourning for their children, even in our days, countenance the fact; the tales of fairy-spiriting may shadow a lamentable verity, and the recovery of the young Montagu be but a solitary instance of good fortune, out of many irreparable and hopeless *defiliations*.

In one of the state-beds at Arundel Castle, a few years since—under a ducal canopy—(that seat of the Howards is an object of curiosity to visitors chiefly for its beds, in which the late duke was especially a connoisseur)—encircled with curtains of delicatest crimson, with starry coronets inwoven— folded between a pair of sheets whiter and softer than the lap where Venus lulled Ascanius—was discovered by chance, after all methods of search had failed, at noon-day, fast asleep, a lost chimney-sweeper. The little creature, having somehow confounded his passage among the intricacies of those lordly chimneys, by some unknown aperture had alighted upon this magnificent chamber; and, tired with his tedious explorations, was unable to resist the delicious invitement to repose, which he there saw exhibited; so, creeping between the sheets very quietly, laid his black head upon the pillow, and slept like a young Howard.

Such is the account given to the visitors at the Castle.— But I cannot help seeming to perceive a confirmation of what I have just hinted at in this story. A high instinct was at work in the case, or I am mistaken. Is it probable that a poor child of that description, with whatever weariness he might be visited, would have ventured, under such a penalty as he would be taught to expect, to uncover the sheets of a Duke's bed, and deliberately to lay himself down between them, when the rug, or the carpet, presented an obvious couch, still far above his pretensions—is this probable, I would ask, if the great power of nature, which I contend for, had not been manifested within him, prompting to the adventure? Doubtless this young nobleman (for such my mind misgives me that

he must be) was allured by some memory, not amounting to
full consciousness, of his condition in infancy, when he was
used to be lapt by his mother, or his nurse, in just such sheets
as he there found, into which he was but now creeping back
as into his proper *incunabula*, and resting-place.—By no other
theory, than by this sentiment of a pre-existent state (as I may
call it), can I explain a deed so venturous, and, indeed, upon
any other system, so indecorous, in this tender, but unseasonable, sleeper.

My pleasant friend JEM WHITE was so impressed with a
belief of metamorphoses like this frequently taking place, that
in some sort to reverse the wrongs of fortune in these poor
changelings, he instituted an annual feast of chimney-sweepers,
at which it was his pleasure to officiate as host and waiter. It
was a solemn supper held in Smithfield, upon the yearly return
of the fair of St. Bartholomew. Cards were issued a week before to the master-sweeps in and about the metropolis, confining the invitation to their younger fry. Now and then an
elderly stripling would get in among us, and be good-
naturedly winked at; but our main body were infantry. One
unfortunate wight, indeed, who relying upon his dusky suit,
had intruded himself into our party, but by tokens was
providentially discovered in time to be no chimney-sweeper
(all is not soot which looks so), was quoited out of the
presence with universal indignation, as not having on the
wedding garment; but in general the greatest harmony prevailed. The place chosen was a convenient spot among the
pens, at the north side of the fair, not so far distant as to be
impervious to the agreeable hubbub of that vanity; but remote
enough not to be obvious to the interruption of every gaping
spectator in it. The guests assembled about seven. In those
little temporary parlours three tables were spread with napery,
not so fine as substantial, and at every board a comely hostess
presided with her pan of hissing sausages. The nostrils of the
young rogues dilated at the savour. JAMES WHITE, as
head waiter, had charge of the first table; and myself, with
our trusty companion BIGOD, ordinarily ministered to the
other two. There was clambering and jostling, you may be

sure, who should get at the first table—for Rochester in his maddest days could not have done the humours of the scene with more spirit than my friend. After some general expression of thanks for the honour the company had done him, his inaugural ceremony was to clasp the greasy waist of old dame Ursula (the fattest of the three), that stood frying and fretting, half-blessing, half-cursing "the gentleman," and imprint upon her chaste lips a tender salute, whereat the universal host would set up a shout that tore the concave, while hundreds of grinning teeth startled the night with their brightness. O it was a pleasure to see the sable younkers lick in the unctuous meat, with *his* more unctuous sayings—how he would fit the tit-bits to the puny mouths, reserving the lengthier links for the seniors—how he would intercept a morsel even in the jaws of some young desperado, declaring it "must to the pan again to be browned, for it was not fit for a gentleman's eating"—how he would recommend this slice of white bread, or that piece of kissing-crust, to a tender juvenile, advising them all to have a care of cracking their teeth, which were their best patrimony,—how genteelly he would deal about the small ale, as if it were wine, naming the brewer, and protesting, if it were not good he should lose their custom; with a special recommendation to wipe the lip before drinking. Then we had our toasts—"The King,"— the "Cloth,"—which, whether they understood or not, was equally diverting and flattering;— and for a crowning sentiment, which never failed, "May the Brush supersede the Laurel!" All these, and fifty other fancies, which were rather felt than comprehended by his guests, would he utter, standing upon tables, and prefacing every sentiment with a "Gentlemen, give me leave to propose so and so," which was a prodigious comfort to those young orphans; every now and then stuffing into his mouth (for it did not do to be squeamish on these occasions) indiscriminate pieces of those reeking sausages, which pleased them mightily, and was the savouriest part, you may believe, of the entertainment.

> Golden lads and lasses must,
> As chimney-sweepers, come to dust—

JAMES WHITE is extinct, and with him these suppers have long ceased. He carried away with him the fun of the world when he died—of my world at least. His old clients look for him among the pens; and, missing him, reproach the altered feast of St. Bartholomew, and the glory of Smithfield departed for ever.

William Hazlitt

1778 · 1830

*William Hazlitt was trained for the Unitarian
ministry, chose to become a portrait painter but
proved to be only mediocre, and in his thirties
began to write dramatic criticism and essays. Other
critics attacked him for his literary views, and so he
began the life-long quarrels that engaged him not
only with his enemies but also with his friends. His
home life was as violent and unhappy as his public
life. Positive opinions on all matters which came to
his attention gave vigor to Hazlitt's essays, and
a clear, uncomplicated style gave them permanence.*

ON FAMILIAR STYLE

IT IS NOT EASY TO WRITE a familiar style. Many
people mistake a familiar for a vulgar style,
and suppose that to write without affectation is to write at
random. On the contrary, there is nothing that requires more
precision, and, if I may so say, purity of expression, than the
style I am speaking of. It utterly rejects not only all unmeaning pomp, but all low, cant phrases, and loose, unconnected,
slipshod allusions. It is not to take the first word that offers, but
the best word in common use; it is not to throw words
together in any combinations we please, but to follow and
avail ourselves of the true idiom of the language. To write a
genuine familiar or truly English style, is to write as any one
would speak in common conversation, who had a thorough
command and choice of words, or who could discourse with
ease, force, and perspicuity, setting aside all pedantic and
oratorical flourishes. Or to give another illustration, to write
naturally is the same thing in regard to common conversation,

as to read naturally is in regard to common speech. It does not follow that it is an easy thing to give the true accent and inflection to the words you utter, because you do not attempt to rise above the level of ordinary life and colloquial speaking. You do not assume indeed the solemnity of the pulpit, or the tone of stage-declamation: neither are you at liberty to gabble on at a venture, without emphasis or discretion, or to resort to vulgar dialect or clownish pronunciation. You must steer a middle course. You are tied down to a given and appropriate articulation, which is determined by the habitual associations between sense and sound, and which you can only hit by entering into the author's meaning, as you must find the proper words and style to express yourself by fixing your thoughts on the subject you have to write about. Any one may mouth out a passage with a theatrical cadence, or get upon stilts to tell his thoughts: but to write or speak with propriety and simplicity is a more difficult task. Thus it is easy to affect a pompous style, to use a word twice as big as the thing you want to express: it is not so easy to pitch upon the very word that exactly fits it. Out of eight or ten words equally common, equally intelligible, with nearly equal pretensions, it is a matter of some nicety and discrimination to pick out the very one, the preferableness of which is scarcely perceptible, but decisive. The reason why I object to Dr. Johnson's style is, that there is no discrimination, no selection, no variety in it. He uses none but "tall, opaque words," taken from the "first row of the rubric":—words with the greatest number of syllables, or Latin phrases with merely English terminations. If a fine style depended on this sort of arbitrary pretension, it would be fair to judge of an author's elegance by the measurement of his words, and the substitution of foreign circumlocutions (with no precise associations) for the mother-tongue. How simple it is to be dignified without ease, to be pompous without meaning! Surely, it is but a mechanical rule for avoiding what is low to be always pedantic and affected. It is clear you cannot use a vulgar English word, if you never use a common English word at all. A fine tact is shewn in adhering to those which are perfectly common, and yet never falling into any expressions which are debased by disgusting circumstances, or which owe their signification and point to technical or professional allusions. A truly natural or familiar style can never be quaint or vulgar, for this reason, that it is of universal force and applicability, and that quaintness and vulgarity arise out of the immediate connection of certain words with coarse and disagreeable, or with confined ideas. The last form what we understand by *cant* or *slang* phrases.—To give an example of what is not very clear in the general statement. I should say that the phrase *To cut with a knife*, or *To cut a piece of wood*, is perfectly free from vulgarity, because it is perfectly common: but to *cut an acquaintance* is not quite unexceptionable, because it is not perfectly common or intelligible, and has hardly yet escaped out of the limits of slang phraseology. I should hardly therefore use the word in this sense without putting it in italics as a license of expression, to be received *cum grano salis*. All provincial or bye-phrases come under the same mark of reprobation—all such as the writer transfers to the page from his fireside or a particular *coterie*, or that he invents for his own sole use and convenience. I conceive that words are like money, not the worse for being common, but that it is the stamp of custom alone that gives them circulation or value. I am fastidious in this respect, and would almost as soon coin the currency of the realm as counterfeit the King's English. I never invented or gave a new and unauthorized meaning to any word but one single one (the term *impersonal* applied to feelings) and that was in an abstruse metaphysical discussion to express a very difficult distinction. I have been (I know) loudly accused of revelling in vulgarisms and broken English. I cannot speak to that point: but so far I plead guilty to the determined use of acknowledged idioms and common elliptical expressions. I am not sure that the critics in question know the one from the other, that is, can distinguish any medium between formal pedantry and the most barbarous solecism. As an author, I endeavour to employ plain words and popular modes of construction, as were I a chapman and dealer, I should common weights and measures.

The proper force of words lies not in the words themselves,

but in their application. A word may be a fine-sounding word, of an unusual length, and very imposing from its learning and novelty, and yet in the connection in which it is introduced, may be quite pointless and irrelevant. It is not pomp or pretension, but the adaptation of the expression to the idea that clenches a writer's meaning:—as it is not the size or glossiness of the materials, but their being fitted each to its place, that gives strength to the arch; or as the pegs and nails are as necessary to the support of the building as the larger timbers, and more so than the mere shewy, unsubstantial ornaments. I hate any thing that occupies more space than it is worth. I hate to see a load of band-boxes go along the street, and I hate to see a parcel of big words without any thing in them. A person who does not deliberately dispose of all his thoughts alike in cumbrous draperies and flimsy disguises, may strike out twenty varieties of familiar everyday language, each coming somewhat nearer to the feeling he wants to convey, and at last not hit upon that particular and only one, which may be said to be identical with the exact impression in his mind. This would seem to shew that Mr. Cobbett is hardly right in saying that the first word that occurs is always the best. It may be a very good one; and yet a better may present itself on reflection or from time to time. It should be suggested naturally, however, and spontaneously, from a fresh and lively conception of the subject. We seldom succeed by trying at improvement, or by merely substituting one word for another that we are not satisfied with, as we cannot recollect the name of a place or person by merely plaguing ourselves about it. We wander farther from the point by persisting in a wrong scent; but it starts up accidentally in the memory when we least expected it, by touching some link in the chain of previous association.

There are those who hoard up and make a cautious display of nothing but rich and rare phraseology;—ancient medals, obscure coins, and Spanish pieces of eight. They are very curious to inspect; but I myself would neither offer nor take them in the course of exchange. A sprinkling of archaisms is not amiss; but a tissue of obsolete expressions is more fit *for keep than wear.* I do not say I would not use any phrase that had been brought into fashion before the middle or the end of the last century; but I should be shy of using any that had not been employed by any approved author during the whole of that time. Words, like clothes, get old-fashioned, or mean and ridiculous, when they have been for some time laid aside. Mr. Lamb is the only imitator of old English style I can read with pleasure; and he is so thoroughly imbued with the spirit of his authors, that the idea of imitation is almost done away. There is an inward unction, a marrowy vein both in the thought and feeling, an intuition, deep and lively, of his subject, that carries off any quaintness or awkwardness arising from an antiquated style and dress. The matter is completely his own, though the manner is assumed. Perhaps his ideas are altogether so marked and individual, as to require their point and pungency to be neutralised by the affectation of a singular but traditional form of conveyance. Tricked out in the prevailing costume, they would probably seem more startling and out of the way. The old English authors, Burton, Fuller, Coryate, Sir Thomas Browne, are a kind of mediators between us and the more eccentric and whimsical modern, reconciling us to his peculiarities. I do not, however, know how far this is the case or not, till he condescends to write like one of us. I must confess that what I like best of his papers under the signature of Elia (still I do not presume, amidst such excellence, to decide what is most excellent) is the account of *Mrs. Battle's Opinions on Whist*, which is also the most free from obsolete allusions and turns of expression—

A well of native English undefiled.

To those acquainted with his admired prototypes, these *Essays* of the ingenious and highly gifted author have the same sort of charm and relish, that Erasmus's *Colloquies* or a fine piece of modern Latin have to the classical scholar. Certainly, I do not know any borrowed pencil that has more power or felicity of execution than the one of which I have here been speaking.

It is as easy to write a gaudy style without ideas, as it is to spread a pallet of shewy colours, or to smear in a flaunting

transparency. "What do you read?"—"Words, words, words."
—"What is the matter?"—"*Nothing*," it might be answered.
The florid style is the reverse of the familiar. The last is
employed as an unvarnished medium to convey ideas; the first
is resorted to as a spangled veil to conceal the want of them.
When there is nothing to be set down but words, it costs
little to have them fine. Look through the dictionary, and cull
out a *florilegium*, rival the *tulip-pomania*. *Rouge* high enough,
and never mind the natural complexion. The vulgar, who are
not in the secret, will admire the look of preternatural health
and vigour; and the fashionable, who regard only appearances,
will be delighted with the imposition. Keep to your sounding
generalities, your tinkling phrases, and all will be well. Swell
out an unmeaning truism to a perfect tympany of style. A
thought, a distinction is the rock on which all this brittle
cargo of verbiage splits at once. Such writers have merely
verbal imaginations, that retain nothing but words. Or their
puny thoughts have dragon-wings, all green and gold. They
soar far above the vulgar failing of the *Sermo humi obrepens*—
their most ordinary speech is never short of an hyperbole,
splendid, imposing, vague, incomprehensible, magniloquent, a
cento of sounding common-places. If some of us, whose "ambition is more lowly," pry a little too narrowly into nooks and
corners to pick up a number of "unconsidered trifles," they
never once direct their eyes or lift their hands to seize on any
but the most gorgeous, tarnished, thread-bare patch-work set
of phrases, the left-off finery of poetic extravagance, transmitted down through successive generations of barren pretenders. If they criticise actors and actresses, a huddled
phantasmagoria of feathers, spangles, floods of light, and
oceans of sound float before their morbid sense, which they
paint in the style of Ancient Pistol. Not a glimpse can you
get of the merits or defects of the performers: they are hidden
in a profusion of barbarous epithets and wilful rhodomontade.
Our hypercritics are not thinking of these little fantoccini
beings—

That strut and fret their hour upon the stage—

but of tall phantoms of words, abstractions, *genera* and *species*, sweeping clauses, periods that unite the Poles, forced alliterations, astounding antitheses—

> And on their pens *Fustian* sits plumed.

If they describe kings and queens, it is an Eastern pageant. The Coronation at either House is nothing to it. We get at four repeated images—a curtain, a throne, a sceptre, and a foot-stool. These are with them the wardrobe of a lofty imagination; and they turn their servile strains to servile uses. Do we read a description of pictures? It is not a reflection of tones and hues which "nature's own sweet and cunning hand laid on," but piles of precious stones, rubies, pearls, emeralds, Golconda's mines, and all the blazonry of art. Such persons are in fact besotted with words, and their brains are turned with the glittering, but empty and sterile phantoms of things. Personifications, capital letters, seas of sunbeams, visions of glory, shining inscriptions, the figures of a tranparency, Britannia with her shield, or Hope leaning on an anchor, make up their stock in trade. They may be considered as *hieroglyphical* writers. Images stand out in their minds isolated and important merely in themselves, without any ground-work of feeling—there is no context in their imaginations. Words affect them in the same way, by the mere sound, that is, by their possible, not by their actual application to the subject in hand. They are fascinated by first appearances, and have no sense of consequences. Nothing more is meant by them than meets the ear: they understand or feel nothing more than meets their eye. The web and texture of the universe, and of the heart of man, is a mystery to them: they have no faculty that strikes a chord in unison with it. They cannot get beyond the daubings of fancy, the varnish of sentiment. Objects are not linked to feelings, words to things, but images revolve in splendid mockery, words represent themselves in their strange rhapsodies. The categories of such a mind are pride and ignorance—pride in outside show, to which they sacrifice every thing, and ignorance of the true worth and hidden structure both of words and things. With a sovereign contempt for what

is familiar and natural, they are the slaves of vulgar affectation—of a routine of high-flown phrases. Scorning to imitate
realities, they are unable to invent any thing, to strike out one
original idea. They are not copyists of nature, it is true: but
they are the poorest of all plagiarists, the plagiarists of words.
All is far-fetched, dear-bought, artificial, oriental in subject
and allusion: all is mechanical, conventional, vapid, formal,
pedantic in style and execution. They startle and confound the
understanding of the reader, by the remoteness and obscurity
of their illustrations: they soothe the ear by the monotony of
the same everlasting round of circuitous metaphors. They are
the *mock-school* in poetry and prose. They flounder about
between fustian in expression, and bathos in sentiment. They
tantalise the fancy but never reach the head nor touch the
heart. Their Temple of Fame is like a shadowy structure raised
by Dulness to Vanity, or like Cowper's description of the
Empress of Russia's palace of ice, as "worthless as in shew
'twas glittering"—

It smiled, and it was cold!

ON GOING A JOURNEY

ONE OF THE PLEASANTEST THINGS in the world is going a
journey; but I like to go by myself. I can enjoy society
in a room; but out of doors, nature is company enough for
me. I am then never less alone than when alone.

The fields his study, nature was his book.

I cannot see the wit of walking and talking at the same
time. When I am in the country, I wish to vegetate like the
country. I am not for criticizing hedge-rows and black cattle.
I go out of town in order to forget the town and all that is
in it. There are those who for this purpose go to watering-
places, and carry the metropolis with them. I like more elbow-
room, and fewer incumbrances. I like solitude, when I give
myself up to it, for the sake of solitude; nor do I ask for

> ——a friend in my retreat,
> Whom I may whisper, solitude is sweet.

The soul of a journey is liberty, perfect liberty, to think, feel, do, just as one pleases. We go a journey chiefly to be free of all impediments and of all inconveniences; to leave ourselves behind, much more to get rid of others. It is because I want a little breathing-space to muse on indifferent matters, where Contemplation

> May plume her feathers and let grow her wings,
> That in the various bustle of resort
> Were all too ruffled, and sometimes impair'd,

that I absent myself from the town for a while, without feeling at a loss the moment I am left by myself. Instead of a friend in a post-chaise or in a Tilbury to exchange good things with and vary the same stale topics over again, for once let me have a truce with impertinence. Give me the clear blue sky over my head, and the green turf beneath my feet, a winding road before me, and a three hours' march to dinner—and then to thinking! It is hard if I cannot start some game on these lone heaths. I laugh, I run, I leap, I sing for joy. From the point of yonder rolling cloud, I plunge into my past being, and revel there, as the sun-burnt Indian plunges headlong into the wave that wafts him to his native shore. Then long-forgotten things, like "sunken wrack and sumless treasuries," burst upon my eager sight, and I begin to feel, think, and be myself again. Instead of an awkward silence, broken by attempts at wit or dull commonplaces, mine is that undisturbed silence of the heart which alone is perfect eloquence. No one likes puns, alliterations, antitheses, argument, and analysis better than I do; but I sometimes had rather be without them. "Leave, oh, leave me to my repose!" I have just now other business in hand, which would seem idle to you, but is with me "very stuff o' the conscience." Is not this wild rose sweet without a comment? Does not this daisy leap to my heart set in its coat of emerald? Yet if I were to explain to you the circumstance that has so endeared it to me, you would only smile. Had I not better then keep it to myself, and let it serve

me to brood over, from here to yonder craggy point, and
from thence onward to the far-distant horizon? I should be
but bad company all that way, and therefore prefer being
alone. I have heard it said that you may, when the moody fit
comes on, walk or ride on by yourself, and indulge your
reveries. But this looks like a breach of manners, a neglect of
others, and you are thinking all the time that you ought to
rejoin your party. "Out upon such half-faced fellowship,"
say I. I like to be either entirely to myself, or entirely at the
disposal of others; to talk or be silent, to walk or sit still, to
be sociable or solitary. I was pleased with an observation of
Mr. Corbett's, that "he thought it a bad French custom to
drink our wine with our meals, and that an Englishman ought
to do only one thing at a time." So I cannot talk and think, or
indulge in melancholy musing and lively conversation by fits
and starts. "Let me have a companion of my way," says
Sterne, "were it but to remark how the shadows lengthen as
the sun declines." It is beautifully said; but in my opinion, this
continual comparing of notes interferes with the involuntary
impression of things upon the mind, and hurts the sentiment.
If you only hint what you feel in a kind of dumb show, it is
insipid: if you have to explain it, it is making a toil of a pleasure. You cannot read the book of nature without being
perpetually put to the trouble of translating it for the benefit
of others.

I am for the synthetical method on a journey in preference
to the analytical. I am content to lay in a stock of ideas then,
and to examine and anatomize them afterwards. I want to see
my vague notions float like the down of the thistle before
the breeze, and not to have them entangled in the briars and
thorns of controversy. For once, I like to have it all my own
way; and this is impossible unless you are alone, or in such
company as I do not covet. I have no objection to argue a
point with any one for twenty miles of measured road, but
not for pleasure. If you remark the scent of a bean-field crossing the road, perhaps your fellow-traveler has no smell. If you
point to a distant object, perhaps he is short-sighted, and has
to take out his glass to look at it. There is a feeling in the air, a

tone in the color of a cloud which hits your fancy, but the effect of which you are unable to account for. There is then no sympathy, but an uneasy craving after it, and a dissatisfaction which pursues you on the way, and in the end probably produces ill-humor. Now I never quarrel with myself, and take all my own conclusions for granted till I find it necessary to defend them against objections. It is not merely that you may not be of accord on the objects and circumstances that present themselves before you—these may recall a number of objects, and lead to associations too delicate and refined to be possibly communicated to others. Yet these I love to cherish, and sometimes still fondly clutch them, when I can escape from the throng to do so. To give way to our feelings before company seems extravagance or affectation; and, on the other hand, to have to unravel this mystery of our being at every turn, and to make others take an equal interest in it (otherwise the end is not answered) is a task to which few are competent. We must "give it an understanding, but no tongue." My old friend Coleridge, however, could do both. He could go on in the most delightful explanatory way over hill and dale a summer's day, and convert a landscape into a didactic poem or a Pindaric ode. "He talked far above singing." If I could so clothe my ideas in sounding and flowing words, I might perhaps wish to have some one with me to admire the swelling theme; or I could be more content, were it possible for me still to hear his echoing voice in the woods of All-Foxden. They had "that fine madness in them which our first poets had"; and if they could have been caught by some rare instrument, would have breathed such strains as the following:

> ——Here be woods as green
> As any, air likewise as fresh and sweet
> As when smooth Zephyrus plays on the fleet
> Face of the curled streams, with flow'rs as many
> As the young spring gives, and as choice as any;
> Here be all new delights, cool streams and wells;
> Arbors o'ergrown with woodbines, caves and dells;
> Choose where thou wilt, while I sit by and sing,

> Or gather rushes, to make many a ring
> For thy long fingers; tell thee tales of love;
> How she pale Phœbe, hunting in a grove,
> First saw the boy Endymion, from whose eyes
> She took eternal fire that never dies;
> How she convey'd him softly in a sleep,
> His temples bound with poppy, to the steep
> Head of old Latmos, where she stoops each night,
> Gilding the mountain with her brother's light,
> To kiss her sweetest.

Had I words and images at command like these, I would attempt to wake the thoughts that lie slumbering on golden ridges in the evening clouds: but at the sight of nature my fancy, poor as it is, droops and closes up its leaves, like flowers at sunset. I can make nothing out on the spot:—I must have time to collect myself.—

In general, a good thing spoils out-of-door prospects: it should be reserved for Table-talk. Lamb is for this reason, I take it, the worst company in the world out of doors; because he is the best within. I grant there is one subject on which it is pleasant to talk on a journey, and that is, what one shall have for supper when we get to our inn at night. The open air improves this sort of conversation or friendly altercation, by setting a keener edge on appetite. Every mile of the road heightens the flavor of the viands we expect at the end of it. How fine it is to enter some old town, walled and turreted, just at the approach of nightfall, or to come to some straggling village, with the lights streaming through the surrounding gloom; and then, after inquiring for the best entertainment that the place affords, to "take one's ease at one's inn!" These eventful moments in our lives' history are too precious, too full of solid, heartfelt happiness to be frittered and dribbled away in imperfect sympathy. I would have them all to myself, and drain them to the last drop: they will do to talk of, or to write about afterwards. What a delicate speculation it is, after drinking whole goblets of tea,

> The cups that cheer, but not inebriate,

and letting the fumes ascend into the brain, to sit considering what we shall have for supper—eggs and a rasher, a rabbit smothered in onions, or an excellent veal cutlet! Sancho in such a situation once fixed upon cow-heel; and his choice, though he could not help it, is not to be disparaged. Then in the intervals of pictured scenery and Shandean contemplation, to catch the preparation and the stir in the kitchen. *Procul, O procul este profani!* These hours are sacred to silence and to musing, to be treasured up in the memory, and to feed the source of smiling thoughts hereafter. I would not waste them in idle talk; or if I must have the integrity of fancy broken in upon, I would rather it were by a stranger than a friend. A stranger takes his hue and character from the time and place; he is a part of the furniture and costume of an inn. If he is a Quaker, or from the West Riding of Yorkshire, so much the better. I do not even try to sympathize with him, and he breaks no squares. I associate nothing with my traveling companion but present objects and passing events. In his ignorance of me and my affairs, I in a manner forget myself. But a friend reminds one of other things, rips up old grievances, and destroys the abstraction of the scene. He comes in ungraciously between us and our imaginary character. Something is dropped in the course of conversation that gives a hint of your profession and pursuits; or from having some one with you that knows the less sublime portions of your history, it seems that other people do. You are no longer a citizen of the world; but your "unhoused free condition is put into circumscription and confine." The *incognito* of an inn is one of its striking privileges—"lord of one's self, uncumbered with a name." Oh! it is great to shake off the trammels of the world and of public opinion—to lose our importunate, tormenting, everlasting personal identity in the elements of nature, and become the creature of the moment, clear of all ties—to hold to the universe only by a dish of sweetbreads, and to owe nothing but the score of the evening—and no longer seeking for applause and meeting with contempt, to be known by no other title than *the Gentleman in the parlor!* One may take one's choice of all characters in this romantic state of uncertainty as to one's real pretensions and become indefinitely respectable and negatively right-worshipful. We baffle prejudice and disappoint conjecture; and from being so to others, begin to be objects of curiosity and wonder even to ourselves. We are no more those hackneyed commonplaces that we appear in the world: an inn restores us to the level of nature, and quits scores with society! I have certainly spent some enviable hours at inns— sometimes when I have been left entirely to myself, and have tried to solve some metaphysical problem, as once at Witham Common, where I found out the proof that likeness is not a case of the association of ideas—at other times, when there have been pictures in the room, as at St. Neot's (I think it was), where I first met with Gribelin's engravings of the Cartoons, into which I entered at once, and at a little inn on the borders of Wales, where there happened to be hanging some of Westall's drawings, which I compared triumphantly (for a theory that I had, not for the admired artist) with the figure of a girl who had ferried me over the Severn, standing up in a boat between me and the twilight—at other times I might mention luxuriating in books, with a peculiar interest in this way, as I remember sitting up half the night to read *Paul and Virginia*, which I picked up at an inn at Bridgewater, after being drenched in the rain all day; and at the same place I got through two volumes of Madam D'Arblay's *Camilla*. It was on the 10th of April, 1798, that I sat down to a volume of the *New Eloise*, at the inn at Llangollen, over a bottle of sherry and a cold chicken. The letter I chose was that in which St. Preux describes his feelings as he first caught a glimpse from the heights of the Jura of the Pays de Vaud, which I had brought with me as a *bon bouche* to crown the evening with. It was my birthday, and I had for the first time come from a place in the neighborhood to visit this delightful spot. The road to Llangollen turns off between Chirk and Wrexham; and on passing a certain point, you come all at once upon the valley, which opens like an amphitheater, broad, barren hills rising in majestic state on either side, with "green upland swells that echo to the bleat of flocks" below and the river Dee babbling over its stony bed in the midst of them. The valley at this time "glittered green with sunny showers," and a budding ashtree dipped its tender branches in the chiding stream. How proud, how glad I was to walk along the high road that overlooks the delicious prospect, repeating the lines which I have just quoted from Mr. Coleridge's poems! But besides the prospect which opened beneath my feet, another also opened to my inward sight, a heavenly vision, on which were written, in letters large as Hope could make them, these four words, LIBERTY, GENIUS, LOVE, VIRTUE; which have since faded into the light of common day, or mock my idle gaze.

The beautiful is vanished, and returns not.

Still I would return some time or other to this enchanted spot; but I would return to it alone. What other self could I find to share that influx of thoughts, of regret, and delight, the fragments of which I could hardly conjure up to myself, so much have they been broken and defaced! I could stand on some tall rock, and overlook the precipice of years that separates me from what I then was. I was at that time going shortly to visit the poet whom I have above named. Where is he now? Not only I myself have changed; the world, which was then new to me, has become old and incorrigible. Yet will I return to thee in thought, O sylvan Dee, in joy, in youth and gladness as thou then wert; and thou shalt always be to me the river of Paradise, where I will drink of the waters of life freely!

There is hardly anything that shows the short-sightedness or capriciousness of the imagination more than traveling does. With change of place we change our ideas; nay, our opinions and feelings. We can by an effort indeed transport ourselves to old and long-forgotten scenes, and then the picture of the mind revives again; but we forget those that we have just left. It seems that we can think but of one place at a time. The canvas of the fancy is but of a certain extent, and if we paint one set of objects upon it, they immediately efface every other. We cannot enlarge our conceptions, we only shift our point of view. The landscape bares its bosom to the enraptured eye, we take our fill of it, and seem as if we could form no other image of beauty or grandeur. We pass on, and think

no more of it: the horizon that shuts it from our sight also
blots it from our memory like a dream. In traveling through a
wild, barren country, I can form no idea of a woody and
cultivated one. It appears to me that all the world must be
barren, like what I see of it. In the country we forget the
town, and in town we despise the country. "Beyond Hyde
Park," says Sir Fopling Flutter, "all is a desert." All that part
of the map that we do not see before us is blank. The world
in our conceit of it is not much bigger than a nutshell. It is not
one prospect expanded into another, county joined to county,
kingdom to kingdom, lands to seas, making an image voluminous and vast;—the mind can form no larger idea of space
than the eye can take in at a single glance. The rest is a name
written in a map, a calculation of arithmetic. For instance,
what is the true signification of that immense mass of territory
and population known by the name of China to us? An inch of
pasteboard on a wooden globe, of no more account than a
China orange! Things near us are seen of the size of life: things
at a distance are diminished to the size of the understanding.
We measure the universe by ourselves, and even comprehend
the texture of our own being only piecemeal. In this way,
however, we remember an infinity of things and places. The
mind is like a mechanical instrument that plays a great variety
of tunes, but it must play them in succession. One idea recalls
another, but it at the same time excludes all others. In trying
to renew old recollections, we cannot as it were unfold the
whole web of our existence; we must pick out the single
threads. So in coming to a place where we have formerly
lived, and with which we have intimate associations, every one
must have found that the feeling grows more vivid the nearer
we approach the spot, from the mere anticipation of the actual
impression: we remember circumstances, feelings, persons,
faces, names that we had not thought of for years; but for the
time all the rest of the world is forgotten!—To return to the
question I have quitted above.

I have no objection to go to see ruins, aqueducts, pictures, in
company with a friend or a party, but rather the contrary, for
the former reason reversed. They are intelligible matters, and

will bear talking about. The sentiment here is not tacit, but communicable and overt. Salisbury Plain is barren of criticism, but Stonehenge will bear a discussion antiquarian, picturesque, and philosophical. In setting out on a party of pleasure, the first consideration always is where we shall go to: in taking a solitary ramble, the question is what we shall meet with by the way. "The mind is its own place"; nor are we anxious to arrive at the end of our journey. I can myself do the honors indifferently well to works of art and curiosity. I once took a party to Oxford with no mean *éclat*—showed them that seat of the Muses at a distance,

> With glistering spires and pinnacles adorn'd—

descanted on the learned air that breathes from the grassy quadrangles and stone walls of halls and colleges—was at home in the Bodleian; and at Blenheim quite superseded the powdered cicerone that attended us and that pointed in vain with his wand to commonplace beauties in matchless pictures. As another exception to the above reasoning, I should not feel confident in venturing on a journey in a foreign country without a companion. I should want at intervals to hear the sound of my own language. There is an involuntary antipathy in the mind of an Englishman to foreign manners and notions that requires the assistance of social sympathy to carry it off. As the distance from home increases, this relief, which was at first a luxury, becomes a passion and an appetite. A person would almost feel stifled to find himself in the deserts of Arabia without friends and countrymen: there must be allowed to be something in the view of Athens or old Rome that claims the utterance of speech; and I own that the Pyramids are too mighty for any single contemplation. In such situations, so opposite to all one's ordinary train of ideas, one seems a species by one's-self, a limb torn off from society, unless one can meet with instant fellowship and support. Yet I did not feel this want or craving very pressing once, when I first set my foot on the laughing shores of France. Calais was peopled with novelty and delight. The confused, busy murmur of the place was like oil and wine poured into my ears; nor did the mariners' hymn, which was sung from the top of an old crazy vessel in the harbor, as the sun went down, send an alien sound into my soul. I only breathed the air of general humanity. I walked over "the vine-covered hills and gay regions of France," erect and satisfied; for the image of man was not cast down and chained to the foot of arbitrary thrones: I was at no loss for language, for that of all the great schools of painting was open to me. The whole is vanished like a shade. Pictures, heroes, glory, freedom, all are fled: nothing remains but the Bourbons and the French people!—There is undoubtedly a sensation in traveling into foreign parts that is to be had nowhere else: but it is more pleasing at the time than lasting. It is too remote from our habitual associations to be a common topic of discourse or reference, and, like a dream or another state of existence, does not piece into our daily modes of life. It is an animated but a momentary hallucination. It demands an effort to exchange our actual for our ideal identity; and to feel the pulse of our old transports revive very keenly, we must "jump" all our present comforts and connections. Our romantic and itinerant character is not to be domesticated. Dr. Johnson remarked how little foreign travel added to the facilities of conversation in those who had been abroad. In fact, the time we have spent there is both delightful, and, in one sense, instructive; but it appears to be cut out of our substantial, downright existence, and never to join kindly on to it. We are not the same, but another, and perhaps more enviable individual, all the time we are out of our own country. We are lost to ourselves, as well as our friends. So the poet somewhat quaintly sings,

> Out of my country and myself I go.

Those who wish to forget painful thoughts, do well to absent themselves for a while from the ties and objects that recall them: but we can be said only to fulfil our destiny in the place that gave us birth. I should on this account like well enough to spend the whole of my life in traveling abroad, if I could anywhere borrow another life to spend afterwards at home!

ON THE FEELING OF
IMMORTALITY IN YOUTH

"Life is a pure flame, and we live by an invisible sun within us."—SIR THOMAS BROWNE

NO YOUNG MAN BELIEVES he shall ever die. It was a saying of my brother's, and a fine one. There is a feeling of Eternity in youth, which makes us amends for everything. To be young is to be as one of the Immortal Gods. One half of time indeed is flown—the other half remains in store for us with all its countless treasures; for there is no line drawn, and we see no limit to our hopes and wishes. We make the coming age our own.—

The vast, the unbounded prospect lies before us.

Death, old age, are words without a meaning, that pass by us like the idle air which we regard not. Others may have undergone, or may still be liable to them—we "bear a charmed life," which laughs to scorn all such sickly fancies. As in setting out on a delightful journey, we strain our eager gaze forward—

Bidding the lovely scenes at distance hail,—

and see no end to the landscape, new objects presenting themselves as we advance; so, in the commencement of life, we set no bounds to our inclinations, nor to the unrestricted opportunities of gratifying them. We have as yet found no obstacle, no disposition to flag; and it seems that we can go on so for ever. We look round in a new world, full of life, and motion, and ceaseless progress; and feel in ourselves all the vigour and spirit to keep pace with it, and do not foresee from any present symptoms how we shall be left behind in the natural course of things, decline into old age, and drop into the grave. It is the simplicity, and as it were *abstractedness* of our feelings in youth, that (so to speak) identifies us with nature, and (our experience being slight and our passions strong) deludes us into a belief of being immortal like it. Our short-lived connection with existence, we fondly flatter ourselves, is an indissoluble and lasting union—a honey-moon that knows neither coldness, jar, nor separation. As infants smile and sleep, we are rocked in the cradle of our wayward fancies, and lulled into security by the roar of the universe around us—we quaff the cup of life with eager haste without draining it, instead of which it only overflows the more—objects press around us, filling the mind with their magnitude and with the throng of desires that wait upon them, so that we have no room for the thoughts of death. From that plenitude of our being, we cannot change all at once to dust and ashes, we cannot imagine "this sensible, warm motion, to become a kneaded clod"—we are too much dazzled by the brightness of the waking dream around us to look into the darkness of the tomb. We no more see our end than our beginning: the one is lost in oblivion and vacancy, as the other is hid from us by the crowd and hurry of approaching events. Or the grim shadow is seen lingering in the horizon, which we are doomed never to overtake, or whose last, faint, glimmering outline touches upon Heaven and translates us to the skies! Nor would the hold that life has taken of us permit us to detach our thoughts from present objects and pursuits, even if we would. What is there more opposed to health, than sickness; to strength and beauty, than decay and dissolution; to the active search of knowledge than mere oblivion? Or is there none of the usual advantage to bar the approach of Death, and mock his idle threats; Hope supplies their place, and draws a veil over the abrupt termination of all our cherished schemes. While the spirit of youth remains unimpaired, ere the "wine of life is drank up" we are like people intoxicated or in a fever, who are hurried away by the violence of their own sensations: it is only as present objects begin to pall upon the sense, as we have been disappointed in our favourite pursuits, cut off from our closest ties, that passion loosens its hold upon the breast, that we by degrees become weaned from the world, and allow ourselves to contemplate, "as in a glass, darkly," the possibility of parting with it for good. The example of others, the voice of experience, has no effect upon us whatever.

Casualties we must avoid: the slow and deliberate advances of age we can play at *hide-and-seek* with. We think ourselves too lusty and too nimble for that blear-eyed decrepit old gentleman to catch us. Like the foolish fat scullion, in Sterne, when she hears that Master Bobby is dead, our only reflection is—"So am not I!" The idea of death, instead of staggering our confidence, rather seems to strengthen and enhance our possession and our enjoyment of life. Others may fall around us like leaves, or be mowed down like flowers by the scythe of Time: these are but tropes and figures to the unreflecting ears and overweening presumption of youth. It is not till we see the flowers of Love, Hope, and Joy, withering around us, and our own pleasures cut up by the roots, that we bring the moral home to ourselves, that we abate something of the wanton extravagance of our pretensions, or that the emptiness and dreariness of the prospect before us reconciles us to the stillness of the grave!

> Life! thou strange thing, that hast a power to feel
> Thou art, and to perceive that others are.

Well might the poet begin his indignant invective against an art, whose professed object is its destruction, with this animated apostrophe to life. Life is indeed a strange gift, and its privileges are most miraculous. Nor is it singular that when the splendid boon is first granted us, our gratitude, our admiration, and our delight should prevent us from reflecting on our own nothingness, or from thinking it will ever be recalled. Our first and strongest impressions are taken from the mighty scene that is opened to us, and we very innocently transfer its durability as well as magnificence to ourselves. So newly found, we cannot make up our minds to parting with it yet and at least put off that consideration to an indefinite term. Like a clown at a fair, we are full of amazement and rapture, and have no thoughts of going home, or that it will soon be night. We know our existence only from external objects, and we measure it by them. We can never be satisfied with gazing; and nature will still want us to look on and applaud. Otherwise, the sumptuous entertainment, "the feast of reason and the flow of soul," to which they were invited seems little better than a mockery and a cruel insult. We do not go from a play till the scene is ended, and the lights are ready to be extinguished. But the fair face of things still shines on; shall we be called away before the curtain falls, or ere we have scarce had a glimpse of what is going on? Like children, our step-mother Nature holds us up to see the raree-show of the universe; and then, as if life were a burthen to support, lets us instantly down again. Yet in that short interval, what "brave sublunary things" does not the spectacle unfold; like a bubble, at one minute reflecting the universe, and the next, shook to air!—To see the golden sun and the azure sky, the outstretched ocean, to walk upon the green earth, and to be lord of a thousand creatures, to look down giddy precipices or over distant flowery vales, to see the world spread out under one's finger in a map, to bring the stars near, to view the smallest insects in a miscroscope, to read history, and witness the revolutions of empires and the succession of generations, to hear of the glory of Sidon and Tyre, or Babylon and Susa, as of a faded pageant, and to say all these were, and are now nothing, to think that we exist in such a point of time, and in such a corner of space, to be at once spectators and a part of the moving scene, to watch the return of the seasons, of spring and autumn, to hear

> —The stockdove plain amid the forest deep,
> That drowsy rustles to the sighing gale—

to traverse desert wildernesses, to listen to the midnight choir, to visit lighted halls, or plunge into the dungeon's gloom, or sit in crowded theatres and see life itself mocked, to feel heat and cold, pleasure and pain, right and wrong, truth and falsehood, to study the works of art and refine the sense of beauty to agony, to worship fame and to dream of immortality, to have read Shakespeare and belong to the same species as Sir Isaac Newton; to be and to do all this, and then in a moment to be nothing, to have it all snatched from one like a juggler's ball or a phantasmagoria; there is something revolting and incredible to sense in the transition, and no wonder that, aided by youth and warm blood, and the flush of enthusiasm, the mind contrives for a long time to reject it with disdain and loathing as a monstrous and improbable fiction, like a monkey on a house-top, that is loath, amidst its fine discoveries and specious antics, to be tumbled head-long into the street, and crushed to atoms, the sport and laughter of the multitude!

The change, from the commencement to the close of life, appears like a fable, after it has taken place; how should we treat it otherwise than as a chimera before it has come to pass? There are some things that happened so long ago, places or persons we have formerly seen, of which such dim traces remain, we hardly know whether it was sleeping or waking they occurred; they are like dreams within the dream of life, a mist, a film before the eye of memory, which, as we try to re-call them more distinctly, elude our notice altogether. It is but natural that the lone interval that we thus look back upon, should have appeared long and endless in prospect. There are others so distinct and fresh, they seem but of yesterday—their very vividness might be deemed a pledge of their permanence. Then, however far back our impressions may go, we find others still older (for our years are multiplied in youth); descriptions of scenes that we had read, and people before our time, Priam and the Trojan war; and even then, Nestor was old and dwelt delighted on his youth, and spoke of the race of heroes that were no more;—what wonder that, seeing this long line of being pictured in our minds, and reviving as it were in us, we should give ourselves involuntary credit for an indeterminate period of existence? In the Cathedral at Peterborough there is a monument to Mary, Queen of Scots, at which I used to gaze when a boy, while the events of the period, all that had happened since, passed in review before me. If all this mass of feeling and imagination could be crowded into a moment's compass, what might not the whole of life be supposed to contain? We are heirs of the past; we count upon the future as our natural reversion. Besides, there are some of our early impressions so exquisitely tempered, it appears that they must always last—nothing can add to or take away from their sweetness and purity—the first breath of spring, the hyacinth dipped in the dew, the mild lustre of the evening-star, the rainbow after a storm—while we have the full enjoyment of these, we must be young; and what can ever alter us in this respect? Truth, friendship, love, books, are also proof against the canker of time; and while we live but for them, we can never grow old. We take out a new lease of existence from the objects on which we set our affections, and become abstracted, impassive, immortal in them. We cannot conceive how certain sentiments should ever decay or grow cold in our breasts; and, consequently, to maintain them in their first youthful glow and vigour, the flame of life must continue to burn as bright as ever, or rather, they are the fuel that feed the sacred lamp, that kindle "the purple light of love," and spread a golden cloud around our heads! Again, we not only flourish and survive in our affections (in which we will not listen to the possibility of a change, any more than we foresee the wrinkles on the brow of a mistress), but we have a farther guarantee against the thoughts of death in our favourite studies and pursuits, and in their continual advance. Art we know is long; life, we feel, should be so too. We see no end of the difficulties we have to encounter: perfection is slow of attainment, and we must have time to accomplish it in. Rubens complained that when he had just learnt his art, he was snatched away from it: we trust we shall be more fortunate! A wrinkle in an old head takes whole days to finish it properly: but to catch "the Raphael grace, the Guido air," no limit should be put to our endeavours. What a prospect for the future! What a task we have entered upon! and shall we be arrested in the middle of it? We do not reckon our time thus employed lost, or our pains thrown away, or our progress slow—we do not droop or grow tired, but "gain new vigour at our endless task";—and shall Time grudge us the opportunity to finish what we have auspiciously begun, and have formed a sort of compact with nature to achieve? The fame of the great names we look up to is also imperishable; and shall not we, who contemplate it with such intense yearnings, imbibe a portion of ethereal fire, the *divinae particula aurae*, which nothing can extinguish? I remember to have looked at a print of Rembrandt for hours together, without being conscious of the flight of time, trying to resolve it into its component parts, to connect its strong and sharp gradations, to learn the secret of its reflected lights, and found neither satiety nor pause in the prosecution of my studies. The print over which I was poring would last long enough; why should the idea in my mind, which was finer, more impalpable, perish before it? At this, I redoubled the ardour of my pursuit, and by the very subtlety and refinement of my inquiries, seemed to bespeak for them an exemption from corruption and the rude grasp of Death.

Objects, on our first acquaintance with them, have that singleness and integrity of impression that it seems as if nothing could destroy or obliterate them, so firmly are they stamped and rivetted on the brain. We repose on them with a sort of voluptuous indolence, in full faith and boundless confidence. We are absorbed in the present moment, or return to the same point—idling away a great deal of time in youth, thinking we have enough and to spare. There is often a local feeling in the air, which is as fixed as if it were of marble; we loiter in dim cloisters, losing ourselves in thought and in their glimmering arches; a winding road before us seems as long as the journey of life, and as full of events. Time and experience dissipate this illusion; and by reducing them to detail, circumscribe the limits of our expectations. It is only as the pageant of life passes by and the masques turn their backs upon us, that we see through the deception, or believe that the train will have an end. In many cases, the slow progress and monotonous texture of our lives, before we mingle with the world and are embroiled in its affairs, has a tendency to aid the same feeling. We have a difficulty, when left to ourselves, and without the resource of books or some more lively pursuit, to "beguile the slow and creeping hours of time," and argue that if it moves on always at this tedious snail's-pace, it can never come to an end. We are willing to skip over certain portions of it that separate us from favourite objects, that irritate ourselves at the unnecessary delay. The young are prodigal of life from a superabundance of it; the old are tenacious on the same score, because they have little left, and cannot enjoy even what remains of it.

For my part, I set out in life with the French Revolution, and that event had considerable influence on my early feelings, as on those of others. Youth was then doubly such. It was the dawn of a new era, a new impulse had been given to men's minds, and the sun of Liberty rose upon the sun of Life in the same day, and both were proud to run their race together. Little did I dream, while my first hopes and wishes went hand in hand with those of the human race, that long before my eyes should close, that dawn would be overcast, and set once more in the night of despotism—"total eclipse!" Happy that I did not. I felt for years, and during the best part of my exist-ence, *heart-whole* in that cause, and triumphed in the tri-umphs over the enemies of man! At that time, while the fairest aspirations of the human mind seemed about to be realized, ere the image of man was defaced and his breast mangled in scorn, philosophy took a higher, poetry could afford a deeper range. At that time, to read the *Robbers*, was indeed delicious, and to hear

> From the dungeon of the tower time-rent,
> That fearful voice, a famish'd father's cry,

could be borne only amidst the fulness of hope, the crash of the fall of the strongholds of power, and the exulting sounds of the march of human freedom. What feelings the death-scene in *Don Carlos* sent into the soul! In that headlong career of lofty enthusiasm, and the joyous opening of the prospects of the world and our own, the thought of death crossing it smote doubly cold upon the mind; there was a stifling sense of oppression and confinement, an impatience of our present knowledge, a desire to grasp the whole of our existence in one strong embrace, to sound the mystery of life and death, and in order to put an end to the agony of doubt and dread, to burst through our prison-house, and confront the King of Terrors in his grisly palace! . . . As I was writing out this passage, my miniature-picture when a child lay on the mantle-piece, and I took it out of the case to look at it. I could perceive few traces of myself in it; but there was the same placid brow, the dimpled mouth, the same timid, inquisitive glance as ever. But its careless smile did not seem to reproach me with having become a recreant to the sentiments that were then sown in my mind, or with having written a sentence that could call up a blush in this image of ingenuous youth!

"That time is past with all its giddy raptures." Since the future was barred to my progress, I have turned for consolation to the past, gathering up the fragments of my early recollections, and putting them into a form that might live. It is thus, that when we find our personal and substantial identity vanishing from us, we strive to gain a reflected and substituted one in our thoughts: we do not like to perish wholly, and wish to bequeath our names at least to posterity. As long as we can keep alive our cherished thoughts and nearest interests in the minds of others, we do not appear to have retired altogether from the stage, we still occupy a place in the estimation of mankind, exercise a powerful influence over them, and it is only our bodies that are trampled into dust or dispersed to air. Our darling speculations still find favour and encouragement, and we make as good a figure in the eyes of our descendants, nay, perhaps, a better than we did in our lifetime. This is one point gained; the demands of our self-love are so far satisfied. Besides, if by the proofs of intellectual superiority we survive ourselves in this world, by exemplary virtue or unblemished faith we are taught to ensure an interest in another and a higher state of being, and to anticipate at the same time the applauses of men and angels.

> Even from the tomb the voice of nature cries;
> Even in our ashes live their wonted fires.

As we advance in life, we acquire a keener sense of the value of time. Nothing else, indeed, seems of any consequence; and we become misers in this respect. We try to arrest its few last tottering steps, and to make it linger on the brink of the grave. We can never leave off wondering how that which has ever been should cease to be, and would still live on, that we may wonder at our own shadow, and when "all the life of life is flown," dwell on the retrospect of the past. This is accompanied by a mechanical tenaciousness of whatever we possess, by a distrust and a sense of fallacious hollowness in all we see. Instead of the full, pulpy feeling of youth, everything is flat and insipid. The world is a painted witch, that puts us off with false shows and tempting appearances. The ease, the jocund gaiety, the unsuspecting security of youth are fled: nor can we, without flying in the face of common sense,

> From the last dregs of life, hope to receive
> What its first sprightly runnings could not give.

If we can slip out of the world without notice or mischance, can tamper with bodily infirmity, and frame our minds to the becoming composure of *still-life*, before we sink into total insensibility, it is as much as we ought to expect. We do not in the regular course of nature die all at once: we have mouldered away gradually long before; faculty after faculty, attachment after attachment, we are torn from ourselves piecemeal while living; year after year takes something from us; and death only consigns the last remnant of what we were to the grave. The revulsion is not so great, and a quiet *euthanasia* is a winding-up of the plot, that is not out of reason or nature.

That we should thus in a manner outlive ourselves, and dwindle imperceptibly into nothing, is not surprising, when even in our prime the strongest impressions leave so little traces of themselves behind, and the last object is driven out by the succeeding one. How little effect is produced on us at any time by the books we have read, the scenes we have witnessed, the sufferings we have gone through! Think only of the variety of feelings we experience in reading an interesting romance, or being present at a fine play—what beauty, what sublimity, what soothing, what heart-rending emotions! You would suppose these would last for ever, or at least subdue the mind to a correspondent tone and harmony—while we turn over the page, while the scene is passing before us, it seems as if nothing could ever after shake our resolution, that "treason domestic, foreign levy, nothing could touch us farther!" The first splash of mud we get, on entering the street, the first pettifogging shop-keeper that cheats us out of twopence, and the whole vanishes clean out of our remembrance, and we become the idle prey of the most petty and annoying circumstances. The mind soars by an effort to the grand and lofty: it is at home in the grovelling, the disagreeable, and the little. This happens in the height and heyday of our existence, when novelty gives a stronger impulse to the blood and takes a faster hold of the brain, (I have known the impression on coming out of a gallery of pictures then last half a day)—as we grow old, we become more feeble and querulous, every object "reverbs its own hollowness," and both worlds are not enough to satisfy the peevish importunity and extravagant presumption of our desires! There are a few superior, happy beings, who are born with a temper exempt from every trifling annoyance. This spirit sits serene and smiling as in its native skies, and a divine harmony (whether heard or not) plays around them. This is to be at peace. Without this, it is in vain to fly into deserts, or to build a hermitage on the top of rocks, if regret and ill-humour follow us there: and with this, it is needless to make the experiment. The only true retirement is that of the heart; the only true leisure is the repose of the passions. To such persons it makes little difference whether they are young or old; and they die as they have lived, with graceful resignation.

Washington Irving

1783 · 1859

Washington Irving was the first major figure in American Literature, even though his style was that of English writers of the eighteenth century and his subjects were only occasionally American. He was born in New York and brought up there, but spent many of his mature years in Europe. His History of New York by Diedrich Knickerbocker *(1809) and many sketches and essays give him first rank among American humorists before Mark Twain. "The Angler" is one of the pieces that make up* The Sketch Book *(1820).*

THE ANGLER

This day dame Nature seem'd in love,
The lusty sap began to move,
Fresh juice did stir th' embracing vines,
And birds had drawn their valentines.
The jealous trout that low did lie,
Rose at a well-dissembled fly.
There stood my friend, with patient skill,
Attending of his trembling quill.—SIR H. WOTTON.

IT IS SAID THAT MANY AN UNLUCKY URCHIN is induced to run away from his family, and betake himself to a seafaring life, from reading the history of Robinson Crusoe; and I suspect that, in like manner, many of those worthy gentlemen who are given to haunt the sides of pastoral streams with anglerods in hand, may trace the origin of their passion to the seductive pages of honest Izaak Walton. I recollect studying his *Complete Angler* several years since, in company with a knot of friends in America, and, moreover, that we were all completely bitten with the angling mania. It was early in the year; but as soon as the weather was auspicious, and that the spring began to melt into the verge of summer, we took rod in hand and sallied into the country, as stark mad as was ever Don Quixote from reading books of chivalry.

One of our party had equalled the Don in the fulness of his equipments; being attired *cap-a-pie* for the enterprise. He wore a broad-skirted fustian coat, perplexed with half a hundred pockets; a pair of stout shoes, and leathern gaiters; a basket slung on one side for fish; a patent rod, a landing-net, and a score of other inconveniences only to be found in the true angler's armory. Thus harnessed for the field, he was as great a matter of stare and wonderment among the country folk, who had never seen a regular angler, as was the steel-clad hero of La Mancha among the goat-herds of the Sierra Morena.

Our first essay was along a mountain brook, among the highlands of the Hudson—a most unfortunate place for the execution of those piscatory tactics which had been invented along the velvet margins of quiet English rivulets. It was one of those wild streams that lavish, among our romantic solitudes, unheeded beauties, enough to fill the sketch-book of a hunter of the picturesque. Sometimes it would leap down rocky shelves, making small cascades, over which the trees threw their broad balancing sprays, and long nameless weeds hung in fringes from the impending banks, dripping with diamond drops. Sometimes it would brawl and fret along a ravine in the matted shade of a forest, filling it with murmurs; and after this termagant career, would steal forth into open day with the most placid demure face imaginable; as I have seen some pestilent shrew of a housewife, after filling her home with uproar and ill-humour, come dimpling out of doors, swimming, and curtsying, and smiling upon all the world.

How smoothly would this vagrant brook glide, at such times, through some bosom of green meadow-land, among

the mountains; where the quiet was only interrupted by the
occasional tinkling of a bell from the lazy cattle among the
clover, or the sound of a wood-cutter's axe from the neighbouring forest!

For my part, I was always a bungler at all kinds of sport
that required either patience or adroitness, and had not angled
above half an hour, before I had completely "satisfied the
sentiment," and convinced myself of the truth of Izaak Walton's opinion, that angling is something like poetry—a man
must be born to it. I hooked myself instead of the fish; tangled
my line in every tree; lost my bait; broke my rod; until I gave
up the attempt in despair, and passed the day under the trees,
reading old Izaak; satisfied that it was his fascinating vein of
honest simplicity and rural feeling that had bewitched me, and
not the passion for angling. My companions, however, were
more persevering in their delusion. I have them at this moment before my eyes, stealing along the border of the brook,
where it lay open to the day, or was merely fringed by shrubs
and bushes. I see the bittern rising with hollow scream, as they
break in upon his rarely-invaded haunt; the kingfisher watching them suspiciously from his dry tree that overhangs the deep
black mill-pond, in the gorge of the hills; the tortoise letting
himself slip sideways from off the stone or log on which he
is sunning himself; and the panic-struck frog plumping in
headlong as they approach, and spreading an alarm throughout
the watery world around.

I recollect, also, that, after toiling and watching and creeping about for the greater part of a day, with scarcely any
success, in spite of all our admirable apparatus, a lubberly
country urchin came down from the hills, with a rod made
from a branch of a tree, a few yards of twine, and, as heaven
shall help me! I believe a crooked pin for a hook, baited with
a vile earth-worm—and in half an hour caught more fish than
we had nibbles throughout the day.

But, above all, I recollect the "good, honest, wholesome,
hungry" repast, which we made under a beech-tree just by
a spring of pure sweet water, that stole out of the side of a
hill; and how, when it was over, one of the party read old

Izaak Walton's scene with the milk-maid, while I lay on the grass and built castles in a bright pile of clouds, until I fell asleep. All this may appear like mere egotism; yet I cannot refrain from uttering these recollections which are passing like a strain of music over my mind, and have been called up by an agreeable scene which I witnessed not long since.

In a morning's stroll along the banks of the Alun, a beautiful little stream which flows down from the Welsh hills and throws itself into the Dee, my attention was attracted to a group seated on the margin. On approaching, I found it to consist of a veteran angler and two rustic disciples. The former was an old fellow with a wooden leg, with clothes very much, but very carefully patched, betokening poverty, honestly come by, and decently maintained. His face bore the marks of former storms, but present fair weather; its furrows had been worn into a habitual smile; his iron-gray locks hung about his ears, and he had altogether the good-humoured air of a constitutional philosopher, who was disposed to take the world as it went. One of his companions was a ragged wight, with the skulking look of an arrant poacher, and I'll warrant could find his way to any gentleman's fish-pond in the neighbourhood in the darkest night. The other was a tall, awkward, country lad, with a lounging gait, and apparently somewhat of a rustic beau. The old man was busied examining the maw of a trout which he had just killed, to discover by its contents what insects were seasonable for bait; and was lecturing on the subject to his companions, who appeared to listen with infinite deference. I have a kind feeling toward all "brothers of the angle," ever since I read Izaak Walton. They are men, he affirms, of a "mild, sweet, and peaceable spirit"; and my esteem for them has been increased since I met with an old *Tretyse of fishing with the Angle*, in which are set forth many of the maxims of their inoffensive fraternity. "Take goode hede," sayth this honest little tretyse, "that in going about your disportes ye open no man's gates but that ye shet them again. Also ye shall not use this foresaid crafti disport for no covetousness to the increasing and sparing of your money only, but principally for your solace and to cause the helth of your body and specyally of your soule."*

I thought that I could perceive in the veteran angler before me an exemplification of what I had read; and there was a cheerful contentedness in his looks, that quite drew me towards him. I could not but remark the gallant manner in which he stumped from one part of the brook to another; waving his rod in the air, to keep the line from dragging on the ground, or catching among the bushes; and the adroitness with which he would throw his fly to any particular place; sometimes skimming it lightly along a little rapid; sometimes casting it into one of those dark holes made by a twisted root or overhanging bank, in which the large trout are apt to lurk. In the meanwhile, he was giving instructions to his two disciples; showing them the manner in which they should handle their rods, fix their flies, and play them along the surface of the stream. The scene brought to my mind the instructions of the sage Piscator to his scholar. The country around was of that pastoral kind which Walton is fond of describing. It was a part of the great plain of Cheshire, close by the beautiful vale of Gessford, and just where the inferior Welsh hills begin to swell up from among fresh-smelling meadows. The day, too, like that recorded in his work, was mild and sunshiny; with now and then a soft dropping shower, that sowed the whole earth with diamonds.

I soon fell into conversation with the old angler, and was so much entertained, that, under pretext of receiving instructions in his art, I kept company with him almost the whole day; wandering along the banks of the stream, and listening to his talk. He was very communicative, having all the easy garrulity of cheerful old age; and I fancy was a little flattered

* *From this same treatise, it would appear that angling is a more industrious and devout employment than it is generally considered. "For when ye purpose to go on your disportes in fishynge, ye will not desyre greatlye many persons with you, which might let you of your game. And that ye may serve God devoutly in sayinge effectually your customable prayers. And thus doyinge, ye shall eschew and also avoyde many vices, as ydleness, which is a principall cause to induce man to many other vices, as it is right well known."*

by having an opportunity of displaying his piscatory lore; for who does not like now and then to play the sage?

He had been much of a rambler in his day; and had passed some years of his youth in America, particularly in Savannah, where he had entered into trade, and had been ruined by the indiscretion of a partner. He had afterwards experienced many ups and downs in life, until he got into the navy, where his leg was carried away by a cannon-ball, at the battle of Camperdown. This was the only stroke of real good fortune he had ever experienced, for it got him a pension, which, together with some small paternal property, brought him in a revenue of nearly forty pounds. On this he retired to his native village, where he lived quietly and independently, and devoted the remainder of his life to the "noble art of angling."

I found that he had read Izaak Walton attentively, and he seemed to have imbibed all his simple frankness and prevalent good-humour. Though he had been sorely buffeted about the world, he was satisfied that the world, in itself, was good and beautiful. Though he had been as roughly used in different countries as a poor sheep that is fleeced by every hedge and thicket, yet he spoke of every nation with candour and kindness, appearing to look only on the good side of things: and above all, he was almost the only man I had ever met with, who had been an unfortunate adventurer in America, and had honesty and magnanimity enough to take the fault to his own door, and not to curse the country.

The lad that was receiving his instructions, I learnt, was the son and heir apparent of a fat old widow, who kept the village inn, and of course a youth of some expectation, and much courted by the idle, gentleman-like personages of the place. In taking him under his care, therefore, the old man had probably an eye to a privileged corner in the taproom, and an occasional cup of cheerful ale free of expense.

There is certainly something in angling, if we could forget, which anglers are apt to do, the cruelties and tortures inflicted on worms and insects, that tends to produce a gentleness of spirit, and a pure serenity of mind. As the English are methodical even in their recreations, and are the most scientific of sportsmen, it has been reduced among them to perfect rule and system. Indeed, it is an amusement peculiarly adapted to the mild and cultivated scenery of England, where every roughness has been softened away from the landscape. It is delightful to saunter along those limpid streams which wander, like veins of silver, through the bosom of this beautiful country; leading one through a diversity of small home scenery; sometimes winding through ornamented grounds; sometimes brimming along through rich pasturage, where the fresh green is mingled with sweet-smelling flowers; sometimes venturing in sight of villages and hamlets; and then running capriciously away into shady retirements. The sweetness and serenity of nature, and the quiet watchfulness of the sport, gradually bring on pleasant fits of musing; which are now and then agreeably interrupted by the song of a bird; the distant whistle of the peasant; or perhaps the vagary of some fish, leaping out of the still water, and skimming transiently about its glassy surface. "When I would beget content," says Izaak Walton, "and increase confidence in the power and wisdom and providence of Almighty God, I will walk the meadows by some gliding stream, and there contemplate the lilies that take no care, and those very many other little living creatures that are not only created, but fed, (man knows not how) by the goodness of the God of nature, and therefore trust in him."

I cannot forbear to give another quotation from one of those ancient champions of angling, which breathes the same innocent and happy spirit:

> Let me live harmlessly, and near the brink
>   Of Trent or Avon have a dwelling-place:
> Where I may see my quill, or cork down sink,
>   With eager bite of Pike, or Bleak, or Dace.
> And on the world and my Creator think:
>   While some men strive ill-gotten goods t' embrace;
> And others spend their time in base excess
>   Of wine, or worse, in war or wantonness.

Let them that will, these pastimes still pursue,
And on such pleasing fancies feed their fill,
So I the fields and meadows green may view,
And daily by fresh rivers walk at will
Among the daisies and the violets blue,
Red hyacinth and yellow daffodil.—J. DAVORS.

On parting with the old angler, I inquired after his place of abode, and happening to be in the neighbourhood of the village a few evenings afterwards, I had the curiosity to seek him out. I found him living in a small cottage, containing only one room, but a perfect curiosity in its method and arrangement. It was on the skirts of the village, on a green bank, a little back from the road, with a small garden in front, stocked with kitchen-herbs, and adorned with a few flowers. The whole front of the cottage was overrun with a honeysuckle. On the top was a ship for a weathercock. The interior was fitted up in a truly nautical style, his ideas of comfort and convenience having been acquired on the berth-deck of a man-of-war. A hammock was slung from the ceiling, which in the day-time was lashed up so as to take but little room. From the centre of the chamber hung a model of a ship, of his own workmanship. Two or three chairs, a table, and a large sea-chest, formed the principal moveables. About the wall were stuck up naval ballads, such as Admiral Hosier's Ghost, All in the Downs, and Tom Bowling, intermingled with pictures of sea-fights, among which the battle of Camperdown held a distinguished place. The mantelpiece was decorated with seashells; over which hung a quadrant, flanked by two woodcuts of most bitter-looking naval commanders. His implements for angling were carefully disposed on nails and hooks about the room. On a shelf was arranged his library, containing a work on angling, much worn; a bible covered with canvas; an odd volume or two of voyages; a nautical almanac; and a book of songs.

His family consisted of a large black cat with one eye, and a parrot which he had caught and tamed, and educated himself, in the course of one of his voyages; and which uttered a variety of sea phrases, with the hoarse rattling tone of a veteran boatswain. The establishment reminded me of that of the renowned Robinson Crusoe; it was kept in neat order, every thing being "stowed away" with the regularity of a ship of war; and he informed me that he "scoured the deck every morning, and swept it between meals."

I found him seated on a bench before the door, smoking his pipe in the soft evening sunshine. His cat was purring soberly on the threshold, and his parrot describing some strange evolutions in an iron ring, that swung in the centre of his cage. He had been angling all day, and gave me a history of his sport with as much minuteness as a general would talk over a campaign; being particularly animated in relating the manner in which he had taken a large trout, which had completely tasked all his skill and wariness, and which he had sent as a trophy to mine hostess of the inn.

How comforting it is to see a cheerful and contented old age; and to behold a poor fellow, like this, after being tempest-tost through life, safely moored in a snug and quiet harbour in the evening of his days! His happiness, however, sprung from within himself, and was independent of external circumstances; for he had that inexhaustible good-nature, which is the most precious gift of Heaven; spreading itself like oil over the troubled sea of thought, and keeping the mind smooth and equable in the roughest weather.

On inquiring further about him, I learnt that he was a universal favourite in the village, and the oracle of the tap-room; where he delighted the rustics with his songs, and, like Sinbad, astonished them with his stories of strange lands, and shipwrecks, and sea-fights. He was much noticed too by gentlemen sportsmen of the neighbourhood; had taught several of them the art of angling; and was a privileged visitor to their kitchens. The whole tenor of his life was quiet and inoffensive, being principally passed about the neighbouring streams, when the weather and season were favourable; and at other times he employed himself at home, preparing his fishing tackle for the next campaign, or manufacturing rods, nets, and flies, for his patrons and pupils among the gentry.

He was a regular attendant at church on Sundays, though

he generally fell asleep during the sermon. He had made it his particular request that when he died he should be buried in a green spot, which he could see from his seat in church, and which he had marked out ever since he was a boy, and had thought of when far from home on the raging sea, in danger of being food for the fishes—it was the spot where his father and mother had been buried.

I have done, for I fear that my reader is growing weary; but I could not refrain from drawing the picture of this worthy "brother of the angle"; who has made me more than ever in love with the theory, though I fear I shall never be adroit in the practice of his art; and I will conclude this rambling sketch in the words of honest Izaak Walton, by craving the blessing of St. Peter's master upon my reader; "and upon all that are true lovers of virtue; and dare trust in his providence; and be quiet; and go a angling."

Leigh Hunt

1784 · 1859

James Henry Leigh Hunt, English journalist, poet,
critic, and playwright, appears at his best in the
periodical essays which he wrote for The Examiner,
The Indicator, *and other publications which he*
edited. A liberal and an idealist, he paid for holding
independent views by suffering several prosecutions
and even a two-year jail sentence, imposed in 1813,
for an article reflecting on the Prince Regent.
During his own time, his reputation was great,
but it has diminished in comparison with that
of Lamb, Hazlitt, Coleridge and others, all
of whom were his friends and acquaintances.

DEATHS OF LITTLE CHILDREN

A GRECIAN PHILOSOPHER being asked why he wept for the death of his son, since the sorrow was in vain, replied, "I weep on that very account." And his answer became his wisdom. It is only for sophists to pretend that we, whose eyes contain the fountains of tears, need never give way to them. It would be unwise not to do so on some occasions. Sorrow unlocks them in her balmy moods. The first bursts may be bitter and overwhelming; but the soil on which they pour would be worse without them. They refresh the fever of the soul—the dry misery which parches the countenance into furrows, and renders us liable to our most terrible "flesh-quakes."

There are sorrows, it is true, so great, that to give them some of the ordinary vents is to run a hazard of being overthrown. These we must rather strengthen ourselves to resist, or bow quietly and drily down, in order to let them pass over us, as the traveller does the wind of the desert. But where we feel that tears would relieve us, it is false philosophy to deny ourselves at least that first refreshment; and it is always false consolation to tell people that because they cannot help a thing, they are not to mind it. The true way is, to let them grapple with the unavoidable sorrow, and try to win it into gentleness by a reasonable yielding. There are griefs so gentle in their very nature that it would be worse than false heroism to refuse them a tear. Of this kind are the deaths of infants. Particular circumstances may render it more or less advisable to indulge in grief for the loss of a little child; but, in general, parents should be no more advised to repress their first tears on such an occasion, than to repress their smiles towards a child surviving, or to indulge in any other sympathy. It is an appeal to the same gentle tenderness; and such appeals are never made in vain. The end of them is an acquittal from the harsher bonds of affliction—from the tying down of the spirit to one melancholy idea.

It is the nature of tears of this kind, however strongly they may gush forth, to run into quiet waters at last. We cannot easily, for the whole course of our lives, think with pain of any good and kind person whom we have lost. It is the divine nature of their qualities to conquer pain and death itself; to turn the memory of them into pleasure; to survive with a placid aspect in our imaginations. We are writing at this moment just opposite a spot which contains the grave of one inexpressibly dear to us. We see from our window the trees about it, and the church spire. The green fields lie around. The clouds are travelling overhead, alternately taking away the sunshine and restoring it. The vernal winds, piping of the flowery summer-time, are nevertheless calling to mind the far-distant and dangerous ocean, which the heart that lies in that grave had many reasons to think of. And yet the sight of this spot does not give us pain. So far from it, it is the existence of that grave which doubles every charm of the spot; which links the pleasures of our childhood and manhood together; which puts a hushing tenderness in the winds, and a patient joy upon the landscape; which seems to unite heaven and earth, mortality and immortality, the grass of the tomb and the grass of the green field; and gives a more maternal aspect to the whole kindness of nature. It does not hinder gaiety itself. Happiness was what its tenant, through all her troubles, would have diffused. To diffuse happiness, and to enjoy it, is not only carrying on her wishes, but realising her hopes; and gaiety, freed from its only pollutions, malignity and want of sympathy, is but a child playing about the knees of its mother.

The remembered innocence and endearments of a child stand us instead of virtues that have died older. Children have not exercised the voluntary offices of friendship; they have not chosen to be kind and good to us; nor stood by us, from conscious will, in the hour of adversity. But they have shared their pleasures and pains with us as well as they could; the interchange of good offices between us has, of necessity, been less mingled with the troubles of the world; the sorrow arising from their death is the only one which we can associate with their memories. These are happy thoughts that cannot die. Our loss may always render them pensive; but they will not always be painful. It is a part of the benignity of Nature that pain does not survive like pleasure, at any time, much less where the cause of it is an innocent one. The smile will remain reflected by memory, as the moon reflects the light upon us when the sun has gone into heaven.

When writers like ourselves quarrel with earthly pain (we mean writers of the same intentions, without implying, of course, anything about abilities or otherwise), they are misunderstood if they are supposed to quarrel with pains of every sort. This would be idle and effeminate. They do not pretend, indeed, that humanity might not wish, if it could, to be entirely free from pain; for it endeavours, at all times, to turn pain into pleasure: or at least to set off the one with the other, to make the former a zest and the latter a refreshment. The most unaffected dignity of suffering does this, and, if wise, acknowledges it. The greatest benevolence towards others, the most unselfish relish of their pleasures, even at its own expense, does but look to increasing the general stock of happiness, though content, if it could, to have its identity swallowed up in that splendid contemplation. We are far from meaning that this is to be called selfishness. We are far, indeed, from thinking so, or of so confounding words. But neither is it to be called pain when most unselfish, if disinterestedness be truly understood. The pain that is in it softens into pleasure, as the darker hue of the rainbow melts into the brighter. Yet even if a harsher line is to be drawn between the pain and pleasure of the most unselfish mind (and ill-health, for instance, may draw it), we should not quarrel with it if it contributed to the general mass of comfort, and were of a nature which general kindliness could not afford. Made as we are, there are certain pains without which it would be difficult to conceive certain great and overbalancing pleasures. We may conceive it possible for beings to be made entirely happy; but in our composition something of pain seems to be a necessary ingredient, in order that the materials may turn to as fine account as possible, though our clay, in the course of ages and experience, may be refined more and more. We may get rid of the worst earth, though not of earth itself.

Now the liability to the loss of children—or rather what renders us sensible of it, the occasional loss itself—seems to be one of these necessary bitters thrown into the cup of humanity. We do not mean that everybody must lose one of his children in order to enjoy the rest; or that every individual loss afflicts us in the same proportion. We allude to the deaths of infants in general. These might be as few as we could render them. But if none at all ever took place, we should regard every little child as a man or woman secured; and it will easily be conceived what a world of endearing cares and hopes this security would endanger. The very idea of infancy would lose its continuity with us. Girls and boys would be future men and women, not present children. They would have attained their full growth in our imaginations, and might as well have been men and women at once. On the other hand, those who have lost an infant, are never, as it were, without an infant child. They are the only persons who, in one sense, retain it always, and they furnish their neighbours with the same idea. The other children grow up to manhood and womanhood, and suffer all the changes of mortality. This one alone is rendered an immortal child. Death has arrested it with his kindly harshness, and blessed it into an eternal image of youth and innocence.

Of such as these are the pleasantest shapes that visit our fancy and our hopes. They are the ever-smiling emblems of joy; the prettiest pages that wait upon imagination. Lastly, "Of these are the kingdom of heaven." Wherever there is a province of that benevolent and all-accessible empire, whether on earth or elsewhere, such are the gentle spirits that must inhabit it. To such simplicity, or the resemblance of it, must they come. Such must be the ready confidence of their hearts and creativeness of their fancy. And so ignorant must they be of the "knowledge of good and evil," losing their discernment of that self-created trouble, by enjoying the garden before them, and not being ashamed of what is kindly and innocent.

ON THE REALITIES OF IMAGINATION

THERE IS NOT A MORE UNTHINKING WAY of talking than to say such and such pains and pleasures are only imaginary, and therefore to be got rid of or undervalued accordingly. There is nothing imaginary in the common acceptation of the word. The logic of Moses in the *Vicar of Wakefield* is good argument here:—"Whatever is, is." Whatever touches us, whatever moves us, does touch and does move us. We recognise the reality of it, as we do that of a hand in the dark. We might as well say that a sight which makes us laugh, or a blow which brings tears into our eyes, is imaginary, as that anything else is imaginary which makes us laugh or weep. We can only judge of things by their effects. Our perception constantly deceives us, in things with which we suppose ourselves perfectly conversant; but our reception of their effect is a different matter. Whether we are materialists or immaterialists, whether things be about us or within us, whether we think the sun is a substance, or only the image of a divine thought, an idea, a thing imaginary, we are equally agreed as to the notion of its warmth. But on the other hand, as this warmth is felt differently by different temperaments, so what we call imaginary things affect different minds. What we have to do is not to deny their effect, because we do not feel in the same proportion, or whether we even feel it at all; but to see whether our neighbours may not be moved. If they are, there is, to all intents and purposes, a moving cause. But we do not see it? No;—neither perhaps do they. They only feel it; they are only sentient—a word which implies the sight given to the imagination by the feelings. But what do you mean, we may ask in return, by seeing? Some rays of light come in contact with the eye; they bring a sensation to it; in a word, they touch it; and the impression left by this touch we call sight. How far does this differ in effect from the impression left by any other touch, however mysterious? An ox knocked down by a butcher, and a man knocked down by a fit of apoplexy, equally feel themselves compelled to drop. The tickling of a straw and of a comedy equally move the muscles about the mouth. The look of a beloved eye will so thrill the frame, that old philosophers have had recourse to a doctrine of beams and radiant particles flying from one sight to another. In fine, what is contact itself, and why does it affect us? There is no one cause more mysterious than another, if we look into it.

Nor does the question concern us like moral causes. We may be content to know the earth by its fruits; but how to increase and improve them is a more attractive study. If, instead of saying that the causes which moved in us this or that pain or pleasure were imaginary, people were to say that the causes themselves were removable, they would be nearer the truth. When a stone trips us up, we do not fall to disputing its existence: we put it out of the way. In like manner, when we suffer from what is called an imaginary pain, our business is not to canvass the reality of it. Whether there is any cause or not in that or any other perception, or whether everything consist not in what is called effect, it is sufficient for us that the effect is real. Our sole business is to remove those second causes, which always accompany the original idea. As in deliriums, for instance, it would be idle to go about persuading the patient that he did not behold the figures he says he does. He might reasonably ask us, if he could, how we know anything about the matter; or how we can be sure that in the infinite wonders of the universe certain realities may not become apparent to certain eyes, whether diseased or not. Our business would be to put him into that state of health in which human beings are not diverted from their offices and comforts by a liability to such imaginations. The best reply to his question would be, that such a morbidity is clearly no more a fit state for a human being than a disarranged or incomplete state of works is for a watch; and that seeing the general tendency of nature to this completeness or state of comfort, we naturally conclude that the imaginations in question, whether substantial or not, are at least not of the same lasting or prevailing description.

We do not profess metaphysics. We are indeed so little conversant with the masters of that art, that we are never sure whether we are using even its proper terms. All that we may know on the subject comes to us from some reflection and some experience; and this all may be so little as to make a metaphysician smile; which, if he be a true one, he will do good-naturedly. The pretender will take occasion, from our very confession, to say that we know nothing. Our faculty, such as it is, is rather instinctive than reasoning; rather physical than metaphysical; rather sentient because it loves much, than because it knows much; rather calculated by a certain retention of boyhood, and by its wanderings in the green places of thought, to light upon a piece of the old golden world, than to tire ourselves, and conclude it unattainable, by too wide and scientific a search. We pretend to see farther than none but the worldly and the malignant. And yet those who see farther may not see so well. We do not blind our eyes with looking upon the sun in the heavens. We believe it to be there, but we find its light upon earth also; and we would lead humanity, if we could, out of misery and coldness into the shine of it. Pain might still be there; must be so, as long as we are mortal;

For oft we still must weep, since we are human:

but it should be pain for the sake of others, which is noble; not unnecessary pain inflicted by or upon them, which it is absurd not to remove. The very pains of mankind struggle towards pleasures; and such pains as are proper for them have this inevitable accompaniment of true humanity—that they cannot but realise a certain gentleness of enjoyment. Thus the true bearer of pain would come round to us; and he would not grudge us a share of his burden, though in taking from his trouble it might diminish his pride. Pride is but a bad pleasure at the expense of others. The great object of humanity is to enrich everybody. If it is a task destined not to succeed, it is a good one from its very nature; and fulfils at least a glad destiny of its own. To look upon it austerely is in reality the reverse of austerity. It is only such an impatience of the want of pleasure as leads us to grudge it in others; and this impatience itself, if the sufferer knew how to use it, is but another impulse, in the general yearning, towards an equal wealth of enjoyment.

But we shall be getting into other discussions.—The ground-work of all happiness is health. Take care of this ground, and the doleful imaginations that come to warn us against its abuse will avoid it. Take care of this ground, and let as many glad imaginations throng to it as possible. Read the magical works of the poets, and they will come. If you doubt their existence, ask yourself whether you feel pleasure at the idea of them; whether you are moved into delicious smiles, or tears as delicious. If you are, the result is the same to you, whether they exist or not. It is not mere words to say that he who goes through a rich man's park, and sees things in it which never bless the mental eyesight of the possessor, is richer than he. He is richer. More results of pleasure come home to him. The ground is actually more fertile to him: the place haunted with finer shapes. He has more servants to come at his call, and administer to him with full hands. Knowledge, sympathy, imagination, are all divining-rods, with which he discovers treasure. Let a painter go through the grounds, and he will see not only the general colours of green and brown, but their combinations and contrasts, and the modes in which they might again be combined and contrasted. He will also put figures in the landscape if there are none there, flocks and herds, or a solitary spectator, or Venus lying with her white body among the violets and primroses. Let a musician go through, and he will hear "differences discreet" in the notes of the birds and the lapsing of the water-fall. He will fancy a serenade of wind instruments in the open air at a lady's window, with a voice rising through it; or the horn of the hunter; or the musical cry of the hounds,

> Matched in mouth-like bells,
> Each under each;

or a solitary voice in a bower, singing for an expected lover; or the chapel organ, waking up like the fountain of the winds. Let a poet go through the grounds and he will heighten and increase all these sounds and images. He will bring the colours from heaven, and put an unearthly meaning into the voice. He will have stories of the sylvan inhabitants; will shift the population through infinite varieties; will put a sentiment upon every sight and sound; will be human, romantic, supernatural; will make all nature send tribute into that spot.

We may say of the love of nature what Shakespeare says of another love, that it

> Adds a precious seeing to the eye.

And we may say also, upon the like principle, that it adds a precious hearing to the ear. This and imagination, which ever follows upon it, are the two purifiers of our sense, which rescue us from the deafening babble of common cares, and enable us to hear all the affectionate voices of earth and heaven. The starry orbs, lapsing about in their smooth and sparkling dance, sing to us. The brooks talk to us of solitude. The birds are the animal spirits of nature, carolling in the air, like a careless lass.

> The gentle gales,
> Fanning their odoriferous wings, dispense
> Native perfumes; and whisper whence they stole
> Those balmy spoils.—*Paradise Lost*, iv, 156–9.

The poets are called creators, because with their magical words they bring forth to our eyesight the abundant images and beauties of creation. They put them there, if the reader pleases; and so are literally creators. But whether put there or discovered, whether created or invented (for invention means nothing but finding out), there they are. If they touch us, they exist to as much purpose as anything else which touches us. If a passage in *King Lear* brings the tears into our eyes, it is real as the touch of a sorrowful hand. If the flow of a song of Anacreon's intoxicates us, it is as true to a pulse within us as the wine he drank. We hear not their sounds with ears, nor see their sights with eyes; but we hear and see both so truly, that we are moved with pleasure; and the advantage, nay even the test, of seeing and hearing, at any time, is not in the seeing and hearing, but in the ideas we realise, and the pleasure we derive. Intellectual objects, therefore, inasmuch as they come home to us, are as true a part of the stock of nature as visible ones; and they are infinitely more abundant. Between the tree of a country clown and the tree of a Milton or Spenser, what a difference in point of productiveness! Between the plodding of a sexton through a church-yard and the walk of a Gray, what a difference! What a difference between the Bermudas of a ship-builder and the Bermoothes of Shakespeare! the isle

> Full of noises,
> Sounds, and sweet airs, that give delight, and hurt not;

the isle of elves and fairies, that chased the tide to and fro on the sea-shore; of coral-bones and the knell of sea-nymphs; of spirits dancing on the sands, and singing amidst the hushes of the wind; of Caliban, whose brute nature enchantment had made poetical; of Ariel, who lay in cowslip bells, and rode

upon the bat; of Miranda, who wept when she saw Ferdinand
work so hard, and begged him to let her help; telling him,

> I am your wife, if you will marry me;
> If not, I'll die your maid. To be your fellow
> You may deny me; but I'll be your servant,
> Whether you will or no.

Such are the discoveries which the poets make for us; worlds
to which that of Columbus was but a handful of brute matter. America began to be richer for us the other day, when
Humboldt came back and told us of its luxuriant and gigantic
vegetation; of the myriads of shooting lights, which revel at
evening in the southern sky; and of that grand constellation,
at which Dante seems to have made so remarkable a guess
(*Purgatorio*, cant. i., v, 22). The natural warmth of the Mexican and Peruvian genius, set free from despotism, will soon
do all the rest for it; awaken the sleeping riches of its eyesight,
and call forth the glad music of its affections.

Imagination enriches everything. A great library contains
not only books, but

> The assembled souls of all that men held wise.
>
> —DAVENANT.

The moon is Homer's and Shakespeare's moon, as well as the
one we look at. The sun comes out of his chamber in the east,
with a sparkling eye, "rejoicing like a bridegroom." The commonest thing becomes like Aaron's rod, that budded. Pope
called up the spirits of the Cabala to wait upon a lock of hair,
and justly gave it the honours of a constellation; for he has
hung it, sparkling for ever in the eyes of posterity. A common
meadow is a sorry thing to a ditcher or a coxcomb; but by
the help of its dues from imagination and the love of nature,
the grass brightens for us, the air soothes us, we feel as we
did in the daisied hours of childhood. Its verdures, its sheep, its
hedge-row elms—all these, and all else which sight, and sound,
and associations can give it, are made to furnish a treasure of

pleasant thoughts. Even brick and mortar are vivified, as of old, at the harp of Orpheus. A metropolis becomes no longer a mere collection of houses or of trades. It puts on all the grandeur of its history, and its literature; its towers, and rivers; its art, and jewellery, and foreign wealth; its multitude of human beings all intent upon excitement, wise or yet to learn; the huge and sullen dignity of its canopy of smoke by day; the wide gleam upwards of its lighted lustre at night-time; and the noise of its many chariots, heard at the same hour, when the wind sets gently towards some quiet suburb.

Thomas De Quincey

1785 · 1859

*Thomas De Quincey, a sensitive, studious, precocious
boy, went to Oxford from his native Manchester
well trained in both Latin and Greek and informed
of the ways of the world through two experiences
in running away from home, once to Wales and
once to the slums of London. Severe headaches
caused him to start taking laudanum, which
eventually made him a confirmed opium addict.
In 1820, Lamb introduced him to the editors of*
The London Magazine, *who encouraged him
to write* Confessions of an English Opium Eater,
the work which brought him fame.

LEVANA AND OUR LADIES OF SORROW

OFTENTIMES AT OXFORD I saw Levana in my
dreams. I knew her by her Roman symbols.
Who is Levana? Reader, that do not pretend to have leisure
for very much scholarship, you will not be angry with me for
telling you. Levana was the Roman goddess that performed
for the new-born infant the earliest office of ennobling kindness—typical, by its mode, of that grandeur which belongs to
man everywhere, and of that benignity in powers invisible
which even in pagan worlds sometimes descends to sustain
it. At the very moment of birth, just as the infant tasted for
the first time the atmosphere of our troubled planet, it was
laid on the ground. But immediately, lest so grand a creature
should grovel there for more than one instant, either the
paternal hand, as proxy for the goddess Levana, or some near
kinsman, as proxy for the father, raised it upright, bade it
look erect as the king of all this world, and presented its fore-

head to the stars, saying, perhaps, in his heart, "Behold what is greater than yourselves!" This symbolic act represented the function of Levana. And that mysterious lady, who never revealed her face (except to me in dreams), but always acted by delegation, had her name from the Latin verb (as still it is the Italian verb) *levare*, to raise aloft.

This is the explanation of Levana, and hence it has arisen that some people have understood by Levana the tutelary power that controls the education of the nursery. She, that would not suffer at his birth even a prefigurative or mimic degradation for her awful ward, far less could be supposed to suffer the real degradation attaching to the non-development of his powers. She therefore watches over human education. Now, the word *edŭco*, with the penultimate short, was derived (by a process often exemplified in the crystallisation of languages) from the word *edūco*, with the penultimate long. Whatever *educes* or develops, *educates*. By the education of Levana, therefore, is meant—not the poor machinery that moves by spelling-books and grammars, but by that mighty system of central forces hidden in the deep bosom of human life, which by passion, by strife, by temptation, by the energies of resistance, works for ever upon children—resting not day or night, any more than the mighty wheel of the day and night themselves, whose moments, like restless spokes, are glimmering for ever as they revolve.

If, then, *these* are the ministries by which Levana works, how profoundly must she reverence the agencies of grief. But you, reader, think that children generally are not liable to grief such as mine. There are two senses in the word *generally*—the sense of Euclid, where it means *universally* (or in the whole extent of the *genus*), and a foolish sense of this word, where it means *usually*. Now, I am far from saying that children universally are capable of grief like mine. But there are more than you ever heard of who die of grief in this island of ours. I will tell you a common case. The rules of Eton require that a boy on the *foundation* should be there twelve years: he is superannuated at eighteen, consequently he must come at six. Children torn away from mothers and sisters at that age not unfrequently die. I speak of what I know. The complaint is not entered by the registrar as grief; but *that* it is. Grief of that sort, and at that age, has killed more than have ever been counted amongst its martyrs.

Therefore it is that Levana often communes with the powers that shake man's heart: therefore it is that she dotes on grief. "These ladies," said I softly to myself, on seeing the ministers with whom Levana was conversing, "these are the Sorrows; and they are three in number, as the *Graces* are three, who dress man's life with beauty; the *Parcae* are three, who weave the dark arras of man's life in their mysterious loom always with colours sad in part, sometimes angry with tragic crimson and black; the *Furies* are three, who visit with retribution called from the other side of the grave offences that walk upon this; and once even the *Muses* were but three, who fit the harp, the trumpet, or the lute, to the great burdens of man's impassioned creations. These are the Sorrows, all three of whom I know." The last words I say *now;* but in Oxford I said, "One of whom I know, and the others too surely I *shall* know." For already, in my fervent youth, I saw (dimly relieved upon the dark background of my dreams) the imperfect lineaments of the awful sisters. These sisters—by what name shall we call them?

If I say simply, "The Sorrows," there will be a chance of mistaking the term; it might be understood of individual sorrow—separate cases of sorrow—whereas I want a term expressing the mighty abstractions that incarnate themselves in all individual sufferings of man's heart; and I wish to have these abstractions presented as impersonations, that is, as clothed with human attributes of life, and with functions pointing to flesh. Let us call them, therefore, *Our Ladies of Sorrow.* I know them thoroughly, and have walked in all their kingdoms. Three sisters they are, of one mysterious household; and their paths are wide apart; but of their dominion there is no end. Them I saw often conversing with Levana, and sometimes about myself. Do they talk, then? Oh, no! Mighty phantoms like these disdain the infirmities of language. They may utter voices through the organs of man when they dwell in human hearts, but amongst themselves is no voice nor sound; eternal silence reigns in *their* kingdoms. *They* spoke not as they talked with Levana. *They* whispered not. *They* sang not. Though oftentimes methought they *might* have sung; for I upon earth had heard their mysteries oftentimes deciphered by harp and timbrel, by dulcimer and organ. Like God, whose servants they are, they utter their pleasure, not by sounds that perish, or by words that go astray, but by signs in heaven, by changes on earth, by pulses in secret rivers, heraldries painted on darkness, and hieroglyphics written on the tablets of the brain. *They* wheeled in mazes; *I* spelled the steps. *They* telegraphed from afar; *I* read the signals. *They* conspired together; and on the mirrors of darkness *my* eye traced the plots. *Theirs* were the symbols; *mine* are the words.

What is it the sisters are? What is it that they do? Let me describe their form, and their presence: if form it were that still fluctuated in its outline, or presence it were that for ever advanced to the front, or for ever receded amongst shades.

The eldest of the three is named *Mater Lachrymarum*, Our Lady of Tears. She it is that night and day raves and moans, calling for vanished faces. She stood in Rama, where a voice was heard of lamentation—Rachel weeping for her children, and refusing to be comforted. She it was that stood in Bethlehem on the night when Herod's sword swept its nurseries of Innocents, and the little feet were stiffened for ever, which, heard at times as they tottered along floors overhead, woke pulses of love in household hearts that were not unmarked in heaven. Her eyes are sweet and subtle, wild and sleepy by turns; oftentimes rising to the clouds, oftentimes challenging the heavens. She wears a diadem round her head. And I knew by childish memories that she could go abroad upon the winds, when she heard the sobbing of litanies or the thundering of organs, and when she beheld the mustering of summer clouds. This sister, the eldest, it is that carries keys more than papal at her girdle, which open every cottage and every palace. She, to my knowledge, sat all last summer by the bed-side of the blind beggar, him that so often and so gladly I talked with, whose pious daughter, eight years old, with the sunny countenance, resisted the temptations of play and village mirth to travel all day long on dusty roads with her afflicted father. For this did God send her a great reward. In the springtime of the year, and whilst yet her own Spring was budding, He recalled her to Himself. But her blind father mourns for ever over *her;* still he dreams at midnight that the little guiding hand is locked within his own; and still he wakens to a darkness that is *now* within a second and a deeper darkness. This *Mater Lachrymarum* also has been sitting all this winter of 1844–5 within the bedchamber of the Czar, bringing before his eyes a daughter (not less pious) that vanished to God not less suddenly, and left behind her a darkness not less profound. By the power of the keys it is that Our Lady of Tears glides a ghostly intruder into the chambers of sleepless men, sleepless women, sleepless children, from Ganges to Nile, from Nile to Mississippi. And her, because she is the first-born of her house, and has the widest empire, let us honour with the title of "Madonna."

The second sister is called *Mater Suspiriorum,* Our Lady of Sighs. She never scales the clouds, nor walks abroad upon the winds. She wears no diadem. And her eyes, if they were ever seen, would be neither sweet nor subtle; no man could read their story; they would be found filled with perishing dreams, and with wrecks of forgotten delirium. But she raises not her eyes; her head, on which sits a dilapidated turban, droops for ever, for ever fastens on the dust. She weeps not. She groans not. But she sighs inaudibly at intervals. Her sister, Madonna, is oftentimes stormy and frantic, raging in the highest against heaven, and demanding back her darlings. But Our Lady of Sighs never clamours, never defies, dreams not of rebellious aspirations. She is humble to abjectness. Hers is the meekness that belongs to the hopeless. Murmur she may, but it is in her sleep. Whisper she may, but it is to herself in the twilight. Mutter she does at times, but it is in solitary places that are desolate as she is desolate, in ruined cities, and when the sun has gone down to his rest. This sister is the visitor of the Pariah, of the Jew, of the bondsman to the oar

in Mediterranean galleys, and of the English criminal in
Norfolk Island, blotted out from the books of remembrance
in sweet far-off England, of the baffled penitent reverting his
eyes for ever upon a solitary grave, which to him seems the
altar overthrown of some past and bloody sacrifice, on which
altar no oblations can now be availing, whether towards
pardon that he might implore, or towards reparation that he
might attempt. Every slave that at noonday looks up to the
tropical sun with timid reproach, as he points with one hand
to the earth, our general mother, but for *him* a stepmother, as
he points with the other hand to the Bible, our general teacher,
but against *him* sealed and sequestered; every woman sitting
in darkness, without love to shelter her head, or hope to
illumine her solitude, because the heaven-born instincts kin-
dling in her nature germs of holy affections, which God im-
planted in her womanly bosom, having been stifled by social
necessities, now burn sullenly to waste, like sepulchral lamps
amongst the ancients; every nun defrauded of her unreturning
Maytime by wicked kinsmen, whom God will judge; every
captive in every dungeon; all that are betrayed, and all that
are rejected outcasts by traditionary law, and children of
hereditary disgrace—all these walk with Our Lady of Sighs.
She also carries a key; but she needs it little. For her kingdom
is chiefly amongst the tents of Shem, and the houseless vagrant
of every clime. Yet in the very highest walks of man she finds
chapels of her own; and even in glorious England there are
some that, to the world, carry their heads as proudly as the
reindeer, who yet secretly have received her mark upon their
foreheads.

But the third sister, who is also the youngest!—Hush,
whisper whilst we talk of *her!* Her kingdom is not large, or
else no flesh should live; but within that kingdom all power
is hers. Her head, turreted like that of Cybele, rises almost
beyond the reach of sight. She droops not; and her eyes
rising so high *might* be hidden by distance; but, being what
they are, they cannot be hidden; through the treble veil of
crape which she wears, the fierce light of a blazing misery, that
rests not for matins or for vespers, for noon of day or noon of

night, for ebbing or for flowing tide, may be read from the very ground. She is the defier of God. She is also the mother of lunacies, and the suggestress of suicides. Deep lie the roots of her power; but narrow is the nation that she rules. For she can approach only those in whom a profound nature has been upheaved by central convulsions; in whom the heart trembles and the brain rocks under conspiracies of tempest from without and tempest from within. Madonna moves with uncertain steps, fast or slow, but still with tragic grace. Our Lady of Sighs creeps timidly and stealthily. But this youngest sister moves with incalculable motions, bounding, and with a tiger's leaps. She carries no key; for, though coming rarely amongst men, she storms all doors at which she is permitted to enter at all. And *her* name is *Mater Tenebrarum*—Our Lady of Darkness.

These were the *Semnai Theai*, or Sublime Goddesses; these were the *Eumenides* or Gracious Ladies (so called by antiquity in shuddering propitiation), of my Oxford dreams. Madonna spoke. She spoke by her mysterious hand. Touching my head, she beckoned to Our Lady of Sighs; and *what* she spoke, translated out of the signs which (except in dreams) no man reads, was this:—

"Lo! here is he whom in childhood I dedicated to my altars. This is he that once I made my darling. Him I led astray, him I beguiled, and from heaven I stole away his young heart to mine. Through me did he become idolatrous; and through me it was, by languishing desires, that he worshipped the worm, and prayed to the wormy grave. Holy was the grave to him; lovely was its darkness; saintly its corruption. Him, this young idolater, I have seasoned for thee, dear gentle Sister of Sighs! Do thou take him now to *thy* heart, and season him for our dreadful sister. And thou"—turning to the *Mater Tenebrarum*, she said—"wicked sister, that temptest and hatest, do thou take him from *her*. See that thy sceptre lie heavy on his head. Suffer not woman and her tenderness to sit near him in his darkness. Banish the frailties of hope, wither the relentings of love, scorch the fountains of tears, curse him as only thou canst curse. So shall he be accomplished in the furnace, so shall he see the things that ought *not* to be seen, sights that are abominable, and secrets that are unutterable. So shall he read elder truths, sad truths, grand truths, fearful truths. So shall he rise again *before* he dies, and so shall our commission be accomplished which from God we had—to plague his heart until we had unfolded the capacities of his spirit."

THE LITERATURE OF KNOWLEDGE
AND THE LITERATURE OF POWER

WHAT IS IT THAT WE MEAN BY LITERATURE? Popularly, and amongst the thoughtless, it is held to include everything that is printed in a book. Little logic is required to disturb that definition. The most thoughtless person is easily made aware that in the idea of literature one essential element is some relation to a general and common interest of man, so that what applies only to a local or professional or merely personal interest, even though presenting itself in the shape of a book, will not belong to literature. So far the definition is easily narrowed; and it is as easily expanded. For not only is much that takes a station in books not literature; but inversely, much that really is literature never reaches a station in books. The weekly sermons of Christendom, that vast pulpit literature which acts so extensively upon the popular mind—to warn, to uphold, to renew, to comfort, to alarm—does not attain the sanctuary of libraries in the ten-thousandth part of its extent. The drama, again, as for instance the finest of Shakespeare's plays in England and all leading Athenian plays in the noontide of the Attic stage, operated as a literature on the public mind, and were (according to the strictest letter of that term) published through the audiences that witnessed their representation some time before they were published as things to be read; and they were published in the scenical mode of publication with much more effect than they could have had as books during ages of costly copying or of costly printing.

Books, therefore, do not suggest an idea coextensive and interchangeable with the idea of literature; since much literature, scenic, forensic, or didactic (as from lecturers and public orators), may never come into books, and much that does come into books may connect itself with no literary interest. But a far more important correction, applicable to the common vague idea of literature, is to be sought not so much in a better definition of literature as in a sharper distinction of the two functions which it fulfils. In that great social organ which, collectively, we call literature, there may be distinguished two separate offices that may blend and often do so, but capable, severally, of a severe insulation, and naturally fitted for reciprocal repulsion. There is, first, the literature of knowledge; and secondly, the literature of power. The function of the first is to teach; the function of the second is to move: the first is a rudder, the second an oar or a sail. The first speaks to the mere discursive understanding; the second speaks ultimately, it may happen, to the higher understanding or reason, but always through affections of pleasure and sympathy. Remotely, it may travel towards an object seated in what Lord Bacon calls dry light; but proximately, it does and must operate —else it ceases to be a literature of power—on and through that humid light which clothes itself in the mists and glittering iris of human passions, desires, and genial emotions. Men have so little reflected on the higher functions of literature as to find it a paradox if one should describe it as a mean or subordinate purpose of books to give information. But this is a paradox only in the sense which makes it honorable to be paradoxical. Whenever we talk in ordinary language of seeking information or gaining knowledge, we understand the words as connected with something of absolute novelty. But it is the grandeur of all truth which can occupy a very high place in human interests that it is never absolutely novel to the meanest of minds: it exists eternally by way of germ or latent principle in the lowest as in the highest, needing to be developed, but never to be planted. To be capable of transplantation is the immediate criterion of a truth that ranges on a lower scale. Besides which, there is a rarer thing than truth—namely, power, or deep sympathy with truth. What is the effect, for instance, upon society, of children? By the pity, by the tenderness, and by the peculiar modes of admiration, which connect themselves with the helplessness, with the innocence, and with the simplicity of children, not only are the primal affections strengthened and continually renewed, but the qualities which are dearest in the sight of heaven—the frailty, for instance, which appeals to forbearance, the innocence which symbolizes the heavenly, and the simplicity which is most alien from the worldly—are kept up in perpetual remembrance, and their ideals are continually refreshed. A purpose of the same nature is answered by the higher literature, *viz.*, the literature of power. What do you learn from *Paradise Lost?* Nothing at all. What do you learn from a cookery-book? Something new, something that you did not know before, in every paragraph. But would you therefore put the wretched cookery-book on a higher level of estimation than the divine poem? What you owe to Milton is not any knowledge, of which a million separate items are still but a million of advancing steps on the same earthly level; what you owe is power— that is, exercise and expansion to your own latent capacity of sympathy with the infinite, where every pulse and each separate influx is a step upwards, a step ascending as upon a Jacob's ladder from earth to mysterious altitudes above the earth. All the steps of knowledge, from first to last, carry you further on the same plane, but could never raise you one foot above your ancient level of earth: whereas the very first step in power is a flight—is an ascending movement into another element where earth is forgotten.

Were it not that human sensibilities are ventilated and continually called out into exercise by the great phenomena of infancy, or of real life as it moves through chance and change, or of literature as it recombines these elements in the mimicries of poetry, romance, *etc.*, it is certain that, like any animal power or muscular energy falling into disuse, all such sensibilities would gradually droop and dwindle. It is in relation to these great moral capacities of man that the literature of power, as contradistinguished from that of knowledge, lives and has its field of action. It is concerned with what is highest in man; for the Scriptures themselves never condescended to deal by suggestion or co-operation with the mere discursive understanding: when speaking of man in his intellectual capacity, the Scriptures speak not of the understanding, but of "the understanding heart"—making the heart, *i.e.*, the great intuitive (or non-discursive) organ, to be the interchangeable formula for man in his highest state of capacity for the infinite. Tragedy, romance, fairy tale, or epopee, all alike restore to man's mind the ideals of justice, of hope, of truth, of mercy, of retribution, which else (left to the support of daily life in its realities) would languish for want of sufficient illustration.

What is meant, for instance, by poetic justice? It does not mean a justice that differs by its object from the ordinary justice of human jurisprudence, for then it must be confessedly a very bad kind of justice; but it means a justice that differs from common forensic justice by the degree in which it attains its object, a justice that is more omnipotent over its own ends, as dealing—not with the refractory elements of earthly life, but with the elements of its own creation, and with materials flexible to its own purest preconceptions. It is certain that, were it not for the literature of power, these ideals would often remain amongst us as mere arid notional forms; whereas, by the creative forces of man put forth in literature, they gain a vernal life of restoration, and germinate into vital activities. The commonest novel, by moving in alliance with human fears and hopes, with human instincts of wrong and right, sustains and quickens those affections. Calling them into action, it rescues them from torpor. And hence the pre-eminency over all authors that merely teach, of the meanest that moves, or that teaches, if at all, indirectly by moving. The very highest work that has ever existed in the literature of knowledge is but a provisional work—a book upon trial and sufferance, and *quamdiu bene se gesserit*. Let its teaching be even partially revised, let it be but expanded—nay, even let its teaching be but placed in a better order—and instantly it is superseded. Whereas the feeblest works in the literature of power, surviving at all, survive as finished and unalterable amongst men. For instance, the *Principia* of Sir Isaac Newton was a book militant on earth from the first. In all stages of its progress it would have to fight for its existence: first, as regards absolute truth; secondly, when that combat was over, as regards its form or mode of presenting the truth. And as soon as a Laplace, or anybody else, builds higher upon the foundations laid by this book, effectually he throws it out of the sunshine into decay and darkness; by weapons won from this book he superannuates and destroys this book, so that soon the name of Newton remains as a mere *nominis umbra*, but his book, as a living power, has transmigrated into other forms. Now, on the contrary, the *Iliad*, the *Prometheus* of Aeschylus, the *Othello* or *King Lear*, the *Hamlet* or *Macbeth*, and the *Paradise Lost*, are not militant, but triumphant forever, as long as the languages exist in which they speak or can be taught to speak. They never can transmigrate into new incarnations. To reproduce these in new forms, or variations, even if in some things they should be improved, would be to plagiarize. A good steam-engine is properly superseded by a better. But one lovely pastoral valley is not superseded by another, nor a statue of Praxiteles by a statue of Michael Angelo. These things are separated not by imparity but by disparity. They are not thought of as unequal under the same standard, but as different in kind, and, if otherwise equal, as equal under a different standard. Human works of immortal beauty and works of nature in one respect stand on the same footing: they never absolutely repeat each other, never approach so near as not to differ; and they differ not as better and worse, or simply by more and less: they differ by undecipherable and incommunicable differences, that cannot be caught by mimicries, that cannot be reflected in the mirror of copies, that cannot become ponderable in the scales of vulgar comparison.

Applying these principles to Pope as a representative of fine literature in general, we would wish to remark the claim which he has, or which any equal writer has, to the attention and jealous winnowing of those critics in particular who watch over public morals. Clergymen, and all organs of public criticism put in motion by clergymen, are more especially concerned in the just appreciation of such writers, if the two canons are remembered which we have endeavored to illustrate, *viz.*, that all works in this class, as opposed to those in the literature of knowledge, first, work by far deeper agencies, and, secondly, are more permanent; in the strictest sense they are permanent possessions; and what evil they do, or what good they do, is commensurate with the national language, sometimes long after the nation has departed. At this hour, five hundred years since their creation, the tales of Chaucer, never equaled on this earth for their tenderness, and for life of picturesqueness, are read familiarly by many in the charming language of their natal day, and by others in the modernisations of Dryden, of Pope, and Wordsworth. At this hour, one thousand eight hundred years since their creation, the Pagan tales of Ovid, never equaled on this earth for the gaiety of their movement and the capricious graces of their narrative, are read by all Christendom. This man's people and their monuments are dust; but he is alive: he has survived them, as he told us that he had it in his commission to do, by a thousand years "and shall a thousand more."

All the literature of knowledge builds only ground-nests, that are swept away by floods, or confounded by the plow; but the literature of power builds nests in aerial altitudes of temples sacred from violation, or of forests inaccessible to fraud. This is a great prerogative of the power literature; and it is a greater which lies in the mode of its influence. The knowledge literature, like the fashion of this world, passeth away. An Encyclopædia is its abstract; and, in this respect, it may be taken for its speaking symbol—that before one generation has passed an Encyclopædia is superannuated; for it speaks through the dead memory and unimpassioned understanding, which have not the repose of higher faculties, but are continually enlarging and varying their phylacteries. But all literature properly so called—literature *par excellence*—for the very same reason that it is so much more durable than the literature of knowledge, is (and by the very same proportion it is) more intense and electrically searching in its impressions. The directions in which the tragedy of this planet has trained our human feelings to play, and the combinations into which the poetry of this planet has thrown our human passions of love and hatred, of admiration and contempt, exercise a power for bad or good over human life that cannot be contemplated, when stretching through many generations, without a sentiment allied to awe. And of this let everyone be assured—that he owes to the impassioned books which he has read many a thousand more of emotions than he can consciously trace back to them. Dim by their origination, these emotions yet arise in him and mold him through life, like forgotten incidents of his childhood. . . .

Ralph Waldo Emerson

1803 · 1882

Ralph Waldo Emerson, American essayist, poet, lecturer, and transcendental philosopher, began his professional career as minister to the Second Church in Boston. In 1832, he left his pastorate because his religious views had changed. After a trip to Europe, on which he met Landor, Coleridge, Wordsworth, and Carlyle, he returned home and settled in Concord, where he was neighbor to Hawthorne, Thoreau, and Alcott. He lectured frequently to lyceum audiences and published the substance of his lectures in essays. As the leading spokesman for the transcendental movement, he was influential in various practical applications of the idealistic philosophy which he taught: the Brook Farm Institute, which he supported but did not join, and The Dial, *a journal of the transcendental movement, which he edited for two years (1842–1844).*

ILLUSIONS

SOME YEARS AGO, in company with an agreeable party, I spent a long summer day in exploring the Mammoth Cave in Kentucky. We traversed, through spacious galleries affording a solid masonry foundation for the town and county overhead, the six or eight black miles from the mouth of the cavern to the innermost recess which tourists visit—a niche or grotto made of one seamless stalactite, and called, I believe, "Serena's Bower." I lost the light of one day. I saw high domes and bottomless pits; heard the voice of unseen waterfalls; paddled three quarters of a mile in the deep Echo River, whose waters are peopled with the blind fish; crossed the streams "Lethe" and "Styx"; plied with music and guns the echoes in these alarming galleries; saw every form of stalagmite and stalactite in the sculptured and fretted chambers—icicle, orange-flower, acanthus, grapes, and snowball. We shot Bengal lights into the vaults and groins of the sparry cathedrals and examined all the masterpieces which the four combined engineers, water, limestone, gravitation, and time, could make in the dark.

The mysteries and scenery of the cave had the same dignity that belongs to all natural objects, and which shames the fine things to which we foppishly compare them. I remarked especially the mimetic habit with which nature, on new instruments, hums her old tunes, making night to mimic day, and chemistry to ape vegetation. But I then took notice and still chiefly remember that the best thing which the cave had to offer was an illusion. On arriving at what is called the "Star-Chamber," our lamps were taken from us by the guide and extinguished or put aside, and, on looking upwards, I saw or seemed to see the night heaven thick with stars glimmering more or less brightly over our heads, and even what seemed a comet flaming among them. All the party were touched with astonishment and pleasure. Our musical friends sung with much feeling a pretty song, "The stars are in the quiet sky," etc., and I sat down on the rocky floor to enjoy the serene picture. Some crystal specks in the black ceiling high overhead, reflecting the light of a half-hid lamp, yielded this magnificent effect.

I own I did not like the cave so well for eking out its sublimities with this theatrical trick. But I have had many experiences like it, before and since; and we must be content to be pleased without too curiously analyzing the occasions. Our conversation with nature is not just what it seems. The cloud-rack, the sunrise and sunset glories, rainbows and Northern Lights are not quite so spheral as our childhood thought them, and the part our organization plays in them is too large. The senses interfere everywhere and mix their own structure with all they report of. Once we fancied the earth a plane, and stationary. In admiring the sunset we do not yet deduct the rounding, coordinating, pictorial powers of the eye.

The same interference from our organization creates the most of our pleasure and pain. Our first mistake is the belief that the circumstance gives the joy which we give to the circumstance. Life is an ecstasy. Life is sweet as nitrous oxide; and the fisherman dripping all day over a cold pond, the switchman at the railway intersection, the farmer in the field, the Negro in the rice-swamp, the fop in the street, the hunter in the woods, the barrister with the jury, the belle at the ball, all ascribe a certain pleasure to their employment, which they themselves give it. Health and appetite impart the sweetness to sugar, bread, and meat. We fancy that our civilization has got on far, but we still come back to our primers.

We live by our imaginations, by our admirations, by our sentiments. The child walks amid heaps of illusions, which he does not like to have disturbed. The boy, how sweet to him is his fancy! how dear the story of barons and battles! What a hero he is, whilst he feeds on his heroes! What a debt is his to imaginative books! He has no better friend or influence than Scott, Shakspeare, Plutarch, and Homer. The man lives to other objects, but who dare affirm that they are more real? Even the prose of the streets is full of refractions. In the life of the dreariest alderman, fancy enters into all details and colors them with rosy hue. He imitates the air and actions of people whom he admires, and is raised in his own eyes. He pays a debt quicker to a rich man than to a poor man. He wishes the bow and compliment of some leader in the state or in society; weighs what he says; perhaps he never comes nearer to him for that, but dies at last better contented for this amusement of his eyes and his fancy.

The world rolls, the din of life is never hushed. In London, in Paris, in Boston, in San Francisco, the carnival, the masquerade is at its height. Nobody drops his domino. The unities, the fictions of the piece it would be an impertinence to break. The chapter of fascinations is very long. Great is paint; nay, God is the painter, and we rightly accuse the critic who destroys too many illusions. Society does not love its unmaskers. It was wittily if somewhat bitterly said by D'Alembert, "*qu'un état de vapeur était un état très fâcheux, parce-qu'il nous faisait voir les choses comme elles sont.*" I find men victims of illusion in all parts of life. Children, youths, adults and old men, all are led by one bauble or another. Yoganidra, the goddess of illusion, Proteus, or Momus, or Gylfi's Mocking— for the Power has many names—is stronger than the Titans, stronger than Apollo. Few have overheard the gods or surprised their secret. Life is a succession of lessons which must be lived to be understood. All is riddle, and the key to a riddle is another riddle. There are as many pillows of illusion as flakes in a snowstorm. We wake from one dream into another dream. The toys to be sure are various, and are graduated in refinement to the quality of the dupe. The intellectual man requires a fine bait; the sots are easily amused. But everybody is drugged with his own frenzy, and the pageant marches at all hours, with music and banner and badge.

Amid the joyous troop who give in to the charivari, comes now and then a sad-eyed boy whose eyes lack the requisite refractions to clothe the show in due glory, and who is afflicted with a tendency to trace home the glittering miscellany of fruits and flowers to one root. Science is a search after identity, and the scientific whim is lurking in all corners. At the State Fair a friend of mine complained that all the varieties of fancy pears in our orchards seem to have been selected by somebody who had a whim for a particular kind of pear, and only cultivated such as had that perfume; they were all alike. And I remember the quarrel of another youth with the confectioners, that when he racked his wit to choose the best comfits in the shops, in all the endless varieties of sweetmeat he could find only three flavors, or two. What then? Pears and cakes are good for something; and because you unluckily have an eye or nose too keen, why need you spoil the comfort which the rest of us find in them? I knew a humorist who in a good deal of rattle had a grain or two of sense. He shocked the company by maintaining that the attributes of God were two—power and risibility, and that it was the duty of every pious man to keep up the comedy.

And I have known gentlemen of great stake in the community, but whose sympathies were cold—presidents of colleges and governors and senators—who held themselves bound to sign every temperance pledge, and act with Bible societies and missions and peace-makers, and cry *Hist-a-boy!* to every good dog. We must not carry comity too far, but we all have kind impulses in this direction. When the boys come into my yard for leave to gather horse-chestnuts, I own I enter into nature's game, and effect to grant the permission reluctantly, fearing that any moment they will find out the imposture of that showy chaff. But this tenderness is quite unnecessary; the enchantments are laid on very thick. Their young life is thatched with them. Bare and grim to tears is the lot of the children in the hovel I saw yesterday; yet not the less they hung it round with frippery romance, like the children of the happiest fortune, and talked of "the dear cottage where so many joyful hours had flown." Well, this thatching of hovels is the custom of the country. Women, more than all, are the element and kingdom of illusion. Being fascinated, they fascinate. They see through Claude-Lorraines. And how dare anyone, if he could, pluck away the *coulisses*, stage effects and ceremonies, by which they live? Too pathetic, too pitiable, is the region of affection, and its atmosphere always liable to *mirage*.

We are not very much to blame for our bad marriages. We live amid hallucinations; and this especial trap is laid to trip up our feet with, and all are tripped up first or last. But the mighty Mother who had been so sly with us, as if she felt that she owed us some indemnity, insinuates into the Pandora-box of marriage some deep and serious benefits and some great joys. We find a delight in the beauty and happiness of children that makes the heart too big for the body. In the worst-assorted connections there is ever some mixture of true marriage. Teague and his jade get some just relations of mutual respect, kindly observation, and fostering of each other; learn something, and would carry themselves wiselier if they were now to begin.

'Tis fine for us to point at one or another fine madman, as

if there were any exempts. The scholar in his library is none. I, who have all my life heard any number of orations and debates, read poems and miscellaneous books, conversed with many geniuses, am still the victim of any new page; and if Marmaduke, or Hugh, or Moosehead, or any other, invent a new style or mythology, I fancy that the world will be all brave and right if dressed in these colors, which I had not thought of. Then at once I will daub with this new paint; but it will not stick. 'Tis like the cement which the peddler sells at the door; he makes broken crockery hold with it, but you can never buy of him a bit of the cement which will make it hold when he is gone.

Men who make themselves felt in the world avail themselves of a certain fate in their constitution which they know how to use. But they never deeply interest us unless they lift a corner of the curtain, or betray, never so slightly, their penetration of what is behind it. 'Tis the charm of practical men that outside of their practicality are a certain poetry and play, as if they led the good horse Power by the bridle, and preferred to walk, though they can ride so fiercely. Bonaparte is intellectual, as well as Cæsar; and the best soldiers, sea-captains, and railway men have a gentleness when off duty, a good-natured admission that there are illusions, and who shall say that he is not their sport? We stigmatize the cast-iron fellows who cannot so detach themselves, as "dragon-ridden," "thunder-stricken," and fools of fate, with whatever powers endowed.

Since our tuition is through emblems and indirections, it is well to know that there is method in it, a fixed scale and rank above rank in the phantasms. We begin low with coarse masks and rise to the most subtle and beautiful. The red men told Columbus "they had an herb which took away fatigue"; but he found the illusion of "arriving from the east at the Indies" more composing to his lofty spirit than any tobacco. Is not our faith in the impenetrability of matter more sedative than narcotics? You play with jackstraws, balls, bowls, horse and gun, estates and politics; but there are finer games before you. Is not time a pretty toy? Life will show you masks that are worth all your carnivals. Yonder mountain must migrate into your mind. The fine stardust and nebulous blur in Orion, "the portentous year of Mizar and Alcor," must come down and be dealt with in your household thought. What if you shall come to discern that the play and playground of all this pompous history are radiations from yourself, and that the sun borrows his beams? What terrible questions we are learning to ask! The former men believed in magic, by which temples, cities, and men were swallowed up, and all trace of them gone. We are coming on the secret of a magic which sweeps out of men's minds all vestige of theism and beliefs which they and their fathers held and were framed upon.

There are deceptions of the senses, deceptions of the passions, and the structural, beneficent illusions of sentiment and of the intellect. There is the illusion of love, which attributes to the beloved person all which that person shares with his or her family, sex, age, or condition, nay, with the human mind itself. 'Tis these which the lover loves, and Anna Matilda gets the credit of them. As if one shut up always in a tower, with one window through which the face of heaven and earth could be seen, should fancy that all the marvels he beheld belonged to that window. There is the illusion of time, which is very deep; who has disposed of it?—or come to the conviction that what seems the *succession* of thought is only the distribution of wholes into causal series? The intellect sees that every atom carries the whole of nature; that the mind opens to omnipotence; that, in the endless striving and ascents, the metamorphosis is entire, so that the soul doth not know itself in its own act when the act is perfected. There is illusion that shall deceive even the elect. There is illusion that shall deceive even the performer of the miracle. Though he make his body, he denies that he makes it. Though the world exist from thought, thought is daunted in presence of the world. One after the other we accept the mental laws, still resisting those which follow, which however must be accepted. But all our concessions only compel us to new profusion. And what avails it that science has come to treat space and time as simply forms of thought, and the material world as hypothetical, and withal our pretension of *property* and even of self-hood are fading with the rest, if, at last, even our thoughts are not finalities, but the incessant flowing and ascension reach these also, and each thought which yesterday was a finality, today is yielding to a larger generalization?

With such volatile elements to work in, 'tis no wonder if our estimates are loose and floating. We must work and affirm, but we have no guess of the value of what we say or do. The cloud is now as big as your hand, and now it covers a county. That story of Thor, who was set to drain the drinking-horn in Asgard and to wrestle with the old woman and to run with the runner Lok, and presently found that he had been drinking up the sea, and wrestling with Time, and racing with Thought, describes us, who are contending, amid these seeming trifles, with the supreme energies of nature. We fancy we have fallen into bad company and squalid condition, low debts, shoe-bills, broken glass to pay for, pots to buy, butcher's meat, sugar, milk, and coal. "Set me some great task, ye gods! and I will show my spirit." "Not so," says the good Heaven; "plod and plough, vamp your old coats and hats, weave a shoestring; great affairs and the best wine by and by." Well, 'tis all phantasm; and if we weave a yard of tape in all humility and as well as we can, long hereafter we shall see it was no cotton tape at all but some galaxy which we braided, and that the threads were Time and Nature.

We cannot write the order of the variable winds. How can we penetrate the law of our shifting moods and susceptibility? Yet they differ as all and nothing. Instead of the firmament of yesterday, which our eyes require, it is today an eggshell which coops us in; we cannot even see what or where our stars of destiny are. From day to day the capital facts of human life are hidden from our eyes. Suddenly the mist rolls up and reveals them, and we think how much good time is gone that might have been saved had any hint of these things been shown. A sudden rise in the road shows us the system of mountains, and all the summits, which have been just as near us all the year, but quite out of mind. But these alternations are not without their order, and we are parties to our various fortune. If life seem a succession of dreams, yet poetic justice is done in dreams also. The visions of good men are good; it is the undisciplined will that is whipped with bad thoughts and bad fortunes. When we break the laws, we lose our hold on the central reality. Like sick men in hospitals, we change only from bed to bed, from one folly to another; and it cannot signify much what becomes of such castaways, wailing, stupid, comatose creatures, lifted from bed to bed, from the nothing of life to the nothing of death.

In this kingdom of illusions we grope eagerly for stays and foundations. There is none but a strict and faithful dealing at home and a severe barring out of all duplicity or illusion there. Whatever games are played with us, we must play no games with ourselves, but deal in our privacy with the last honesty and truth. I look upon the simple and childish virtues of veracity and honesty as the root of all that is sublime in character. Speak as you think, be what you are, pay your debts of all kinds. I prefer to be owned as sound and solvent, and my word as good as my bond, and to be what cannot be skipped, or dissipated, or undermined, to all the *éclat* in the universe. This reality is the foundation of friendship, religion, poetry, and art. At the top or at the bottom of all illusions, I set the cheat which still leads us to work and live for appearances; in spite of our conviction, in all sane hours, that it is what we really are that avails, with friends, with strangers, and with fate or fortune.

One would think from the talk of men that riches and poverty were a great matter; and our civilization mainly respects it. But the Indians say that they do not think the white man, with his brow of care, always toiling, afraid of heat and cold, and keeping within doors, has any advantage of them. The permanent interest of every man is never to be in a false position, but to have the weight of Nature to back him in all that he does. Riches and poverty are a thick or thin costume; and our life—the life of all of us—identical. For we transcend the circumstance continually and taste the real quality of existence; as in our employments, which only differ in the manipulations but express the same laws; or in our thoughts, which wear no silks and taste no ice creams. We see God face to face every hour, and know the savor of nature.

The early Greek philosophers Heraclitus and Xenophanes measured their force on this problem of identity. Diogenes of Apollonia said that unless the atoms were made of one stuff, they could never blend and act with one another. But the Hindoos, in their sacred writings, express the liveliest feeling, both of the essential identity and of that illusion which they conceive variety to be. "The notions, '*I am*,' and '*This is mine*,' which influence mankind, are but delusions of the mother of the world. Dispel, O Lord of all creatures! the conceit of knowledge which proceeds from ignorance." And the beatitude of man they hold to lie in being freed from fascination.

The intellect is stimulated by the statement of truth in a trope, and the will by clothing the laws of life in illusions. But the unities of Truth and of Right are not broken by the disguise. There need never be any confusion in these. In a crowded life of many parts and performers, on a stage of nations, or in the obscurest hamlet in Maine or California, the same elements offer the same choices to each new comer, and, according to his election, he fixes his fortune in absolute Nature. It would be hard to put more mental and moral philosophy than the Persians have thrown into a sentence:

> *Fooled thou must be, though wisest of the wise:*
> *Then be the fool of virtue, not of vice.*

There is no chance and no anarchy in the universe. All is system and gradation. Every god is there sitting in his sphere. The young mortal enters the hall of the firmament; there is he alone with them alone, they pouring on him benedictions and gifts, and beckoning him up to their thrones. On the instant, and incessantly, fall snowstorms of illusions. He fancies himself in a vast crowd which sways this way and that and whose movement and doings he must obey: he fancies himself poor, orphaned, insignificant. The mad crowd drives hither and thither, now furiously commanding this thing to be done, now that. What is he that he should resist their will, and think or act for himself? Every moment new changes and new showers of deceptions to baffle and distract him. And when, by and by, for an instant, the air clears and the cloud lifts a little, there are the gods still sitting around him on their thrones—they alone with him alone.

Oliver Wendell Holmes

1809 · 1894

*Oliver Wendell Holmes, American physician, poet,
teacher, essayist, novelist, and inventor, ruled
Boston as a literary dictator much as Johnson had
dominated London a century earlier. He was little
interested in the intellectual ferment in Boston in
the nineteenth century—transcendentalism, and such
movements. Instead, he held to a conservative,
common sense set of beliefs about humanity,
decency, and the value of sentiment and expressed
these beliefs with becoming restraint and humor.*

TO REACH PORT

I FIND THE GREAT THING IN THIS WORLD is not
so much where we stand, as in what direction
we are moving: To reach the port of heaven, we must sail
sometimes with the wind and sometimes against it—but we
must sail, and not drift, nor lie at anchor. There is one very
sad thing in old friendships, to every mind which is really
moving onward. It is this: that one cannot help using his early
friends as the seaman uses the log, to mark his progress. Every
now and then we throw an old schoolmate over the stern with
a string of thought tied to him, and look—I am afraid with a
kind of luxurious and sanctimonious compassion—to see the
rate at which the string reels off, while he lies there bobbing
up and down, poor fellow! and we are dashing along with
the white foam and bright sparkle at our bows—the ruffled
bosom of prosperity and progress, with a sprig of diamonds
stuck in it! But this is only the sentimental side of the matter;
for grow we must, if we outgrow all that we love.

Don't misunderstand that metaphor of heaving the log, I

beg you. It is merely a smart way of saying that we cannot avoid measuring our rate of movement by those with whom we have long been in the habit of comparing ourselves; and when they once become stationary, we can get our reckoning from them with painful accuracy. We see just what we were when they were our peers, and can strike the balance between that and whatever we may feel ourselves to be now. No doubt we may sometimes be mistaken. If we change our last simile to that very old and familiar one of a fleet leaving the harbor and sailing in company for some distant region, we can get what we want out of it. There is one of our companions—her streamers were torn into rags before she had got into the open sea, then by and by her sails blew out of the ropes one after another, the waves swept her deck, and as night came on we left her a seeming wreck, as we flew under our pyramid of canvas. But lo! at dawn she is still in sight—it may be in advance of us. Some deep ocean-current has been moving her on, strong, but silent—yes, stronger than these noisy winds that puff our sails until they are swollen as the cheeks of jubilant cherubim. And when at last the black steam-tug with the skeleton arms, which comes out of the mist sooner or later and takes us all in tow, grapples her and goes off panting and groaning with her, it is to that harbor where all wrecks are refitted and where, alas! we, towering in our pride, may never come.

So you will not think I mean to speak lightly of old friendships, because we cannot help instituting comparisons between our present and former selves by the aid of those who were what we were, but are not what we are. Nothing strikes one more, in the race of life, than to see how many give out in the first half of the course. "Commencement day" always reminds me of the start for the "Derby," when the beautiful high-bred three-year-olds of the season are brought up for trial. That day is the start, and life is the race. Here we are at Cambridge, and a class is just "graduating." Poor Harry! he was to have been there too, but he has paid forfeit; step out here into the grass behind the church; ah! there it is:—

"Hunc lapidem posuerunt
Soch mœrentes."

But this is the start, and here they are—coats bright as silk, and manes as smooth as *eau lustrale* can make them. Some of the best of the colts are pranced round, a few minutes each, to show their paces. What is that old gentleman crying about? and the old lady by him, and the three girls, what are they all covering their eyes for? Oh, that is *their* colt which has just been trotted up on the stage. Do they really think those little thin legs can do anything in such a slashing sweepstakes as is coming off in these next forty years? Oh, this terrible gift of second-sight that comes to some of us when we begin to look through the silvered rings of the *arcus senilis!*

Ten years gone. First turn in the race. A few broken down; two or three bolted. Several show in advance of the ruck. *Cassock*, a black colt, seems to be ahead of the rest; those black colts commonly get the start, I have noticed, of the others, in the first quarter. *Meteor* has pulled up.

Twenty years. Second corner turned. *Cassock* has dropped from the front, and *Judex*, an iron-gray, has the lead. But look! how they have thinned out! Down flat—five—six—how many? They lie still enough! they will not get up again in this race, be very sure! And the rest of them, what a "tailing off"! Anybody can see who is going to win—perhaps.

Thirty years. Third corner turned. *Dives*, bright sorrel, ridden by the fellow in a yellow jacket, begins to make play fast; is getting to be the favorite with many. But who is that other one that has been lengthening his stride from the first, and now shows close up to the front? Don't you remember the quiet brown colt *Asteroid*, with the star in his forehead? That is he; he is one of the sort that lasts; look out for him! The black "colt," as we used to call him, is in the background, taking it easily in a gentle trot. There is one they used to call *the Filly*, on account of a certain feminine air he had; well up, you see; the Filly is not to be despised, my boy!

Forty years. More dropping off—but places much as before.
Fifty years. Race over. All that are on the course are com-

ing in at a walk; no more running. Who is ahead? Ahead? What! and the winning-post a slab of white or gray stone standing out from that turf where there is no more jockeying or straining for victory! Well, the world marks their places in its betting-book; but be sure that these matter very little, if they have run as well as they knew how!

—Did I not say to you a little while ago that the universe swam in an ocean of similitudes and analogies? I will not quote Cowley, or Burns, or Wordsworth, just now, to show you what thoughts were suggested to them by the simplest natural objects, such as a flower or a leaf; but I will read you a few lines, if you do not object, suggested by looking at a section of one of those chambered shells to which is given the name of Pearly Nautilus. We need not trouble ourselves about the distinction between this and the Paper Nautilus, the *Argonauta* of the ancients. The name applied to both shows that each has long been compared to a ship, as you may see more fully in Webster's Dictionary, or the "Encyclopædia," to which he refers. If you will look into Roget's Bridgewater Treatise, you will find a figure of one of these shells and a section of it. The last will show you the series of enlarging compartments successively dwelt in by the animal that inhabits the shell, which is built in a widening spiral. Can you find no lesson in this?

THE CHAMBERED NAUTILUS

This is the ship of pearl, which, poets feign,
    Sails the unshadowed main—
    The venturous bark that flings
On the sweet summer wind its purpled wings
In gulfs enchanted, where the siren sings,
    And coral reefs lie bare,
Where the cold sea-maids rise to sun their streaming hair.

Its webs of living gauze no more unfurl;
    Wrecked is the ship of pearl!
    And every chambered cell,
Where its dim dreaming life was wont to dwell,

As the frail tenant shaped his growing shell,
    Before thee lies revealed—
Its irised ceiling rent, its sunless crypt unsealed!

Year after year beheld the silent toil
    That spread his lustrous coil;
    Still, as the spiral grew,
He left the past year's dwelling for the new,
Stole with soft step its shining archway through,
    Built up its idle door,
Stretched in his last-found home, and knew the old no more.

Thanks for the heavenly message brought by thee,
    Child of the wandering sea,
    Cast from her lap forlorn!
From thy dead lips a clearer note is born
Than ever Triton blew from wreathéd horn!
    While on mine ear it rings,
Through the deep caves of thought I hear a voice that sings:—

Build thee more stately mansions, O my soul,
    As the swift seasons roll!
    Leave thy low-vaulted past!
Let each new temple, nobler than the last,
Shut thee from heaven with a dome more vast,
    Till thou at length art free,
Leaving thine outgrown shell by life's unresting sea!

THE GREEN STATE

I DON'T THINK THE POEMS I READ YOU sometimes can be fairly appreciated, given to you as they are in the green state.

—You don't know what I mean by the *green state?* Well, then, I will tell you. Certain things are good for nothing until they have been kept a long while; and some are good for nothing until they have been long kept and *used.* Of the first, wine is the illustrious and immortal example. Of those

which must be kept and used I will name three—meerschaum
pipes, violins, and poems. The meerschaum is but a poor
affair until it has burned a thousand offerings to the cloud-
compelling deities. It comes to us without complexion or
flavor—born of the sea-foam, like Aphrodite, but colorless
as *pallida Mors* herself. The fire is lighted in its central shrine,
and gradually the juices which the broad leaves of the Great
Vegetable had sucked up from an acre and curdled into a
drachm are diffused through its thirsting pores. First a dis-
coloration, then a stain, and at last a rich, glowing, umber tint
spreading over the whole surface. Nature true to her old
brown autumnal hue, you see—as true in the fire of the
meerschaum as in the sunshine of October! And then the
cumulative wealth of its fragrant reminiscences! he who in-
hales its vapors takes a thousand whiffs in a single breath;
and one cannot touch it without awakening the old joys that
hang around it as the smell of flowers clings to the dresses of
the daughters of the house of Farina!

[Don't think I use a meerschaum myself, for *I do not*,
though I have owned a calumet since my childhood, which
from a naked Pict (of the Mohawk species) my grandsire
won, together with a tomahawk and beaded knife-sheath;
paying for the lot with a bullet-mark on his right cheek.
On the maternal side I inherit the loveliest silver-mounted
tobacco-stopper you ever saw. It is a little box-wood Triton, carved with charming liveliness and truth. I have often
compared it to a figure in Raphael's "Triumph of Galatea."
It came to me in an ancient shagreen case—how old it is I
do not know—but it must have been made since Sir Walter
Raleigh's time. If you are curious, you shall see it any day.
Neither will I pretend that I am so unused to the more per-
ishable smoking contrivance that a few whiffs would make
me feel as if I lay in a ground-swell on the Bay of Biscay.
I am not unacquainted with that fusiform, spiral-wound
bundle of chopped stems and miscellaneous incombustibles,
the *cigar*, so called, of the shops—which to "draw" asks the
suction-power of a nursling infant Hercules, and to relish,
the leathery palate of an old Silenus. I do not advise you,

young man, even if my illustration strike your fancy, to consecrate the flower of your life to painting the bowl of a pipe, for, let me assure you, the stain of a reverie-breeding narcotic may strike deeper than you think for. I have seen the green leaf of early promise grow brown before its time under such Nicotian regimen, and thought the umbered meerschaum was dearly bought at the cost of a brain enfeebled and a will enslaved.]

Violins, too—the sweet old Amati!—the divine Stradivarius! Played on by ancient *maestros* until the bow-hand lost its power and the flying fingers stiffened. Bequeathed to the passionate young enthusiast, who made it whisper his hidden love, and cry his inarticulate longings, and scream his untold agonies, and wail his monotonous despair. Passed from his dying hand to the cold *virtuoso*, who let it slumber in its case for a generation, till, when his hoard was broken up, it came forth once more and rode the stormy symphonies of royal orchestras, beneath the rushing bow of their lord and leader. Into lonely prisons with improvident artists; into convents from which arose, day and night, the holy hymns with which its tones were blended; and back again to orgies in which it learned to howl and laugh as if a legion of devils were shut up in it; then again to the gentle *dilettante* who calmed it down with easy melodies until it answered him softly as in the days of the old *maestros*. And so given into our hands, its pores all full of music; stained, like the meerschaum, through and through, with the concentrated hue and sweetness of all the harmonies which have kindled and faded on its strings.

Now I tell you a poem must be kept *and used*, like a meerschaum, or a violin. A poem is just as porous as the meerschaum—the more porous it is, the better. I mean to say that a genuine poem is capable of absorbing an indefinite amount of the essence of our own humanity—its tenderness, its heroism, its regrets, its aspirations, so as to be gradually stained through with a divine secondary color derived from ourselves. So you see it must take time to bring the sentiment of a poem into harmony with our nature, by staining ourselves through every thought and image our being can penetrate.

Then again as to the mere music of a new poem, why, who can expect anything more from that than from the music of a violin fresh from the maker's hands? Now you know very well that there are no less than fifty-eight different pieces in a violin. These pieces are strangers to each other, and it takes a century, more or less, to make them thoroughly acquainted. At last they learn to vibrate in harmony and the instrument becomes an organic whole, as if it were a great seed-capsule which had grown from a garden-bed in Cremona, or elsewhere. Besides, the wood is juicy and full of sap for fifty years or so, but at the end of fifty or a hundred more gets tolerably dry and comparatively resonant.

Don't you see that all this is just as true of a poem? Counting each word as a piece, there are more pieces in an average copy of verses than in a violin. The poet has forced all these words together, and fastened them, and they don't understand it at first. But let the poem be repeated aloud and murmured over in the mind's muffled whisper often enough, and at length the parts become knit together in such absolute solidarity that you could not change a syllable without the whole world's crying out against you for meddling with the harmonious fabric. Observe, too, how the drying process takes place in the stuff of a poem just as in that of a violin. Here is a Tyrolese fiddle that is just coming to its hundredth birthday— (Pedro Klauss, Tyroli, fecit, 1760)—the sap is pretty well out of it. And here is the song of an old poet whom Neæra cheated:—

> "Nox erat, et cœlo fulgebat Luna sereno
> Inter minora sidera,
> Cum tu magnorum numen læsura deorum
> In verba jurabas mea."

Don't you perceive the sonorousness of these old dead Latin phrases? Now I tell you that every word fresh from the dictionary brings with it a certain succulence; and though I cannot expect the sheets of the "Pactolian," in which, as I told you, I sometimes print my verses, to get so dry as the crisp papyrus that held those words of Horatius Flaccus, yet you may be sure, that, while the sheets are damp, and while the lines hold their sap, you can't fairly judge of my performances, and that, if made of the true stuff, they will ring better after a while.

William Makepeace Thackeray

1811 · 1863

*William Makepeace Thackeray was born in India
and educated at Cambridge, where he did not take a
degree but where he formed friendships with
Tennyson and Fitzgerald. He began a journalistic
career as proprietor of* The National Standard, *
for which he was an artist as well as a writer. After
the failure of the* Standard, *he studied drawing and
continued writing for many journals, including*
Punch. Vanity Fair, Pendennis, *and other
novels made him one of the most popular and
successful of English writers, and at the height of
his fame he achieved further acclaim as a
lecturer in England and in the United States.*

DE FINIBUS

WHEN SWIFT WAS IN LOVE WITH STELLA, and
despatching her a letter from London thrice
a month by the Irish packet, you may remember how he
would begin Letter No. xxiii, we will say, on the very day
when xxii had been sent away, stealing out of the coffee-
house or the assembly so as to be able to prattle with his dear;
"never letting go her kind hand, as it were," as some com-
mentator or other has said in speaking of the Dean and his
amour. When Mr. Johnson, walking to Dodsley's, and touching the posts in Pall Mall as he walked, forgot to pat the head
of one of them, he went back and imposed his hands on it,—
impelled I know not by what superstition. I have this I hope
not dangerous mania too. As soon as a piece of work is out of
hand, and before going to sleep, I like to begin another; it
may be to write only half-a-dozen lines: but that is something

towards Number the Next. The printer's boy has not yet
reached Green Arbour Court with the copy. Those people
who were alive half-an-hour since, Pendennis, Clive Newcome, and (what do you call him? what was the name of the
last hero? I remember now!) Philip Firmin, have hardly
drunk their glass of wine, and the mammas have only this
minute got the children's cloaks on, and have been bowed out
of my premises—and here I come back to the study again:
tamen usque recurro. How lonely it looks now all these
people are gone! My dear good friends, some folks are utterly
tired of you, and say, "What a poverty of friends the man
has! He is always asking us to meet those Pendennises, Newcomes, and so forth. Why does he not introduce us to some
new characters? Why is he not thrilling like Twostars, learned
and profound like Threestars, exquisitely humorous and human like Fourstars? Why, finally, is he not somebody else?"
My good people, it is not only impossible to please you all, but
it is absurd to try. The dish which one man devours, another
dislikes. Is the dinner of to-day not to your taste? Let us hope
to-morrow's entertainment will be more agreeable. . . . I resume my original subject. What an odd, pleasant, humorous,
melancholy feeling it is to sit in the study, alone and quiet,
now all these people are gone who have been boarding and
lodging with me for twenty months! They have interrupted
my rest: they have plagued me at all sorts of minutes: they
have thrust themselves upon me when I was ill, or wished to
be idle, and I have growled out a "Be hanged to you, can't
you leave me alone now?" Once or twice they have prevented
my going out to dinner. Many and many a time they have
prevented my coming home, because I knew they were there
waiting in the study, and a plague take them! and I have left
home and family, and gone to dine at the Club, and told nobody where I went. They have bored me, those people. They
have plagued me at all sorts of uncomfortable hours. They
have made such a disturbance in my mind and house, that
sometimes I have hardly known what was going on in my
family, and scarcely have heard what my neighbour said to
me. They are gone at last; and you would expect me to be at

ease? Far from it. I should almost be glad if Woolcomb would walk in and talk to me; or Twysden reappear, take his place in that chair opposite me, and begin one of his tremendous stories.

Madmen, you know, see visions, hold conversations with, even draw the likeness of, people invisible to you and me. Is this making of people out of fancy madness? and are novel-writers at all entitled to strait-waistcoats? I often forget people's names in life; and in my own stories contritely own that I make dreadful blunders regarding them; but I declare, my dear sir, with respect to the personages introduced into your humble servant's fables, I know the people utterly—I know the sound of their voices. A gentleman came in to see me the other day, who was so like the picture of Philip Firmin in Mr. Walker's charming drawings in the *Cornhill Magazine* that he was quite a curiosity to me. The same eyes, beard, shoulders, just as you have seen them from month to month. Well, he is not like the Philip Firmin in my mind. Asleep, asleep in the grave, lies the bold, the generous, the reckless, the tender-hearted creature whom I have made to pass through those adventures which have just been brought to an end. It is years since I heard the laughter ringing, or saw the bright blue eyes. When I knew him both were young. I become young as I think of him. And this morning he was alive again in this room, ready to laugh, to fight, to weep. As I write, do you know, it is the grey of evening; the house is quiet; everybody is out; the room is getting a little dark, and I look rather wistfully up from the paper with perhaps ever so little fancy that HE MAY COME IN.——No? No movement. No grey shade, growing more palpable, out of which at last look the well-known eyes. No, the printer came and took him away with the last page of the proofs. And with the printer's boy did the whole cortège of ghosts flit away, invisible? Ha! stay! what is this? Angels and ministers of grace! The door opens, and a dark form—enters, bearing a black—a black suit of clothes. It is John. He says it is time to dress for dinner.

.   .   .   .

Every man who has had his German tutor, and has been

coached through the famous *Faust* of Goethe (thou wert my instructor, good old Weissenborn, and these eyes beheld the great master himself in dear little Weimar town!) has read those charming verses which are prefixed to the drama, in which the poet reverts to the time when his work was first composed, and recalls the friends now departed, who once listened to his song. The dear shadows rise up around him, he says; he lives in the past again. It is to-day which appears vague and visionary. We humbler writers cannot create Fausts, or raise up monumental works that shall endure for all ages; but our books are diaries, in which our own feelings must of necessity be set down. As we look to the page written last month, or ten years ago, we remember the day and its events; the child ill, mayhap, in the adjoining room, and the doubts and fears which racked the brain as it still pursued its work; the dear old friend who read the commencement of the tale, and whose gentle hand shall be laid in ours no more. I own for my part that, in reading pages which this hand penned formerly, I often lose sight of the text under my eyes. It is not the words I see; but that past day; that bygone page of life's history; that tragedy, comedy it may be, which our little home company was enacting; that merry-making which we shared; that funeral which we followed; that bitter, bitter grief which we buried.

And, such being the state of my mind, I pray gentle readers to deal kindly with their humble servant's manifold shortcomings, blunders, and slips of memory. As sure as I read a page of my own composition, I find a fault or two, half a dozen. Jones is called Brown. Brown, who is dead, is brought to life. Aghast, and months after the number was printed, I saw that I had called Philip Firmin, Clive Newcome. Now Clive Newcome is the hero of another story by the reader's most obedient writer. The two men are as different in my mind's eye, as—as Lord Palmerston and Mr. Disraeli let us say. But there is that blunder at page 990, line 76, volume 84 of the *Cornhill Magazine*, and it is past mending; and I wish in my life I had made no worse blunders or errors than that which is hereby acknowledged.

De Finibus

Another Finis written. Another mile-stone passed on this journey from birth to the next world! Sure it is a subject for solemn cogitation. Shall we continue this story-telling business and be voluble to the end of our age? Will it not be presently time, O prattler, to hold your tongue, and let younger people speak? I have a friend, a painter, who, like other persons who shall be nameless, is growing old. He has never painted with such laborious finish as his works now show. This master is still the most humble and diligent of scholars. Of Art, his mistress, he is always an eager reverent pupil. In his calling, in yours, in mine, industry and humility will help and comfort us. A word with you. In a pretty large experience I have not found the men who write books superior in wit or learning to those who don't write at all. In regard of mere information, non-writers must often be superior to writers. You don't expect a lawyer in full practice to be conversant with all kinds of literature; he is too busy with his law; and so a writer is commonly too busy with his own books to be able to bestow attention on the works of other people. After a day's work (in which I have been depicting, let us say, the agonies of Louisa on parting with the Captain, or the atrocious behaviour of the wicked Marquis to Lady Emily) I march to the Club, proposing to improve my mind and keep myself "posted up," as the Americans phrase it, with the literature of the day. And what happens? Given a walk after luncheon, a pleasing book, and a most comfortable arm-chair by the fire, and you know the rest. A doze ensues. Pleasing book drops suddenly, is picked up once with an air of some confusion, is laid presently softly in lap: head falls on comfortable armchair cushion: eyes close: soft nasal music is heard. Am I telling Club secrets? Of afternoons, after lunch, I say, scores of sensible fogies have a doze. Perhaps I have fallen asleep over that very book to which "Finis" has just been written. "And if the writer sleeps, what happens to the readers?" says Jones, coming down upon me with his lightning wit. What? You *did* sleep over it? And a very good thing too. These eyes have more than once seen a friend dozing over pages which this hand has written. There is a vignette somewhere in one of my books of a friend so caught napping with *Pendennis,* or *The Newcomes,* in his lap; and if a writer can give you a sweet, soothing, harmless sleep, has he not done you a kindness? So is the author who excites and interests you worthy of your thanks and benedictions. I am troubled with fever and ague, that seizes me at odd intervals and prostrates me for a day. There is cold fit, for which, I am thankful to say, hot brandy-and-water is prescribed, and this induces hot fit, and so on. In one or two of these fits I have read novels with the most fearful contentment of mind. Once on the Mississippi, it was my dearly beloved *Jacob Faithful:* once at Frankfort O. M., the delightful *Vingt Ans Après* of Monsieur Dumas: once at Tunbridge Wells, the thrilling *Woman in White:* and these books gave me amusement from morning till sunset. I remember those ague fits with a great deal of pleasure and gratitude. Think of a whole day in bed, and a good novel for a companion! No cares: no remorse about idleness: no visitors: and the Woman in White or the Chevalier d'Artagnan to tell me stories from dawn to night! "Please, ma'am, my master's compliments, and can he have the third volume?" (This message was sent to an astonished friend and neighbour who lent me, volume by volume, the *W. in W.*) How do you like your novels? I like mine strong, "hot with," and no mistake: no love-making: no observations about society: little dialogue, except where the characters are bullying each other: plenty of fighting: and a villain in the cupboard, who is to suffer tortures just before Finis. I don't like your melancholy Finis. I never read the history of a consumptive heroine twice. If I might give a short hint to an impartial writer (as the *Examiner* used to say in old days), it would be to act, *not* à la mode le pays de Pole (I think that was the phraseology), but *always* to give quarter. In the story of Philip, just come to an end, I have the permission of the author to state that he was going to drown the two villains of the piece—a certain Doctor F—— and a certain Mr. T. H—— on board the *President,* or some other tragic ship—but you see I relented. I pictured to myself Firmin's ghastly face amid the crowd of shuddering people on that reeling deck in the lonely ocean and thought, "Thou ghastly lying wretch, thou shalt not be drowned: thou shalt have a fever only; a knowledge of thy danger; and a chance—ever so small a chance—of repentance." I wonder whether he *did* repent when he found himself in the yellow-fever, in Virginia? The probability is, he fancied that his son had injured him very much, and forgave him on his death-bed. Do you imagine there is a great deal of genuine right-down remorse in the world? Don't people rather find excuses which make their minds easy; endeavour to prove to themselves that they have been lamentably belied and misunderstood; and try and forgive the persecutors who *will* present that bill when it is due; and not bear malice against the cruel ruffian who takes them to the police-office for stealing the spoons? Years ago I had a quarrel with a certain well-known person (I believed a statement regarding him which his friends imparted to me, and which turned out to be quite incorrect). To his dying day that quarrel was never quite made up. I said to his brother, "Why is your brother's soul still dark against me? It is I who ought to be angry and unforgiving: for I was in the wrong." In the region which they now inhabit (for Finis has been set to the volumes of the lives of both here below), if they take any cognisance of our squabbles, and tittle-tattles, and gossips on earth here, I hope they admit that my little error was not of a nature unpardonable. If you have never committed a worse, my good sir, surely the score against you will not be heavy. Ha, *dilectissimi fratres!* It is in regard of sins *not* found out that we may say or sing (in an undertone, in a most penitent and lugubrious minor key), *Miserere nobis miseris peccatoribus.*

Among the sins of commission which novel-writers not seldom perpetrate, is the sin of grandiloquence, or tall-talking against which, for my part, I will offer up a special *libra me.* This is the sin of schoolmasters, governesses, critics, sermoners, and instructors of young or old people. Nay (for I am making a clean breast, and liberating my soul), perhaps of all the novel-spinners now extant, the present speaker is the most addicted to preaching. Does he not stop perpetually in his story and begin to preach to you? When he ought to be engaged with business, is he not for ever taking the Muse by the sleeve, and plaguing her with some of his cynical sermons? I cry *peccavi* loudly and heartily. I tell you I would like to be able to write a story which should show no egotism whatever —in which there should be no reflections, no cynicism, no vulgarity (and so forth), but an incident in every other page, a villain, a battle, a mystery in every chapter. I should like to be able to feed a reader so spicily as to leave him hungering and thirsting for more at the end of every monthly meal.

Alexandre Dumas describes himself, when inventing the plan of a work, as lying silent on his back for two whole days on the deck of a yacht in a Mediterranean port. At the end of the two days he arose and called for dinner. In those two days he had built his plot. He had moulded a mighty clay, to be cast presently in perennial brass. The chapters, the characters, the incidents, the combinations were all arranged in the artist's brain ere he set a pen to paper. My Pegasus won't fly, so as to let me survey the field below me. He has no wings, he is blind of one eye certainly, he is restive, stubborn, slow; crops a hedge when he ought to be galloping, or gallops when he ought to be quiet. He never will show off when I want him. Sometimes he goes at a pace which surprises me. Sometimes, when I most wish him to make the running, the brute turns restive, and I am obliged to let him take his own time. I wonder do other novel-writers experience this fatalism? They *must* go a certain way, in spite of themselves. I have been surprised at the observations made by some of my characters. It seems as if an occult Power was moving the pen. The personage does or says something, and I ask, how the dickens did he come to think of that? Every man has remarked in dreams, the vast dramatic power which is sometimes evinced; I won't say the surprising power, for nothing does surprise you in dreams. But those strange characters you meet make instant observations of which you never can have thought previously. In like manner, the imagination foretells things. We spake anon of the inflated style of some writers. What also if there is an *afflated* style,—when a writer is like a Pythoness on her oracle tripod, and mighty words, words which he cannot help, come blowing, and bellowing, and whistling, and moaning through the speaking pipes of his bodily organ? I have told you it was a very queer shock to me the other day when, with a letter of introduction in his hand, the artist's (not my) Philip Firmin walked into this room, and sat down in the chair opposite. In the novel of *Pendennis*, written ten years ago, there is an account of a certain Costigan, whom I had invented (as I suppose authors invent their personages out of scraps, heeltaps, odds and ends of characters). I was smoking in a tavern parlour one night—and this Costigan came into the room alive —the very man:—the most remarkable resemblance of the printed sketches of the man, of the rude drawings in which I had depicted him. He had the same little coat, the same battered hat, cocked on one eye, the same twinkle in that eye. "Sir," said I, knowing him to be an old friend whom I had met in unknown regions, "sir," I said, "may I offer you a glass of brandy-and-water?" "*Bedad, ye may,*" says he, "*and I'll sing ye a song tu.*" Of course he spoke with an Irish brogue. Of course he had been in the army. In ten minutes he pulled out an Army Agent's account, whereon his name was written. A few months after we read of him in a police-court. How had I come to know him, to divine him? Nothing shall convince me that I have not seen that man in the world of spirits. In the world of spirits and water I know I did: but that is a mere quibble of words. I was not surprised when he spoke in an Irish brogue. I had had cognisance of him before somehow. Who has not felt that little shock which arises when a person, a place, some words in a book (there is always a collocation) present themselves to you, and you know that you have before met the same person, words, scene, and so forth?

They used to call the good Sir Walter the "Wizard of the North." What if some writer should appear who can write so *enchantingly* that he shall be able to call into actual life the people whom he invents? What if Mignon, and Margaret, and Goetz von Berlichingen are alive now (though I don't say they are visible), and Dugald Dalgetty and Ivanhoe were to step in at that open window by the little garden yonder? Suppose Uncas and our noble old Leather-stocking were to glide silently in? Suppose Athos, Porthos, and Aramis should enter with a noiseless swagger, curling their moustaches? And dearest Amelia Booth, on Uncle Toby's arm; and Tittlebat Titmouse, with his hair dyed green; and all the Crummles company of comedians, with the Gil Blas troop; and Sir Roger de Coverley; and the greatest of all crazy gentlemen, the Knight of La Mancha, with his blessed squire? I say to you, I look rather wistfully towards the window, musing upon these people. Were any of them to enter, I think I should not be very much frightened. Dear old friends, what pleasant hours I have had with them! We do not see each other very often, but when we do, we are ever happy to meet. I had a capital half-hour with Jacob Faithful last night; when the last sheet was corrected, when "Finis," had been written, and the printer's boy, with the copy, was safe in Green Arbour Court.

So you are gone, little printer's boy, with the last scratches and corrections on the proof, and a fine flourish by way of Finis at the story's end. The last corrections? I say those last corrections seem never to be finished. A plague upon the weeds! Every day, when I walk in my own little literary garden-plot, I spy some, and should like to have a spud, and root them out. Those idle words, neighbour, are past remedy. That turning back to the old pages produces anything but elation of mind. Would you not pay a pretty fine to be able to cancel some of them? Oh, the sad old pages, the dull old pages! Oh, the cares, the *ennui*, the squabbles, the repetitions, the old conversations over and over again! But now and again a kind thought is recalled, and now and again a dear memory. Yet a few chapters more, and then the last: after which, behold Finis itself come to an end, and the Infinite begun.

Henry David Thoreau

1817 · 1862

Henry David Thoreau, American essayist, lecturer, and naturalist, was born in Concord, Massachusetts, and spent most of his life there. Emerson sponsored him, and Hawthorne was his friend. After leaving Harvard, he tried teaching but soon gave it up and supported himself by working with his hands at carpentry, surveying, and odd jobs. Walden (1854) is in part an account of his life during two years spent in a cabin which he built near Walden Pond, and in part an expression of his protest against the complexities of modern civilization, which, as an extreme individualist, he deplored. "Civil Disobedience" is said to have influenced Mahatma Gandhi, who made use of Thoreau's thesis in developing his doctrine of passive resistance.

CIVIL DISOBEDIENCE

I HEARTILY ACCEPT THE MOTTO,—"That government is best which governs least"; and I should like to see it acted up to more rapidly and systematically. Carried out, it finally amounts to this, which also I believe,— "That government is best which governs not at all"; and when men are prepared for it, that will be the kind of government which they will have. Government is at best but an expedient; but most governments are usually, and all governments are sometimes, inexpedient. The objections which have been brought against a standing army, and they are many and weighty, and deserve to prevail, may also at last be brought against a standing government. The standing army is only an arm of the standing government. The government itself, which is only the mode which the people have chosen to execute their will, is equally liable to be abused and perverted before the people can act through it. Witness the present Mexican war, the work of comparatively a few individuals using the standing government as their tool; for, in the outset, the people would not have consented to this measure.

This American government,—what is it but a tradition, though a recent one, endeavoring to transmit itself unimpaired to posterity, but each instant losing some of its integrity? It has not the vitality and force of a single living man; for a single man can bend it to his will. It is a sort of wooden gun to the people themselves. But it is not the less necessary for this; for the people must have some complicated machinery or other, and hear its din, to satisfy that idea of government which they have. Governments show thus how successfully men can be imposed on, even impose on themselves, for their own advantage. It is excellent, we must all allow. Yet this government never of itself furthered any enterprise, but by the alacrity with which it got out of its way. *It* does not keep the country free. *It* does not settle the West. *It* does not educate. The character inherent in the American people has done all that has been accomplished; and it would have done somewhat more, if the government had not sometimes got in its way. For government is an expedient by which men would fain succeed in letting one another alone; and, as has been said, when it is most expedient, the governed are most let alone by it. Trade and commerce, if they were not made of India-rubber, would never manage to bounce over the obstacles which legislators are continually putting in their way; and, if one were to judge these men wholly by the effects of their actions and not partly by their intentions, they would deserve to be classed and punished with those mischievous persons who put obstructions on the railroads.

But, to speak practically and as a citizen, unlike those who call themselves no-government men, I ask for, not at once no government, but *at once* a better government. Let every man make known what kind of government would command his respect, and that will be one step toward obtaining it.

After all, the practical reason why, when the power is once in the hands of the people, a majority are permitted, and for a long period continue, to rule is not because they are most likely to be in the right, nor because this seems fairest to the minority, but because they are physically the strongest. But a government in which the majority rule in all cases cannot be based on justice, even as far as men understand it. Can there not be a government in which majorities do not virtually decide right and wrong, but conscience?—in which majorities decide only those questions to which the rule of expediency is applicable? Must the citizen ever for a moment, or in the least degree, resign his conscience to the legislator? Why has every man a conscience, then? I think that we should be men first, and subjects afterward. It is not desirable to cultivate a respect for the law, so much as for the right. The only obligation which I have a right to assume is to do at any time what I think right. It is truly enough said, that a corporation has no conscience; but a corporation of conscientious men is a corporation *with* a conscience. Law never made men a whit more just; and, by means of their respect for it, even the well-disposed are daily made the agents of injustice. A common and natural result of an undue respect for law is, that you may see a file of soldiers, colonel, captain, corporal, privates, powder-monkeys, and all, marching in admirable order over hill and dale to the wars, against their wills, ay, against their common sense and consciences, which makes it very steep marching indeed, and produces a palpitation of the heart. They have no doubt that it is a damnable business in which they are concerned; they are all peaceably inclined. Now, what are they? Men at all? or small movable forts and magazines, at the service of some unscrupulous man in power? Visit the Navy-Yard, and behold a marine, such a man as an American government can make, or such as it can make a man with its black arts,—a mere shadow and reminiscence of humanity, a man laid out alive and standing, and already, as one may say, buried under arms with funeral accompaniments, though it may be,—

> "Not a drum was heard, not a funeral note,
>   As his corse to the rampart we hurried;
>   Not a soldier discharged his farewell shot
>   O'er the grave where our hero we buried."

The mass of men serve the state thus, not as men mainly, but as machines, with their bodies. They are the standing army, and the militia, jailors, constables, posse comitatus, etc. In most cases there is no free exercise whatever of the judgment or of the moral sense; but they put themselves on a level with wood and earth and stones; and wooden men can perhaps be manufactured that will serve the purpose as well. Such command no more respect than men of straw or a lump of dirt. They have the same sort of worth only as horses and dogs. Yet such as these even are commonly esteemed good citizens. Others—as most legislators, politicians, lawyers, ministers, and office-holders—serve the state chiefly with their heads; and, as they rarely make any moral distinctions, they are as likely to serve the Devil, without *intending* it, as God. A very few, as heroes, patriots, martyrs, reformers in the great sense, and *men*, serve the state with their consciences also, and so necessarily resist it for the most part; and they are commonly treated as enemies by it. A wise man will only be useful as a man, and will not submit to be "clay," and "stop a hole to keep the wind away," but leave that office to his dust at least:—

> "I am too high-born to be propertied,
>   To be a secondary at control,
>   Or useful serving-man and instrument
>   To any sovereign state throughout the world."

He who gives himself entirely to his fellow-men appears to them useless and selfish; but he who gives himself partially to them is pronounced a benefactor and philanthropist.

How does it become a man to behave toward this American government to-day? I answer, that he cannot without disgrace be associated with it. I cannot for an instant recognize that political organization as *my* government which is the *slave's* government also.

All men recognize the right of revolution; that is, the right to refuse allegiance to, and to resist, the government, when its tyranny or its inefficiency are great and unendurable. But almost all say that such is not the case now. But such was the case, they think, in the Revolution of '75. If one were to tell me that this was a bad government because it taxed certain foreign commodities brought to its ports, it is most probable that I should not make an ado about it, for I can do without them. All machines have their friction; and possibly this does enough good to counterbalance the evil. At any rate, it is a great evil to make a stir about it. But when the friction comes to have its machine, and oppression and robbery are organized, I say, let us not have such a machine any longer. In other words, when a sixth of the population of a nation which has undertaken to be the refuge of liberty are slaves, and a whole country is unjustly overrun and conquered by a foreign army, and subjected to military law, I think that it is not too soon for honest men to rebel and revolutionize. What makes this duty the more urgent is the fact that the country so overrun is not our own, but ours is the invading army. . . .

All voting is a sort of gaming, like checkers or backgammon, with a slight moral tinge to it, a playing with right and wrong, with moral questions; and betting naturally accompanies it. The character of the voters is not staked. I cast my vote, perchance, as I think right; but I am not vitally concerned that that right should prevail. I am willing to leave it to the majority. Its obligation, therefore, never exceeds that of expediency. Even voting *for the right* is *doing* nothing for it. It is only expressing to men feebly your desire that it should prevail. A wise man will not leave the right to the mercy of chance, nor wish it to prevail through the power of the majority. There is but little virtue in the action of masses of men. When the majority shall at length vote for the abolition of slavery, it will be because they are indifferent to slavery, or because there is but little slavery left to be abolished by their vote. *They* will then be the only slaves. Only *his* vote can hasten the abolition of slavery who asserts his own freedom by his vote. . . .

The broadest and most prevalent error requires the most disinterested virtue to sustain it. The slight reproach to which the virtue of patriotism is commonly liable, the noble are most likely to incur. Those who, while they disapprove of the character and measures of a government, yield to it their allegiance and support are undoubtedly its most conscientious supporters, and so frequently the most serious obstacles to reform. Some are petitioning the state to dissolve the Union, to disregard the requisitions of the President. Why do they not dissolve it themselves,—the union between themselves and the state,—and refuse to pay their quota into its treasury? Do not they stand in the same relation to the state that the state does to the Union? And have not the same reasons prevented the state from resisting the Union which have prevented them from resisting the state?

How can a man be satisfied to entertain an opinion merely, and enjoy *it?* Is there any enjoyment in it, if his opinion is that he is aggrieved? If you are cheated out of a single dollar by your neighbor, you do not rest satisfied with knowing that you are cheated, or with saying that you are cheated, or even with petitioning him to pay you your due; but you take effectual steps at once to obtain the full amount, and see that you are never cheated again. Action from principle, the perception and the performance of right, changes things and relations; it is essentially revolutionary, and does not consist wholly with anything which was. It not only divides states and churches, it divides families; ay, it divides the *individual*, separating the diabolical in him from the divine.

Unjust laws exist: shall we be content to obey them, or shall we endeavor to amend them, and obey them until we have succeeded, or shall we transgress them at once? Men generally, under such a government as this, think that they ought to wait until they have persuaded the majority to alter them. They think that, if they should resist, the remedy would be worse than the evil. But it is the fault of the government itself that the remedy *is* worse than the evil. *It* makes it worse. Why is it not more apt to anticipate and provide for reform? Why does it not cherish its wise minority?

Why does it cry and resist before it is hurt? Why does it not encourage its citizens to be on the alert to point out its faults and *do* better than it would have them? Why does it always crucify Christ, and excommunicate Copernicus and Luther, and pronounce Washington and Franklin rebels?

One would think, that a deliberate and practical denial of its authority was the only offense never contemplated by government; else, why has it not assigned its definite, its suitable and proportionate penalty? If a man who has no property refuses but once to earn nine shillings for the state, he is put in prison for a period unlimited by any law that I know, and determined only by the discretion of those who placed him there; but if he should steal ninety times nine shillings from the state, he is soon permitted to go at large again.

If the injustice is part of the necessary friction of the machine of government, let it go, let it go: perchance it will wear smooth,—certainly the machine will wear out. If the injustice has a spring, or a pulley, or a rope, or a crank, exclusively for itself, then perhaps you may consider whether the remedy will not be worse than the evil; but if it is of such a nature that it requires you to be the agent of injustice to another, then, I say, break the law. Let your life be a counter friction to stop the machine. What I have to do is to see, at any rate, that I do not lend myself to the wrong which I condemn.

As for adopting the ways which the state has provided for remedying the evil, I know not of such ways. They take too much time, and a man's life will be gone. I have other affairs to attend to. I came into this world, not chiefly to make this a good place to live in, but to live in it, be it good or bad. A man has not everything to do, but something; and because he cannot do *everything*, it is not necessary that he should do *something* wrong. It is not my business to be petitioning the Governor or the Legislature any more than it is theirs to petition me; and if they should not hear my petition, what should I do then? But in this case the state has provided no way: its very Constitution is the evil. This may seem to be harsh and stubborn and unconciliatory; but it is to treat with the utmost kindness and consideration the only spirit that can appreciate or deserves it. So is all change for the better, like birth and death, which convulse the body.

I do not hesitate to say, that those who call themselves Abolitionists should at once effectually withdraw their support, both in person and property, from the government of Massachusetts and not wait till they constitute a majority of one, before they suffer the right to prevail through them. I think that it is enough if they have God on their side, without waiting for that other one. Moreover, any man more right than his neighbors constitutes a majority of one already.

I meet this American government, or its representative, the state government, directly, and face to face, once a year—no more—in the person of its tax-gatherer; this is the only mode in which a man situated as I am necessarily meets it; and it then says distinctly, Recognize me; and the simplest, most effectual, and, in the present posture of affairs, the indispensablest mode of treating with it on this head, of expressing your little satisfaction with and love for it, is to deny it then. My civil neighbor, the tax-gatherer, is the very man I have to deal with,—for it is, after all, with men and not with parchment that I quarrel,—and he has voluntarily chosen to be an agent of the government. How shall he ever know well what he is and does as an officer of the government, or as a man, until he is obliged to consider whether he shall treat me, his neighbor, for whom he has respect, as a neighbor and well-disposed man, or as a maniac and disturber of the peace, and see if he can get over this obstruction to his neighborliness without a ruder and more impetuous thought or speech corresponding with his action? . . .

Some years ago, the State met me in behalf of the Church, and commanded me to pay a certain sum toward the support of a clergyman whose preaching my father attended, but never I myself. "Pay," it said, "or be locked up in the jail." I declined to pay. But, unfortunately, another man saw fit to pay it. I did not see why the schoolmaster should be taxed to support the priest, and not the priest the schoolmaster; for I was not the State's schoolmaster, but I supported myself by

voluntary subscription. I did not see why the lyceum should
not present its tax-bill, and have the State to back its demand,
as well as the Church. However, at the request of the select-
men, I condescended to make some such statement as this in
writing:—"Know all men by these presents, that I, Henry
Thoreau, do not wish to be regarded as a member of any
incorporated society which I have not joined." This I gave
to the town clerk; and he has it. The State, having thus learned
that I did not wish to be regarded as a member of that church,
has never made a like demand on me since; though it said that
it must adhere to its original presumption that time. If I had
known how to name them, I should then have signed off in
detail from all the societies which I never signed on to; but I
did not know where to find a complete list.

I have paid no poll-tax for six years. I was put into a jail
once on this account, for one night; and, as I stood considering
the walls of solid stone, two or three feet thick, the door of
wood and iron, a foot thick, and the iron grating which
strained the light, I could not help being struck with the fool-
ishness of that institution which treated me as if I were mere
flesh and blood and bones, to be locked up. I wondered that
it should have concluded at length that this was the best use it
could put me to, and had never thought to avail itself of my
services in some way. I saw that, if there was a wall of stone
between me and my townsmen, there was a still more difficult
one to climb or break through before they could get to be as
free as I was. I did not for a moment feel confined, and the
walls seemed a great waste of stone and mortar. I felt as if I
alone of all my townsmen had paid my tax. They plainly did
not know how to treat me, but behaved like persons who are
underbred. In every threat and in every compliment there was
a blunder; for they thought that my chief desire was to
stand the other side of that stone wall. I could not but smile
to see how industriously they locked the door on my meditations, which followed them out again without let or hindrance,
and *they* were really all that was dangerous. As they could
not reach me, they had resolved to punish my body; just as
boys, if they cannot come at some person against whom they

have a spite, will abuse his dog. I saw that the State was half-witted, that it was timid as a lone woman with her silver spoons, and that it did not know its friends from its foes, and I lost all my remaining respect for it, and pitied it.

Thus the State never intentionally confronts a man's sense, intellectual or moral, but only his body, his senses. It is not armed with superior wit or honesty, but with superior physical strength. I was not born to be forced. I will breathe after my own fashion. Let us see who is the strongest. What force has a multitude? They only can force me who obey a higher law than I. They force me to become like themselves. I do not hear of *men* being *forced* to live this way or that by masses of men. What sort of life were that to live? When I meet a government which says to me, "Your money or your life," why should I be in haste to give it my money? It may be in a great strait, and not know what to do: I cannot help that. It must help itself; do as I do. It is not worth the while to snivel about it. I am not responsible for the successful working of the machinery of society. I am not the son of the engineer. I perceive that, when an acorn and a chestnut fall side by side, the one does not remain inert to make way for the other, but both obey their own laws, and spring and grow and flourish as best they can, till one, perchance, overshadows and destroys the other. If a plant cannot live according to its nature, it dies; and so a man.

The night in prison was novel and interesting enough. The prisoners in their shirt-sleeves were enjoying a chat and the evening air in the doorway, when I entered. But the jailer said, "Come, boys, it is time to lock up"; and so they dispersed, and I heard the sound of their steps returning into the hollow apartments. My room-mate was introduced to me by the jailer as "a first-rate fellow and a clever man." When the door was locked, he showed me where to hang my hat, and how he managed matters there. The rooms were white-washed once a month; and this one, at least, was the whitest, most simply furnished, and probably the neatest apartment in the town. He naturally wanted to know where I came from, and what brought me there; and, when I had told him, I asked him in my turn how he came there, presuming him to be an honest man, of course; and, as the world goes, I believe he was. "Why," said he, "they accuse me of burning a barn; but I never did it." As near as I could discover, he had probably gone to bed in a barn when drunk, and smoked his pipe there; and so a barn was burnt. He had the reputation of being a clever man, had been there some three months waiting for his trial to come on, and would have to wait as much longer; but he was quite domesticated and contented, since he got his board for nothing, and thought that he was well treated.

He occupied one window, and I the other; and I saw that if one stayed there long, his principal business would be to look out the window. I had soon read all the tracts that were left there, and examined where former prisoners had broken out, and where a grate had been sawed off, and heard the history of the various occupants of that room; for I found that even here there was a history and a gossip which never circulated beyond the walls of the jail. Probably this is the only house in the town where verses are composed, which are afterward printed in a circular form, but not published. I was shown quite a long list of verses which were composed by some young men who had been detected in an attempt to escape, who avenged themselves by singing them.

I pumped my fellow-prisoner as dry as I could, for fear I should never see him again; but at length he showed me which was my bed, and left me to blow out the lamp.

It was like travelling into a far country, such as I had never expected to behold, to lie there for one night. It seemed to me that I never had heard the town-clock strike before, nor the evening sounds of the village; for we slept with the windows open, which were inside the grating. It was to see my native village in the light of the Middle Ages, and our Concord was turned into a Rhine stream, and visions of knights and castles passed before me. They were the voices of old burghers that I heard in the streets. I was an involuntary spectator and auditor of whatever was done and said in the kitchen of the adjacent village-inn,—a wholly new and rare experience to me. It was a closer view of my native town. I was fairly inside of it. I never had seen its institutions before. This is one of its peculiar institutions; for it is a shire town. I began to comprehend what its inhabitants were about.

In the morning, our breakfasts were put through the hole in the door, in small oblong-square tin pans, made to fit, and holding a pint of chocolate, with brown bread, and an iron spoon. When they called for the vessels again, I was green enough to return what bread I had left; but my comrade seized it, and said that I should lay that up for lunch or dinner. Soon after he was let out to work at haying in a neighboring field, whither he went every day, and would not be back till noon; so he bade me good-day, saying that he doubted if he should see me again.

When I came out of prison,—for some one interfered, and paid that tax,—I did not perceive that great changes had taken place on the common, such as he observed who went in a youth and emerged a tottering and gray-headed man; and yet a change had to my eyes come over the scene,—the town, and State, and country,—greater than any that mere time could effect. I saw yet more distinctly the State in which I lived. I saw to what extent the people among whom I lived could be trusted as good neighbors and friends; that their friendship was for summer weather only; that they did not greatly propose to do right; that they were a distinct race from me by their prejudices and superstitions, as the Chinamen and Malays are; that in their sacrifices to humanity they ran no risks, not even to their property; that after all they were not so noble but they treated the thief as he had treated them, and hoped, by a certain outward observance and a few prayers, and by walking in a particular straight though useless path from time to time, to save their souls. This may be to judge my neighbors harshly; for I believe that many of them are not aware that they have such an institution as the jail in their village.

It was formerly the custom in our village, when a poor debtor came out of jail, for his acquaintances to salute him, looking through their fingers, which were crossed to represent the grating of a jail window, "How do ye do?" My

neighbors did not thus salute me, but first looked at me, and
then at one another, as if I had returned from a long journey.
I was put into jail as I was going to the shoemaker's to get a
shoe which was mended. When I was let out the next morning, I proceeded to finish my errand, and, having put on my
mended shoe, joined a huckleberry party, who were impatient
to put themselves under my conduct; and in half an hour,—for
the horse was soon tackled,—was in the midst of a huckleberry
field, on one of our highest hills, two miles off, and then the
State was nowhere to be seen.

This is the whole history of "My Prisons."

I have never declined paying the highway tax, because
I am as desirous of being a good neighbor as I am of being
a bad subject; and as for supporting schools, I am doing my
part to educate my fellow-countrymen now. It is for no
particular item in the tax-bill that I refuse to pay it. I simply
wish to refuse allegiance to the State, to withdraw and stand
aloof from it effectually. I do not care to trace the course of
my dollar, if I could, till it buys a man or a musket to shoot
one with,—the dollar is innocent,—but I am concerned to trace
the effects of my allegiance. In fact, I quietly declare war with
the State, after my fashion, though I will still make what use
and get what advantage of her I can, as is usual in such cases.

If others pay the tax which is demanded of me, from a
sympathy with the State, they do but what they have already done in their own case, or rather they abet injustice to
a greater extent than the State requires. If they pay the tax
from a mistaken interest in the individual taxed, to save his
property, or prevent his going to jail, it is because they have
not considered wisely how far they let their private feelings
interfere with the public good.

This, then, is my position at present. But one cannot be
too much on his guard in such a case, lest his action be biased
by obstinacy or an undue regard for the opinions of men. Let
him see that he does only what belongs to himself and to the
hour.

I think sometimes, Why, this people mean well, they are

only ignorant; they would do better if they knew how: why give your neighbors this pain to treat you as they are not inclined to? But I think again, This is no reason why I should do as they do, or permit others to suffer much greater pain of a different kind. Again, I sometimes say to myself, When many millions of men, without heat, without ill will, without personal feeling of any kind, demand of you a few shillings only, without the possibility, such is their constitution, of retracting or altering their present demand, and without the possibility, on your side, of appeal to any other millions, why expose yourself to this overwhelming brute force? You do not resist cold and hunger, the winds and the waves, thus obstinately; you quietly submit to a thousand similar necessities. You do not put your head into the fire. But just in proportion as I regard this as not wholly a brute force, but partly a human force, and consider that I have relations to those millions as to so many millions of men, and not of mere brute or inanimate things, I see that appeal is possible, first and instantaneously, from them to the Maker of them, and, secondly, from them to themselves. But if I put my head deliberately into the fire, there is no appeal to fire or to the Maker of fire, and I have only myself to blame. If I could convince myself that I have any right to be satisfied with men as they are, and to treat them accordingly, and not according, in some respects, to my requisitions and expectations of what they and I ought to be, then, like a good Mussulman and fatalist, I should endeavor to be satisfied with things as they are, and say it is the will of God. And, above all, there is this difference between resisting this and a purely brute or natural force, that I can resist this with some effect; but I cannot expect, like Orpheus, to change the nature of the rocks and trees and beasts.

I do not wish to quarrel with any man or nation. I do not wish to split hairs, to make fine distinctions, or set myself up as better than my neighbors. I seek rather, I may say, even an excuse for conforming to the laws of the land. I am but too ready to conform to them. Indeed, I have reason to suspect myself on this head; and each year, as the tax-gatherer comes round, I find myself disposed to review the acts and position of the general and State governments, and the spirit of the people, to discover a pretext for conformity.

> "We must affect our country as our parents,
> And if at any time we alienate
> Our love or industry from doing it honor,
> We must respect effects and teach the soul
> Matter of conscience and religion,
> And not desire of rule or benefit."

I believe that the State will soon be able to take all my work of this sort out of my hands, and then I shall be no better a patriot than my fellow-countrymen. Seen from a lower point of view, the Constitution, with all its faults, is very good; the law and the courts are very respectable; even this State and this American government are, in many respects, very admirable, and rare things, to be thankful for, such as a great many have described them; but seen from a point of view a little higher, they are what I have described them; seen from a higher still, and the highest, who shall say what they are, or that they are worth looking at or thinking of at all?

However, the government does not concern me much, and I shall bestow the fewest possible thoughts on it. It is not many moments that I live under a government, even in this world. If a man is thought-free, fancy-free, imagination-free, that which *is not* never for a long time appearing *to be* to him, unwise rulers or reformers cannot fatally interrupt him. . . .

They who know of no purer sources of truth, who have traced up its stream no higher, stand, and wisely stand, by the Bible and the Constitution, and drink at it there with reverence and humility; but they who behold where it comes trickling into this lake or that pool, gird up their loins once more, and continue their pilgrimage toward its fountainhead.

No man with a genius for legislation has appeared in America. They are rare in the history of the world. There are orators, politicians, and eloquent men, by the thousand; but the speaker has not yet opened his mouth to speak who is capable of settling the much-vexed questions of the day. We love eloquence for its own sake, and not for any truth which it may utter, or any heroism it may inspire. Our legislators have not yet learned the comparative value of free-trade and of freedom, of union, and of rectitude, to a nation. They have no genius or talent for comparatively humble questions of taxation and finance, commerce and manufactures and agriculture. If we were left solely to the wordy wit of legislators in Congress for our guidance, uncorrected by the seasonable experience and the effectual complaints of the people, America would not long retain her rank among the nations. For eighteen hundred years, though perchance I have no right to say it, the New Testament has been written; yet where is the legislator who has wisdom and practical talent enough to avail himself of the light which it sheds on the science of legislation?

The authority of government, even such as I am willing to submit to,—for I will cheerfully obey those who know and can do better than I, and in many things even those who neither know nor can do so well,—is still an impure one: to be strictly just, it must have the sanction and consent of the governed. It can have no pure right over my person and property but what I concede to it. The progress from an absolute to a limited monarchy, from a limited monarchy to a democracy, is a progress toward a true respect for the individual. Even the Chinese philosopher was wise enough to regard the individual as the basis of the empire. Is a democracy, such as we know it, the last improvement possible in government? Is it not possible to take a step further towards recognizing and organizing the rights of man? There will never be a really free and enlightened State until the State comes to recognize the individual as a higher and independent power, from which all its own power and authority are derived, and treats him accordingly. I please myself with imagining a State at last which can afford to be just to all men, and to treat the individual with respect as a neighbor; which even would not think it inconsistent with its own repose if a few were to live aloof from it, not meddling with it, nor embraced by it, who fulfilled all the duties of neighbors and fellowmen. A State which bore this kind of fruit, and suffered it to drop off as fast as it ripened, would prepare the way for a still more perfect and glorious State, which also I have imagined, but not yet anywhere seen.

John Ruskin

1819 · 1900

*John Ruskin was the son of a wealthy wine
merchant, from whom he inherited a large fortune.
In his youth he was given careful tutoring in the
arts, science, and the Bible. He began a defense of
Turner in* Modern Painters *(1843–1860), and by the
time the fifth and last volume was published, he was
famous as a critic of art and of society. His concern
with moral and social theories carried him to
extremes such as spending most of his money to
improve the lot of poor people in order, one may
suppose, to raise the level of artistic production.*

OF THE PATHETIC FALLACY

1. GERMAN DULNESS, AND ENGLISH AFFECTATION,
have of late much multiplied among us the
use of two of the most objectionable words that were ever
coined by the troublesomeness of metaphysicians—namely,
'Objective' and 'Subjective.'

No words can be more exquisitely, and in all points, useless; and I merely speak of them that I may, at once and for
ever, get them out of my way, and out of my reader's. But
to get that done, they must be explained.

The word 'Blue,' say certain philosophers, means the sensation of colour which the human eye receives in looking at
the open sky, or at a bell gentian.

Now, say they farther, as this sensation can only be felt
when the eye is turned to the object, and as, therefore, no
such sensation is produced by the object when nobody looks
at it, therefore the thing, when it is not looked at, is not blue;
and thus (say they) there are many qualities of things which

depend as much on something else as on themselves. To be sweet, a thing must have a taster; it is only sweet while it is being tasted, and if the tongue had not the capacity of taste, then the sugar would not have the quality of sweetness.

And then they agree that the qualities of things which thus depend upon our perception of them, and upon our human nature as affected by them, shall be called Subjective; and the qualities of things which they always have, irrespective of any other nature, as roundness or squareness, shall be called Objective.

From these ingenious views the step is very easy to a farther opinion, that it does not much matter what things are in themselves, but only what they are to us; and that the only real truth of them is their appearance to, or effect upon, us. From which position, with a hearty desire for mystification, and much egotism, selfishness, shallowness, and impertinence, a philosopher may easily go so far as to believe, and say, that everything in the world depends upon his seeing or thinking of it, and that nothing, therefore, exists, but what he sees or thinks of.

2. Now, to get rid of all these ambiguities and troublesome words at once, be it observed that the word 'Blue' does *not* mean the *sensation* caused by a gentian on the human eye; but it means the *power* of producing that sensation; and this power is always there, in the thing, whether we are there to experience it or not, and would remain there though there were not left a man on the face of the earth. Precisely in the same way gunpowder has a power of exploding. It will not explode if you put no match to it. But it has always the power of so exploding, and is therefore called an explosive compound, which it very positively and assuredly is, whatever philosophy may say to the contrary.

In like manner, a gentian does not produce the sensation of blueness if you don't look at it. But it has always the power of doing so; its particles being everlastingly so arranged by its Maker. And, therefore, the gentian and the sky are always verily blue, whatever philosophy may say to the contrary; and if you do not see them blue when you look at them, it is not their fault but yours.

3. Hence I would say to these philosophers: If, instead of using the sonorous phrase, 'It is objectively so,' you will use the plain old phrase, 'It *is* so,' and if instead of the sonorous phrase, 'It is subjectively so,' you will say, in plain old English, 'It does so,' or 'It seems so to me,' you will, on the whole, be more intelligible to your fellow-creatures; and besides, if you find that a thing which generally 'does so' to other people (as a gentian looks blue to most men), does *not* so to you, on any particular occasion, you will not fall into the impertinence of saying, that the thing is not so, or did not so, but you will say simply (what you will be all the better for speedily finding out), that something is the matter with you. If you find that you cannot explode the gunpowder, you will not declare that all gunpowder is subjective, and all explosion imaginary, but you will simply suspect and declare yourself to be an ill-made match. Which, on the whole, though there may be a distant chance of a mistake about it, is, nevertheless, the wisest conclusion you can come to until farther experiment.

4. Now, therefore, putting these tiresome and absurd words quite out of our way, we may go on at our ease to examine the point in question—namely, the difference between the ordinary, proper, and true appearances of things to us; and the extraordinary, or false appearances, when we are under the influence of emotion, or contemplative fancy; false appearances, I say, as being entirely unconnected with any real power or character in the object, and only imputed to it by us.

For instance—

> The spendthrift crocus, bursting through the mould
> Naked and shivering, with his cup of gold.

This is very beautiful, and yet very untrue. The crocus is not a spendthrift, but a hardy plant; its yellow is not gold, but saffron. How is it that we enjoy so much the having it put into our heads that it is anything else than a plain crocus?

It is an important question. For, throughout our past reasonings about art, we have always found that nothing could be good, or useful, or ultimately pleasurable, which was untrue. But here is something pleasurable in written poetry which is nevertheless *un*true. And what is more, if we think over our favourite poetry, we shall find it full of this kind of fallacy, and that we like it all the more for being so.

5. It will appear also, on consideration of the matter, that this fallacy is of two principal kinds. Either, as in this case of the crocus, it is the fallacy of wilful fancy, which involves no real expectation that it will be believed; or else it is a fallacy caused by an excited state of the feelings, making us, for the time, more or less irrational. Of the cheating of the fancy we shall have to speak presently; but, in this chapter, I want to examine the nature of the other error, that which the mind admits when affected strongly by emotion. Thus, for instance, in *Alton Locke*—

> They rowed her in across the rolling foam—
> The cruel, crawling foam.

The foam is not cruel, neither does it crawl. The state of mind which attributes to it these characters of a living creature is one in which the reason is unhinged by grief. All violent feelings have the same effect. They produce in us a falseness in all our impressions of external things, which I would generally characterize as the 'Pathetic Fallacy.'

6. Now we are in the habit of considering this fallacy as eminently a character of poetical description, and the temper of mind in which we allow it, as one eminently poetical, because passionate. But, I believe, if we look well into the matter, that we shall find the greatest poets do not often admit this kind of falseness—that it is only the second order of poets who much delight in it.

Thus, when Dante describes the spirits falling from the bank of Acheron 'as dead leaves flutter from a bough,' he gives the most perfect image possible of their utter lightness, feebleness, passiveness, and scattering agony of despair, without, however, for an instant losing his own clear perception that *these* are souls, and *those* are leaves; he makes no confusion of one with the other. But when Coleridge speaks of

> The one red leaf, the last of its clan,
> That dances as often as dance it can,

he has a morbid, that is to say, a so far false, idea about the leaf: he fancies a life in it, and will, which there are not; confuses its powerlessness with choice, its fading death with merriment, and the wind that shakes it with music. Here, however, there is some beauty, even in the morbid passage; but take an instance in Homer and Pope. Without the knowledge of Ulysses, Elpenor, his youngest follower, has fallen from an upper chamber in the Circean palace, and has been left dead, unmissed by his leader or companions, in the haste of their departure. They cross the sea to the Cimmerian land; and Ulysses summons the shades from Tartarus. The first which appears is that of the lost Elpenor. Ulysses, amazed, and in exactly the spirit of bitter and terrified lightness which is seen in Hamlet, addresses the spirit with the simple, startled words: —

> Elpenor! How camest thou under the shadowy darkness?
> Hast thou come faster on foot than I in my black ship?

Which Pope renders thus: —

> O, say, what angry power Elpenor led
> To glide in shades, and wander with the dead?
> How could thy soul, by realms and seas disjoined,
> Outfly the nimble sail, and leave the lagging wind?

I sincerely hope the reader finds no pleasure here, either in the nimbleness of the sail, or the laziness of the wind! And yet how is it that these conceits are so painful now, when they have been pleasant to us in the other instances?

7. For a very simple reason. They are not a *pathetic* fallacy at all, for they are put into the mouth of the wrong passion —a passion which never could possibly have spoken them— agonized curiosity. Ulysses wants to know the facts of the matter; and the very last thing his mind could do at the moment would be to pause, or suggest in anywise what was *not* a fact. The delay in the first three lines, and conceit in the last, jar upon us instantly, like the most frightful discord in music. No poet of true imaginative power could possibly have written the passage.

Therefore, we see that the spirit of truth must guide us in some sort, even in our enjoyment of fallacy. Coleridge's fallacy has no discord in it, but Pope's has set our teeth on edge. Without farther questioning, I will endeavour to state the main bearings of this matter.

8. The temperament which admits the pathetic fallacy, is, as I said above, that of a mind and body in some sort too weak to deal fully with what is before them or upon them; borne away, or over-clouded, or over-dazzled by emotion; and it is a more or less noble state, according to the force of the emotion which has induced it. For it is no credit to a man that he is not morbid or inaccurate in his perceptions, when he has no strength of feeling to warp them; and it is in general a sign of higher capacity and stand in the ranks of being, that the emotions should be strong enough to vanquish, partly, the intellect, and make it believe what they choose. But it is still a grander condition when the intellect also rises, till it is strong enough to assert its rule against, or together with, the utmost efforts of the passions; and the whole man stands in an iron glow, white hot, perhaps, but still strong, and in no wise evaporating; even if he melts, losing none of his weight.

So, then, we have the three ranks: the man who perceives rightly, because he does not feel, and to whom the primrose is very accurately the primrose, because he does not love it. Then, secondly, the man who perceives wrongly, because he feels, and to whom the primrose is anything else than a primrose: a star, or a sun, or a fairy's shield, or a forsaken maiden. And then, lastly, there is the man who perceives rightly in spite of his feelings, and to whom the primrose is for ever nothing else than itself—a little flower, apprehended in the very plain and leafy fact of it, whatever and how many soever the associations and passions may be that crowd around it. And, in general, these three classes may be rated in comparative order, as the men who are not poets at all, and the poets of the second order, and the poets of the first; only however great a man may be, there are always some subjects which *ought* to throw him off his balance; some, by which his poor human capacity of thought should be conquered, and brought into the inaccurate and vague state of perception, so that the language of the highest inspiration becomes broken, obscure, and wild in metaphor, resembling that of the weaker man, overborne by weaker things.

9. And thus, in full, there are four classes: the men who feel nothing, and therefore see truly; the men who feel strongly, think weakly, and see untruly (second order of poets); the men who feel strongly, think strongly, and see truly (first order of poets); and the men who, strong as human creatures can be, are yet submitted to influences stronger than they, and see in a sort untruly, because what they see is inconceivably above them. This last is the usual condition of prophetic inspiration.

10. I separate these classes, in order that their character may be clearly understood; but of course they are united each to the other by imperceptible transitions, and the same mind, according to the influences to which it is subjected, passes at different times into the various states. Still, the difference between the great and less man is, on the whole, chiefly in this point of *alterability*. That is to say, the one knows too much, and perceives and feels too much of the past and future, and of all things beside and around that which immediately affects him, to be in anywise shaken by it. His mind is made up; his thoughts have an accustomed current; his ways are steadfast; it is not this or that new sight which will at once unbalance him. He is tender to impression at the surface, like a rock with deep moss upon it; but there is too much mass of him to be moved. The smaller man, with the same degree of sensibility, is at once carried off his feet; he wants to do something he did not want to do before; he views all the universe in a new light through his tears; he is gay or enthusiastic, melancholy or passionate, as things come and go to him. Therefore the high creative poet might even be thought, to a great extent, impassive (as shallow people think Dante stern), receiving indeed all feelings to the full, but having a great centre of reflection and knowledge in which he stands serene, and watches the feeling, as it were, from far off.

Dante, in his most intense moods, has entire command of

himself, and can look around calmly, at all moments, for the image or the word that will best tell what he sees to the upper or lower world. But Keats and Tennyson, and the poets of the second order, are generally themselves subdued by the feelings under which they write, or, at least, write as choosing to be so, and therefore admit certain expressions and modes of thought which are in some sort diseased or false.

11. Now so long as we see that the *feeling* is true, we pardon, or are even pleased by, the confessed fallacy of sight which it induces: we are pleased, for instance, with those lines of Kingsley's above quoted, not because they fallaciously describe foam, but because they faithfully describe sorrow. But the moment the mind of the speaker becomes cold, that moment every such expression becomes untrue, as being for ever untrue in the external facts. And there is no greater baseness in literature than the habit of using these metaphorical expressions in cold blood. An inspired writer, in full impetuosity of passion, may speak wisely and truly of 'raging waves of the sea, foaming out of their own shame'; but it is only the basest writer who cannot speak of the sea without talking of 'raging waves,' 'remorseless floods,' 'ravenous billows,' &c.; and it is one of the signs of the highest power in a writer to check all such habits of thought, and to keep his eyes fixed firmly on the *pure fact*, out of which if any feeling comes to him or his reader, he knows it must be a true one.

To keep to the waves, I forget who it is who represents a man in despair, desiring that his body may be cast into the sea,

> *Whose changing mound, and foam that passed away,*
> Might mock the eye that questioned where I lay.

Observe, there is not here a single false, or even overcharged, expression. 'Mound' of the sea wave is perfectly simple and true; 'changing' is as familiar as may be; 'foam that passed away,' strictly literal; and the whole line descriptive of the reality with a degree of accuracy which I know not any other verse, in the range of poetry, that altogether equals. For most people have not a distinct idea of the clumsiness and massiveness of a large wave. The word

wave' is used too generally of ripples and breakers, and bend-
ings in light drapery or grass: it does not by itself convey a
perfect image. But the word 'mound' is heavy, large, dark,
definite; there is no mistaking the kind of wave meant, nor
missing the sight of it. Then the term 'changing' has a peculiar
force also. Most people think of waves as rising and falling.
But if they look at the sea carefully, they will perceive that
the waves do not rise and fall. They change. Change both
place and form, but they do not fall; one wave goes on, and
on, and still on; now lower, now higher, now tossing its mane
like a horse, now building itself together like a wall, now
shaking, now steady, but still the same wave, till at last it
seems struck by something, and changes, one knows not how—
becomes another wave.

The close of the line insists on this image, and paints it
still more perfectly—'foam that passed away.' Not merely
melting, disappearing, but passing on, out of sight, on the
career of the wave. Then, having put the absolute ocean fact
as far as he may before our eyes, the poet leaves us to feel
about it as we may, and to trace for ourselves the opposite
fact—the image of the green mounds that do not change, and
the white and written stones that do not pass away; and
thence to follow out also the associated images of the calm
life with the quiet grave, and the despairing life with the
fading foam:

> Let no man move his bones.
As for Samaria, her king is cut off like the foam upon the water.

But nothing of this is actually told or pointed out, and the
expressions, as they stand, are perfectly severe and accurate,
utterly uninfluenced by the firmly governed emotion of the
writer. Even the word 'mock' is hardly an exception, as it
may stand merely for 'deceive' or 'defeat,' without implying
any impersonation of the waves.

14. . . . A poet is great, first in proportion to the strength
of his passion, and then, that strength being granted, in proportion to his government of it; there being, however, always
a point beyond which it would be inhuman and monstrous

if he pushed this government, and, therefore, a point at which all feverish and wild fancy becomes just and true. Thus the destruction of the kingdom of Assyria cannot be contemplated firmly by a prophet of Israel. The fact is too great, too wonderful. It overthrows him, dashes him into a confused element of dreams. All the world is, to his stunned thought, full of strange voices. 'Yea, the fir-trees rejoice at thee, and the cedars of Lebanon, saying, "Since thou art gone down to the grave, no feller is come up against us." ' So, still more, the thought of the presence of Deity cannot be borne without this great astonishment. 'The mountains and the hills shall break forth before you into singing, and all the trees of the field shall clap their hands.'

15. But by how much this feeling is noble when it is justified by the strength of its cause, by so much it is ignoble when there is not cause enough for it; and beyond all other ignobleness is the mere affectation of it, in hardness of heart. Simply bad writing may almost always, as above noticed, be known by its adoption of these fanciful metaphorical expressions, as a sort of current coin; yet there is even a worse, at least a more harmful, condition of writing than this, in which such expressions are not ignorantly and feelinglessly caught up, but, by some master, skilful in handling, yet insincere, deliberately wrought out with chill and studied fancy; as if we should try to make an old lava-stream look red-hot again, by covering it with dead leaves, or white-hot, with hoar-frost.

When Young is lost in veneration, as he dwells on the character of a truly good and holy man, he permits himself for a moment to be overborne by the feeling so far as to exclaim:

> Where shall I find him? angels, tell me where.
> You know him; he is near you; point him out.
> Shall I see glories beaming from his brow,
> Or trace his footsteps by the rising flowers?

This emotion has a worthy cause, and is thus true and right. But now hear the cold-hearted Pope say to a shepherd girl:

Where'er you walk, cool gales shall fan the glade;
Trees, where you sit, shall crowd into a shade;
Your praise the birds shall chant in every grove,
And winds shall waft it to the powers above.
But would you sing, and rival Orpheus' strain,
The wondering forests soon should dance again;
The moving mountains hear the powerful call,
And headlong streams hang, listening, in their fall.

This is not, nor could it for a moment be mistaken for, the language of passion. It is simple falsehood, uttered by hypocrisy; definite absurdity, rooted in affectation, and coldly asserted in the teeth of nature and fact. Passion will indeed go far in deceiving itself; but it must be a strong passion, not the simple wish of a lover to tempt his mistress to sing. Compare a very closely parallel passage in Wordsworth, in which the lover has lost his mistress:

Three years had Barbara in her grave been laid,
When thus his moan he made:—
'Oh move, thou cottage, from behind yon oak,
    Or let the ancient tree uprooted lie,
That in some other way yon smoke
    May mount into the sky.
If still behind yon pine-tree's ragged bough,
    Headlong, the waterfall must come,
    Oh, let it, then, be dumb—
Be anything, sweet stream, but that which thou
    art now.'

Here is a cottage to be moved, if not a mountain, and a waterfall to be silent, if it is not to hang listening: but with what different relation to the mind that contemplates them! Here, in the extremity of its agony, the soul cries out wildly for relief, which at the same moment it partly knows to be impossible, but partly believes possible, in a vague impression that a miracle *might* be wrought to give relief even to a less sore distress—that nature is kind, and God is kind, and that grief is strong: it knows not well what *is* possible to such grief. To silence a stream, to move a cottage wall—one might think it could do as much as that!

16. I believe these instances are enough to illustrate the main point I insist upon respecting the pathetic fallacy—that so far as it *is* a fallacy, it is always the sign of a morbid state of mind, and comparatively of a weak one. Even in the most inspired prophet it is a sign of the incapacity of his human sight or thought to bear what has been revealed to it. In ordinary poetry, if it is found in the thoughts of the poet himself, it is at once a sign of his belonging to the inferior school; if in the thoughts of the characters imagined by him, it is right or wrong according to the genuineness of the emotion from which it springs; always, however, implying necessarily *some* degree of weakness in the character.

Take two most exquisite instances from master hands. The Jessy of Shenstone, and the Ellen of Wordsworth have both been betrayed and deserted. Jessy, in the course of her most touching complaint, says:

> If through the garden's flowery tribes I stray,
> Where bloom the jasmines that could once allure,
> 'Hope not to find delight in us,' they say,
> 'For we are spotless, Jessy; we are pure.'

Compare with this some of the words of Ellen:

> 'Ah, why,' said Ellen, sighing to herself,
> 'Why do not words, and kiss, and solemn pledge,
> And nature, that is kind in woman's breast,
> And reason, that in man is wise and good,
> And fear of Him who is a righteous Judge,—
> Why do not these prevail for human life,
> To keep two hearts together, that began
> Their springtime with one love, and that have need
> Of mutual pity and forgiveness, sweet
> To grant, or be received; while that poor bird—
> O, come and hear him! Thou who hast to me
> Been faithless, hear him;—though a lowly creature,
> One of God's simple children, that yet know not

The Universal Parent, *how* he sings!
As if he wished the firmament of heaven
Should listen, and give back to him the voice
Of his triumphant constancy and love.
The proclamation that he makes, how far
His darkness doth transcend our fickle light.'

The perfection of both these passages, as far as regards truth and tenderness of imagination in the two poets, is quite insuperable. But, of the two characters imagined, Jessy is weaker than Ellen, exactly in so far as something appears to her to be in nature which is not. The flowers do not really reproach her. God meant them to comfort her, not to taunt her; they would do so if she saw them rightly.

Ellen, on the other hand, is quite above the slightest erring emotion. There is not the barest film of fallacy in all her thoughts. She reasons as calmly as if she did not feel. And, although the singing of the bird suggests to her the idea of its desiring to be heard in heaven, she does not for an instant admit any veracity in the thought. 'As if,' she says, 'I know he means nothing of the kind; but it does verily seem as if.' The reader will find, by examining the rest of the poem, that Ellen's character is throughout consistent in this clear though passionate strength.

It is, I hope, now made clear to the reader in all respects that the pathetic fallacy is powerful only so far as it is pathetic, feeble so far as it is fallacious, and, therefore, that the dominion of Truth is entire, over this, as over every other natural and just state of the human mind.

Matthew Arnold

1822 · 1888

*Matthew Arnold was the son of Dr. Thomas
Arnold, the famous Head Master of Rugby, who
brought him up in classical traditions. Habits of
order, respect for right reason, belief in the
importance of right conduct, and acceptance of
authority became fixed principles in him. He was
Inspector of Schools and for ten years was Professor
of Poetry at Oxford. As critic and poet, he stands
among the greatest English writers of the
Victorian period. In his life, as in his poetry and his
essays, he strove to exemplify the ideal culture
which he described as "a study of perfection."*

LITERATURE AND SCIENCE

PRACTICAL PEOPLE TALK WITH A SMILE of Plato
and of his absolute ideas; and it is impossible
to deny that Plato's ideas do often seem unpractical and im-
practicable, and especially when one views them in connection
with the life of a great work-a-day world like the United
States. The necessary staple of the life of such a world Plato
regards with disdain; handicraft and trade and the working
professions he regards with disdain; but what becomes of the
life of an industrial modern community if you take handicraft and trade and the working professions out of it? The
base mechanic arts and handicrafts, says Plato, bring about
a natural weakness in the principle of excellence in a man,
so that he cannot govern the ignoble growths in him, but
nurses them, and cannot understand fostering any other.

*From DISCOURSES IN AMERICA, by Matthew Arnold. Used by
permission of The Macmillan Company, publishers.*

Those who exercise such arts and trades, as they have their bodies, he says, marred by their vulgar businesses, so they have their souls, too, bowed and broken by them. And if one of these uncomely people has a mind to seek self-culture and philosophy, Plato compares him to a bald little tinker, who has scraped together money, and has got his release from service, and has had a bath, and bought a new coat, and is rigged out like a bridegroom about to marry the daughter of his master who has fallen into poor and helpless estate.

Nor do the working professions fare any better than trade at the hands of Plato. He draws for us an inimitable picture of the working lawyer, and of his life of bondage; he shows how this bondage from his youth up has stunted and warped him, and made him small and crooked of soul, encompassing him with difficulties which he is not man enough to rely on justice and truth as means to encounter, but has recourse, for help out of them, to falsehood and wrong. And so, says Plato, this poor creature is bent and broken, and grows up from boy to man without a particle of soundness in him, although exceedingly smart and clever in his own esteem.

One cannot refuse to admire the artist who draws these pictures. But we say to ourselves that his ideas show the influence of a primitive and obsolete order of things, when the warrior caste and the priestly caste were alone in honour, and the humble work of the world was done by slaves. We have now changed all that; the modern majority consists in work, as Emerson declares; and in work, we may add, principally of such plain and dusty kind as the work of cultivators of the ground, handicraftsmen, men of trade and business, men of the working professions. Above all is this true in a great industrious community such as that of the United States.

Now education, many people go on to say, is still mainly governed by the ideas of men like Plato, who lived when the warrior caste and the priestly or philosophical class were alone in honour, and the really useful part of the community were slaves. It is an education fitted for persons of leisure in such a community. This education passed from Greece and Rome to the feudal communities of Europe, where also the warrior caste and the priestly caste were alone held in honour, and where the really useful and working part of the community, though not nominally slaves as in the pagan world, were practically not much better off than slaves, and not more seriously regarded. And how absurd it is, people end by saying, to inflict this education upon an industrious modern community, where very few indeed are persons of leisure, and the mass to be considered has not leisure, but is bound, for its own great good, and for the great good of the world at large, to plain labour and to industrial pursuits, and the education in question tends necessarily to make men dissatisfied with these pursuits and unfitted for them!

That is what is said. So far I must defend Plato, as to plead that his view of education and studies is in the general, as it seems to me, sound enough, and fitted for all sorts and conditions of men, whatever their pursuits may be. "An intelligent man," says Plato, "will prize those studies which result in his soul getting soberness, righteousness, and wisdom, and will less value the others." I cannot consider *that* a bad description of the aim of education, and of the motives which should govern us in the choice of studies, whether we are preparing ourselves for a hereditary seat in the English House of Lords or for the pork trade in Chicago.

Still I admit that Plato's world was not ours, that his scorn of trade and handicraft is fantastic, that he had no conception of a great industrial community such as that of the United States, and that such a community must and will shape its education to suit its own needs. If the usual education handed down to it from the past does not suit it, it will certainly before long drop this and try another. The usual education in the past has been mainly literary. The question is whether the studies which were long supposed to be the best for all of us are practically the best now; whether others are not better. The tyranny of the past, many think, weighs on us injuriously in the predominance given to letters in education. The question is raised whether, to meet the needs of our modern life, the predominance ought not now to pass from letters to science; and naturally the question is nowhere raised with more energy than here in the United States. The design of abasing what is called "mere literary instruction and education," and of exalting what is called "sound, extensive, and practical scientific knowledge," is, in this intensely modern world of the United States, even more perhaps than in Europe, a very popular design, and makes great and rapid progress.

I am going to ask whether the present movement for ousting letters from their old predominance in education, and for transferring the predominance in education to the natural sciences, whether this brisk and flourishing movement ought to prevail, and whether it is likely that in the end it really will prevail. An objection may be raised which I will anticipate. My own studies have been almost wholly in letters, and my visits to the field of the natural sciences have been very slight and inadequate, although those sciences have always strongly moved my curiosity. A man of letters, it will perhaps be said, is not competent to discuss the comparative merits of letters and natural science as means of education. To this objection I reply, first of all, that his incompetence, if he attempts the discussion but is really incompetent for it, will be abundantly visible; nobody will be taken in; he will have plenty of sharp observers and critics to save mankind from that danger. But the line I am going to follow is, as you will soon discover, so extremely simple, that perhaps it may be followed without failure even by one who for a more ambitious line of discussion would be quite incompetent.

Some of you may possibly remember a phrase of mine which has been the object of a good deal of comment; an observation to the effect that in our culture, the aim being *to know ourselves and the world*, we have, as the means to this end, *to know the best which has been thought and said in the world*. A man of science, who is also an excellent writer and the very prince of debaters, Professor Huxley, in a discourse at the opening of Sir Josiah Mason's college at Birmingham, laying hold of this phrase, expanded it by quoting some more words of mine, which are these: "The civilized world is to be regarded as now being, for intellectual and spiritual purposes, one great confederation, bound to a joint action and working to a common result; and whose members have for their proper outfit a knowledge of Greek, Roman, and Eastern antiquity, and of one another. Special local and temporary advantages being put out of account, that modern nation will in the intellectual and spiritual sphere make most progress, which most thoroughly carries out this programme."

Now on my phrase, thus enlarged, Professor Huxley remarks that when I speak of the above-mentioned knowledge as enabling us to know ourselves and the world, I assert *literature* to contain the materials which suffice for thus making us know ourselves and the world. But it is not by any means clear, says he, that after having learnt all which ancient and modern literatures have to tell us, we have laid a sufficiently broad and deep foundation for that criticism of life, that knowledge of ourselves and the world, which constitutes culture. On the contrary, Professor Huxley declares that he finds himself "wholly unable to admit that either nations or individuals will really advance, if their outfit draws nothing from the stores of physical science. An army without weapons of precision, and with no particular base of operations, might more hopefully enter upon a campaign on the Rhine, than a man, devoid of a knowledge of what physical science has done in the last century, upon a criticism of life."

This shows how needful it is for those who are to discuss any matter together, to have a common understanding as to the sense of the terms they employ,—how needful, and how difficult. What Professor Huxley says, implies just the reproach which is so often brought against the study of *belles lettres*, as they are called: that the study is an elegant one, but slight and ineffectual; a smattering of Greek and Latin and other ornamental things, of little use for anyone whose object is to get at truth, and to be a practical man. So, too, M. Renan talks of the "superficial humanism" of a school-course which treats us as if we were all going to be poets, writers, preachers, orators, and he opposes this humanism to positive science, or the critical search after truth. And there is always a tendency in those who are remonstrating against the predominance of letters in education, to understand by letters *belles lettres*, and by *belles lettres* a superficial humanism, the opposite of science or true knowledge.

But when we talk of knowing Greek and Roman antiquity, for instance, which is the knowledge people have called the humanities, I for my part mean a knowledge which is something more than a superficial humanism, mainly decorative. "I call all teaching *scientific*," says Wolf, the critic of Homer, "which is systematically laid out and followed up to its original sources. For example: a knowledge of classical antiquity is scientific when the remains of classical antiquity are correctly studied in the original languages." There can be no doubt that Wolf is perfectly right; that all learning is scientific which is systematically laid out and followed up to its original sources, and that a genuine humanism is scientific.

When I speak of knowing Greek and Roman antiquity, therefore, as a help to knowing ourselves and the world, I mean more than a knowledge of so much vocabulary, so much grammar, so many portions of authors in the Greek and Latin languages, I mean knowing the Greeks and Romans, and their life and genius, and what they were and did in the world; what we get from them, and what is its value. That, at least, is the ideal; and when we talk of endeavouring to know Greek and Roman antiquity, as a help to knowing ourselves and the world, we mean endeavouring so to know them as to satisfy this ideal, however much we may still fall short of it.

The same also as to knowing our own and other modern nations, with the like aim of getting to understand ourselves and the world. To know the best that has been thought and said by the modern nations, is to know, says Professor Huxley, "only what modern *literatures* have to tell us; it is the criticism of life contained in modern literature." And yet "the distinctive character of our times," he urges, "lies in the vast and constantly increasing part which is played by natural knowledge." And how, therefore, can a man, devoid of knowledge of what physical science has done in the last century, enter hopefully upon a criticism of modern life?

Let us, I say, be agreed about the meaning of the terms we are using. I talk of knowing the best which has been thought and uttered in the world; Professor Huxley says this means knowing *literature*. Literature is a large word; it may mean everything written with letters or printed in a book. Euclid's *Elements* and Newton's *Principia* are thus literature. All knowledge that reaches us through books is literature. But by literature Professor Huxley means *belles lettres*. He means to make me say, that knowing the best which has been thought and said by the modern nations is knowing their *belles lettres* and no more. And this is no sufficient equipment, he argues, for a criticism of modern life. But as I do not mean, by knowing ancient Rome, knowing merely more or less of Latin *belles lettres*, and taking no account of Rome's military, and political, and legal, and administrative work in the world; and as, by knowing ancient Greece, I understand knowing her as the giver of Greek art, and the guide to a free and right use of reason and to scientific method, and the founder of our mathematics and physics and astronomy and biology,—I understand knowing her as all this, and not merely knowing certain Greek poems, and histories, and treatises, and speeches,—so as to the knowledge of modern nations also. By knowing modern nations, I mean not merely knowing their *belles lettres*, but knowing also what has been done by such men as Copernicus, Galileo, Newton, Darwin. "Our ancestors learned," says Professor Huxley, "that the earth is the centre of the visible universe, and that man is the cynosure of things terrestrial; and more especially was it inculcated that the course of nature had no fixed order, but that it could be, and constantly was, altered." But for us now, continues Professor Huxley, "the notions of the beginning and the end of the world entertained by our forefathers are no longer credible. It is very certain that the earth is not the chief body in the material universe, and that the world is not subordinated to man's use. It is even more certain that nature is the expression of a definite order, with which nothing interferes." "And yet," he cries, "the purely classical education advocated by the representatives of the humanists in our day gives no inkling of all this!"

In due place and time I will just touch upon that vexed question of classical education; but at present the question is as to what is meant by knowing the best which modern nations have thought and said. It is not knowing their *belles lettres* merely which is meant. To know Italian *belles lettres* is not to know Italy, and to know English *belles lettres* is not to know England. Into knowing Italy and England there comes a great deal more, Galileo and Newton amongst it. The reproach of being a superficial humanism, a tincture of *belles lettres*, may attach rightly enough to some other disciplines; but to the particular discipline recommended when I proposed knowing the best that has been thought and said in the world, it does not apply. In that best I certainly include what in modern times has been thought and said by the great observers and knowers of nature.

There is, therefore, really no question between Professor Huxley and me as to whether knowing the great results of the modern scientific study of nature is not required as a part of our culture, as well as knowing the products of literature and art. But to follow the processes by which those results are reached, ought, say the friends of physical science, to be made the staple of education for the bulk of mankind. And here there does arise a question between those whom Professor Huxley calls with playful sarcasm "the Levites of culture," and those whom the poor humanist is sometimes apt to regard as its Nebudchadnezzars.

The great results of the scientific investigation of nature we are agreed upon knowing, but how much of our study are we bound to give to the processes by which those results are reached? The results have their visible bearing on human life. But all the processes, too, all the items of fact, by which those results are reached and established, are interesting. All knowledge is interesting to a wise man, and the knowledge of nature is interesting to all men. It is very interesting to know, that, from the albuminous white of the egg, the chick in the egg gets the materials for its flesh, bones, blood, and feathers; while, from the fatty yolk of the egg, it gets the heat and energy which enable it at length to break its shell and begin the world. It is less interesting, perhaps, but still it is interesting, to know that when a taper burns, the wax is converted into carbonic acid and water. Moreover, it is quite true that the habit of dealing with facts, which is given by the study of nature, is, as the friends of physical science praise it for being, an excellent discipline. The appeal, in the study of nature, is constantly to observation and experiment; not only is it said that the thing is so, but we can be made to see that it is so. Not only does a man tell us that when a taper burns the wax is converted into carbonic acid and water, as a man may tell us, if he likes, that Charon is punting his ferry-boat on the river Styx, or that Victor Hugo is a sublime poet, or Mr. Gladstone the most admirable of statesmen; but we are made to see that the conversion into carbonic acid and water does actually happen. This reality of natural knowledge it is, which makes the friends of physical science contrast it, as a knowledge of things, with the humanist's knowledge, which is, say they, a knowledge of words. And hence Professor Huxley is moved to lay it down that, "for the purpose of attaining real culture, an exclusively scientific education is at least as effectual as an exclusively literary education." And a certain President of the Section for Mechanical Science in the British Association is, in Scripture phrase, "very bold," and declares that if a man, in his mental training, "has substituted literature and history for natural science, he has chosen the less useful alternative." But whether we go these lengths or not, we must all admit that in natural science the habit gained of dealing with facts is a most valuable discipline, and that every one should have some experience of it.

More than this, however, is demanded by the reformers. It is proposed to make the training in natural science the main part of education, for the great majority of mankind at any rate. And here, I confess, I part company with the friends of physical science, with whom up to this point I have been agreeing. In differing from them, however, I wish to proceed with the utmost caution and diffidence. The smallness of my own acquaintance with the disciplines of natural science is ever before my mind, and I am fearful of doing these disciplines an injustice. The ability and pugnacity of the partisans of natural science make them formidable persons to contradict. The tone of tentative inquiry, which befits a being of dim faculties and bounded knowledge, is the tone I would wish to take and not to depart from. At present it seems to me, that those who are for giving to natural knowledge, as they call it, the chief place in the education of the majority of mankind, leave one important thing out of their account: the constitution of human nature. But I put this forward on the strength of some facts not at all recondite, very far from it; facts capable of being stated in the simplest possible fashion, and to which, if I so state them, the man of science will, I am sure, be willing to allow their due weight.

Deny the facts altogether, I think, he hardly can. He can hardly deny, that when we set ourselves to enumerate the powers which go to the building up of human life, and say that they are the power of conduct, the power of intellect and knowledge, the power of beauty, and the power of social life and manners,—he can hardly deny that this scheme, though drawn in rough and plain lines enough, and not pretending to scientific exactness, does yet give a fairly true representation of the matter. Human nature is built up by these powers; we have the need for them all. When we have rightly met and adjusted the claims of them all, we shall then be in a fair way for getting soberness and righteousness, with wisdom. This is evident enough, and the friends of physical science would admit it.

But perhaps they may not have sufficiently observed another thing: namely, that the several powers just mentioned are not isolated, but there is, in the generality of mankind, a perpetual tendency to relate them one to another in divers ways. With one such way of relating them I am particularly concerned now. Following our instinct for intellect and knowledge, we acquire pieces of knowledge; and presently, in the generality of men, there arises the desire to relate these pieces of knowledge to our sense for conduct, to our sense for beauty,—and there is weariness and dissatisfaction if the desire is balked. Now in this desire lies, I think, the strength of that hold which letters have upon us.

All knowledge is, as I said just now, interesting; and even

items of knowledge which from the nature of the case cannot well be related, but must stand isolated in our thoughts, have their interest. Even lists of exceptions have their interest. If we are studying Greek accents, it is interesting to know that *pais* and *pas*, and some other monosyllables of the same form of declension, do not take the circumflex upon the last syllable of the genitive plural, but vary, in this respect, from the common rule. If we are studying physiology, it is interesting to know that the pulmonary artery carries dark blood and the pulmonary vein carries bright blood, departing in this respect from the common rule for the division of labour between the veins and the arteries. But every one knows how we seek naturally to combine the pieces of our knowledge together, to bring them under general rules, to relate them to principles; and how unsatisfactory and tiresome it would be to go on forever learning lists of exceptions, or accumulating items of fact which must stand isolated.

Well, that same need of relating our knowledge, which operates here within the sphere of our knowledge itself, we shall find operating, also, outside that sphere. We experience, as we go on learning and knowing,—the vast majority of us experience,—the need of relating what we have learned and known to the sense which we have in us for conduct, to the sense which we have in us for beauty.

A certain Greek prophetess of Mantineia in Arcadia, Diotima by name, once explained to the philosopher Socrates that love, and impulse, and bent of all kinds, is, in fact, nothing else but the desire in men that good should forever be present to them. This desire for good, Diotima assured Socrates, is our fundamental desire, of which fundamental desire every impulse in us is only some one particular form. And therefore this fundamental desire it is, I suppose,—this desire in men that good should be forever present to them,—which acts in us when we feel the impulse for relating our knowledge to our sense for conduct and to our sense for beauty. At any rate, with men in general the instinct exists. Such is human nature. And the instinct, it will be admitted, is innocent, and human nature is preserved by our following the lead of its innocent instincts. Therefore, in seeking to gratify this instinct in question, we are following the instinct of self-preservation in humanity.

But, no doubt, some kinds of knowledge cannot be made to directly serve the instinct in question, cannot be directly related to the sense for beauty, to the sense for conduct. These are instrument-knowledges; they lead on to other knowledges, which can. A man who passes his life in instrument-knowledges is a specialist. They may be invaluable as instruments to something beyond, for those who have the gift thus to employ them; and they may be disciplines in themselves wherein it is useful for every one to have some schooling. But it is inconceivable that the generality of men should pass all their mental life with Greek accents or with formal logic. My friend Professor Sylvester, who is one of the first mathematicians in the world, holds transcendental doctrines as to the virtue of mathematics, but those doctrines are not for common men. In the very Senate House and heart of our English Cambridge I once ventured, though not without an apology for my profaneness, to hazard the opinion that for the majority of mankind a little of mathematics, even, goes a long way. Of course this is quite consistent with their being of immense importance as an instrument to something else; but it is the few who have the aptitude for thus using them, not the bulk of mankind.

The natural sciences do not, however, stand on the same footing with these instrument-knowledges. Experience shows us that the generality of men will find more interest in learning that, when a taper burns, the wax is converted into carbonic acid and water, or in learning the explanation of the phenomenon of dew, or in learning how the circulation of the blood is carried on, than they find in learning that the genitive plural of *pais* and *pas* does not take the circumflex on the termination. And one piece of natural knowledge is added to another, and others are added to that, and at last we come to propositions so interesting as Mr. Darwin's famous proposition that "our ancestor was a hairy quadruped furnished with a tail and pointed ears, probably arboreal in his habits." Or we come to propositions of such reach and magnitude as those which Professor Huxley delivers, when he says that the notions of our forefathers about the beginning and the end of the world were all wrong, and that nature is the expression of a definite order with which nothing interferes.

Interesting, indeed, these results of science are, important they are, and we should all of us be acquainted with them. But what I now wish you to mark is, that we are still, when they are propounded to us and we receive them, we are still in the sphere of intellect and knowledge. And for the generality of men there will be found, I say, to arise, when they have duly taken in the proposition that their ancestor was "a hairy quadruped furnished with a tail and pointed ears, probably arboreal in his habits," there will be found to arise an invincible desire to relate this proposition to the sense in us for conduct, and to the sense in us for beauty. But this the men of science will not do for us, and will hardly even profess to do. They will give us other pieces of knowledge, other facts, about other animals and their ancestors, or about plants, or about stones, or about stars; and they may finally bring us to those great "general conceptions of the universe, which are forced upon us all," says Professor Huxley, "by the progress of physical science." But still it will be *knowledge* only which they give us; knowledge not put for us into relation with our sense for conduct, our sense for beauty, and touched with emotion by being so put; not thus put for us, and therefore, to the majority of mankind, after a certain while, unsatisfying, wearying.

Not to the born naturalist, I admit. But what do we mean by a born naturalist? We mean a man in whom the zeal for observing nature is so uncommonly strong and eminent, that it marks him off from the bulk of mankind. Such a man will pass his life happily in collecting natural knowledge and reasoning upon it, and will ask for nothing, or hardly anything, more. I have heard it said that the sagacious and admirable naturalist whom we lost not very long ago, Mr. Darwin, once owned to a friend that for his part he did not experience the necessity for two things which most men find so necessary to them,—religion and poetry; science and the domestic affections, he thought, were enough. To a born naturalist, I can well understand that this should seem so. So absorbing is his occupation with nature, so strong his love for his occupation, that he goes on acquiring natural knowledge and reasoning upon it, and has little time or inclination for thinking about getting it related to the desire in man for conduct, the desire in man for beauty. He relates it to them for himself as he goes along, so far as he feels the need; and he draws from the domestic affections all the additional solace necessary. But then Darwins are extremely rare. Another great and admirable master of natural knowledge, Faraday, was a Sandemanian. That is to say, he related his knowledge to his instinct for conduct and to his instinct for beauty, by the aid of that respectable Scottish sectary, Robert Sandeman. And so strong, in general, is the demand of religion and poetry to have their share in a man, to associate themselves with his knowing, and to relieve and rejoice it, that, probably, for one man amongst us with the disposition to do as Darwin did in this respect, there are at least fifty with the disposition to do as Faraday.

Education lays hold upon us, in fact, by satisfying this demand. Professor Huxley holds up to scorn mediæval education, with its neglect of the knowledge of nature, its poverty even of literary studies, its formal logic devoted to "showing how and why that which the Church said was true must be true." But the great mediæval Universities were not brought into being, we may be sure, by the zeal for giving a jejune and contemptible education. Kings have been their nursing fathers, and queens have been their nursing mothers, but not for this. The mediæval Universities came into being, because the supposed knowledge, delivered by Scripture and the Church, so deeply engaged men's hearts, by so simply, easily, and powerfully relating itself to their desire for conduct, their desire for beauty. All other knowledge was dominated by this supposed knowledge and was subordinated to it, because of the surpassing strength of the hold which it gained upon the affections of men, by allying itself profoundly with their sense for conduct, their sense for beauty.

But now, says Professor Huxley, conceptions of the universe fatal to the notions held by our forefathers have been forced upon us by physical science. Grant to him that they are thus fatal, that the new conceptions must and will soon become current everywhere, and that every one will finally perceive them to be fatal to the beliefs of our forefathers. The need of humane letters, as they are truly called, because they serve the paramount desire in men that good should be forever present to them,—the need of humane letters, to establish a relation between the new conceptions, and our instinct for beauty, our instinct for conduct, is only the more visible. The Middle Age could do without humane letters, as it could do without the study of nature, because its supposed knowledge was made to engage its emotions so powerfully. Grant that the supposed knowledge disappears, its power of being made to engage the emotions will of course disappear along with it,—but the emotions themselves, and their claim to be engaged and satisfied, will remain. Now if we find by experience that humane letters have an undeniable power of engaging the emotions, the importance of humane letters in a man's training becomes not less, but greater, in proportion to the success of modern science in extirpating what it calls "mediæval thinking."

Have humane letters, then, have poetry and eloquence, the power here attributed to them of engaging the emotions, and do they exercise it? And if they have it and exercise it, *how* do they exercise it, so as to exert an influence upon man's sense for conduct, his sense for beauty? Finally, even if they both can and do exert an influence upon the senses in question, how are they to relate to them the results,—the modern results,—of natural science? All these questions may be asked. First, have poetry and eloquence the power of calling out the emotions? The appeal is to experience. Experience shows that for the vast majority of men, for mankind in general, they have the power. Next, do they exercise it? They do. But then, *how* do they exercise it so as to affect man's sense for conduct, his sense for beauty? And this is perhaps a case for applying the Preacher's words: "Though a man labor to seek it out, yet he shall not find it; yea, farther, though a wise man think to know it, yet shall he not be able to find it." Why should it be one thing, in its effect upon the emotions, to say, "Patience is a virtue," and quite another thing, in its effect upon the emotions, to say with Homer,

τλητὸν γὰρ Μοῖραι θυμὸν θέσαν ἀνθρώποισιν—

"for an enduring heart have the destinies appointed to the children of men"? Why should it be one thing, in its effect upon the emotions, to say with the philosopher Spinoza, *Felicitas in eo consistit quod homo suum esse conservare potest*—"Man's happiness consists in his being able to preserve his own essence," and quite another thing, in its effect upon the emotions, to say with the Gospel, "What is a man advantaged, if he gain the whole world, and lose himself, forfeit himself?" How does this difference of effect arise? I cannot tell, and I am not much concerned to know; the important thing is that it does arise, and that we can profit by it. But how, finally, are poetry and eloquence to exercise the power of relating the modern results of natural science to man's instinct for conduct, his instinct for beauty? And here again I answer that I do not know *how* they will exercise it, but that they can and will exercise it I am sure. I do not mean that modern philosophical poets and modern philosophical moralists are to come and relate for us, in express terms, the results of modern scientific research to our instinct for conduct, our instinct for beauty. But I mean that we shall find, as a matter of experience, if we know the best that has been thought and uttered in the world, we shall find that the art and poetry and eloquence of men who lived, perhaps, long ago, who had the most limited natural knowledge, who had the most erroneous conceptions about many important matters, we shall find that this art, and poetry, and eloquence, have in fact not only the power of refreshing and delighting us, they have also the power,—such is the strength and worth, in essentials, of their authors' criticism of life,—they have a fortifying, and elevating, and quickening, and suggestive power, capable of wonderfully helping us to relate the results of modern science to our need for conduct, our need for beauty. Homer's conceptions of the physical universe were, I imagine, grotesque; but really, under the shock of hearing from modern science that "the world is not subordinated to man's use, and that man is not the cynosure of things terrestrial," I could, for my own part, desire no better comfort than Homer's line which I quoted just now,

τλητὸν γὰρ Μοῖραι θυμὸν θέσαν ἀνθρώποισιν—

"for an enduring heart have the destinies appointed to the children of men"!

And the more that men's minds are cleared, the more that the results of science are frankly accepted, the more that poetry and eloquence come to be received and studied as what in truth they really are,—the criticism of life by gifted men, alive and active with extraordinary power at an unusual number of points;—so much the more will the value of humane letters, and of art also, which is an utterance having a like kind of power with theirs, be felt and acknowledged, and their place in education be secured.

Let us therefore, all of us, avoid indeed as much as possible any invidious comparison between the merits of humane letters, as means of education, and the merits of the natural sciences. But when some President of a Section for Mechanical Science insists on making the comparison, and tells us that "he who in his training has substituted literature and history for natural science has chosen the less useful alternative," let us make answer to him that the student of humane letters only, will, at least, know also the great general conceptions brought in by modern physical science; for science, as Professor Huxley says, forces them upon us all. But the student of the natural sciences only, will, by our very hypothesis, know nothing of humane letters; not to mention that in setting himself to be perpetually accumulating natural knowledge, he sets himself to do what only specialists have in general the gift for doing genially. And so he will probably be unsatisfied, or at any rate incomplete, and even more incomplete than the student of humane letters only.

I once mentioned in a school-report, how a young man

in one of our English training colleges having to paraphrase the passage in *Macbeth* beginning,

> Can'st thou not minister to a mind diseased?

turned this line into, "Can you not wait upon the lunatic?" And I remarked what a curious state of things it would be, if every pupil of our national schools knew, let us say, that the moon is two thousand one hundred and sixty miles in diameter, and thought at the same time that a good paraphrase for

> Can'st thou not minister to a mind diseased?

was, "Can you not wait upon the lunatic?" If one is driven to choose, I think I would rather have a young person ignorant about the moon's diameter, but aware that "Can you not wait upon the lunatic?" is bad, than a young person whose education had been such as to manage things the other way.

Or to go higher than the pupils of our national schools. I have in my mind's eye a member of our British Parliament who comes to travel here in America, who afterwards relates his travels, and who shows a really masterly knowledge of the geology of this great country and of its mining capabilities, but who ends by gravely suggesting that the United States should borrow a prince from our Royal Family, and should make him their king, and should create a House of Lords of great landed proprietors after the pattern of ours; and then America, he thinks, would have her future happily and perfectly secured. Surely, in this case, the President of the Section for Mechanical Science would himself hardly say that our member of Parliament, by concentrating himself upon geology and mineralogy, and so on, and not attending to literature and history, had "chosen the more useful alternative."

If then there is to be separation and option between humane letters on the one hand, and the natural sciences on the other, the great majority of mankind, all who have not exceptional and overpowering aptitudes for the study of nature, would do well, I cannot but think, to choose to be educated in humane letters rather than in the natural sciences. Letters will call out their being at more points, will make them live more.

I said that before I ended I would just touch on the question of classical education, and I will keep my word. Even if literature is to retain a large place in our education, yet Latin and Greek, say the friends of progress, will certainly have to go. Greek is the grand offender in the eyes of these gentlemen. The attackers of the established course of study think that against Greek, at any rate, they have irresistible arguments. Literature may perhaps be needed in education, they say; but why on earth should it be Greek literature? Why not French or German? Nay, "has not an Englishman models in his own literature of every kind of excellence?" As before, it is not on any weak pleadings of my own that I rely for convincing the gainsayers; it is on the constitution of human nature itself, and on the instinct of self-preservation in humanity. The instinct for beauty is set in human nature, as surely as the instinct for knowledge is set there, or the instinct for conduct. If the instinct for beauty is served by Greek literature and art as it is served by no other literature and art, we may trust to the instinct of self-preservation in humanity for keeping Greek as part of our culture. We may trust to it for even making the study of Greek more prevalent than it is now. Greek will come, I hope, some day to be studied more rationally than at present; but it will be increasingly studied as men increasingly feel the need in them for beauty, and how powerfully Greek art and Greek literature can serve this need. Women will again study Greek, as Lady Jane Grey did; I believe that in that chain of forts, with which the fair host of the Amazons are now engirdling our English universities, I find that here in America, in colleges like Smith College in Massachusetts, and Vassar College in the State of New York, and in the happy families of the mixed universities out West, they are studying it already.

Defuit una mihi symmetria prisca,—"The antique symmetry was the one thing wanting to me," said Leonardo da Vinci; and he was an Italian. I will not presume to speak for the Americans, but I am sure that, in the Englishman, the want of this admirable symmetry of the Greeks is a thousand times more great and crying than in any Italian. The results of the want show themselves most glaringly, perhaps, in our architecture, but they show themselves, also, in all our art. *Fit details strictly combined, in view of a large general result nobly conceived;* that is just the beautiful *symmetria prisca* of the Greeks, and it is just where we English fail, where all our art fails. Striking ideas we have, and well-executed details we have; but that high symmetry which, with satisfying and delightful effect, combines them, we seldom or never have. The glorious beauty of the Acropolis at Athens did not come from single fine things stuck about on that hill, a statue here, a gateway there;—no, it arose from all things being perfectly combined for a supreme total effect. What must not an Englishman feel about our deficiencies in this respect, as the sense for beauty, whereof this symmetry is an essential element, awakens and strengthens within him! what will not one day be his respect and desire for Greece and its *symmetria prisca*, when the scales drop from his eyes as he walks the London streets, and he sees such a lesson in meanness as the Strand, for instance, in its true deformity! But here we are coming to our friend Mr. Ruskin's province, and I will not intrude upon it, for he is its very sufficient guardian.

And so we at last find, it seems, we find flowing in favour of the humanities the natural and necessary stream of things, which seemed against them when we started. The "hairy quadruped furnished with a tail and pointed ears, probably arboreal in his habits," this good fellow carried hidden in his nature, apparently, something destined to develop into a necessity for humane letters. Nay, more; we seem finally to be even led to the further conclusion that our hairy ancestor carried in his nature, also, a necessity for Greek.

And therefore, to say the truth, I cannot really think that humane letters are in much actual danger of being thrust out from their leading place in education, in spite of the array of authorities against them at this moment. So long as human nature is what it is, their attractions will remain irresistible. As with Greek, so with letters generally: they will some day come, we may hope, to be studied more rationally, but they will not lose their place. What will happen will rather be that there will be crowded into education other matters besides, far too many; there will be, perhaps, a period of unsettlement and confusion and false tendency; but letters will not in the end lose their leading place. If they lose it for a time, they will get it back again. We shall be brought back to them by our wants and aspirations. And a poor humanist may possess his soul in patience, neither strive nor cry, admit the energy and brilliancy of the partisans of physical science, and their present favour with the public, to be far greater than his own, and still have a happy faith that the nature of things works silently on behalf of the studies which he loves, and that, while we shall all have to acquaint ourselves with the great results reached by modern science, and to give ourselves as much training in its disciplines as we can conveniently carry, yet the majority of men will always require humane letters; and so much the more, as they have the more and the greater results of science to relate to the need in man for conduct, and to the need in him for beauty.

Robert Louis Stevenson

1850 · 1894

Robert Louis Stevenson was born and brought up in Edinburgh, where, at the request of his father, he studied law. His preference for the writing profession led him to work toward a mastery of literary style. Despite ill health, he produced an astonishing number of essays, articles, poems, stories, and novels in a relatively short lifetime. He traveled extensively in search of health in France, in the United States, and finally in the islands of the South Pacific.

A GOSSIP ON ROMANCE

IN ANYTHING FIT TO BE CALLED by the name of reading, the process itself should be absorbing and voluptuous; we should gloat over a book, be rapt clean out of ourselves, and rise from the perusal, our mind filled with the busiest kaleidoscopic dance of images, incapable of sleep or of continuous thought. The words, if the book be eloquent, should run thenceforward in our ears like the noise of breakers, and the story, if it be a story, repeat itself in a thousand colored pictures to the eye. It was for this last pleasure that we read so closely, and loved our books so dearly, in the bright, troubled period of boyhood. Eloquence and thought, character and conversation, were but obstacles to brush aside as we dug blithely after a certain sort of incident, like a pig for truffles. For my part, I liked a story to begin with an old wayside inn where, "towards the close of the year 17—," several gentlemen in three-cocked hats were playing

Reprinted from MEMORIES AND PORTRAITS by Robert Louis Stevenson; used by permission of the publishers, Charles Scribner's Sons.

bowls. A friend of mine preferred the Malabar coast in a storm, with a ship beating to windward, and a scowling fellow of Herculean proportions striding along the beach; he, to be sure, was a pirate. This was further afield than my home-keeping fancy loved to travel, and designed altogether for a larger canvas than the tales that I affected. Give me a highwayman and I was full to the brim; a Jacobite would do, but the highwayman was my favorite dish. I can still hear that merry clatter of the hoofs along the moonlit lane; night and the coming of the day are still related in my mind with the doings of John Rann or Jerry Abershaw; and the words "postchaise," the "great North road," "ostler," and "nag," still sound in my ears like poetry. One and all, at least, and each with his particular fancy, we read storybooks in childhood, not for eloquence or character or thought, but for some quality of the brute incident. That quality was not mere bloodshed or wonder. Although each of these was welcome in its place, the charm for the sake of which we read depended on something different from either. My elders used to read novels aloud; and I can still remember four different passages which I heard, before I was ten, with the same keen and lasting pleasure. One I discovered long afterwards to be the admirable opening of *What Will He Do with It:* it was no wonder I was pleased with that. The other three still remain unidentified. One is a little vague; it was about a dark, tall house at night, and people groping on the stairs by the light that escaped from the open door of a sickroom. In another, a lover left a ball, and went walking in a cool, dewy park, whence he could watch the lighted windows and the figures of the dancers as they moved. This was the most sentimental impression I think I had yet received, for a child is somewhat deaf to the sentimental. In the last, a poet, who had been tragically wrangling with his wife, walked forth on the sea-beach on a tempestuous night and witnessed the horrors of a wreck. Different as they are, all these early favorites have a common note—they have all a touch of the romantic.

Drama is the poetry of conduct, romance the poetry of circumstance. The pleasure that we take in life is of two sorts—

the active and the passive. Now we are conscious of a great command over our destiny; anon we are lifted up by circumstance, as by a breaking wave, and dashed we know not how into the future. Now we are pleased by our conduct, anon merely pleased by our surroundings. It would be hard to say which of these modes of satisfaction is the more effective, but the latter is surely the more constant. Conduct is three parts of life, they say; but I think they put it high. There is a vast deal in life and letters both which is not immoral, but simply a-moral; which either does not regard the human will at all, or deals with it in obvious and healthy relations; where the interest turns, not upon what a man shall choose to do, but on how he manages to do it; not on the passionate slips and hesitations of the conscience, but on the problems of the body and of the practical intelligence, in clean, open-air adventure, the shock of arms or the diplomacy of life. With such material as this it is impossible to build a play, for the serious theater exists solely on moral grounds, and is a standing proof of the dissemination of the human conscience. But it is possible to build, upon this ground, the most joyous of verses, and the most lively, beautiful, and buoyant tales.

One thing in life calls for another; there is a fitness in events and places. The sight of a pleasant arbor puts it in our mind to sit there. One place suggests work, another idleness, a third early rising and long rambles in the dew. The effect of night, of any flowing water, of lighted cities, of the peep of day, of ships, of the open ocean, calls up in the mind an army of anonymous desires and pleasures. Something, we feel, should happen; we know not what, yet we proceed in quest of it. And many of the happiest hours of life fleet by us in this vain attendance on the genius of the place and moment. It is thus that tracts of young fir, and low rocks that reach into deep soundings, particularly torture and delight me. Something must have happened in such places, and perhaps ages back, to members of my race; and when I was a child I tried in vain to invent appropriate games for them, as I still try, just as vainly, to fit them with the proper story. Some places speak distinctly. Certain dank gardens cry aloud for a murder; certain old houses demand to be haunted; certain coasts are set apart for shipwreck. Other spots again seem to abide their destiny, suggestive and impenetrable, "miching mallecho." The inn at Burford Bridge, with its arbors and green garden and silent, eddying river—though it is known already as the place where Keats wrote some of his *Endymion* and Nelson parted from his Emma—still seems to wait the coming of the appropriate legend. Within these ivied walls, behind these old green shutters, some further business smolders, waiting for its hour. The old Hawes Inn at the Queen's Ferry makes a similar call upon my fancy. There it stands, apart from the town, beside the pier, in a climate of its own, half inland, half marine—in front, the ferry bubbling with the tide and the guardship swinging to her anchor; behind, the old garden with the trees. Americans seek it already for the sake of Lovel and Oldbuck, who dined there at the beginning of *The Antiquary.* But you need not tell me—that is not all; there is some story, unrecorded or not yet complete, which must express the meaning of that inn more fully. So it is with names and faces; so it is with incidents that are idle and inconclusive in themselves, and yet seem like the beginning of some quaint romance, which the all-careless author leaves untold. How many of these romances have we not seen determined at their birth; how many people have met us with a look of meaning in their eye, and sunk at once into trivial acquaintances; to how many places have we not drawn near, with express intimations —"here my destiny awaits me"—and we have but dined there and passed on! I have lived both at the Hawes and Burford in a perpetual flutter, on the heels, as it seemed, of some adventure that should justify the place; but though the feeling had me to bed at night and called me again at morning in one unbroken round of pleasure and suspense, nothing befell me in either worth remark. The man of the hour had not yet come; but some day, I think, a boat shall put off from the Queen's Ferry, fraught with a dear cargo, and some frosty night a horseman, on a tragic errand, rattle with his whip upon the green shutters of the inn at Burford.

Now, this is one of the natural appetites with which any

lively literature has to count. The desire for knowledge, I had almost added the desire for meat, is not more deeply seated than this demand for fit and striking incident. The dullest of clowns tells, or tries to tell, himself a story, as the feeblest of children uses invention in his play; and even as the imaginative grown person, joining in the game, at once enriches it with many delightful circumstances, the great creative writer shows us the realization and the apotheosis of the day-dreams of common men. His stories may be nourished with the realities of life, but their true mark is to satisfy the nameless longings of the reader, and to obey the ideal laws of the day-dream. The right kind of thing should fall out in the right kind of place; the right kind of thing should follow; and not only the characters talk aptly and think naturally, but all the circumstances in a tale answer one to another like notes in music. The threads of a story come from time to time together and make a picture in the web; the characters fall from time to time into some attitude to each other or to nature, which stamps the story home like an illustration. Crusoe recoiling from the footprint, Achilles shouting over against the Trojans, Ulysses bending the great bow, Christian running with his fingers in his ears, these are each culminating moments in the legend, and each has been printed on the mind's eye forever. Other things we may forget; we may forget the words, although they are beautiful; we may forget the author's comment, although perhaps it was ingenious and true; but these epoch-making scenes, which put the last mark of truth upon a story and fill up, at one blow, our capacity for sympathetic pleasure, we so adopt into the very bosom of our mind that neither time nor tide can efface or weaken the impression. This, then, is the plastic part of literature: to embody character, thought, or emotion in some act or attitude that shall be remarkably striking to the mind's eye. This is the highest and hardest thing to do in words; the thing which, once accomplished, equally delights the schoolboy and the sage, and makes, in its own right, the quality of epics. Compared with this, all other purposes in literature, except the purely lyrical or the purely philosophic, are bastard in nature, facile of execution, and feeble in result.

344

It is one thing to write about the inn at Burford, or to describe scenery with the word-painters; it is quite another to seize on the heart of the suggestion and make a country famous with a legend. It is one thing to remark and to dissect, with the most cutting logic, the complications of life and of the human spirit; it is quite another to give them body and blood in the story of Ajax or of Hamlet. The first is literature, but the second is something besides, for it is likewise art.

English people of the present day are apt, I know not why, to look somewhat down on incident, and reserve their admiration for the clink of teaspoons and the accents of the curate. It is thought clever to write a novel with no story at all, or at least with a very dull one. Reduced even to the lowest terms, a certain interest can be communicated by the art of narrative; a sense of human kinship stirred; and a kind of monotonous fitness, comparable to the words and air of *Sandy's Mull*, preserved among the infinitesimal occurrences recorded. Some people work in this manner, with even a strong touch. Mr. Trollope's inimitable clergymen arise to the mind in this connection. But even Mr. Trollope does not confine himself to chronicling small beer. Mr. Crawley's collision with the Bishop's wife, Mr. Mclnotte dallying in the deserted banquet-room, are typical incidents, epically conceived, fitly embodying a crisis. Or again look at Thackeray. If Rawdon Crawley's blow were not delivered, *Vanity Fair* would cease to be a work of art. That scene is the chief ganglion of the tale; and the discharge of energy from Rawdon's fist is the reward and consolation of the reader. The end of *Esmond* is a yet wider excursion from the author's customary fields; the scene at Castlewood is pure Dumas; the great and wily English borrower has here borrowed from the great unblushing French thief; as usual, he has borrowed admirably well, and the breaking of the sword rounds off the best of all his books with a manly, martial note. But perhaps nothing can more strongly illustrate the necessity for marking incident than to compare the living fame of *Robinson Crusoe* with the discredit of *Clarissa Harlowe*. *Clarissa* is a book of a far more startling import, worked out, on a great canvas, with inimitable courage and unflagging art. It contains wit, character, passion, plot, conversations full of spirit and insight, letters sparkling with unstrained humanity; and if the death of the heroine be somewhat frigid and artificial, the last days of the hero strike the only note of what we now call Byronism, between the Elizabethans and Byron himself. And yet a little story of a shipwrecked sailor, with not a tenth part of the style nor a thousandth part of the wisdom, exploring none of the arcana of humanity and deprived of the perennial interest of love, goes on from edition to edition, ever young, while *Clarissa* lies upon the shelves unread. A friend of mine, a Welsh blacksmith, was twenty-five years old and could neither read nor write, when he heard a chapter of *Robinson* read aloud in a farm kitchen. Up to that moment he had sat content, huddled in his ignorance, but he left that farm another man. There were daydreams, it appeared, divine day-dreams, written and printed and bound, and to be bought for money and enjoyed at pleasure. Down he sat that day, painfully learned to read Welsh, and returned to borrow the book. It had been lost, nor could he find another copy but one that was in English. Down he sat once more, learned English, and at length, and with entire delight, read *Robinson*. It was like the story of a love-chase. If he had heard a letter from *Clarissa*, would he have been fired with the same chivalrous ardor? I wonder. Yet *Clarissa* has every quality that can be shown in prose, one alone excepted—pictorial or picture-making romance. While *Robinson* depends, for the most part and with the overwhelming majority of its readers, on the charm of circumstance.

In the highest achievements of the art of words, the dramatic and the pictorial, the moral and romantic interest, rise and fall together by a common and organic law. Situation is animated with passion, passion clothed upon with situation. Neither exists for itself, but each inheres indissolubly with the other. This is high art; and not only the highest art possible in words, but the highest art of all, since it combines the greatest mass and diversity of the elements of truth and pleasure. Such are epics, and the few prose tales that have the epic

346

weight. But as from a school of works, aping the creative, incident and romance are ruthlessly discarded, so may character and drama be omitted or subordinated to romance. There is one book, for example, more generally loved than Shakespeare, that captivates in childhood, and still delights in age—I mean the *Arabian Nights*—where you shall look in vain for moral or for intellectual interest. No human face or voice greets us among that wooden crowd of kings and genies, sorcerers and beggarmen. Adventure, in the most naked terms, furnishes forth the entertainment, and is found enough. Dumas approaches perhaps nearest of any modern to these Arabian authors in the purely material charm of some of his romances. The early part of *Monte Cristo*, down to the finding of the treasure, is a piece of perfect story-telling; the man never breathed who shared these moving incidents without a tremor; and yet Faria is a thing of packthread and Dantès little more than a name. The sequel is one long-drawn error, gloomy, bloody, unnatural, and dull; but as for these early chapters, I do not believe there is another volume extant where you can breathe the same unmingled atmosphere of romance. It is very thin and light, to be sure, as on a high mountain; but it is brisk and clear and sunny in proportion. I saw the other day, with envy, an old and very clever lady setting forth on a second or third voyage into *Monte Cristo*. Here are stories which powerfully affect the reader, which can be reperused at any age, and where the characters are no more than puppets. The bony fist of the showman visibly propels them; their springs are an open secret; their faces are of wood; their bellies filled with bran; and yet we thrillingly partake of their adventures. And the point may be illustrated still further. The last interview between Lucy and Richard Feverel is pure drama; more than that, it is the strongest scene, since Shakespeare, in the English tongue. Their first meeting by the river, on the other hand, is pure romance; it has nothing to do with character; it might happen to any other boy and maiden, and be none the less delightful for the change. And yet I think he would be a bold man who should choose between these passages. Thus, in the same book, we may have two scenes, each capital in its order: in the one, human passion, deep calling unto deep, shall utter its genuine voice; in the second, according circumstances, like instruments in tune, shall build up a trivial but desirable incident, such as we love to prefigure for ourselves; and in the end, in spite of the critics, we may hesitate to give the preference to either. The one may ask more genius—I do not say it does; but at least the other dwells as clearly in the memory.

True romantic art, again, makes a romance of all things. It reaches into the highest abstraction of the ideal; it does not refuse the most pedestrian realism. *Robinson Crusoe* is as realistic as it is romantic: both qualities are pushed to an extreme, and neither suffers. Nor does romance depend upon the material importance of the incidents. To deal with strong and deadly elements, banditti, pirates, war and murder, is to conjure with great names, and, in the event of failure, to double the disgrace. The arrival of Haydn and Consuelo at the Canon's villa is a very trifling incident; yet we may read a dozen boisterous stories from beginning to end, and not receive so fresh and stirring an impression of adventure. It was the scene of Crusoe at the wreck, if I remember rightly, that so bewitched my blacksmith. Nor is the fact surprising. Every single article the castaway recovers from the hulk is "a joy for ever" to the man who reads of them. They are the things that should be found, and bare enumeration stirs the blood. I found a glimmer of the same interest the other day in a new book, *The Sailor's Sweetheart*, by Mr. Clark Russell. The whole business of the brig *Morning Star* is very rightly felt and spiritedly written; but the clothes, the books and the money satisfy the reader's mind like things to eat. We are dealing here with the old cut-and-dry, legitimate interest of treasure trove. But even treasure trove can be made dull. There are few people who have not groaned under the plethora of goods that fell to the lot of the *Swiss Family Robinson*, that dreary family. They found article after article, creature after creature, from milk kine to pieces of ordnance, a whole consignment; but no informing taste had presided over the selection,—there was no smack or relish in the invoice, and these riches left the fancy cold. The box of goods in Verne's *Mysterious Island* is another case in point: there was no gusto and no glamour about that; it might have come from a shop. But the two hundred and seventy-eight Australian sovereigns on board the *Morning Star* fell upon me like a surprise that I had expected; whole vistas of secondary stories, besides the one in hand, radiated forth from that discovery, as they radiate from a striking particular in life; and I was made for the moment as happy as a reader has a right to be.

To come at all at the nature of this quality of romance, we must bear in mind the peculiarity of our attitude to any art. No art produces illusion; in the theater we never forget that we are in the theater; and while we read a story, we sit wavering between two minds, now merely clapping our hands at the merit of the performance, now condescending to take an active part in fancy with the characters. This last is the triumph of romantic story-telling: when the reader consciously plays at being the hero, the scene is a good scene. Now, in character-studies the pleasure that we take is critical; we watch, we approve, we smile at incongruities, we are moved to sudden heats of sympathy with courage, suffering, or virtue. But the characters are still themselves, they are not us; the more clearly they are depicted, the more widely do they stand away from us, the more imperiously do they thrust us back into our place as a spectator. I cannot identify myself with Rawdon Crawley or with Eugène de Rastignac, for I have scarce a hope or fear in common with them. It is not character but incident that woos us out of our reserve. Something happens as we desire to have it happen to ourselves; some situation, that we have long dallied with in fancy, is realized in the story with enticing and appropriate details. Then we forget the characters; then we push the hero aside; then we plunge into the tale in our own person and bathe in fresh experience; and then, and then only, do we say we have been reading a romance. It is not only pleasurable things that we imagine in our day-dreams; there are lights in which we are willing to contemplate even the idea of our own death; ways in which it seems as if it would amuse us to be cheated, wounded, or calumniated. It is thus possible to construct a story, even of tragic import, in which every incident, detail, and trick of circumstance shall be welcome to the reader's thoughts. Fiction is to the grown man what play is to the child; it is there that he changes the atmosphere and tenor of his life; and when the game so chimes with his fancy that he can join in it with all his heart, when it pleases him with every turn, when he loves to recall it and dwells upon its recollection with entire delight, fiction is called romance.

Walter Scott is out and away the king of the romantics. *The Lady of the Lake* has no indisputable claim to be a poem beyond the inherent fitness and desirability of the tale. It is just such a story as a man would make up for himself, walking, in the best health and temper, through just such scenes as it is laid in. Hence it is that a charm dwells undefinable among these slovenly verses, as the unseen cuckoo fills the mountains with his note; hence, even after we have flung the book aside, the scenery and adventures remain present to the mind, a new and green possession, not unworthy of that beautiful name, *The Lady of the Lake*, or that direct, romantic opening—one of the most spirited and poetical in literature—"The stag at eve had drunk his fill." The same strength and the same weaknesses adorn and disfigure the novels. In that ill-written, ragged book, *The Pirate*, the figure of Cleveland—cast up by the sea on the resounding foreland of Dunrossness—moving, with the blood on his hands and the Spanish words on his tongue, among the simple islanders—singing a serenade under the window of his Shetland mistress—is conceived in the very highest manner of romantic invention. The words of his song, "Through groves of palm," sung in such a scene and by such a lover, clench, as in a nutshell, the emphatic contrast upon which the tale is built. In *Guy Mannering*, again, every incident is delightful to the imagination; and the scene when Harry Bertram lands at Ellangowan is a model instance of romantic method.

" 'I remember the tune well,' he says, 'though I cannot guess what should at present so strongly recall it to my memory.' He took his flageolet from his pocket and played a simple

melody. Apparently the tune awoke the corresponding associations of a damsel. . . . She immediately took up the song—

> " 'Are these the links of Forth,' she said;
> 'Or are they the crooks of Dee,
> Or the bonny woods of Warroch Head
> That I so fain would see?'

" 'By heaven!' said Bertram, 'it is the very ballad.' "

On this quotation two remarks fall to be made. First, as
an instance of modern feeling for romance, this famous touch
of the flageolet and the old song is selected by Miss Braddon
for omission. Miss Braddon's idea of a story, like Mrs. Tod-
gers's idea of a wooden leg, were something strange to have
expounded. As a matter of personal experience, Meg's appearance to old Mr. Bertram on the road, the ruins of Dern-
cleugh, the scene of the flageolet, and the Dominie's recognition of Harry, are the four strong notes that continue to ring
in the mind after the book is laid aside. The second point is
still more curious. The reader will observe a mark of excision
in the passage as quoted by me. Well, here is how it runs in
the original: "a damsel who, close behind a fine spring about
half-way down the descent, and which had once supplied the
castle with water, was engaged in bleaching linen." A man
who gave in such copy would be discharged from the staff of a
daily paper. Scott has forgotten to prepare the reader for
the presence of the "damsel"; he has forgotten to mention the
spring and its relation to the ruin; and now, face to face with
his omission, instead of trying back and starting fair, crams
all this matter, tail foremost, into a single shambling sentence.
It is not merely bad English, or bad style; it is abominably
bad narrative besides.

Certainly the contrast is remarkable; and it is one that
throws a strong light upon the subject of this paper. For here
we have a man of the finest creative instinct touching with
perfect certainty and charm the romantic junctures of his
story; and we find him utterly careless, almost, it would seem,
incapable, in the technical matter of style, and not only frequently weak, but frequently wrong in points of drama. In

character parts, indeed, and particularly in the Scotch, he was delicate, strong, and truthful; but the trite, obliterated features of too many of his heroes have already wearied two generations of readers. At times his characters will speak with something far beyond propriety with a true heroic note; but on the next page they will be wading wearily forward with an ungrammatical and undramatic rigmarole of words. The man who could conceive and write the character of Elspeth of the Craigburnfoot, as Scott has conceived and written it, had not only splendid romantic, but splendid tragic gifts. How comes it, then, that he could so often fob us off with languid, inarticulate twaddle?

It seems to me that the explanation is to be found in the very quality of his surprising merits. As his books are play to the reader, so were they play to him. He conjured up the romantic with delight, but he had hardly patience to describe it. He was a great day-dreamer, a seer of fit and beautiful and humorous visions, but hardly a great artist; hardly, in the manful sense, an artist at all. He pleased himself, and so he pleases us. Of the pleasures of his art he tasted fully; but of its toils and vigils and distresses never man knew less. A great romantic—an idle child.

Joseph Conrad

1857 · 1924

Joseph Conrad, born in the Ukraine of Polish parents, overcame handicaps of language and training to become one of the greatest modern writers of English fiction. As a boy he went to sea in a British merchant ship, and eventually he rose to command his own ships. His experience with ships and the sea provides a background for his portrayal of character, and his sensitivity to human tragedy lends to his stories a feeling of urgency.

PREFACE TO *THE NIGGER OF THE NARCISSUS*

A WORK THAT ASPIRES, however humbly, to the condition of art should carry its justification in every line. And art itself may be defined as a single-minded attempt to render the highest kind of justice to the visible universe, by bringing to light the truth, manifold and one, underlying its every aspect. It is an attempt to find in its forms, in its colors, in its light, in its shadows, in the aspects of matter and in the facts of life, what of each is fundamental, what is enduring and essential—their one illuminating and convincing quality—the very truth of their existence. The artist, then, like the thinker or the scientist, seeks the truth and makes his appeal. Impressed by the aspect of the world the thinker plunges into ideas, the scientist into facts—whence, presently, emerging they make their appeal to those qualities of our being that fit us best for the hazardous enterprise of living. They speak authoritatively to our common-sense, to our intelligence,

Reprinted from THE NIGGER OF THE NARCISSUS by Joseph Conrad. Used by permission of J. M. Dent & Sons Ltd., London, England.

to our desire of peace or to our desire of unrest; not seldom to our prejudices, sometimes to our fears, often to our egoism —but always to our credulity. And their words are heard with reverence, for their concern is with weighty matters: with the cultivation of our minds and the proper care of our bodies, with the attainment of our ambitions, with the perfection of the means and the glorification of our precious aims.

It is otherwise with the artist.

Confronted by the same enigmatical spectacle the artist descends within himself, and in that lonely region of stress and strife, if he be deserving and fortunate, he finds the terms of his appeal. His appeal is made to our less obvious capacities: to that part of our nature which, because of the warlike conditions of existence, is necessarily kept out of sight within the more resisting and hard qualities—like the vulnerable body within a steel armor. His appeal is less loud, more profound, less distinct, more stirring—and sooner forgotten. Yet its effect endures forever. The changing wisdom of successive generations discards ideas, questions facts, demolishes theories. But the artist appeals to that part of our being which is not dependent on wisdom: to that in us which is a gift and not an acquisition—and, therefore, more permanently enduring. He speaks to our capacity for delight and wonder, to the sense of mystery surrounding our lives; to our sense of pity, and beauty, and pain; to the latent feeling of fellowship with all creation—and to the subtle but invincible conviction of solidarity that knits together the loneliness of innumerable hearts, to the solidarity in dreams, in joy, in sorrow, in aspirations, in illusions, in hope, in fear, which binds men to each other, which binds together all humanity—the dead to the living and the living to the unborn.

It is only some such train of thought, or rather of feeling, that can in a measure explain the aim of the attempt, made in the tale which follows, to present an unrestful episode in the obscure lives of a few individuals out of all the disregarded multitude of the bewildered, the simple and the voiceless. For, if any part of truth dwells in the belief confessed above, it becomes evident that there is not a place of splendor or a dark corner of the earth that does not deserve, if only a passing glance of wonder and pity. The motive, then, may be held to justify the matter of the work; but this preface, which is simply an avowal of endeavor, cannot end here—for the avowal is not yet complete.

Fiction—if it at all aspires to be art—appeals to temperament. And in truth it must be, like painting, like music, like all art, the appeal of one temperament to all the other innumerable temperaments whose subtle and resistless power endows passing events with their true meaning, and creates the moral, the emotional atmosphere of the place and time. Such an appeal to be effective must be an impression conveyed through the senses; and, in fact, it cannot be made in any other way, because temperament, whether individual or collective, is not amenable to persuasion. All art, therefore, appeals primarily to the senses, and the artistic aim when expressing itself in written words must also make its appeal through the senses, if its high desire is to reach the secret spring of responsive emotions. It must strenuously aspire to the plasticity of sculpture, to the color of painting, and to the magic suggestiveness of music—which is the art of arts. And it is only through complete, unswerving devotion to the perfect blending of form and substance; it is only through an unremitting never-discouraged care for the shape and ring of sentences that an approach can be made to plasticity, to color, and that the light of magic suggestiveness may be brought to play for an evanescent instant over the commonplace surface of words: of the old, old words, worn thin, defaced by ages of careless usage.

The sincere endeavor to accomplish that creative task, to go as far on that road as his strength will carry him, to go undeterred by faltering, weariness or reproach, is the only valid justification for the worker in prose. And if his conscience is clear, his answer to those who, in the fullness of a wisdom which looks for an immediate profit, demand specifically to be edified, consoled, amused; who demand to be promptly improved, or encouraged, or frightened, or shocked, or charmed, must run thus:—My task which I am trying to achieve is, by the power of the written word, to make you hear, to make you feel—it is, before all, to make you *see*. That—and no more, and it is everything. If I succeed, you shall find there according to your deserts: encouragement, consolation, fear, charm—all you demand—and, perhaps, also that glimpse of truth for which you have forgotten to ask.

To snatch in a moment of courage, from the remorseless rush of time, a passing phase of life, is only the beginning of the task. The task approached in tenderness and faith is to hold up unquestioningly, without choice and without fear, the rescued fragment before all eyes in the light of a sincere mood. It is to show its vibration, its color, its form; and through its movement, its form, and its color, reveal the substance of its truth—disclose its inspiring secret: the stress and passion within the core of each convincing moment. In a single-minded attempt of that kind, if one be deserving and fortunate, one may perchance attain to such clearness of sincerity that at last the presented vision of regret or pity, of terror or mirth, shall awaken in the hearts of the beholders that feeling of unavoidable solidarity; of the solidarity in mysterious origin, in toil, in joy, in hope, in uncertain fate, which binds men to each other and all mankind to the visible world.

It is evident that he who, rightly or wrongly, holds by the convictions expressed above cannot be faithful to any one of the temporary formulas of his craft. The enduring part of them—the truth which each only imperfectly veils—should abide with him as the most precious of his possessions, but they all: Realism, Romanticism, Naturalism, even the unofficial sentimentalism (which like the poor, is exceedingly difficult to get rid of) all these gods must, after a short period of fellowship, abandon him—even on the very threshold of the temple—to the stammerings of his conscience and to the outspoken consciousness of the difficulties of his work. In that uneasy solitude the supreme cry of Art for Art itself, loses the exciting ring of its apparent immorality. It sounds far off. It has ceased to be a cry, and is heard only as a whisper, often incomprehensible, but at times and faintly encouraging.

Sometimes, stretched at ease in the shade of a roadside tree, we watch the motions of a laborer in a distant field, and after a time, begin to wonder languidly as to what the fellow may be at. We watch the movements of his body, the waving of his arms, we see him bend down, stand up, hesitate, begin again. It may add to the charm of an idle hour to be told the purpose of his exertions. If we know he is trying to lift a stone, to dig a ditch, to uproot a stump, we look with a more real interest at his efforts; we are disposed to condone the jar of his agitation upon the restfulness of the landscape; and even, if in a brotherly frame of mind, we may bring ourselves to forgive his failure. We understood his object, and, after all, the fellow has tried, and perhaps he had not the strength— and perhaps he had not the knowledge. We forgive, go on our way—and forget.

And so it is with the workman of art. Art is long and life is short, and success is very far off. And thus, doubtful of strength to travel so far, we talk a little about the aim—the aim of art, which, like life itself, is inspiring, difficult—obscured by mists. It is not in the clear logic of a triumphant conclusion; it is not in the unveiling of one of those heartless secrets which are called the Laws of Nature. It is not less great, but only more difficult.

To arrest, for the space of a breath, the hands busy about the work of the earth, and compel men entranced by the sight of distant goals to glance for a moment at the surrounding vision of form and color, of sunshine and shadows; to make them pause for a look, for a sigh, for a smile—such is the aim, difficult and evanescent, and reserved only for a very few to achieve. But sometimes, by the deserving and the fortunate, even that task is accomplished. And when it is accomplished— behold!—all the truth of life is there: a moment of vision, a sigh, a smile—and the return to an eternal rest.

George Santayana

1863 · 1952

> *George Santayana was born in Madrid and educated in the United States. From 1889 until 1912, he taught philosophy at Harvard, and since 1914 he had lived in Europe. In addition to several distinguished philosophical works, he wrote poems and a novel,* The Last Puritan *(1936). A materialist and skeptic, he rejected all mysticism and stressed the intellectual life.*

PENITENT ART

ART IS LIKE A CHARMING WOMAN who once had her age of innocence in the nursery, when she was beautiful without knowing it, being wholly intent on what she was making or telling or imagining.

Then she has had a season of passion and vanity, when having discovered how beautiful she was, she decked herself out in all possible pomp and finery, invented fashion after fashion to keep admiration alive, and finally began to put on rouge and false hair and too much scent, in the hope of still being a belle at seventy.

But it sometimes happens, during her long decline, that she hears a call to repentance, and thinks of being converted. Naturally, such a fine lady cannot give up her carriage; she is obliged occasionally to entertain her old friends at dinner, and to be seen now and then at the opera. Habit and the commitments she has in the world, where no function is complete without her, are too strong for her to be converted suddenly, or altogether; but henceforth something in her, in her most sensitive and thoughtful hours, upbraids her for the hollowness of her old airs and graces. It is really a sorry business, this perpetual pretence of being important and charming and charmed and beautiful.

Art seems to be passing at present through a lenten mood of this sort. Not all art, of course: somebody must still manufacture official statues and family portraits, somebody must design apartment houses, clubs, churches, skyscrapers, and stations. Visible through the academic framework of these inevitable objects, there is often much professional learning and judgment; there is even, sometimes, a hint of poetic life, or a suggestion of exotic beauty. In Mr. Sargent's painting, for instance, beneath the photographic standards of the studio, we often catch a satirical intention, or a philosophic idea, or love of the sensuous qualities in the model and in the accessories; a technical echo of Velasquez and Goya, though without plastic vitality or dramatic ease; a sort of Van Dyke, as it were, for the days of Edward VII; the dreadful lapse in refinement not being greater, perhaps, than is requisite for the documentary value of a true mirror of fashion in the later age. Taste of the old honest worldly sort is far from dead; it is found still in milliners and designers of fashionable garments, of furniture and ornaments. All this luxurious traditional art is as far as possible from repentance. Yet as the Magdalene was potentially a saint—perhaps always a saint really—so the most meretricious contrivances in the arts may sometimes include and betray the very principle of redemption, which is love; in this case the love of beauty. For example, here is the Russian ballet, doubling the dose of luxurious stimulation in every direction, erotic, tragic, historical, and decorative; yet see how it glides at times into simplicity, and in spite of all the paraphernalia of expert æstheticism, issues in forms of unmistakably penitent art, like pure colour and caricature.

I call pure colour and caricature penitent art, because it is only disappointment in other directions that drives artists back to these primary effects. By an austere and deliberate abstinence from everything that naturally tempts them, they achieve in this way a certain peace; but they would far rather have found it by genuinely recovering their naïveté. Sensuous splendour and caricature would then have seemed to them not the acme of abstract art, but the obvious truth of things; they would have doted on puppets and pantomime as a child dotes on dolls, without ever noticing how remote they are from reality. In the nineteenth century some romantic artists, poets, and philosophers actually tried being rebaptized, hoping that a fresh dip in the Jordan might rejuvenate them; but it was of no use. The notion of *recovering innocence* is a contradiction in terms; conversion can only initiate a non-natural life of grace; death must intervene before corruption can put on incorruption. That age was accordingly an age of revivals, of antiquaries, nothing in art and religion but retrospective; it was progressive only in things material and in the knowledge of them. Even its philosophical idealism and psychology were meant to be historical and descriptive of facts, literary and egotistical as the view of the facts might be. Romanticism thought it was exquisitely sensitive to the spirit of remote things, but in reality it was sensitive only to material perspectives, to costume and stage-setting; it grew sentimental over legends and ruins, and being moon-struck, thought it was imbibing the spirit of the past. But the past had not been consciously romantic; what the ancients actually thought and felt was understood much better before the nineteenth century than since; for formerly they were regarded simply as men, essentially contemporary—which comes much nearer the truth. Of course, the passion that can drive people to such earnest affectations must be itself genuine. Keats or Ruskin or Oscar Wilde had abundant vitality and expressed, each in his studied archaism, the profound helplessness that beset him; but what was vital in them was some sensuous or moral or revolutionary instinct of their own, such as in Shelley had existed pure; only in them it was contorted by their terrible preoccupation with being early, or rich, or choice. They were hypnotized by dead beauty; and not having invention nor influence enough to remodel their own age,

they fled from it to exotic delights, sometimes primitive, sometimes luxurious, sometimes religious, and sometimes all these
things at once. Similarly the revivals in architecture and in the
minor crafts expressed a genuine love of colour, ornament,
and beauty; they gave the snobbish middle classes a taste of
cheap luxury; they could sip culture in a teacup. Yet the
particular fashions revived were unstable; each successive
affectation had hardly ceased to seem exquisite when it began
to look foolish. Art at best is subject to fashion, because there
is a margin of arbitrary variation in its forms, even when
their chief lines are determined by their function; but in revived art fashion is all; it is a fancy-dress, unsatisfying even
in the glamour of the ballroom, which we are positively
ashamed to be seen in in the morning.

Fortunately revivals now seem to be over. Ruins and muse-
ums are interesting to the antiquary; they stir the historical
imagination, and dazzle us here and there with some ray of
living beauty, like that of a jewel; but they cannot supply
inspiration. In art, in poetry, unless you become as a little
child you cannot enter the kingdom of heaven. Little children
is what artists and poets are now striving hard to be; little
children who instead of blowing a tin trumpet blow by
chance through a whole orchestra, but with the same emotion
as the child; or who, instead of daubing a geometrical skeleton
with a piece of chalk, can daub a cross-eyed cross-section of
the entire spectrum or a compound fracture of a nightmare.
Such is Cubism: by no means an inexpert or meaningless thing.
Before you can compose a chaos or paint the unnamable, you
must train yourself to a severe abstention from all practical
habits of perception; you must heroically suppress the understanding. The result, when the penance is genuinely performed, has a very deep and recondite charm; you revert to
what the spinal column might feel if it had a separate consciousness, or to what the retina might see if it could be pain-
lessly cut off from the brain; lights, patterns, dynamic sugges-
tions, sights and memories fused together, hypnotic harmonies
such as may visit a vegetative or even mineral sensibility; you
become a thousand prisms and mirrors reflecting one another.

This is one kind of æsthetic repentance. Vain, vain, it says to it-self, was the attempt to depict or beautify external objects; let material things be what they will; what are they to the artist? Nature has the urgency of life, which art cannot rival; it has the lure, the cruelty, of actual existence, where all is sin and confusion and vanity, a hideous strife of forms devouring one another, in which all are mutilated and doomed. What is that to the spirit? Let it confess its own impotence in that field, and abandon all attempts to observe or preserve what are called *things:* let it devote itself instead to cleansing the inside of the cup, to purifying its sensibility, which is after all what nature plays upon when she seems to us to be beautiful. Perhaps in that way spirit may abstract the gold of beauty and cast the dross away—all that alloy of preoccupation with material forms and external events and moral sentiments and vain ani-mal adventures which has so long distracted the misguided artist, when he could paint the whole world and had lost his own soul. It is always the play of sensibility, and nothing else, that lends interest to external themes; and it was an evil obses-sion with alien things that dragged sensibility into a slavery to things which stifled and degraded it: *salvation lies in emanci-pating the medium.*

To renounce representation, or be representative only by accident, is accordingly one sort of penitent art; but there is another sort, more humble and humorous. This second sort makes no attempt to resist the impulse to observe and to ex-press external things. It does not proudly imagine that the medium, which is the human contribution to representation, can be sufficient unto itself. On the contrary, in its sensuous orchestration it is content to be rudimentary, to work in clay or in wood, and to dress in homespun. It is all feeling, all child-like tenderness, all sense of life. Persons and animals fascinate it. At the same time, warned by the fate of explicit poets and realistic painters, it does not attempt, in its portraiture, to give more than a pregnant hint, some large graphic sign, some pro-found caricature. Don't be rhetorical, it says; don't try to be exhaustive; all that is worth saying can be said in words of one syllable. Look long, and be brief. It is not in their material entirety and detail that things penetrate to the soul, but in their simple large identity, as a child knows his mother, nurse, or dog. Fresh inchoate forms, voices draped in mantles, people the mind, and return to it in dreams. Monsters and dwarfs were the first gods; the half, said a Greek proverb, is better than the whole. The implicit is alone important where life is concerned: nothing is more eloquent than an abstract posture, an immovable single gesture. Let art abandon reproduction and become indication. If it threatens thereby to become caricature, know that profound art can never be anything else. If men, when seen truly, take on the aspect of animals or puppets, it is because they are animals and puppets at bottom. But all caricature need not be unkind; it may be tender, or even sublime. The distortion, the single emphasis, the extreme simplification may reveal a soul which rhetoric and self-love had hidden in a false rationality. The absurd is the naked truth, the pathetic appeal of sheer fact, attempting to come into existence, like a featherless chick peeping out of its eggshell. All this pompous drapery of convention was a disguise; strip it away. Do not make maps of your images; make companions of them, make idols. Be reticent, emphatic, moody, bold; *salvation lies in caricature.*

Accustomed as they are to revivals, some critics have called this form of æsthetic penance a revival of savage art; but the mood is reversed. Savages were never rudimentary on purpose; they were not experimenting in the distortion or simplification of forms; much less, of course, did they voluntarily eliminate all representation of objects in order to deepen sensibility for the medium. They simply painted as well as they could. We have got far beyond that. Penitent art, childish as it may seem at times, is a refinement, perhaps an over-refinement; it is not so much crude or incompetent, as ascetic or morbid. It is also sometimes a little vulgar; because one of the forms of caricature and self-revelation is to be brutal, to flaunt what is out of place, what spoils the picture. Tragedy used to be noble; there is a new refinement in seeing how often it is ignoble; there is a second tragedy in that. Perhaps what we regard at first sight as a terrible decline in art may be sometimes the awakening of this sort of self-scorn. See how ugly I am, it cries, how brutish, common, and deformed! There are remains of sculpture and paintings of the late Roman Empire in some respects like our latest experiments. The decorative splendour (which was very marked) is lost; we miss the coloured marbles, the gold, the embroideries, the barbaric armour and jewels; but the stunted pathetic human figures remain in crowds. It seems that the spirit had no joy in man any more; it hid him in hieratic garments or pityingly recorded his gregarious misery. He was a corpse laid out in pontifical vestments. We too are dying; but in nature the death of one thing is commonly the birth of another. Instead of decorating a Byzantine sanctuary, our artists do penance in a psychological desert, studying their own sensations, the mysteries of sheer light and sound; and as music was long ago divorced from poetry and instrumental music from singing, so a luxurious but strident art is detaching itself from everything but its own medium. This on the decorative side; in representation the same retrenchment stops at another level. Representation too has a psychological medium; fancy must create the images which the observer or reproducer of things conceives to be their forms. These images are not the forms of things at all; not only is their perspective created by the observer, but their character, when it is truly considered, is amazingly summary, variable, and fantastic—a mere wraith, a mere hint, a mere symbol. What we suppose we see, what we *say* things look like, is rather an inventory, collected in memory and language, of many successive observations; it is discursive study, registered perhaps in discursive painting. But as the total composition never was nor ever could be a living image, so its parts are not images any longer; in being arrested they have acquired new boundaries and lost half their primitive essence. We may paint the things we see, we cannot arrest the images by which we see them; all we can do—if the images and not the things are what interest us—is to paint something that, by some occult trick of optics, may revive the image in some particular; and then, although the picture when studied discursively may not resemble the thing at all, it may bring back to us, as it were by scent, the feeling which the thing originally gave us; and we may say that it has caught the *spirit* of the thing. It is the medium that in such a case animates the object, and seems to obscure it; and this medium which we call sense in so far as things affect us through it, we call spirit in so far as it modifies our view of the things. The more we transform things in seeing them, the more we seem to spiritualize them and turn them into forms of our own sensibility, regarding the living image in us as the dramatic essence of the object. It is the business of science to correct this illusion; but the penitent artist—who has taken refuge in the spirit and is not striving to stretch his apprehension into literal truth, since the effort to depict things discursively has proved a vain and arid ambition—the penitent artist is content with the rhythms, echoes, or rays which things awaken within him; and in proportion as these reverberations are actually renewed, the poem remains a cry, the story a dream, the building a glimpse, the portrait a caricature.

PRIMARY POETRY

THERE IS BOTH TRUTH AND ILLUSION in the saying that primitive poets are sublime. *Genesis* and the *Iliad* (works doubtless backed by a long tradition) are indeed sublime. Primitive men, having perhaps developed language before the other arts, used it with singular directness to describe the chief episodes of life, which was all that life as yet contained. They had frank passions and saw things from single points of view. A breath from that early world seems to enlarge our natures, and to restore to language, which we have sophisticated, all its magnificence and truth. But there is more, for language is spontaneous; it constitutes an act before it registers an observation. It gives vent to emotion before it is adjusted to things external and reduced, as it were, to its own echo rebounding from a refractory world. The lion's roar, the bellowing of bulls, even the sea's cadence has a great sublimity.

Reprinted from LITTLE ESSAYS by George Santayana; used by permission of the publishers, Charles Scribner's Sons.

Though hardly in itself poetry, an animal cry, when still audible in human language, renders it also the unanswerable, the ultimate voice of nature. Nothing can so pierce the soul as the uttermost sigh of the body. An intense, inhospitable mind, filled with a single idea, in which all animal, social, and moral interests are fused together, speaks a language of incomparable force. Thus the Hebrew prophets, in their savage concentration, poured into one torrent all that their souls possessed or could dream of. What other men are wont to pursue in politics, business, religion, or art, they looked for from one wave of national repentance and consecration. Their age, swept by this ideal passion, possessed at the same time a fresh and homely vocabulary; and the result was an eloquence so elemental and combative, so imaginative and so bitterly practical, that the world has never heard its like. Such single-mindedness, with such heroic simplicity in words and images, is hardly possible in a late civilization. Cultivated poets are not unconsciously sublime.

The sublimity of early utterances should not be hailed, however, with unmixed admiration. It is a sublimity born of defect or at least of disproportion. The will asserts itself magnificently; images, like thunderclouds, seem to cover half the firmament at once. But such a will is sadly inexperienced; it has hardly tasted or even conceived any possible or high satisfactions. Its lurid firmament is poor in stars. To throw the whole mind upon something is not so great a feat when the mind has nothing else to throw itself upon. Every animal when goaded becomes intense; and it is perhaps merely the apathy in which mortals are wont to live that keeps them from being habitually sublime in their sentiments. The sympathy that makes a sheep hasten after its fellows, in vague alarm or in vague affection; the fierce premonitions that drive a bull to the heifer; the patience with which a hen sits on her eggs; the loyalty which a dog shows to his master—what thoughts may not all these instincts involve, which it needs only a medium of communication to translate into poetry?

Memorable nonsense, or sound with a certain hypnotic power, is the really primitive and radical form of poetry.

Nor is such poetry yet extinct: children still love and compose it, and every genuine poet, on one side of his genius, reverts to it from explicit speech. As all language has acquired its meaning, and did not have it in the beginning, so the man who launches a new locution, the poet who creates a symbol, must do so without knowing what significance it may eventually acquire, and conscious at best only of the emotional background from which it emerged. Pure poetry is pure experiment; and it is not strange that nine-tenths of it should be pure failure. For it matters little what unutterable things may have originally gone together with a phrase in the dreamer's mind; if they were not uttered and the phrase cannot call them back, this verbal relic is none the richer for the high company it may once have kept. Expressiveness is a most accidental matter. What a line suggests at one reading, it may never suggest again even to the same person. For this reason, among others, poets are partial to their own compositions; they truly discover there depths of meaning which exist for nobody else. Those readers who appropriate a poet and make him their own fall into a similar illusion; they attribute to him what they themselves supply, and whatever he reels out, lost in his own personal reverie, seems to them, like *sortes biblicae*, written to fit their own case.

Justice has never been done to Plato's remarkable consistency and boldness in declaring that poets are inspired by a divine madness and yet, when they transgress rational bounds, are to be banished from an ideal republic, though not without some marks of platonic regard. Instead of fillets, a modern age might assign them a coterie of flattering dames, and instead of banishment, starvation; but the result would be the same in the end. A poet is inspired because what occurs in his brain is a true experiment in creation. His apprehension plays with words and their meanings as nature, in any spontaneous variation, plays with her own structure. A mechanical force shifts the kaleidoscope; a new direction is given to growth or a new gist to signification. This inspiration, moreover, is mad, being wholly ignorant of its own issue; and though it has a confused fund of experience and verbal habit on which to draw, it draws on this fund blindly and quite at random, consciously possessed by nothing but a certain stress and pregnancy and the pains, as it were, of parturition. Finally the new birth has to be inspected critically by the public censor before it is allowed to live; most probably it is too feeble and defective to prosper in the common air, or is a monster that violates some primary rule of civic existence, tormenting itself to disturb others.

Plato seems to have exaggerated the havoc which these poetic dragons can work in the world. They are in fact more often absurd than venomous, and no special legislation is needed to abolish them. They soon die quietly of universal neglect. The poetry that ordinarily circulates among a people is poetry of a secondary and conventional sort that propagates established ideas in trite metaphors. Popular poets are the parish priests of the Muse, retailing her ancient divinations to a long since converted public. As a tree in the autumn sheds leaves and seeds together, so a ripening experience comes indifferently to various manifestations, some barren and without further function, others fit to carry the parent experience over into another mind, and give it a new embodiment there. Expressiveness in the former case is dead, like that of a fossil; in the latter it is living and efficacious, recreating its original. The first is idle self-manifestation, the second rational art.

A poet, spokesman of his full soul at a given moment, cannot consider eventualities or think of anything but the message he is sent to deliver, whether the world can then hear it or not. God, he may feel sure, understands him, and in the eternal the beauty he sees and loves immortally justifies his enthusiasm. Nevertheless, critics must view his momentary ebullition from another side. They do not come to justify the poet in his own eyes; he amply relieves them of such a function. They come only to inquire how significant the poet's expressions are for humanity at large or for whatever public he addresses. They come to register the social or representative value of the poet's soul. His inspiration may have been an odd cerebral rumbling, a perfectly irrecoverable and wasted intuition; the exquisite quality it doubtless had to his own sense is now not to the purpose. A work of art is a public possession; it is addressed to the world. By taking on a material embodiment, a spirit solicits attention and claims some kinship with the prevalent gods. Has it, critics should ask, the affinities needed for such intercourse? Is it humane, is it rational, is it friendly to the rest of the soul? To its inherent incommunicable charms it must add a kind of courtesy. If it wants other approval than its own, it cannot afford to regard no other aspiration.

INDUSTRIAL IDEALISM

A PEOPLE ONCE HAVING BECOME INDUSTRIAL will hardly be happy if sent back to Arcadia; it will have formed busy habits which it cannot relax without tedium; it will have developed a restlessness and avidity which will crave matter, like any other kind of hunger. Every experiment in living qualifies the initial possibilities of life, and the moralist would reckon without his host if he did not allow for the change which forced exercise makes in instinct, adjusting it more or less to extant conditions originally, perhaps, unwelcome. It is too late for the highest good to prescribe flying for quadrupeds or peace for the sea waves. Knowledge of what is possible is the beginning of happiness.

The acceptable side of industrialism, which is supposed to be inspired exclusively by utility, is not utility at all but pure achievement. If we wish to do such an age justice we must judge it as we should a child and praise its feats without inquiring after its purposes. That is its own spirit: a spirit dominant at the present time, particularly in America, where industrialism appears most free from alloy. There is a curious delight in turning things over, changing their shape, discovering their possibilities, making of them some new contrivance. Use, in these experimental minds, as in nature, is only incidental. There is an irrational creative impulse, a zest in novelty, in progression, in beating the other man, or, as they say, in breaking the record. There is also a fascination in seeing the world un-

Reprinted from LITTLE ESSAYS by George Santayana; used by permission of the publishers, Charles Scribner's Sons.

bosom itself of ancient secrets, obey man's coaxing, and take on unheard-of shapes. The highest building, the largest steamer, the fastest train, the book reaching the widest circulation have, in America, a clear title to respect. When the just functions of things are as yet not discriminated, the superlative in any direction seems naturally admirable. Again, many possessions, if they do make a man better, are at least expected to make his children happier; and this pathetic hope is behind many exertions. An experimental materialism, spontaneous and divorced from reason and from everything useful, is also confused in some minds with traditional duties; and a school of popular hierophants is not lacking that turns it into a sort of religion and perhaps calls it idealism. Impulse is more visible in all this than purpose, imagination more than judgment; but it is pleasant for the moment to abound in invention and effort and to let the future cash the account.

Stephen Leacock
1869 · 1944

Stephen Butler Leacock was born in England and reared in America. After taking a B.A. degree at Toronto and a Ph.D. at Chicago, he began, in 1903, a long and distinguished career as Professor of Economics at McGill University. Although he achieved an enviable reputation as an economist, he became known best as a writer of humorous essays, many of which are keen and discerning criticism of contemporary life.

HUMOUR AS I SEE IT

IT IS ONLY FAIR that I should be allowed a few pages to myself to put down some things that I really think. Once I might have taken my pen in hand to write about humour with the confident air of an acknowledged professional.

But that time is past. Such claim as I had has been taken from me. In fact I stand unmasked. An English reviewer writing in a literary journal, the very name of which is enough to put contradiction to sleep, has said of my writing, "What is there, after all, in Professor Leacock's humour but a rather ingenious mixture of hyperbole and myosis?"

The man was right. How he stumbled upon this trade secret, I do not know. But I am willing to admit, since the truth is out, that it has long been my custom in preparing an article of a humorous nature to go down to the cellar and mix up half a gallon of myosis with a pint of hyperbole. If I want to give the article a decidedly literary character, I find it well to put in about half a pint of paresis. The whole thing is amazingly simple.

But I only mention this by way of introduction and to dispel any idea that I am conceited enough to write about humour, with the professional authority of Ella Wheeler Wilcox writing about love, or Fred Astaire talking about dancing.

All that I dare claim is that I have as much sense of humour as other people. And, oddly enough, I notice that everybody else makes this same claim. Any man will admit, if need be, that his sight is not good, or that he cannot swim, or shoots badly with a rifle, but to touch upon his sense of humour is to give him a mortal affront.

"No," said a friend of mine the other day, "I never go to Grand Opera," and then he added with an air of pride—"You see, I have absolutely no ear for music."

"You don't say so!" I exclaimed.

"None!" he went on. "I can't tell one tune from another. I don't know *Home, Sweet Home* from *God Save the King*. I can't tell whether a man is tuning a violin or playing a sonata."

He seemed to get prouder and prouder over each item of his own deficiency. He ended by saying that he had a dog at his house that had a far better ear for music than he had. As soon as his wife or any visitor started to play the piano the dog always began to howl—plaintively, he said, as if it were hurt. He himself never did this.

When he had finished I made what I thought a harmless comment.

"I suppose," I said, "that you find your sense of humour deficient in the same way: the two generally go together."

My friend was livid with rage in a moment.

"Sense of humour!" he said. "My sense of humour! Me without a sense of humour! Why, I suppose I've a keener sense of humour than any man, or any two men, in this city!"

From that he turned to bitter personal attack. He said that *my* sense of humour seemed to have withered altogether.

He left me, still quivering with indignation.

Personally, however, I do not mind making the admission, however damaging it may be, that there are certain forms of so-called humour, or, at least, fun, which I am quite unable to appreciate. Chief among these is that ancient thing called the Practical Joke.

"You never knew McGann, did you?" a friend of mine asked me the other day. When I said, "No, I had never known McGann," he shook his head with a sigh, and said:

"Ah, you should have known McGann. He had the greatest sense of humour of any man I ever knew—always full of jokes. I remember one night at the boarding house where we were, he stretched a string across the passageway and then rang the dinner bell. One of the boarders broke his leg. We nearly died laughing."

"Dear me!" I said. "What a humourist! Did he often do things like that?"

"Oh, yes, he was at them all the time. He used to put tar in the tomato soup, and beeswax and tin-tacks on the chairs. He was full of ideas. They seemed to come to him without any trouble."

McGann, I understand, is dead. I am not sorry for it. Indeed I think that for most of us the time has gone by when we can see the fun of putting tacks on chairs, or thistles in beds, or live snakes in people's boots.

To me it has always seemed that the very essence of good humour is that it must be without harm and without malice. I admit that there is in all of us a certain vein of the old original demoniacal humour or joy in the misfortune of another which sticks to us like our original sin. It ought not to be funny to see a man, especially a fat and pompous man, slip suddenly on a banana skin. But it is. When a skater on a pond who is describing graceful circles and showing off before the crowd, breaks through the ice and gets a ducking, everybody shouts with joy. To the original savage, the cream of the joke in such cases was found if the man who slipped broke his neck, or the man who went through the ice never came up again. I can imagine a group of prehistoric men standing round the ice-hole where he had disappeared and laughing till their sides split. If there had been such a thing as a prehistoric newspaper, the affair would have been headed up: *"Amusing Incident. Unknown Gentleman Breaks Through Ice and Is Drowned."*

But our sense of humour under civilization has been weakened. Much of the fun of this sort of thing has been lost on us.

Children, however, still retain a large share of this primitive sense of enjoyment.

I remember once watching two little boys making snowballs at the side of the street and getting ready a little store of them to use. As they worked there came along an old man wearing a silk hat, and belonging by appearance to the class of "jolly old gentlemen." When he saw the boys his gold spectacles gleamed with kindly enjoyment. He began waving his arms and calling, "Now, then, boys, free shot at me! free shot!" In his gaiety he had, without noticing it, edged himself over the sidewalk on to the street. An express cart collided with him and knocked him over on his back in a heap of snow. He lay there gasping and trying to get the snow off his face and spectacles. The boys gathered up their snow-balls and took a run towards him. "Free shot!" they yelled. "Soak him! Soak him!"

I repeat, however, that for me, as I suppose for most of us, it is a prime condition of humour that it must be without harm or malice, nor should it convey even incidentally any real picture of sorrow or suffering or death. There is a great deal in the humour of Scotland (I admit its general merit) which seems to me, not being a Scotchman, to sin in this respect. Take this familiar story (I quote it as something already known and not for the sake of telling it).

A Scotchman had a sister-in-law—his wife's sister—with whom he could never agree. He always objected to going anywhere with her, and in spite of his wife's entreaties always refused to do so. The wife was taken mortally ill and as she lay dying, she whispered, "John, ye'll drive Janet with you to the funeral, will ye no?" The Scotchman, after an internal struggle, answered, "Margaret, I'll do it for ye, but it'll spoil my day."

Whatever humour there may be in this is lost for me by

the actual and vivid picture that it conjures up—the dying wife, the darkened room and the last whispered request.

No doubt the Scotch see things differently. That wonderful people—whom personally I cannot too much admire—always seem to me to prefer adversity to sunshine, to welcome the prospect of a pretty general damnation, and to live with grim cheerfulness within the very shadow of death. Alone among the nations they have converted the devil—under such names as Old Horny—into a familiar acquaintance not without a certain grim charm of his own. No doubt also there enters into their humour something of the original barbaric attitude towards things. For a primitive people who saw death often and at first hand, and for whom the future world was a vivid reality, that could be *felt*, as it were, in the midnight forest and heard in the roaring storm—for such a people it was no doubt natural to turn the flank of terror by forcing a merry and jovial acquaintance with the unseen world. Such a practice as a wake, and the merrymaking about the corpse, carry us back to the twilight of the world, with the poor savage in his bewildered misery, pretending that his dead still lived. Our funeral with its black trappings and its elaborate ceremonies is the lineal descendant of a merrymaking. Our undertaker is, by evolution, a genial master of ceremonies, keeping things lively at the death-dance. Thus have the ceremonies and the trappings of death been transformed in the course of ages till the forced gaiety is gone, and the black hearse and the gloomy mutes betoken the cold dignity of our despair.

But I fear this article is getting serious. I must apologize.

I was about to say, when I wandered from the point, that there is another form of humour which I am also quite unable to appreciate. This is that particular form of story which may be called, par excellence, the English Anecdote. It always deals with persons of rank and birth, and, except for the exalted nature of the subject itself, is, as far as I can see, absolutely pointless.

This is the kind of thing that I mean.

"His Grace the Fourth Duke of Marlborough was noted for the open-handed hospitality which reigned at Blenheim, the family seat, during his régime. One day on going in to luncheon it was discovered that there were thirty guests present, whereas the table only held covers for twenty-one. 'Oh, well,' said the Duke, not a whit abashed, 'some of us will have to eat standing up.' Everybody, of course, roared with laughter."

My only wonder is that they didn't kill themselves with it. A mere roar doesn't seem enough to do justice to such a story as this.

The Duke of Wellington has been made the storm-center of three generations of wit of this sort. In fact the typical Duke of Wellington story had been reduced to a thin skeleton such as this:

"A young subaltern once met the Duke of Wellington coming out of Westminster Abbey. 'Good morning, your Grace,' he said, 'rather a wet morning.' 'Yes,' said the Duke, with a very rigid bow, 'but it was a damn sight wetter, sir, on the morning of Waterloo.' The young subaltern, rightly rebuked, hung his head."

Nor is it only the English who sin in regard to anecdotes.

One can indeed make the sweeping assertion that the telling of stories as a mode of amusing others, ought to be kept within strict limits. Few people realize how extremely difficult it is to tell a story so as to reproduce the real fun of it—to "get it over" as the actors say. The mere "facts" of a story seldom make it funny. It needs the right words, with every word in its proper place. Here and there, perhaps once in a hundred times, a story turns up which needs no telling. The humour of it turns so completely on a sudden twist or incongruity in the dénouement of it that no narrator however clumsy can altogether fumble it.

Take, for example, this well known instance—a story which, in one form or other, everybody has heard.

"George Grossmith, the famous comedian, was once badly run down and went to consult a doctor. It happened that the doctor, though, like everybody else, he had often seen Grossmith on the stage, had never seen him without his make-up and did not know him by sight. He examined his patient, looked at his tongue, felt his pulse and tapped his lungs. Then he shook his head. 'There's nothing wrong with you, sir,' he said, 'except that you're run down from overwork and worry. You need rest and amusement. Take a night off and go and see George Grossmith at the Savoy.'

" 'Thank you,' said the patient, 'I *am* George Grossmith.' "

Let the reader please observe that I have purposely told this story all wrongly, just as wrongly as could be, and yet there is something left of it. Will the reader kindly look back to the beginning of it and see for himself just how it ought to be narrated and what obvious error has been made. If he has any particle of the artist in his make-up, he will see at once that the story ought to begin:

"One day a very haggard and nervous-looking patient called at the office of a fashionable doctor, etc., etc."

In other words, the chief point of the joke lies in keeping it concealed till the moment when the patient says, "Thank you, I am George Grossmith." But the story is such a good one that it cannot be completely spoiled even when told wrongly. This particular anecdote has been variously told of George Grossmith, Coquelin, Joe Jefferson, John Hare, Cyril Maude, and about sixty others. And I have noticed that there is a certain type of man who, on hearing this story about Grossmith, immediately tells it all back again, putting in the name of somebody else, and goes into new fits of laughter over it, as if the change of name made it brand new.

But few people, I repeat, realize the difficulty of reproducing a humorous or comic effect in its original spirit.

"I saw Harry Lauder last night," said Griggs, a Stock-Exchange friend of mine, as we walked up town together the other day. "He came onto the stage in kilts" (here Griggs started to chuckle) "and he had a slate under his arm" (here Griggs began to laugh quite heartily), "and he said, 'I always like to carry a slate with me' (of course he said it in Scotch, but I can't do the Scotch the way he does it) 'just in case there might be any figures I'd be wanting to put down' " (by this time Griggs was almost suffocated with laughter)—"and he took a little bit of chalk out of his pocket, and he said" (Griggs was now almost hysterical), " 'I like to carry a wee bit chalk along because I find the slate is' " (Griggs was now faint with laughter), " 'the slate is—is—not much good without the chalk.' "

Griggs had to stop, with his hand to his side and lean against a lamp post. "I can't, of course, do the Scotch the way Harry Lauder does it," he repeated.

Exactly. He couldn't do the Scotch and he couldn't do the rich mellow voice of Mr. Lauder and the face beaming with merriment, and the spectacles glittering with amusement, and he couldn't do the slate, nor the "wee bit chalk"—in fact he couldn't do any of it. He ought merely to have said, "Harry Lauder," and leaned up against a post and laughed till he had got over it.

Yet in spite of everything, people insist on spoiling conversation by telling stories. I know nothing more dreadful at a dinner table than one of these amateur raconteurs—except perhaps, two of them. After about three stories have been told, there falls on the dinner table an uncomfortable silence, in which everybody is aware that everybody else is trying hard to think of another story, and is failing to find it. There is no peace in the gathering again till some man of firm and quiet mind turns to his neighbour and says—"But after all there is no doubt that whether we like it or not prohibition is coming." Then everybody in his heart says, Thank Heaven! and the whole tableful are happy and contented again, till one of the story tellers "thinks of another," and breaks loose.

Worst of all perhaps is the modest story teller who is haunted by the idea that one has heard his story before. He attacks you after this fashion:

"I heard a very good story the other day on the steamer going to Bermuda"—then he pauses with a certain doubt in his face—"but perhaps you've heard this?"

"No, no, I've never been to Bermuda. Go ahead."

"Well, this is a story that they tell about a man who went down to Bermuda one winter to get cured of rheumatism— but you've heard this?"

"No, no."

"Well, he had rheumatism pretty bad and he went to

Bermuda to get cured of it. And so when he went into the hotel he said to the clerk at the desk—but, perhaps you know this."

"No, no, go right ahead."

"Well, he said to the clerk I want a room that looks out over the sea—but perhaps—"

Now the sensible thing to do is to stop the narrator right at this point. Say to him quietly and firmly, "Yes, I have heard that story. I always liked it ever since it came out in *Titbits* in 1878, and I read it every time I see it. Go on and tell it to me and I'll sit back with my eyes closed and enjoy it."

No doubt the story-telling habit owes much to the fact that ordinary people, quite unconsciously, rate humour very low: I mean, they underestimate the difficulty of "making humour." It would never occur to them that the thing is hard, meritorious and dignified. Because the result is gay and light, they think the process must be. Few people would realize that it is much harder to write one of Owen Seaman's "funny" poems in *Punch* than to write one of the Archbishop of Canterbury's sermons. Mark Twain's *Huckleberry Finn* is a greater work than Kant's *Critique of Pure Reason*, and Charles Dickens' creation of Mr. Pickwick did more for the elevation of the human race—I say it in all seriousness—than Cardinal Newman's *Lead, Kindly Light, Amid the Encircling Gloom*. Newman only cried out for light in the gloom of a sad world. Dickens gave it.

But the deep background that lies behind and beyond what we call humour is revealed only to the few who, by instinct or by effort, have given thought to it. The world's humour, in its best and greatest sense, is perhaps the highest product of our civilization. One thinks here not of the mere spasmodic effects of the comic artist or the black-face expert of the vaudeville show, but of the really great humour which, once or twice in a generation at best, illuminates and elevates our literature. It is no longer dependent upon the mere trick and quibble of words, or the odd and meaningless incongruities in things that strike us as "funny." Its basis lies in the deeper contrasts offered by life itself: the strange incongruity between our aspiration and our achievement, the eager and fretful anxieties of to-day that fade into nothingness to-morrow, the burning pain and the sharp sorrow that are softened in the gentle retrospect of time, till as we look back upon the course that has been traversed we pass in view the panorama of our lives, as people in old age may recall, with mingled tears and smiles, the angry quarrels of their childhood. And here, in its larger aspect, humour is blended with pathos till the two are one, and represent, as they have in every age, the mingled heritage of tears and laughter that is our lot on earth.

Hilaire Belloc

1870 · 1953

Hilaire Belloc was born in France and brought up in England. After attending Balliol College, Oxford, he began a career of journalism and later sat as a member of the House of Commons. Like G. K. Chesterton, he indicated, in many of his essays, great devotion to the Roman Catholic Church. He shunned the materialism of modern living and sought to express his belief in moral and spiritual values.

THE MOWING OF A FIELD

THERE IS A VALLEY in South England remote from ambition and from fear, where the passage of strangers is rare and unperceived, and where the scent of the grass in summer is breathed only by those who are native to that unvisited land. The roads to the Channel do not traverse it; they choose upon either side easier passes over the range. One track alone leads up through it to the hills, and this is changeable: now green where men have little occasion to go, now a good road where it nears the homesteads and the barns. The woods grow steep above the slopes; they reach sometimes the very summit of the heights, or, when they cannot attain them, fill in and clothe the coombes. And, in between, along the floor of the valley, deep pastures and their silence are bordered by lawns of chalky grass and the small yew trees of the Downs.

The clouds that visit its sky reveal themselves beyond the one great rise, and sail, white and enormous, to the other, and

Reprinted from HILLS AND THE SEA by Hilaire Belloc; used by permission of the publishers, Charles Scribner's Sons.

sink beyond that other. But the plains above which they have travelled and the Weald to which they go, the people of the valley cannot see and hardly recall. The wind, when it reaches such fields, is no longer a gale from the salt, but fruitful and soft, an inland breeze; and those whose blood was nourished here feel in that wind the fruitfulness of our orchards and all the life that all things draw from the air.

In this place, when I was a boy, I pushed through a fringe of beeches that made a complete screen between me and the world, and I came to a glade called No Man's Land. I climbed beyond it, and I was surprised and glad, because from the ridge of that glade I saw the sea. To this place very lately I returned.

The many things that I recovered as I came up the country-side were not less charming than when a distant memory had enshrined them, but much more. Whatever veil is thrown by a longing recollection had not intensified nor even made more mysterious the beauty of that happy ground; not in my very dreams of morning had I, in exile, seen it more beloved or more rare. Much also that I had forgotten now returned to me as I approached—a group of elms, a little turn of the parson's wall, a small paddock beyond the graveyard close, cherished by one man, with a low wall of very old stone guarding it all round. And all these things fulfilled and amplified my delight, till even the good vision of the place, which I had kept so many years, left me and was replaced by its better reality. "Here," I said to myself, "is a symbol of what some say is reserved for the soul: pleasure of a kind which cannot be imagined save in a moment when at last it is attained."

When I came to my own gate and my own field, and had before me the house I knew, I looked around a little (though it was already evening), and I saw that the grass was standing as it should stand when it is ready for the scythe. For in this, as in everything that a man can do—of those things at least which are very old—there is an exact moment when they are done best. And it has been remarked of whatever rules us that it works blunderingly, seeing that the good things given to man are not given at the precise moment when they would have filled him with delight. But, whether this be true or false, we can choose the just turn of the seasons in everything we do of our own will, and especially in the making of hay. Many think that hay is best made when the grass is thickest; and so they delay until it is rank and in flower, and has already heavily pulled the ground. And there is another false reason for delay, which is wet weather. For very few will understand (though it comes year after year) that we have rain always in South England between the sickle and the scythe, or say just after the weeks of east wind are over. First we have a week of sudden warmth, as though the South had come to see us all; then we have the weeks of east and southeast wind; and then we have more or less of that rain of which I spoke, and which always astonishes the world. Now it is just before, or during, or at the very end of that rain—but not later—that grass should be cut for hay. True, upland grass, which is always thin, should be cut earlier than the grass in the bottoms and along the water meadows; but not even the latest, even in the wettest seasons, should be left (as it is) to flower and even to seed. For what we get when we store our grass is not a harvest of something ripe, but a thing just caught in its prime before maturity: as witness that our corn and straw are best yellow, but our hay is best green. So also Death should be represented with a scythe and Time with a sickle; for Time can take only what is ripe, but Death comes always too soon. In a word, then, it is always much easier to cut grass too late than too early; and I, under that evening and come back to these pleasant fields, looked at the grass and knew that it was time. June was in full advance: it was the beginning of that season when the night has already lost her foothold of the earth and hovers over it, never quite descending, but mixing sunset with the dawn.

Next morning, before it was yet broad day, I awoke, and thought of the mowing. The birds were already chattering in the trees beside my window, all except the nightingale, which had left and flown away to the Weald, where he sings all summer by day as well as by night in the oaks and the hazel spinneys, and especially along the little river Adur, one of the rivers of the Weald. The birds and the thought of the mowing had awakened me, and I went down the stairs and along the stone floors to where I could find a scythe; and when I took it from its nail, I remembered how, fourteen years ago, I had last gone out with my scythe, just so, into the fields at morning. In between that day and this were many things, cities and armies, and a confusion of books, mountains and the desert, and horrible great breadths of sea.

When I got out into the long grass the sun was not yet risen, but there were already many colours in the eastern sky, and I made haste to sharpen my scythe, so that I might get to the cutting before the dew should dry. Some say that it is best to wait till all the dew has risen, so as to get the grass quite dry from the very first. But, though it is an advantage to get the grass quite dry, yet it is not worth while to wait till the dew has risen. For, in the first place, you lose many hours of work (and those the coolest), and next—which is more important— you lose that great ease and thickness in cutting which comes of the dew. So I at once began to sharpen my scythe.

There is an art also in the sharpening of a scythe, and it is worth describing carefully. Your blade must be dry, and that is why you will see men rubbing the scythe-blade with grass before they whet it. Then also your rubber must be quite dry, and on this account it is a good thing to lay it on your coat and keep it there during all your day's mowing. The scythe you stand upright, with the blade pointing away from you, and you put your left hand firmly on the back of the blade, grasping it: then you pass the rubber first down one side of the blade-edge and then down the other, beginning near the handle and going on to the point and working quickly and hard. When you first do this you will, perhaps, cut your hand; but it is only at first that such an accident will happen to you.

To tell when the scythe is sharp enough this is the rule. First the stone clangs and grinds against the iron harshly; then it rings musically to one note; then, at last, it purrs as though the iron and stone were exactly suited. When you hear this, your scythe is sharp enough; and I, when I heard it that June dawn, with everything quite silent except the birds, let down the scythe and bent myself to mow.

When one does anything anew, after so many years, one fears very much for one's trick or habit. But all things once learnt are easily recoverable, and I very soon recovered the swing and power of the mower. Mowing well and mowing badly—or rather not mowing at all—are separated by very little; as is also true of writing verse, of playing the fiddle, and of dozens of other things, but of nothing more than of believing. For the bad or young or untaught mower without tradition, the mower Promethean, the mower original and contemptuous of the past, does all these things: He leaves great crescents of grass uncut. He digs the point of the scythe hard into the ground with a jerk. He loosens the handles and even the fastening of the blade. He twists the blade with his blunders, he blunts the blade, he chips it, dulls it, or breaks it clean off at the tip. If any one is standing by he cuts him in the ankle. He sweeps up into the air wildly, with nothing to resist his stroke. He drags up earth with the grass, which is like making the meadow bleed. But the good mower who does things just as they should be done and have been for a hundred thousand years, falls into none of these fooleries. He goes forward very steadily, his scythe-blade just barely missing the ground, every grass falling; the swish and rhythm of his mowing are always the same.

So great an art can only be learnt by continual practice; but this much is worth writing down, that, as in all good work, to know the thing with which you work is the core of the affair. Good verse is best written on good paper with an easy pen, not with a lump of coal on a whitewashed wall. The pen thinks for you; and so does the scythe mow for you if you treat it honourably and in a manner that makes it recognize its service. The manner is this. You must regard the scythe as a pendulum that swings, not as a knife that cuts. A good mower puts no more strength into his stroke than into his lifting. Again, stand up to your work. The bad mower, eager and full of pain, leans forward and tries to force the scythe through the grass. The good mower, serene and able, stands as nearly straight as the shape of the scythe will let him, and follows up every stroke closely, moving his left foot forward.

Then also let every stroke get well away. Mowing is a thing of ample gestures, like drawing a cartoon. Then, again, get yourself into a mechanical and repetitive mood: be thinking of anything at all but your mowing, and be anxious only when there seems some interruption to the monotony of the sound. In this mowing should be like one's prayers—all of a sort and always the same, and so made that you can establish a monotony and work them, as it were, with half your mind: that happier half, the half that does not bother.

In this way, when I had recovered the art after so many years, I went forward over the field, cutting lane after lane through the grass, and bringing out its most secret essences with the sweep of the scythe until the air was full of odours. At the end of every lane I sharpened my scythe and looked back at the work done, and then carried my scythe down again upon my shoulder to begin another. So, long before the bell rang in the chapel above me—that is, long before six o'clock, which is the time for the *Angelus*—I had many swathes already lying in order parallel like soldiery; and the high grass yet standing, making a great contrast with the shaven part, looked dense and high. As it says in the *Ballad of Val-ès-Dunes*, where—

> The tall son of the Seven Winds
> Came riding out of Hither-hythe,

and his horse-hoofs (you will remember) trampled into the press and made a gap in it, and his sword (as you know)

> was like a scythe
> In Arcus when the grass is high
> And all the swathes in order lie,
> And there's the bailiff standing by
> A-gathering of the tithe.

So I mowed all that morning, till the houses awoke in the valley, and from some of them rose a little fragrant smoke, and men began to be seen.

I stood still and rested on my scythe to watch the awakening of the village, when I saw coming up to my field a man whom I had known in older times, before I had left the Valley.

He was of that dark silent race upon which all the learned quarrel, but which, by whatever meaningless name it may be called—Iberian, or Celtic, or what you will—is the permanent root of all England, and makes England wealthy and preserves it everywhere, except perhaps in the Fens and in a part of Yorkshire. Everywhere else you will find it active and strong. These people are intensive; their thoughts and their labours turn inward. It is on account of their presence in these islands that our gardens are the richest in the world. They also love low rooms and ample fires and great warm slopes of thatch. They have, as I believe, an older acquaintance with the English air than any other of all the strains that make up England. They hunted in the Weald with stones, and camped in the pines of the green-sand. They lurked under the oaks of the upper rivers, and saw the legionaries go up, up the straight paved road from the sea. They helped the few pirates to destroy the towns, and mixed with those pirates and shared the spoils of the Roman villas, and were glad to see the captains and the priests destroyed. They remain; and no admixture of the Frisian pirates, or the Breton, or the Angevin and Norman conquerors, has very much affected their cunning eyes.

To this race, I say, belonged the man who now approached me. And he said to me, "Mowing?" And I answered, "Ar." Then he also said "Ar," as in duty bound; for so we speak to each other in the Stenes of the Downs.

Next he told me that, as he had nothing to do, he would lend me a hand; and I thanked him warmly, or, as we say, "kindly." For it is a good custom of ours always to treat bargaining as though it were a courteous pastime; and though what he was after was money, and what I wanted was his labour at the least pay, yet we both played the comedy that we were free men, the one granting a grace and the other accepting it. For the dry bones of commerce, avarice and method and need, are odious to the Valley; and we cover them up with a pretty body of fiction and observances. Thus, when it comes to buying pigs, the buyer does not begin to decry the pig and the vendor to praise it, as is the custom with lesser men; but tradition makes them do business in this fashion:—

First the buyer will go up to the seller when he sees him in his own steading, and, looking at the pig with admiration, the buyer will say that rain may or may not fall, or that we shall have snow or thunder, according to the time of year. Then the seller, looking critically at the pig, will agree that the weather is as his friend maintains. There is no haste at all; great leisure marks the dignity of their exchange. And the next step is, that the buyer says: "That's a fine pig you have there, Mr. ——" (giving the seller's name). "Ar, powerful fine pig." Then the seller, saying also "Mr." (for twin brothers rocked in one cradle give each other ceremonious observance here), the seller, I say, admits, as though with reluctance, the strength and beauty of the pig, and falls into deep thought. Then the buyer says, as though moved by a great desire, that he is ready to give so much for the pig, naming half the proper price, or a little less. Then the seller remains in silence for some moments; and at last begins to shake his head slowly, till he says: "I don't be thinking of selling the pig, anyways." He will also add that a party only Wednesday offered him so much for the pig—and he names about double the proper price. Thus all ritual is duly accomplished; and the solemn act is entered upon with reverence and in a spirit of truth. For when the buyer uses this phrase: "I'll tell you what I *will* do," and offers within half a crown of the pig's value, the seller replies that he can refuse him nothing, and names half a crown above its value; the difference is split, the pig is sold, and in the quiet soul of each runs the peace of something accomplished.

Thus do we buy a pig or land or labour or malt or lime, always with elaboration and set forms; and many a London man has paid double and more for his violence and his greedy haste and very unchivalrous higgling. As happened with the land at Underwaltham, which the mortgagees had begged and implored the estate to take at twelve hundred and had privately offered to all the world at a thousand, but which a sharp direct man, of the kind that makes great fortunes, a man in a motor-car, a man in a fur coat, a man of few words, bought for two thousand three hundred before my very eyes, protesting that they might take his offer or leave it; and all because he did not begin by praising the land.

Well then, this man I spoke of offered to help me, and he went to get his scythe. But I went into the house and brought out a gallon jar of small ale for him and for me; for the sun was now very warm, and small ale goes well with mowing. When we had drunk some of this ale in mugs called "I see you," we took each a swathe, he a little behind me because he was the better mower; and so for many hours we swung, one before the other, mowing and mowing at the tall grass of the field. And the sun rose to noon and we were still at our mowing; and we ate food, but only for a little while, and we took again to our mowing. And at last there was nothing left but a small square of grass, standing like a square of linesmen who keep their formation, tall and unbroken, with all the dead lying around them when a battle is over and done.

Then for some little time I rested after all those hours; and the man and I talked together, and a long way off we heard in another field the musical sharpening of a scythe.

The sunlight slanted powdered and mellow over the breadth of the valley; for day was nearing its end. I went to fetch rakes from the steading; and when I had come back the last of the grass had fallen, and all the field lay flat and smooth, with the very green short grass in lanes between the dead and yellow swathes.

These swathes we raked into cocks to keep them from the dew against our return at daybreak; and we made the cocks as tall and steep as we could, for in that shape they best keep off the dew, and it is easier also to spread them after the sun has risen. Then we raked up every straggling blade, till the whole field was a clean floor for the tedding and the carrying of the hay next morning. The grass we had mown was but a little over two acres; for that is all the pasture on my little tiny farm.

When we had done all this, there fell upon us the beneficent and deliberate evening; so that as we sat a little while together near the rakes, we saw the valley more solemn and dim around us, and all the trees and hedgerows quite still, and held by a complete silence. Then I paid my companion his wage, and bade him a good night, till we should meet in the same place before sunrise.

He went off with a slow and steady progress, as all our peasants do, making their walking a part of the easy but continual labour of their lives. But I sat on, watching the light creep around towards the north and change, and the waning moon coming up as though by stealth behind the woods of No Man's Land.

Max Beerbohm

1872 · ——

Max Beerbohm, English essayist, critic, and caricaturist, began to develop his brilliant style while he was a student at Merton College, Oxford. In the 1890's, he contributed essays to The Yellow Book, *and in 1898 he succeeded George Bernard Shaw as dramatic critic for* The Saturday Review. *In addition to several volumes of essays and caricatures, he has published one satiric novel,* Zuleika Dobson. *For many years he has made his home in Rapallo, on the Italian Riviera.*

'A CLERGYMAN'

FRAGMENTARY, PALE, MOMENTARY; almost nothing; glimpsed and gone; as it were, a faint human hand thrust up, never to reappear, from beneath the rolling waters of Time, he forever haunts my memory and solicits my weak imagination. Nothing is told of him but that once, abruptly, he asked a question, and received an answer.

This was on the afternoon of April 7th, 1778, at Streatham, in the well-appointed house of Mr. Thrale. Johnson, on the morning of that day, had entertained Boswell at breakfast in Bolt Court and invited him to dine at Thrale Hall. The two took coach and arrived early. It seems that Sir John Pringle had asked Boswell to ask Johnson 'what were the best English sermons for style.' In the interval before dinner, accordingly, Boswell reeled off the names of several divines whose prose might or might not win commendation. 'Atterbury?' he suggested. JOHNSON: Yes, Sir, one of the best. BOSWELL: Tillotson? JOHNSON: Why, not now. I should not advise any one to imitate Tillotson's style; though I don't know; I should be cautious of censuring anything that has been applauded by so many suffrages.—South is one of the best, if you except his peculiarities, and his violence, and sometimes coarseness of language.—Seed has a very fine style; but he is not very theological.—Jortin's sermons are very elegant.—Sherlock's style, too, is very elegant, though he has not made it his principal study.—And you may add Smalridge. BOSWELL: I like Ogden's Sermons on Prayer very much, both for neatness of style and subtilty of reasoning. JOHNSON: I should like to read all that Ogden has written. BOSWELL: What I want to know is, what sermons afford the best specimen of English pulpit eloquence. JOHNSON: We have no sermons addressed to the passions, that are good for anything; if you mean that kind of eloquence. A CLERGYMAN, whose name I do not recollect: Were not Dodd's sermons addressed to the passions? JOHNSON: They were nothing, Sir, be they addressed to what they may.

The suddenness of it! Bang!—and the rabbit that had popped from its burrow was no more.

I know not which is the more startling—the début of the unfortunate clergyman, or the instantaneousness of his end. Why hadn't Boswell told us there was a clergyman present? Well, we may be sure that so careful and acute an artist had some good reason. And I suppose the clergyman was left to take us unawares because just so did he take the company. Had we been told he was there, we might have expected that sooner or later he would join in the conversation. He would have had a place in our minds. We may assume that in the minds of the company around Johnson he had no place. He sat forgotten, overlooked; so that his self-assertion startled every one just as on Boswell's page it startles us. In Johnson's massive and magnetic presence only some very remarkable man, such as Mr. Burke, was sharply distinguishable from the rest. Others might, if they had something in them, stand out slightly. This unfortunate clergyman may have had something in him, but I judge that he lacked the gift of seeming as if he had. That deficiency, however, does not account for the horrid fate that befell him. One of Johnson's strongest and most inveterate feelings was his veneration for the Cloth. To any one in Holy Orders he habitually listened with a grave and charming deference. To-day, moreover, he was in excellent good humour. He was at the Thrales', where he so loved to be; the day was fine; a fine dinner was in close prospect; and he had had what he always declared to be the sum of human felicity—a ride in a coach. Nor was there in the question put by the clergyman anything likely to enrage him. Dodd was one whom Johnson had befriended in adversity; and it had always been agreed that Dodd in his pulpit was very emotional. What drew the blasting flash must have been not the question itself, but the manner in which it was asked. And I think we can guess what that manner was.

Say the words aloud: 'Were not Dodd's sermons addressed to the passions?' They are words which, if you have any dramatic and histrionic sense, *cannot* be said except in a high, thin voice.

You may, from sheer perversity, utter them in a rich and sonorous baritone or bass. But if you do so, they sound utterly unnatural. To make them carry the conviction of human utterance, you have no choice: you must pipe them.

Remember, now, Johnson was very deaf. Even the people whom he knew well, the people to whose voices he was accustomed, had to address him very loudly. It is probable that this unregarded, young, shy clergyman, when at length he suddenly mustered courage to 'cut in,' let his high, thin voice soar *too* high, insomuch that it was a kind of scream. On no other hypothesis can we account for the ferocity with which Johnson turned and rended him. Johnson didn't, we may be sure, mean to be cruel. The old lion, startled, just struck out blindly. But the force of paw and claws was not the less lethal. We have endless testimony to the strength of Johnson's voice; and the very cadence of those words, 'They were nothing, Sir, be they addressed to what they may,' convinces me that the old lion's jaws never gave forth a louder roar. Boswell does not record that there was any further conversation before the announcement of dinner. Perhaps the whole company had been temporarily deafened. But I am not bothering about *them*. My heart goes out to the poor dear clergyman exclusively.

I said a moment ago that he was young and shy; and I admit that I slipped those epithets in without having justified them to you by due process of induction. Your quick mind will have already supplied what I omitted. A man with a high, thin voice, and without power to impress any one with a sense of his importance, a man so null in effect that even the retentive mind of Boswell did not retain his very name, would assuredly not be a self-confident man. Even if he were not naturally shy, social courage would soon have been sapped in him, and would in time have been destroyed, by experience. That he had not yet given himself up as a bad job, that he still had faint wild hopes, is proved by the fact that he did snatch the opportunity for asking that question. He must, accordingly, have been young. Was he the curate of the neighbouring church? I think so. It would account for his having been invited. I see him as he sits there listening to the great Doctor's pronouncement on Atterbury and those others. He sits on the edge of a chair in the background. He has colourless eyes, fixed earnestly, and a face almost as pale as the clerical bands beneath his somewhat receding chin. His forehead is high and narrow, his hair mouse-coloured. His hands are clasped tight before him, the knuckles standing out sharply. This constriction does not mean that he is steeling himself to speak. He has no positive intention of speaking. Very much, nevertheless, is he wishing in the back of his mind that he *could* say something—something whereat the great Doctor would turn on him and say, after a pause for thought, 'Why yes, Sir. That is most justly observed' or 'Sir, this has never occurred to me. I thank you'—thereby fixing the observer forever high in the esteem of all. And now in a flash the chance presents itself. 'We have,' shouts Johnson, 'no sermons addressed to the passions, that are good for anything.' I see the curate's frame quiver with sudden impulse, and his mouth fly open, and—no, I can't bear it, I shut my eyes and ears. But audible, even so, is something shrill, followed by something thunderous.

Presently I re-open my eyes. The crimson has not yet faded from that young face yonder, and slowly down either cheek falls a glistening tear. Shades of Atterbury and Tillotson! Such weakness shames the Established Church. What would Jortin and Smalridge have said?—what Seed and South? And, by the way, who *were* they, these worthies? It is a solemn thought that so little is conveyed to us by names which to the palæo-Georgians conveyed so much. We discern a dim, composite picture of a big man in a big wig and a billowing black gown, with a big congregation beneath him. But we are not anxious to hear what he is saying. We know it is all very elegant. We know it will be printed and be bound in finely-tooled full calf, and no palæo-Georgian gentleman's library will be complete without it. Literate people in those days were comparatively few; but, bating that, one may say that sermons were as much in request as novels are to-day. I wonder, will mankind continue to be capricious? It is a very solemn thought indeed that no more than a hundred-and-fifty years hence the novelists of our time, with all their moral and political and sociological outlook and influence, will perhaps shine as indistinctly as do those old preachers, with all their elegance, now. 'Yes, Sir,' some great pundit may be telling a disciple at this moment, 'Wells is one of the best. Galsworthy is one of the best, if you except his concern for delicacy of style. Mrs. Ward has a very firm grasp of problems, but is not very creational.—Caine's books are very edifying. I should like to read all that Caine has written. Miss Corelli, too, is very edifying.—And you may add Upton Sinclair.' 'What I want to know,' says the disciple, 'is, what English novels may be selected as specially enthralling.' The pundit answers: 'We have no novels addressed to the passions that are good for anything, if you mean that kind of enthralment.' And here some poor wretch (whose name the disciple will not remember) inquires: 'Are not Mrs. Glyn's novels addressed to the passions?' and is in due form annihilated. Can it be that a time will come when readers of this passage in our pundit's life will take more interest in the poor nameless wretch than in all the bearers of those great names put together, being no more able or anxious to discriminate between (say) Mrs. Ward and Mr. Sinclair than we are to set Ogden above Sherlock, or Sherlock above Ogden? It seems impossible. But we must remember that things are not always what they seem.

Every man illustrious in his day, however much he may be gratified by his fame, looks with an eager eye to posterity for a continuance of past favours, and would even live the remainder of his life in obscurity if by so doing he could insure that future generations would preserve a correct attitude towards him forever. This is very natural and human, but, like so many very natural and human things, very silly. Tillotson and the rest need not, after all, be pitied for our neglect of them. They either know nothing about it, or are above such terrene trifles. Let us keep our pity for the great seething mass of divines who were *not* elegantly verbose, and had no fun or glory while they lasted. And let us keep a specially large portion for one whose lot was so much worse than merely undistinguished. If that nameless curate had not been at the Thrales' that day, or, being there, had kept the silence that so well became him, his life would have been drab enough in all conscience. But at any rate an unpromising career would not have been nipped in the bud. And that is what in fact happened, I'm sure of it. A robust man might have rallied under the blow. Not so our friend. Those who knew him in infancy had not expected that he would be reared. Better for him had they been right. It is well to grow up and be ordained, but not if you are delicate and very sensitive, and shall happen to annoy the greatest, the most stentorian and roughest of contemporary personages. 'A Clergyman' never held up his head or smiled again after the brief encounter recorded for us by Boswell. He sank into a rapid decline. Before the next blossoming of Thrale Hall's almond trees he was no more. I like to think that he died forgiving Dr. Johnson.

H. M. Tomlinson

1873 · ——

Henry Major Tomlinson worked as a boy along the wharves of London and later turned to newspaper work. His experiences with shipping, with travel, and later with the first World War are recorded faithfully and often brilliantly in his essays, novels, and travel books, some of the best of which are London River *(1921),* Tide Marks *(1924), and* All Our Yesterdays *(1930). He has never achieved the popularity of some of his contemporaries, but his writing is much admired by discriminating readers.*

EXPLORATION

THE REPINING BEGAN IN ME through reading Ballantyne's *Hudson's Bay.* The pull of the Magnetic North was felt; I turned to Boothia Felix. I should not like to say how long ago that was; it was when I began to have occasion, in a house of commerce, to consult the *Weekly Shipping List.* That entrancing guide contained such entries as this: "York Factory, Hudson's Bay. *Lady Head*, bk., 457 tons, A. 1. Capt. Anderson. Sailing June 1. South West India Dock."

I was very young then, and so supposed a man went travelling to see what was round the corner; because, as a sage master mariner, later in life, once sadly explained to me in his cabin: When we are young we think all the good things are far away. I did not know, so early, that a man sets out to find himself, and that on such a journey, in a country all

Reprinted from OUT OF SOUNDINGS *by H. M. Tomlinson; used by the kind permission of Mr. H. M. Tomlinson and the British Society of Authors*

unknown, he may get lost. When young Herman Melville shipped in a whaler, he little guessed his voyage would never end, not while men fancy they discern a Great Bear in the night sky, from which their brave harpoons ever return to earth.

Ballantyne unsettled me, and Butler's *Great Lone Land*, and *Wild North Land* made matters worse; it was the dream that was real. Lake Athabasca and the Mackenzie River were desolate; and how noble were their names! But the Hudson's Bay Company, at whose door in Lime Street, London, I knocked, generously spared my proffered service. It amused me once to hear Joseph Conrad confess—it was to my ear alone, and I had made no confession to him—that his earliest effort to find employment as a ship's officer was with the H. B. C.; and he, too, failed, for the H. B. C. is Scotch, and most careful and particular. There was not a book on the exploration of North America and the Arctic, in the Guildhall Library of the City of London, for which I did not save or steal time to read. It came to nothing. But the very name, Canadian Barren Grounds, still works a faint reminiscent enchantment; yet resolutely but regretfully I resist the Northern Lights.

The ease with which a man may get into the outer blue, which is uncharted, and is not at all kenspeckled, I learned a little later, from *A Week on the Concord*. Once you have started you may find yourself anywhere. The transit may be instant. There is no oracle to warn you where you may be at night. You may be so different that the world itself will be changed. Then what will you do?—for do something you must. When your fellows continue as usual to call your burning bush a briar patch, which is what it is, and will remain for most of us, how is that sign to be doused? There is no return.

There must be categories for books, yet I do not think Books of Travel is precisely the place in the index for the *Arabia Deserta*, or Thoreau's *Week on the Concord*, or even for Bate's *Naturalist on the River Amazon*. The right good book is always a book of travel; it is about a life's journey. It does not matter whether the point of view is got from Egdon Heath, Capri or Kanchenjunga. The *Seven Pillars of Wisdom* was to me less Arabia in war time than Lawrence; the war and its intrigues, the Arabs, the Turks, and the Germans and the desert, were incidental; they chanced to evoke Lawrence, agents of destiny of consequence to us, for they were the cause of a war of thoughts compared with which the desert campaign was only ugly and common tribal bickering. Revolts of Arabs and others against what enrages them may burn up a little rubbish, and perhaps make more, but a revolt from our traditions and accepted verities by bleakly intrepid thoughts may lead us the deuce of an eternal dance. Is *Moby Dick* a yarn of a whaling cruise? Is *Gulliver's Travels* merely a fantastic diversion?

We shall continue to call the *Arabia Deserta* a book of travel, for it is that, though so is the *Pilgrim's Progress*. Nevertheless, it is plain that Doughty, that gaunt and stubborn survival from a pre-Shakespearian England, so much an Englishman that he was a foreigner to the Oxford and London of his day, looms in his book with more startling distinction than the basaltic crags of the Arabian desert. No wonder his spirit held in check the sunstruck fanatics about him, though they wanted to cut his throat. We, too, were in nature as much opposed to him when we began to read him, but he has subdued us. The stark bergs of his desert are not more enduring than the traveller. But for him, would that burnt region of sand and rock with its dangerous and rhapsodical nomads exist for us? While reading Doughty, you begin to sense something of the origin of the Semitic scriptures; we know that Doughty himself, had he been one in the Exile, brooding on lost Jerusalem, would have bowed to the stripes, but have prophesied apart for all those that must hereafter patiently endure by the waters of Babylon.

First and last a poet may write only of himself. The world exists because he sees it. That can be all he knows of it. What then, is he? For the validity of the world depends on the kind of man he is. Whether it is Europe shaken by the French Revolution, or the deserts of Asia, or Walden Pond, the seer is the consummation and reality. His broomstick, if he travel astride of that, may range over deeps as dark as the gulfs in the Milky Way; and yet another kind of traveller may convert the region which holds the culture of the Chinese into a mere album of photographic snapshots and interlined facetiousness.

Seeing is of faith, for faith is not blind. There can be no faith without light. What we do not see may condemn us. What traveller would dare to interpret the world which he thinks he sees today? There is harder travelling now than kept Marco Polo so long from his home. There is no simple problem of a Grand Khan now. There is no Tartary. Cathay is a republic, complete with civic strife. Western ideas, and the machinery of industry. Communists interrupt the railway service of Java. Messer Marco Polo in all his wanderings saw nothing stranger than that, nor more difficult to read. Instead of Venice and Canton we have London and New York. A man flew to Baghdad and back the other week in contemptuously few hours; and Persia weaves prayer-mats, not to point to Mecca, but to help the sentiment of English suburban villas. One may buy Burmese gems by the pint by taking a penny bus from Charing Cross; there is no need to voyage to Cairo, Calicut, and Peking, to see the Orient. It is mostly in the Cutler Street warehouse, by Houndsditch. The Underground Railway serves the Orient.

But we are not satisfied. A vague desperation is suggested in our tours round the world. Something is missing from our civilization. Perhaps we think that the farther we go the more likely we are to recover whatever it is we have lost. It is possible that the Communist risings in the Garden of the East come of the same disquiet which sends rich Westerners circling the globe. Why should the Hindus and Javanese revolt? Their lives are more secure now than they were under their old emperors and rajahs. And why should rich men shut up their ancestral country seats and go to the South Seas for the simplicity which began to die there as soon as Watt learned the way to harness steam? The affliction appears to be world wide. It is felt in Benares, Peking, and Park Lane. The lions of

Africa are being displaced by sisal fibre, just as speedways and coalmines are destroying Kentish orchards. We read that an imaginative explorer, instead of gratitude for his seclusion in a tropical forest, considered that the trees were growing to waste; they ought to be turned into wood-spirit. He was a modern traveller. He did not call the forest *Green Mansions*, nor see Rima there. He saw a potential reservoir of alcohol.

That may be our trouble. The faith may be dying which sees beauty in the world, and without knowing it that may be why we are desperate to escape from our toils. We are no longer able to wonder, even at our own ingenuity. We are not as little children, so the kingdom is lost. It is useless to voyage to Papeete to look for the kingdom. The Venetian noble, Nicolo de Conti, early in the fifteenth century, when his ship was in the Red Sea, was surprised to see elephants equipped for war; but he would have been still more surprised had he heard at night voices that were speaking in Venice; as I heard one night, off Cape Bon, the movements of dancers in a London hotel—through the sough of the dark, far at sea, I could hear London shuffling its feet; and that thought, if sufficiently examined afterwards when one was by the bulwarks alone, was enough to give pause to the heedlessness of idle feet. The very empyrean was listening. It might not be safe to entertain even idle thoughts, for Heaven only knows what registering mystery may hear those as readily as the shuffling of dancers. A poet once cryptically reminded us that we cannot pluck a flower without troubling a star. No doubt it will be difficult to persuade us that Aldebaran cares the least for our dandelions; yet when the gift of reason inclines us to observe only a larger circulation of cheap newspapers in pine woods, or alcohol in the forest of the Amazon, one begins to fear that the sweet influences of Pleiades are then loosened to a slight degree; perhaps when we trample the bloom off the earth, and replace it with smoke, clinker heaps, and hovels, the bands of Orion remain as fast as ever; yet the dread that the deliberate darkening of our own star may affect the Galaxy, though that dread does not arise from any logic that we know, may not be without a reason.

That dread, and we are beginning to feel it, is no less remarkable than wireless telephony. It is a thought new to the world of men, though the squalor with which we continue to disfigure our place in our efforts to make it fruitful is as ancient as man's activities. Pero Tafur, who began travelling and adventuring about 1425, reports for his day a Europe which in most respects is inexplicable to us. There was no New Learning then. When Tafur entered France, Joan of Arc had been dead only seven years. The English had been driven out of Paris, but were still in Rouen. The Mediterranean was still the centre of gravity of European commerce; not then had Portuguese navigators made the discoveries which would shift that commerce to the Atlantic seaboard, though, curiously enough, Tafur shows that one mart of Flanders was then richer than Venice, and the shipping of Sluys enormous in its tonnage. America was unknown. The Turks were encamped about Constantinople, where the Eastern Empire was about to fall. The Pope was an exile. The plague was in France, and that land was desolate with the wars of the fourteenth and early fifteenth centuries. We cannot, with those reminders, picture such a Europe. But in some chance ways, and without conscious design, Tafur does that for us. It is the wayside incidents of his story which betray a Europe we know quite well. He had been astonished by the riches of Bruges, and he went to Sluys to see the ships. At Mass there a woman approached him in secret, and wondering, he went home with her. There she offered him one of her two young daughters. The family was starving. All that commercial activity of Flanders and its wealth of luxuries, and this family had nothing to eat! How far, since Tafur's day, have our many inventions taken us? Have we got any distance, in our flying-machines?

Even while a doubt about our progress begins to disturb us, old habits compel the consideration of the conversion of beauty into still more starvation and smoke. We are not sufficiently afraid of troubling the stars by darkening the splendour of our planet; yet a doubt grows that what we think and do may not be inconsequential beyond the orbit of the earth.

In that space beyond, where we cannot go, it is possible that some emanation from our liveliness finds its way, and not fortuitously. We may make a mark without knowing it. It is irrelevant to the story, no doubt, that one night at sea we chanced to hear revellers at Charing Cross, yet it was a warning not easily quieted. We have now learned beyond question that our various noises are indeed registered where we had supposed there was nothing but the impersonal sough of the dark.

There was a sometime Archdeacon of Westminster, Richard Hakluyt, who celebrated the earlier English seamen and travellers. His tablet in Bristol Cathedral reads: "His studious Imagination discovered new Paths for geographical Science and his patriotic Labours rescued from oblivion not a few of those who went down to the Sea in ships to be Harbingers of Empire, descrying new Lands, and finding larger Room for their Race."

That tablet is but just to Hakluyt. Yet consider its implications. The Westminster Archdeacon, without meaning to do it, who desired indeed to light an imperial desire in an adventurous people, did much to prompt the pall over the Black Country. His patriotic labours at length poured out as smoke from our factory chimneys; an odd outcome of a pure and selfless personal devotion. That dark sign of profit to an imperial people was the inevitable result of the valour and enterprise of Elizabethan seamen. Those harbingers of Empire and their celebrant, as now we see them, were moved in their age by an influence which stirred even its poets; they were compelled by a law of growth in a changing world, we may suppose, to which their community had to respond as though it had no more conscious control of its destiny than the annual flowers of the field. All these men together gave our country, gave the civilization we call Western, a mighty shove towards the place where now we find it. The glorious flower of the civilization which romantically they predestined for us unfolded vast and strange at the end of a factory chimney. Thus so different may be man's pure intent from its issue. Drake, returned from the shades, we will imagine, with

Hakluyt, to view what substance we have given to the dreams they had of other lands and seas, would have to agree with the poet of their own day that there is a destiny which shapes our ends whatever ardent measures we take. Hakluyt, while contemplating, as a shade, our motor-ships, our problem of credit, our bickering over the size of the guns we shall use against each other, and the difficulties involved, as in India, in that larger Room for the Race, and the air route to Malacca, might recall his visit, as a boy, a visit evidently so fruitful, to his cousin, a Gentleman of the Middle Temple. It was a trivial incident, that half-holiday visit, to have had its casual part in shaping the problem of the protection of British trade routes without giving America a cause for war. For his cousin but gave him a first lesson in geography. Young Richard found lying in that chamber of the Middle Temple "certaine bookes of Cosmographie, with an universall Mappe."

There is no doubt the Westminster scholar was wakened by his cousin. The subject of geography was given, even on a holiday, quite a cheerful appearance; but the year of that lesson, we must remember, was little more than a decade after Sir Hugh Willoughby tried to reach Cathay and the Moluccas by the Siberian coast. From the map the Gentleman of the Middle Temple turned to the Bible, and directed the boy to read the 107th Psalm. Young Hakluyt did so, and his own contribution towards the industrial era and his country's imperial destiny was at once made certain.

"Which wordes of the Prophet together with my cousins discourse (things of rare and high delight to my young nature) tooke in me so deepe an impression, that I constantly resolved, if ever I were preferred to the University . . . I would by God's assistance prosecute that knowledge and kinde of literature, the doores whereof (after a sort) were so happily opened before me."

We are told that a civilization must grow to its height and then decline, like a flower of the field in its due season. Yet unlike the weed, a civilization passes through its predictable phases to its sere, though to no harvest; it only dies; its seed is potent for no future spring. The philosophers do not explain what lunar influence governs its rhythmic rise and fall; they tell us largely but of powers which bring a civilization to its height, from which it shall lapse till only the barren sands show where its hearths used to be warm, and its priests to chant to its gods. It has its pioneers, its early explorers and prophets; then its period when the profit-makers are assured of a bounteous continuity through a special favour of Providence, for they know they are more worthy than the lesser breeds; and follow them its patriots and celebrators, who praise the familiar scene, now flushed in a serene autumn that is everlasting, as they hope and believe. Will not their assurance of their own worth hold in perpetuity the splendour of the after-glow? No. We see now there never was and cannot be an empire on which the sun shall never set. All civilizations and empires must make their predestined curves and fulfil their cycles.

Yet theories, though they seem flawless, should not cause us to brood. No theory can be right which satisfactorily encloses all that is known. We do not know all. Little alien and unimportant items are left out of the reckoning, forlornly overlooked and unaccounted, yet presently to make the balance and fulfilment of a perfect formula as useless as a net when there are no fish. It is the way of a wilful mystery that its bottom is no sooner viewed than it falls out. Old night is still below.

It is true that the relative objective world may be almost anything a philosopher desires to name it, yet occasionally it does break into his subjectivity with an extrinsic brick, as it were, an interruption which causes him to surmise that something must have thrown it at him. We have been forced of late to develop theories explaining this age of machines, and to see omens of its impending doom. When our machines stop, so shall we. Civilized man, it appears, has passed out of the phase of imaginative exploration and experiment; he has created engines to do his work for him, but his soul has lost its daring, and he is now a subdued captive, chained to the wheels, a helpless slave in the mechanical establishment he created.

But maybe the urgency of this age of machines will slacken.

Some Doughty may explore its polished and efficient desert, and his word may begin to rust it; its impulse will falter and its wheels slow down. Though man now can fly to explore the skies, he may cease to want to—anyhow, for the reasons which now lift him from the earth. After all, it is certain that in time man will see that the relentless cranks and wheels, for which he never had more than a boyish and fevered love, are only the thoughts of his youth. He got those wheels because he wanted them. Does he want them now? Presently we may pause to consider this devotion of ours in a temple which is a factory, where the dynamo is the presiding god, the ritual exacting and numbing, and engineers the priests. That would be natural in us. The theory of the rise and fall of a civilization may be able to stand all known tests as easily as a bright and perfect machine accurately revolving; but suppose we change our mind about it? The machine stops. The subservience of men to the despotism of the polished steel rods and the ordained revolutions of the wheels may weary. The boy may tire of his engine.

Mankind is not of the automatic stuff to worship any god beyond the period of the god's most severe exactions. In the long run men and women cease to do what gives them no fun. Over goes Dagon when he demands more than his worshippers care to give. He will be lucky if he gets much attention after he has compelled that crisis. His late worshippers are sure to discover another world beyond his temple, for it exists; and then down falls the theory, all too neat, of a civilization's inevitable doom. It begins anew. There will be more adventuring and exploring, and in another direction. Life, we may find, has other probabilities and meanings. There can be fairer temples to gods more gracious.

G. K. Chesterton

1874 · 1936

Gilbert Keith Chesterton was a prolific English writer of fiction, biography, verse, and criticism. From 1905 until almost the time of his death, a volume of his essays, drawn from the periodicals for which he wrote, appeared annually. His fictional detective, Father Brown, one of the more remarkable characters of his kind, enabled Chesterton to express in acceptable form the religious and social opinions about which he felt deeply.

SCIENCE AND THE SAVAGES

A PERMANENT DISADVANTAGE of the study of folklore and kindred subjects is that the man of science can hardly be in the nature of things very frequently a man of the world. He is a student of nature; he is scarcely ever a student of human nature. And even where this difficulty is overcome, and he is in some sense a student of human nature, this is only a very faint beginning of the painful progress towards being human. For the study of primitive race and religion stands apart in one important respect from all, or nearly all, the ordinary scientific studies. A man can understand astronomy only by being an astronomer; he can understand entomology only by being an entomologist (or, perhaps, an insect); but he can understand a great deal of anthropology merely by being a man. He is himself the animal which he studies. Hence arises the fact which strikes

the eye everywhere in the records of ethnology and folklore—
the fact that the same frigid and detached spirit which leads to
success in the study of astronomy or botany leads to disaster
in the study of mythology or human origins. It is necessary
to cease to be a man in order to do justice to a microbe; it is
not necessary to cease to be a man in order to do justice to
men. That same suppression of sympathies, that same waving
away of intuitions or guesswork which make a man preternaturally clever in dealing with the stomach of a spider, will
make him preternaturally stupid in dealing with the heart of
man. He is making himself inhuman in order to understand
humanity. An ignorance of the other world is boasted by
many men of science; but in this matter their defect arises, not
from ignorance of the other world, but from ignorance of
this world. For the secrets about which anthropologists concern themselves can be best learnt, not from books or voyages,
but from the ordinary commerce of man with man. The secret
of why some savage tribe worships monkeys or the moon is
not to be found even by traveling among those savages and
taking down their answers in a notebook, although the clever-
est man may pursue this course. The answer to the riddle is in
England; it is in London; nay, it is in his own heart. When a
man has discovered why men in Bond Street wear black hats
he will at the same moment have discovered why men in Tim-
buctoo wear red feathers. The mystery in the heart of some
savage war-dance should not be studied in books of scientific
travel; it should be studied at a subscription ball. If a man desires to find out the origins of religions, let him not go to the
Sandwich Islands; let him go to church. If a man wishes to
know the origin of human society, to know what society,
philosophically speaking, really is, let him not go into the
British Museum; let him go into society.

This total misunderstanding of the real nature of ceremonial gives rise to the most awkward and dehumanized
versions of the conduct of men in rude lands and ages. The
man of science, not realizing that ceremonial is essentially a
thing which is done without a reason, has to find a reason for
every sort of ceremonial, and, as might be supposed, the rea-

son is generally a very absurd one—absurd because it originates not in the simple mind of the barbarian, but in the sophisticated mind of the professor. The learned man will say, for instance, "The natives of Mumbojumbo Land believe that the dead man can eat, and will require food upon his journey to the other world. This is attested by the fact that they place food in the grave, and that any family not complying with this rite is the object of the anger of the priests and the tribe." To anyone acquainted with humanity this way of talking is topsy-turvy. It is like saying, "The English in the twentieth century believed that a dead man could smell. This is attested by the fact that they always covered his grave with lilies, violets, or other flowers. Some priestly and tribal terrors were evidently attached to the neglect of this action, as we have records of several old ladies who were very much disturbed in mind because their wreaths had not arrived in time for the funeral." It may be of course that savages put food with a dead man because they think that a dead man can eat, or weapons with a dead man because they think that a dead man can fight. But personally I do not believe that they think anything of the kind. I believe they put food or weapons on the dead for the same reason that we put flowers, because it is an exceedingly natural and obvious thing to do. We do not understand, it is true, the emotion which makes us think it obvious and natural; but that is because, like all the important emotions of human existence, it is essentially irrational. We do not understand the savage for the same reason that the savage does not understand himself. And the savage does not understand himself for the same reason that we do not understand ourselves either.

The obvious truth is that the moment any matter has passed through the human mind it is finally and forever spoilt for all purposes of science. It has become a thing incurably mysterious and infinite; this mortal has put on immortality. Even what we call our material desires are spiritual, because they are human. Science can analyse a pork-chop, and say how much of it is phosphorus and how much is protein; but science cannot analyse any man's wish for a pork-chop, and say how much of it is hunger, how much custom, how much nervous fancy, how much a haunting love of the beautiful. The man's desire for the pork-chop remains literally as mystical and ethereal as his desire for heaven. All attempts, therefore, at a science of any human things, at a science of history, a science of folklore, a science of sociology, are by their nature not merely hopeless, but crazy. You can no more be certain in economic history that a man's desire for money was merely a desire for money than you can be certain in hagiology that a saint's desire for God was merely a desire for God. And this kind of vagueness in the primary phenomena of the study is an absolutely final blow to anything in the nature of a science. Men can construct a science with very few instruments, or with very plain instruments; but no one on earth could construct a science with unreliable instruments. A man might work out the whole of mathematics with a handful of pebbles, but not with a handful of clay which was always falling apart into new fragments, and falling together into new combinations. A man might measure heaven and earth with a reed, but not with a growing reed.

As one of the enormous follies of folklore, let us take the case of the transmigration of stories, and the alleged unity of their source. Story after story the scientific mythologists have cut out of its place in history, and pinned side by side with similar stories in their museum of fables. The process is industrious, it is fascinating, and the whole of it rests on one of the plainest fallacies in the world. That a story has been told all over the place at some time or other, not only does not prove that it really never happened; it does not even faintly indicate or make slightly more probable that it never happened. That a large number of fishermen have falsely asserted that they have caught a pike two feet long, does not in the least affect the question of whether anyone ever really did so. That numberless journalists announce a Franco-German war merely for money is no evidence one way or the other upon the dark question of whether such a war ever occurred. Doubtless in a few hundred years the innumerable Franco-German wars that did not happen will have cleared the scientific mind of any belief in the legendary war of '70 which did. But that will be because if folklore students remain at all, their nature will be unchanged; and their services to folklore will be still as they are at present, greater than they know. For in truth these men do something far more godlike than studying legends; they create them.

There are two kinds of stories which the scientists say cannot be true, because everybody tells them. The first class consists of the stories which are told everywhere, because they are somewhat odd or clever; there is nothing in the world to prevent their having happened to somebody as an adventure any more than there is anything to prevent their having occurred, as they certainly did occur, to somebody as an idea. But they are not likely to have happened to many people. The second class of their "myths" consists of the stories that are told everywhere for the simple reason that they happen everywhere. Of the first class, for instance, we might take such an example as the story of William Tell, now generally ranked among legends upon the sole ground that it is found in the tales of other peoples. Now, it is obvious that this was told everywhere because whether true or fictitious it is what is called "a good story"; it is odd, exciting, and it has a climax. But to suggest that some such eccentric incident can never have happened in the whole history of archery, or that it did not happen to any particular person of whom it is told, is stark impudence. The idea of shooting at a mark attached to some valuable or beloved person is an idea doubtless that might easily have occurred to any inventive poet. But it is also an idea that might easily occur to any boastful archer. It might be one of the fantastic caprices of some story-teller. It might equally well be one of the fantastic caprices of some tyrant. It might occur first in real life and afterwards occur in legends. Or it might just as well occur first in legends and afterwards occur in real life. If no apple has ever been shot off a boy's head from the beginning of the world, it may be done to-morrow morning, and by somebody who has never heard of William Tell.

This type of tale, indeed, may be pretty fairly paralleled with the ordinary anecdote terminating in a repartee or an

Irish bull. Such a retort as the famous *"Je ne vois pas la nécessité"* we have all seen attributed to Talleyrand, to Voltaire, to Henri Quatre, to an anonymous judge, and so on. But this variety does not in any way make it more likely that the thing was never said at all. It is highly likely that it was really said by somebody unknown. It is highly likely that it was really said by Talleyrand. In any case, it is not any more difficult to believe that the *mot* might have occurred to a man in conversation than to a man writing memoirs. It might have occurred to any of the men I have mentioned. But there is this point of distinction about it, that it is not likely to have occurred to all of them. And this is where the first class of so-called myth differs from the second to which I have previously referred. For there is a second class of incident found to be common to the stories of five or six heroes, say to Sigurd, to Hercules, to Rustem, to the Cid, and so on. And the peculiarity of this myth is that not only is it highly reasonable to imagine that it really happened to one hero, but it is highly reasonable to imagine that it really happened to all of them. Such a story, for instance, is that of a great man having his strength swayed or thwarted by the mysterious weakness of a woman. The anecdotal story, the story of William Tell, is as I have said, popular because it is peculiar. But this kind of story, the story of Samson and Delilah, of Arthur and Guinevere, is obviously popular because it is not peculiar. It is popular as good, quiet fiction is popular, because it tells the truth about people. If the ruin of Samson by a woman, and the ruin of Hercules by a woman, have a common legendary origin, it is gratifying to know that we can also explain, as a fable, the ruin of Nelson by a woman and the ruin of Parnell by a woman. And, indeed, I have no doubt whatever that, some centuries hence, the students of folklore will refuse altogether to believe that Elizabeth Barrett eloped with Robert Browning, and will prove their point up to the hilt by the unquestionable fact that the whole fiction of the period was full of such elopements from end to end.

Possibly the most pathetic of all the delusions of the modern students of primitive belief is the notion they have about the thing they call anthropomorphism. They believe that primitive men attributed phenomena to a god in human form in order to explain them, because his mind in its sullen limitation could not reach any further than his own clownish existence. The thunder was called the voice of a man, the lightning the eyes of a man, because by this explanation they were made more reasonable and comfortable. The final cure for all this kind of philosophy is to walk down a lane at night. Anyone who does so will discover very quickly that men pictured something semihuman at the back of all things, not because such a thought was natural, but because it was supernatural; not because it made things more comprehensible, but because it made them a hundred times more incomprehensible and mysterious. For a man walking down a lane at night can see the conspicuous fact that as long as nature keeps to her own course, she has no power with us at all. As long as a tree is a tree, it is a top-heavy monster with a hundred arms, a thousand tongues, and only one leg. But so long as a tree is a tree, it does not frighten us at all. It begins to be something alien, to be something strange, only when it looks like ourselves. When a tree really looks like a man our knees knock under us. And when the whole universe looks like a man we fall on our faces.

Winston S. Churchill

1874 · ——

Winston Spencer Churchill, Prime Minister of Great Britain from 1940 until 1945, is properly regarded as one of the great masters of English style. After completing his formal education at Harrow and Sandhurst, he began a career which combined military service, journalism, and politics. Few men in modern times have participated in more decisive events or shared more responsibility for shaping history. To his essays on non-professional subjects, such as painting, Mr. Churchill brings the same vigorous, thoughtful treatment that distinguishes his expressions of political and social opinion.

PAINTING AS A PASTIME

To HAVE REACHED THE AGE OF FORTY without ever handling a brush or fiddling with a pencil, to have regarded with mature eye the painting of pictures of any kind as a mystery, to have stood agape before the chalk of the pavement artist, and then suddenly to find oneself plunged in the middle of a new and intense form of interest and action with paints and palettes and canvases, and not to be discouraged by results, is an astonishing and enriching experience. I hope it may be shared by others. I should be glad if these lines induced others to try the experiment which I have tried, and if some at least were to find themselves dowered with an absorbing new amusement delightful to themselves, and at any rate not violently harmful to man or beast.

I hope this is modest enough: because there is no subject on which I feel more humble or yet at the same time more natural. I do not presume to explain how to paint, but only how to get enjoyment. Do not turn the superior eye of critical passivity upon these efforts. Buy a paint-box and have a try. If you need something to occupy your leisure, to divert your mind from the daily round, to illuminate your holidays, do not be too ready to believe that you cannot find what you want here. Even at the advanced age of forty! It would be a sad pity to shuffle or scramble along through one's playtime with golf and bridge, pottering, loitering, shifting from one heel to the other, wondering what on earth to do—as perhaps is the fate of some unhappy beings—when all the while, if you only knew, there is close at hand a wonderful new world of thought and craft, a sunlit garden gleaming with light and colour of which you have the key in your waist-coat-pocket. Inexpensive independence, a mobile and perennial pleasure apparatus, new mental food and exercise, the old harmonies and symmetries in an entirely different language, an added interest to every common scene, an occupation for every idle hour, an unceasing voyage of entrancing discovery —these are high prizes. Make quite sure they are not yours. After all, if you try, and fail, there is not much harm done. The nursery will grab what the studio has rejected. And then you can always go out and kill some animal, humiliate some rival on the links, or despoil some friend across the green table. You will not be worse off in any way. In fact you will be better off. You will know 'beyond a peradventure,' to quote a phrase disagreeably reminiscent, that that is really what you were meant to do in your hours of relaxation.

But if, on the contrary, you are inclined—late in life though it be—to reconnoitre a foreign sphere of limitless extent, then be persuaded that the first quality that is needed is Audacity. There really is no time for the deliberate approach. Two years of drawing-lessons, three years of copying woodcuts, five years of plaster casts—these are for the young. They have enough to bear. And this thorough grounding is for those who, hearing the call in the morning of their days, are able to make painting their paramount lifelong vocation. The truth and beauty of line and form which by the slightest touch or twist of the brush a real artist imparts to every feature of his design must be founded on long, hard, persevering apprenticeship and a practice so habitual that it has become instinctive. We must not be too ambitious. We cannot aspire to masterpieces. We may content ourselves with a joy ride in a paint-box. And for this Audacity is the only ticket.

I shall now relate my personal experience. When I left the Admiralty at the end of May, 1915, I still remained a member of the Cabinet and of the War Council. In this position I knew everything and could do nothing. The change from the intense executive activities of each day's work at the Admiralty to the narrowly-measured duties of a counsellor left me gasping. Like a sea-beast fished up from the depths, or a diver too suddenly hoisted, my veins threatened to burst from the fall in pressure. I had great anxiety and no means of relieving it; I had vehement convictions and small power to give effect to them. I had to watch the unhappy casting-away of great opportunities, and the feeble execution of plans which I had launched and in which I heartily believed. I had long hours of utterly unwonted leisure in which to contemplate the frightful unfolding of the War. At a moment when every fibre of my being was inflamed to action, I was forced to remain a spectator of the tragedy, placed cruelly in a front seat. And then it was that the Muse of Painting came to my rescue —out of charity and out of chivalry, because after all she had nothing to do with me—and said, 'Are these toys any good to you? They amuse some people.'

Some experiments one Sunday in the country with the children's paint-box led me to procure the next morning a complete outfit for painting in oils.

Having bought the colours, an easel, and a canvas, the next step was *to begin*. But what a step to take! The palette gleamed with beads of colour; fair and white rose the canvas; the empty brush hung poised, heavy with destiny, irresolute in the air. My hand seemed arrested by a silent veto. But after all the sky on this occasion was unquestionably blue, and a pale blue at that. There could be no doubt that blue paint mixed with white should be put on the top part of the canvas. One really does not need to have had an artist's training to see that. It is a starting-point open to all. So very gingerly I mixed a little blue paint on the palette with a very small brush, and then with infinite precaution made a mark about as big as a bean upon the affronted snow-white shield. It was a challenge, a deliberate challenge; but so subdued, so halting, indeed so cataleptic, that it deserved no response. At that moment the loud approaching sound of a motor-car was heard in the drive. From this chariot there stepped swiftly and lightly none other than the gifted wife of Sir John Lavery. 'Painting! But what are you hesitating about? Let me have a brush—the big one.' Splash into the turpentine, wallop into the blue and the white, frantic flourish on the palette—clean no longer— and then several large, fierce strokes and slashes of blue on the absolutely cowering canvas. Anyone could see that it could not hit back. No evil fate avenged the jaunty violence. The canvas grinned in helplessness before me. The spell was broken. The sickly inhibitions rolled away. I seized the largest brush and fell upon my victim with Berserk fury. I have never felt any awe of a canvas since.

Everyone knows the feelings with which one stands shivering on a spring-board, the shock when a friendly foe steals up behind and hurls you into the flood, and the ardent glow which thrills you as you emerge breathless from the plunge.

This beginning with Audacity, or being thrown into the middle of it, is already a very great part of the art of painting. But there is more in it than that.

> La peinture à l'huile
> Est bien difficile,
> Mais c'est beaucoup plus beau
> Que la peinture à l'eau.

I write no word in disparagement of water-colours. But there really is nothing like oils. You have a medium at your disposal which offers real power, if you only can find out how to use it. Moreover, it is easier to get a certain distance along the road by its means than by water-colour. First of all, you can correct mistakes much more easily. One sweep of the palette-knife 'lifts' the blood and tears of a morning from the canvas and enables a fresh start to be made; indeed the canvas is all the better for past impressions. Secondly, you can approach your problem from any direction. You need not build downwards awkwardly from white paper to your darkest dark. You may strike where you please, beginning if you will with a moderate central arrangement of middle tones, and then hurling in the extremes when the psychological moment comes. Lastly, the pigment itself is such nice stuff to handle (if it does not retaliate). You can build it on layer after layer if you like. You can keep on experimenting. You can change your plan to meet the exigencies of time or weather. And always remember you can scrape it all away.

Just to paint is great fun. The colours are lovely to look at and delicious to squeeze out. Matching them, however crudely, with what you see is fascinating and absolutely absorbing. Try it if you have not done so—before you die. As one slowly begins to escape from the difficulties of choosing the right colours and laying them on in the right places and in the right way, wider considerations come into view. One begins to see, for instance, that painting a picture is like fighting a battle; and trying to paint a picture is, I suppose, like trying to fight a battle. It is, if anything, more exciting than fighting it successfully. But the principle is the same. It is the same kind of problem, as unfolding a long, sustained, interlocked argument. It is a proposition which, whether of few or numberless parts, is commanded by a single unity of conception. And we think—though I cannot tell—that painting a great picture must require an intellect on the grand scale. There must be that all-embracing view which presents the beginning and the end, the whole and each part, as one instantaneous impression retentively and untiringly held in the mind. When we look at the larger Turners—canvases yards wide and tall—and observe that they are all done in one piece and represent one single second of time, and that every innumerable detail, however small, however distant, however subordinate, is set forth naturally and in its true proportion and relation, without effort, without failure, we must feel in presence of an intellectual manifestation the equal in quality and intensity of the finest achievements of warlike action, of forensic argument, or of scientific or philosophical adjudication.

In all battles two things are usually required of the Commander-in-Chief: to make a good plan for his army and, secondly, to keep a strong reserve. Both these are also obligatory upon the painter. To make a plan, thorough reconnaissance of the country where the battle is to be fought is needed. Its fields, its mountains, its rivers, its bridges, its trees, its flowers, its atmosphere—all require and repay attentive observation from a special point of view. One is quite astonished to find how many things there are in the landscape, and in every object in it, one never noticed before. And this is a tremendous new pleasure and interest which invests every walk or drive with an added object. So many colours on the hillside, each different in shadow and in sunlight; such brilliant reflections in the pool, each a key lower than what they repeat; such lovely lights gilding or silvering surface or outline, all tinted exquisitely with pale colour, rose, orange, green, or violet. I found myself instinctively as I walked noting the tint and character of a leaf, the dreamy purple shades of mountains, the exquisite lacery of winter branches, the dim pale silhouettes of far horizons. And I had lived for over forty years without ever noticing any of them except in a general way, as one might look at a crowd and say, 'What a lot of people!'

I think this heightened sense of observation of Nature is one of the chief delights that have come to me through trying to paint. No doubt many people who are lovers of art have acquired it in a high degree without actually practising. But I expect that nothing will make one observe more quickly or more thoroughly than having to face the difficulty of representing the thing observed. And mind you, if you do observe accurately and with refinement, and if you do record what you have seen with tolerable correspondence, the result follows on the canvas with startling obedience. Even if only four or five main features are seized and truly recorded, these by themselves will carry a lot of ill-success or half-success. Answer five big questions out of all the hundreds in the examination paper correctly and well, and though you may not win a prize, at any rate you will not be absolutely ploughed.

But in order to make his plan, the General must not only reconnoitre the battle-ground, he must also study the achievements of the great Captains of the past. He must bring the observations he has collected in the field into comparison with the treatment of similar incidents by famous chiefs. Then the galleries of Europe take on a new—and to me at least a severely practical—interest. 'This, then, is how —— painted a cataract. Exactly, and there is that same light I noticed last week in the waterfall at ——.' And so on. You see the difficulty that baffled you yesterday; and you see how easily it has been overcome by a great or even by a skilful painter. Not only is your observation of Nature sensibly improved and developed, but you look at the masterpieces of art with an analysing and a comprehending eye.

The whole world is open with all its treasures. The simplest objects have their beauty. Every garden presents innumerable fascinating problems. Every land, every parish, has its own tale to tell. And there are many lands differing from each other in countless ways, and each presenting delicious variants of colour, light, form, and definition. Obviously, then, armed with a paint-box, one cannot be bored, one cannot be left at a loose end, one cannot 'have several days on one's hands.' Good gracious! what there is to admire and how little time there is to see it in! For the first time one begins to envy Methuselah. No doubt he made a very indifferent use of his opportunities.

But it is in the use and withholding of their reserves that the great commanders have generally excelled. After all, when once the last reserve has been thrown in, the commander's part is played. If that does not win the battle, he has nothing else to give. The event must be left to luck and to the fighting troops. But these last, in the absence of high direction, are apt to get into sad confusion, all mixed together in a nasty mess without order or plan—and consequently without effect. Mere masses count no more. The largest brush, the brightest colours cannot even make an impression. The pictorial battle-field becomes a sea of mud mercifully veiled by the fog of war. It is evident there has been a serious defeat. Even though the General plunges in himself and emerges bespattered, as he sometimes does, he will not retrieve the day.

In painting, the reserves consist in Proportion or Relation. And it is here that the art of the painter marches along the road which is traversed by all the greatest harmonies in thought. At one side of the palette there is white, at the other black; and neither is ever used 'neat.' Between these two rigid limits all the action must lie, all the power required must be generated. Black and white themselves placed in juxtaposition make no great impression; and yet they are the most that you can do in pure contrast. It is wonderful—after one has tried and failed often—to see how easily and surely the true artist is able to produce every effect of light and shade, of sunshine and shadow, of distance or nearness, simply by expressing justly the relations between the different planes and surfaces with which he is dealing. We think that this is founded upon a sense of proportion, trained no doubt by practice, but which in its essence is a frigid manifestation of mental power and size. We think that the same mind's eye that can justly survey and appraise and prescribe beforehand the values of a truly great picture in one all-embracing regard, in one flash of simultaneous and homogeneous comprehension, would also with a certain acquaintance with the special technique be able to pronounce with sureness upon any other high activity of the human intellect. This was certainly true of the great Italians.

I have written in this way to show how varied are the de-lights which may be gained by those who enter hopefully and thoughtfully upon the pathway of painting; how enriched they will be in their daily vision, how fortified in their inde-pendence, how happy in their leisure. Whether you feel that your soul is pleased by the conception or contemplation of harmonies, or that your mind is stimulated by the aspect of magnificent problems, or whether you are content to find fun in trying to observe and depict the jolly things you see, the vistas of possibility are limited only by the shortness of life. Every day you may make progress. Every step may be fruitful. Yet there will stretch out before you an ever-lengthening, ever-ascending, ever-improving path. You know you will never get to the end of the journey. But this, so far from discouraging, only adds to the joy and glory of the climb.

Try it, then, before it is too late and before you mock at me. Try it while there is time to overcome the preliminary difficulties. Learn enough of the language in your prime to open this new literature to your age. Plant a garden in which you can sit when digging days are done. It may be only a small garden, but you will see it grow. Year by year it will bloom and ripen. Year by year it will be better cultivated. The weeds will be cast out. The fruit-trees will be pruned and trained. The flowers will bloom in more beautiful combinations. There will be sunshine there even in the winter-time, and cool shade, and the play of shadow on the pathway in the shining days of June.

I must say I like bright colours. I agree with Ruskin in his denunciation of that school of painting who 'eat slate-pencil and chalk, and assure everybody that they are nicer and purer than strawberries and plums.' I cannot pretend to feel impartial about the colours. I rejoice with the brilliant ones, and am genuinely sorry for the poor browns. When I get to heaven I mean to spend a considerable portion of my first million years in painting, and so get to the bottom of the subject. But then I shall require a still gayer palette than I get here below. I expect orange and vermilion will be the darkest, dullest colours upon it, and beyond them there will be a whole range of wonderful new colours which will delight the celestial eye.

Chance led me one autumn to a secluded nook on the Côte d'Azur, between Marseilles and Toulon, and there I fell in with one or two painters who revelled in the methods of the modern French school. These were disciples of Cézanne. They view Nature as a mass of shimmering light in which forms and surfaces are comparatively unimportant, indeed hardly visible, but which gleams and glows with beautiful harmonies and contrasts of colour. Certainly it was of great interest to me to come suddenly in contact with this entirely different way of looking at things. I had hitherto painted the sea flat, with long, smooth strokes of mixed pigment in which the tints varied only by gradations. Now I must try to represent it by innumerable small separate lozenge-shaped points and patches of colour—often pure colour—so that it looked more like a tessellated pavement than a marine picture. It sounds curious. All the same, do not be in a hurry to reject the method. Go back a few yards and survey the result. Each of these little points of colour is now playing his part in the general effect. Individually invisible, he sets up a strong radiation, of which the eye is conscious without detecting the cause. Look also at the blue of the Mediterranean. How can you depict and record it? Certainly not by any single colour that was ever manufactured. The only way in which that luminous intensity of blue can be simulated is by this multitude of tiny points of varied colour all in true relation to the rest of the scheme. Difficult? Fascinating!

Nature presents itself to the eye through the agency of these individual points of light, each of which sets up the vibrations peculiar to its colour. The brilliancy of a picture must therefore depend partly upon the frequency with which these points are found on any given area of the canvas, and partly on their just relation to one another. Ruskin says in his *Elements of Drawing*, from which I have already quoted, 'You will not, in Turner's largest oil pictures, perhaps six or seven feet long by four or five high, find one spot of colour as large as a grain of wheat ungradated.' But the gradations of Turner differ from those of the modern French school by being gently and almost imperceptibly evolved one from another instead of being bodily and even roughly separated; and the brush of Turner followed the form of the objects he depicted, while our French friends often seem to take a pride in directly opposing it. For instance, they would prefer to paint a sea with up and down strokes rather than with horizontal; or a tree-trunk from right to left rather than up and down.

This, I expect, is due to falling in love with one's theories, and making sacrifices of truth to them in order to demonstrate fidelity and admiration.

But surely we owe a debt to those who have so wonderfully vivified, brightened, and illuminated modern landscape painting. Have not Manet and Monet, Cézanne and Matisse, rendered to painting something of the same service which Keats and Shelley gave to poetry after the solemn and ceremonious literary perfections of the eighteenth century? They have brought back to the pictorial art a new draught of *joie de vivre;* and the beauty of their work is instinct with gaiety, and floats in sparkling air.

I do not expect these masters would particularly appreciate my defence, but I must avow an increasing attraction to their work. Lucid and exact expression is one of the characteristics of the French mind. The French language has been made the instrument of the admirable gift. Frenchmen talk and write just as well about painting as they have done about love, about war, about diplomacy, or cooking. Their terminology is precise and complete. They are therefore admirably equipped to be teachers in the theory of any of these arts. Their critical faculty is so powerfully developed that it is perhaps some restraint upon achievement. But it is a wonderful corrective to others as well as to themselves.

My French friend, for instance, after looking at some of my daubs, took me round the galleries of Paris, pausing here and there. Wherever he paused, I found myself before a picture which I particularly admired. He then explained that it was quite easy to tell, from the kind of things I had been trying to do, what were the things I liked. Never having taken any interest in pictures till I tried to paint, I had no preconceived opinions. I just felt, for reasons I could not fathom, that I liked some much more than others. I was astonished that anyone else should, on the most cursory observation of my work, be able so surely to divine a taste which I had never consciously formed. My friend said that it is not a bad thing to know nothing at all about pictures, but to have a matured mind trained in other things and a new strong interest for painting. The elements are there from which a true taste in art can be formed with time and guidance, and there are no obstacles or imperfect conceptions in the way. I hope this is true. Certainly the last part is true.

Once you begin to study it, all Nature is equally interesting and equally charged with beauty. I was shown a picture by Cézanne of a blank wall of a house, which he had made instinct with the most delicate lights and colours. Now I often amuse myself when I am looking at a wall or a flat surface of any kind by trying to distinguish all the different colours and tints which can be discerned upon it, and considering whether these arise from reflections or from natural hue. You would be astonished the first time you tried this to see how many and what beautiful colours there are even in the most commonplace objects, and the more carefully and frequently you look the more variations do you perceive.

But these are no reasons for limiting oneself to the plainest and most ordinary objects and scenes. Mere prettiness of scene, to be sure, is not needed for a beautiful picture. In fact, artificially-made pretty places are very often a hindrance to a good picture. Nature will hardly stand a double process of beautification: one layer of idealism on top of another is too much of a good thing. But a vivid scene, a brilliant atmosphere, novel and charming lights, impressive contrasts, if they strike the eye all at once, arouse an interest and an ardour which will certainly be reflected in the work which you try to do, and will make it seem easier.

It would be interesting if some real authority investigated carefully the part which memory plays in painting. We look at the object with an intent regard, then at the palette, and thirdly at the canvas. The canvas receives a message dispatched usually a few seconds before from the natural object. But it has come through a post-office *en route*. It has been transmitted in code. It has been turned from light into paint. It reaches the canvas a cryptogram. Not until it has been placed in its correct relation to everything else that is on the canvas can it be deciphered, is its meaning apparent, is it translated once again from mere pigment into light. And the light this time is not of Nature but of Art. The whole of this considerable process is carried through on the wings or the wheels of memory. In most cases we think it is the wings—airy and quick like a butterfly from flower to flower. But all heavy traffic and all that has to go a long journey must travel on wheels.

In painting in the open air the sequence of actions is so rapid that the process of translation into and out of pigment may seem to be unconscious. But all the greatest landscapes have been painted indoors, and often long after the first impressions were gathered. In a dim cellar the Dutch or Italian master recreated the gleaming ice of a Netherlands carnival or the lustrous sunshine of Venice or the Campagna. Here, then, is required a formidable memory of the visual kind. Not only do we develop our powers of observation, but also those of carrying the record—of carrying it through an extraneous medium and of reproducing it, hours, days, or even months after the scene has vanished or the sunlight died.

I was told by a friend that when Whistler guided a school in Paris he made his pupils observe their model on the ground floor, and then run upstairs and paint their picture piece by piece on the floor above. As they became more proficient he put their easels up a storey higher, till at last the *élite* were scampering with their decision up six flights into the attic—praying it would not evaporate on the way. This is, perhaps, only a tale. But it shows effectively of what enormous importance a trained, accurate, retentive memory must be to an artist; and conversely what a useful exercise painting may be for the development of an accurate and retentive memory.

There is no better exercise for the would-be artist than to study and devour a picture, and then, without looking at it again, to attempt the next day to reproduce it. Nothing can more exactly measure the progress both of observation and memory. It is still harder to compose out of many separate, well-retained impressions, aided though they be by sketches and colour notes, a new complete conception. But this is the only way in which great landscapes have been painted—or can be painted. The size of the canvas alone precludes its being handled out of doors. The fleeting light imposes a rigid time-limit. The same light never returns. One cannot go back day after day without the picture getting stale. The painter must choose between a rapid impression, fresh and warm and living, but probably deserving only of a short life, and the cold, profound, intense effort of memory, knowledge, and will-power, prolonged perhaps for weeks, from which a masterpiece can alone result. It is much better not to fret too much about the latter. Leave to the masters of art trained by a lifetime of devotion the wonderful process of picture-building and picture-creation. Go out into the sunlight and be happy with what you see.

Painting is complete as a distraction. I know of nothing which, without exhausting the body, more entirely absorbs the mind. Whatever the worries of the hour or the threats of the future, once the picture has begun to flow along, there is no room for them in the mental screen. They pass out into shadow and darkness. All one's mental light, such as it is, becomes concentrated on the task. Time stands respectfully aside, and it is only after many hesitations that luncheon knocks gruffly at the door. When I have had to stand up on parade, or even, I regret to say, in church, for half an hour at a time, I have always felt that the erect position is not natural to man, has only been painfully acquired, and is only with fatigue and difficulty maintained. But no one who is fond of painting finds the slightest inconvenience, as long as the interest holds, in standing to paint for three or four hours at a stretch.

Lastly, let me say a word on painting as a spur to travel. There is really nothing like it. Every day and all day is provided with its expedition and its occupation—cheap, attainable, innocent, absorbing, recuperative. The vain racket of the tourist gives place to the calm enjoyment of the philosopher, intensified by an enthralling sense of action and endeavour. Every country where the sun shines and every district in it has a theme of its own. The lights, the atmosphere, the aspect, the spirit, are all different; but each has its native charm. Even if you are only a poor painter you can feel the influence of the scene, guiding your brush, selecting the tubes you squeeze on to the palette. Even if you cannot portray it as you see it, you feel it, you know it, and you admire it for ever. When people rush about Europe in the train from one glittering centre of work or pleasure to another, passing—at enormous expense—through a series of mammoth hotels and blatant carnivals, they little know what they are missing, and how cheaply priceless things can be obtained. The painter wanders and loiters contentedly from place to place, always on the look out for some brilliant butterfly of a picture which can be caught and set up and carried safely home.

Now I am learning to like painting even on dull days. But in my hot youth I demanded sunshine. Sir William Orpen advised me to visit Avignon on account of its wonderful light, and certainly there is no more delightful centre for a would-be painter's activities: then Egypt, fierce and brilliant, presenting in infinite variety the single triplex theme of the Nile, the desert, and the sun; or Palestine, a land of rare beauty—the beauty of the turquoise and the opal—which well deserves the attention of some real artist, and has never been portrayed to the extent that is its due. And what of India? Who has ever interpreted its lurid splendours? But after all, if only the sun will shine, one does not need to go beyond one's own country. There is nothing more intense than the burnished steel and gold of a Highland stream; and at the beginning and close of almost every day the Thames displays to the citizens of London glories and delights which one must travel far to rival.

H. L. Mencken

1880 · ——

Henry Louis Mencken, editor, journalist, and critic, has spent fifty years vigorously attacking what he considers sham and hypocrisy in politics, education, religion, and the arts. His antagonism toward academic persons and institutions may have resulted in part from his scanty formal schooling, as some of his critics have charged, but it is more likely that he hates pedantry so much that he challenges anything that smacks of academic narrowness. As editor of the American Mercury *(1924–1933) he delighted a large audience that shared his "debunking" tendencies.*

CRITICISM OF CRITICISM OF CRITICISM

EVERY NOW AND THEN, a sense of the futility of their daily endeavors falling suddenly upon them, the critics of Christendom turn to a somewhat sour and depressing consideration of the nature and objects of their own craft. That is to say, they turn to criticizing criticism. What is it in plain words? What is its aim, exactly stated in legal terms? How far can it go? What good can it do? What is its normal effect upon the artist and the work of art?

Such a spell of self-searching has been in progress for several years past, and the critics of various countries have contributed theories of more or less lucidity and plausibility to the discussion. Their views of their own art, it appears, are quite as divergent as their views of the arts they more commonly deal with. One group argues, partly by direct statement and partly by attacking all other groups, that the one defensible purpose of the critic is to encourage the virtuous and oppose the sinful—in brief, to police the fine arts and so hold them in tune with the moral order of the world. Another group, repudiating this constabulary function, argues hotly that the arts have nothing to do with morality whatsoever—that their concern is solely with pure beauty. A third group holds that the chief aspect of a work of art, particularly in the field of literature, is its aspect as psychological document—that if it doesn't help men to know themselves it is nothing. A fourth group reduces the thing to an exact science, and sets up standards that resemble algebraic formulae—this is the group of metrists, of contrapuntists and of those who gabble of lightwaves. And so, in order, follow groups five, six, seven, eight, nine, ten, each with its theory and its proofs.

Against the whole corps, moral and aesthetic, psychological and algebraic, stands Major J. E. Spingarn, U.S.A. Major Spingarn lately served formal notice upon me that he had abandoned the life of the academic grove for that of the armed array, and so I give him his military title, but at the time he wrote his "Creative Criticism" he was a professor in Columbia University, and I still find myself thinking of him, not as a soldier extraordinarily literate, but as a professor in rebellion. For his notions, whatever one may say in opposition to them, are at least magnificently unprofessorial—they fly violently in the face of the principles that distinguish the largest and most influential group of campus critics. As witness: "To say that poetry is moral or immoral is as meaningless as to say that an equilateral triangle is moral and an isosceles triangle immoral." Or, worse: "It is only conceivable in a world in which dinner-table conversation runs after this fashion: 'This cauliflower would be good if it had only been prepared in accordance with international law.' " One imagines, on hearing such atheism flying about, the amazed indignation of Prof. Dr. William Lyon Phelps, with his discovery that Joseph Conrad preaches "the axiom of the moral law"; the "Hey, what's that!" of Prof. Dr. W. C. Brownell, the Amherst

Aristotle, with his eloquent plea for standards as iron-clad as the Westminster Confession; the loud, patriotic alarm of the gifted Prof. Dr. Stuart P. Sherman, of Iowa, with his maxim that Puritanism is the official philosophy of America, and that all who dispute it are enemy aliens and should be deported. Major Spingarn, in truth, here performs a treason most horrible upon the reverend order he once adorned, and having achieved it, he straightway performs another and then another. That is to say, he tackles all the antagonistic groups of orthodox critics seriatim, and knocks them about unanimously —first the aforesaid agents of the sweet and pious; then the advocates of unities, meters, all rigid formulae; then the experts in imaginary psychology; then the historical comparers, pigeonholers and makers of categories; finally, the professors of pure aesthetic. One and all, they take their places upon his operating table, and one and all they are stripped and anatomized.

But what is the anarchistic ex-professor's own theory?—for a professor must have a theory, as a dog must have fleas. In brief, what he offers is a doctrine borrowed from the Italian, Benedetto Croce, and by Croce filched from Goethe—a doctrine anything but new in the world, even in Goethe's time, but nevertheless long buried in forgetfulness—to wit, the doctrine that it is the critic's first and only duty, as Carlyle once put it, to find out "what the poet's aim really and truly was, how the task he had to do stood before his eye, and how far, with such materials as were afforded him, he has fulfilled it." For poet, read artist, or, if literature is in question, substitute the Germanic word *Dichter*—that is, the artist in words, the creator of beautiful letters, whether in verse or in prose. Ibsen always called himself a *Digter*, not a *Dramatiker* or *Skuespiller*. So, I daresay, did Shakespeare. . . . Well, what is this generalized poet trying to do? asks Major Spingarn, and how has he done it? That, and no more, is the critic's quest. The morality of the work does not concern him. It is not his business to determine whether it heeds Aristotle or flouts Aristotle. He passes no judgment on its rhyme scheme, its length and breadth, its iambics, its politics, its patriotism, its piety, its psychological exactness, its good taste. He may note these things, but he may not protest about them—he may not complain if the thing criticized fails to fit into a pigeonhole. Every sonnet, every drama, every novel is *sui generis;* it must stand on its own bottom; it must be judged by its own inherent intentions. "Poets," says Major Spingarn, "do not really write epics, pastorals, lyrics, however much they may be deceived by these false abstractions; they express *themselves, and this expression is their only form.* There are not, therefore, only three or ten or a hundred literary kinds; there are as many kinds as there are individual poets." Nor is there any valid appeal *ad hominem.* The character and background of the poet are beside the mark; the poem itself is the thing. Oscar Wilde, a bounder and a swine, wrote beautiful prose. To reject that prose on the ground that Wilde was no gentleman is as absurd as to reject "What Is Man?" on the ground that its theology is beyond the intelligence of the editor of the New York *Times.*

This Spingarn-Croce-Carlyle-Goethe theory, of course, throws a heavy burden upon the critic. It presupposes that he is a civilized and tolerant man, hospitable to all intelligible ideas and capable of reading them as he runs. This is a demand that at once rules out nine-tenths of the grown-up sophomores who carry on the business of criticism in America. Their trouble is simply that they lack the intellectual resilience necessary for taking in ideas, and particularly new ideas. The only way they can ingest one is by transforming it into the nearest related formula—usually a harsh and devastating operation. This fact accounts for their chronic inability to understand all that is most personal and original and hence most forceful and significant in the emerging literature of the country. They can get down what has been digested and re-digested, and so brought into forms that they know, and carefully labeled by predecessors of their own sort—but they exhibit alarm immediately they come into the presence of the extraordinary. Here we have an explanation of Brownell's loud appeal for a tightening of standards—*i.e.,* a larger respect for precedents, patterns, rubber-stamps—and here we have an explanation of Phelps's inability to comprehend the colossal phenomenon of

Dreiser, and of Boynton's childish nonsense about realism, and of Sherman's effort to apply the Espionage Act to the arts, and of More's querulous enmity to romanticism, and of all the fatuous pigeon-holing that passes for criticism in the more solemn literary periodicals.

As practiced by all such learned and diligent but essentially ignorant and unimaginative men, criticism is little more than a branch of homiletics. They judge a work of art, not by its clarity and sincerity, not by the force and charm of its ideas, not by the technical virtuosity of the artist, not by his originality and artistic courage, but simply and solely by his orthodoxy. If he is what is called a "right thinker," if he devotes himself to advocating the transient platitudes in a sonorous manner, then he is worthy of respect. But if he lets fall the slightest hint that he is in doubt about any of them, or, worse still, that he is indifferent, then he is a scoundrel, and hence, by their theory, a bad artist. Such pious piffle is horribly familiar among us. I do not exaggerate its terms. You will find it running through the critical writings of practically all the dull fellows who combine criticism with tutoring; in the words of many of them it is stated in the plainest way and defended with much heat, theological and pedagogical. In its baldest form it shows itself in the doctrine that it is scandalous for an artist—say a dramatist or a novelist—to depict vice as attractive. The fact that vice, more often than not, undoubtedly *is* attractive—else why should it ever gobble any of us?—is disposed of with a lofty gesture. What of it? say these birchmen. The artist is not a reporter, but a Great Teacher. It is not his business to depict the world as it is, but as it ought to be.

Against this notion American criticism makes but feeble headway. We are, in fact, a nation of evangelists; every third American devotes himself to improving and lifting up his fellow-citizens, usually by force; the messianic delusion is our national disease. Thus the moral *Privatdozenten* have the crowd on their side, and it is difficult to shake their authority; even the vicious are still in favor of crying vice down. "Here is a novel," says the artist. "Why didn't you write a tract?" roars the professor—and down the chute go novel and novelist. "This girl is pretty," says the painter. "But she has left off her undershirt," protests the headmaster—and off goes the poor dauber's head. At its mildest, this balderdash takes the form of the late Hamilton Wright Mabie's "White List of Books"; at its worst, it is comstockery, an idiotic and abominable thing. Genuine criticism is as impossible to such inordinately narrow and cocksure men as music is to a man who is tone-deaf. The critic, to interpret his artist, even to understand his artist, must be able to get into the mind of his artist; he must feel and comprehend the vast pressure of the creative passion; as Major Spingarn says, "aesthetic judgment and artistic creation are instinct with the same vital life." This is why all the best criticism of the world has been written by men who have had within them, not only the reflective and analytical faculty of critics, but also the gusto of artists— Goethe, Carlyle, Lessing, Schlegel, Sainte-Beuve, and, to drop a story or two, Hazlitt, Hermann Bahr, Georg Brandes and James Huneker. Huneker, tackling "Also sprach Zarathustra," revealed its content in illuminating flashes. But tackled by Paul Elmer More, it became no more than a dull student's exercise, ill-naturedly corrected. . . .

So much for the theory of Major J. E. Spingarn, U.S.A., late professor of modern languages and literatures in Columbia University. Obviously, it is a far sounder and more stimulating theory than any of those cherished by the other professors. It demands that the critic be a man of intelligence, of toleration, of wide information, of genuine hospitality to ideas, whereas the others only demand that he have learning, and accept anything as learning that has been said before. But once he has stated his doctrine, the ingenious ex-professor, professor-like, immediately begins to corrupt it by claiming too much for it. Having laid and hatched, so to speak, his somewhat stale but still highly nourishing egg, he begins to argue fatuously that the resultant flamingo is the whole mustering of the critical *Aves*. But the fact is, of course, that criticism, as humanly practiced, must needs fall a good deal short of this intuitive re-creation of beauty, and what is more, it must go a good deal further. For one thing, it must be interpretation in terms that are not only exact but are also comprehensible to the reader, else it will leave the original mystery as dark as before—and once interpretation comes in, paraphrase and transliteration come in. What is recondite must be made plainer; the transcendental, to some extent at least, must be done into common modes of thinking. Well, what are morality, trochaics, hexameters, movements, historical principles, psychological maxims, the dramatic unities—what are all these save common modes of thinking, short cuts, rubber stamps, words of one syllable? Moreover, beauty as we know it in this world is by no means the apparition *in vacuo* that Dr. Spingarn seems to see. It has its social, its political, even its moral implications. The finale of Beethoven's C minor symphony is not only colossal as music; it is also colossal as revolt; it says something against something. Yet more, the springs of beauty are not within itself alone, nor even in genius alone, but often in things without. Brahms wrote his Deutsches Requiem, not only because he was a great artist, but also because he was a good German. And in Nietzsche there are times when the divine afflatus takes a back seat, and the *spirochaete* have the floor.

Major Spingarn himself seems to harbor some sense of this limitation on his doctrine. He gives warning that "the poet's intention must be judged at the moment of the creative act"—which opens the door enough for many an ancient to creep in. But limited or not, he at least clears off a lot of moldy rubbish, and gets further toward the truth than any of his former colleagues. They waste themselves upon theories that only conceal the poet's achievement the more, the more diligently they are applied; he, at all events, grounds himself upon the sound notion that there should be free speech in art, and no protective tariffs, and no *a priori* assumptions, and no testing of ideas by mere words. The safe ground probably lies between the contestants, but nearer Spingarn. The critic who really illuminates starts off much as he starts off, but with a due regard for the prejudices and imbecilities of the world. I think the best feasible practice is to be found in certain chapters of Huneker, a critic of vastly more solid influence and of infinitely more value to the arts than all the prating pedagogues since Rufus Griswold. Here, as in the case of Poe, a sensitive and intelligent artist recreates the work of other artists, but there also comes to the ceremony a man of the world, and the things he has to say are apposite and instructive too. To denounce moralizing out of hand is to pronounce a moral judgment. To dispute the categories is to set up a new anti-categorical category. And to admire the work of Shakespeare is to be interested in his handling of blank verse, his social aspirations, his shot-gun marriage and his frequent concessions to the bombastic frenzy of his actors, and to have some curiosity about Mr. W. H. The really competent critic must be an empiricist. He must conduct his exploration with whatever means lie within the bounds of his personal limitation. He must produce his effects with whatever tools will work. If pills fail, he gets out his saw. If the saw won't cut, he seizes a club. . . .

Perhaps, after all, the chief burden that lies upon Major Spingarn's theory is to be found in its label. The word "creative" is a bit too flamboyant; it says what he wants to say, but it probably says a good deal more. In this emergency, I propose getting rid of the misleading label by pasting another over it. That is, I propose the substitution of "catalytic" for "creative," despite the fact that "catalytic" is an unfamiliar word, and suggests the dog-Latin of the seminaries. I borrow it from chemistry, and its meaning is really quite simple. A catalyzer, in chemistry, is a substance that helps two other substances to react. For example, consider the case of ordinary cane sugar and water. Dissolve the sugar in the water and nothing happens. But add a few drops of acid and the sugar changes into glucose and fructose. Meanwhile, the acid itself is absolutely unchanged. All it does is to stir up the reaction between the water and the sugar. The process is called catalysis. The acid is a catalyzer.

Well, this is almost exactly the function of a genuine critic of the arts. It is his business to provoke the reaction between the work of art and the spectator. The spectator, untutored, stands unmoved; he sees the work of art, but it fails to make any intelligible impression on him; if he were spontaneously sensitive to it, there would be no need for criticism. But now comes the critic with his catalysis. He makes the work of art live for the spectator; he makes the spectator live for the work of art. Out of the process comes understanding, appreciation, intelligent enjoyment—and that is precisely what the artist tried to produce.

Stuart P. Sherman

1881 · 1926

Stuart Pratt Sherman was born in Iowa and educated at Williams, where he edited the literary journal, and at Harvard, where he made a distinguished record as a scholar. After twenty years of teaching, first at Northwestern University and later at the University of Illinois, he became literary editor of the New York Herald Tribune. *As a critic, he represented the conservative point of view in literature and morals, even though he supported D. H. Lawrence and Sherwood Anderson against critics who claimed to be more liberal.*

FORTY AND UPWARDS

THERE IS AN INTERESTING and true passage in the letters of Matthew Arnold which spirited young fellows encounter with a chill. It is this: "The aimless and unsettled, but also open and liberal, state of our youth we *must* perhaps all leave and take refuge in our morality and character; but with most of us it is a melancholy passage from which we emerge shorn of so many beams that we are almost tempted to quarrel with the law of nature which imposes it on us."

The revolt of youth, the cries of which are now so audible in our literature, is an attempt to resist as long as possible the imposition of the traditional morality and the traditional character upon the fluent welter of youth's desires and possibilities.

The revolt derives its bright enthusiasm from the belief of the insurgents that as the yoke of custom is something wilfully imposed by tyrannical elders, it may, by a superior wilfulness of the young, be thrown off. The wise young Arnold dashes cold water on that belief by referring to the imposing power as a "law of nature."

What is that law of nature to which, in the end, the rebel necks must bow? What power is it that drives young spirits, trailing clouds of glory, into the austere refuge of morality and character? Suppose, to begin with, we call it the law of self-preservation, individual and racial. That has a formidable sound. And, indeed, it is a formidable power. When we feel its wolfish breath at our back, we lighten our impedimenta; we stiffen our sinews; we lengthen our stride; we fix our gaze on the patch of light beyond the woods; and we become careless of wayside flowers.

Some of us, to be sure, seek for a time, to ignore or evade it. An occasional college boy, stimulated to believe that he is the maker of his own destiny, listens with wonder and eager curiosity to a lecturer commending the "cultural ideal" of Goethe—the seductive notion of the continuous growth and free unfolding of a many-sided personality, developed at all points. He may even, through his undergraduate years, revel a little in his own versatility and caress his multifarious un-formed tastes and talents. By extending the years of schooling and popularizing higher education, by bobbing our hair and keeping our faces clean shaven, and by reading the novels of undergraduate authors and taking counsel of their tailors, a few of us manage to extend the plastic age and the experi-mental and uncertain appearance and opinions of adolescence well into our third decade.

But to pass for a youth beyond that point, requires far more money, leisure, and freedom from the cares of this world than are ordinarily to be had upon the economic tableland of democracy. In a society where the most that the average per-son can expect is to start without a handicap, the occupations of the first four decades are essentially predetermined. Our average man has his work cut out for him if he keeps abreast of normal expectations; and to keep abreast, he is impelled by the strongest instincts in him.

There is nothing forbidding or externally formidable in the deputy powers that take him captive, and abduct him out of the irresponsible company of youth. Quite the contrary. He sees the invitation and the promise of life in a pair of grey eyes and white hands, and he runs to meet them, and while he is explaining in a moment of youthful intoxication, how sweet earth would be if Maytime would last forever and gipsying were in fashion, he is bound hand and foot, and delivered to a power which effectively terminates his roving in the Romany Rye. The law of self-preservation has him in thrall. Or to put the matter in plain terms, he must educate himself and pay for his education; he must find a profession; he must marry and pay for his wife; he must start a family and pay for his family; he must buy a lot and build a house; he must pay for his life insurance and start a fund for his old age; he must begin the education of his children. In this homespun garb the awful "law of nature" enforces itself before he knows what has got hold of him.

He enters upon these tasks with the unreflective gusto of youth—a fluent, unformed, unchanneled energy. All the "boys" are doing likewise. All the prizes are attached to doing likewise. As the heat of the contest heightens, he strips himself one by one of the recreations and accomplishments through which in his vernal days the mounting diffusive sap of his youth burst briefly into flower: dancing, acting, singing, mandolin-playing, drawing, verse-writing, tramping, shooting, camping, tennis, and the rest. He pulls himself together. He concentrates. He specializes. "Three meals a day," he says, "my work, my pipe, and no interruptions!" He is nothing but a driving energy. He drives so hard that the bloom of life is brushed off in his passage. Yet for a long time he does not cease to think of himself as one of the "young fellows." The very intensity and singleness of his effort is due, in fact, to a youthful pride and doggedness developed under a sense that the Old Men are watching the youngster critically.

But by and by comes a season when a lot of things, unimpressive singly, happen together and become impressive. His wife gaily discovers three grey hairs, one above his left ear, two above his right. "Yes," says his daughter, kissing a spot on the back of his head, "but Dad will never be grey!" At about the same time he discovers that he needs a stronger pair of glasses. His dentist, who has hitherto passed him easily through the semi-annual inspection, now suggests an extensive plan of bridge construction. He still feels quite fit; but on the way home he mutters to himself with a playful grimness: "A-ha! Baldness, Blindness, and Toothlessness are scouting out a position before the main army of Death." Then he notices with a realizing eye how tall his sons are growing, and how independent, and how—well, he would call it saucy, if they were not so tall. He has to contradict them firmly because—well, they have no business at their age to know so much more about the point than their father. But he fails to feel impressive in the assertion of his authority, for even when they seem to assent, he has a subtle uneasy sense that they are merely humoring him, with an indulgent filial smile in their sleeves. Presently he overhears one of them referring to him as The Old Man.

"The Old Man! Good Heavens!" he exclaims. "How old am I? Forty?—Forty is nothing, nowadays. President Eliot went bicycling before breakfast, at seventy-five. Lounsbury played the New England tennis champion at seventy-five. At eighty-five or ninety Uncle Joe Cannon and Chauncey Depew had just got started. At forty, a man is a mere fledgling." So he soothes and flatters himself. But, in this season of disillusion, another fact gradually establishes itself in his awakened consciousness—a fact full of pathos and mystery: he discovers that the unchallengeably young people really prefer their own society to his, while he himself prefers their society to that of the men of forty. There is nothing like that to plunge a sword into a man's viscera and twist it about in the wound. He tries to conceal his hurt. He rallies his gaiety and makes a desperate effort to retrace his steps and rejoin the merrymakers who are going a-Maying. But even when he presents himself in scenes dewy with sentiment, sparkling with young desires, and rich with dreams, somehow he does not seem to "enter in." He feels—he confides it soberly and in the utmost confidence to his own heart—he feels like Leonard Merrick's hero in quest of his youth, who fell asleep, and snored softly—didn't he?—while his old sweetheart bent over him, bitterly, in the trysting hour.

He feels "the fierce necessity to feel" but lacks the power. What is the trouble with him? He knows. He knows. He faces a tragedy. It isn't that he is forty. Other men have been forty. 'Tis common, Madam! His tragedy is that he possesses a character. No: his character possesses him. He is imprisoned in his morality and his character. He overhears the respectful rumor of his contemporaries: "Yes, Brown has achieved a character. We can count on Brown. We know where he stands."

The object of this applause inwardly squirms. He squirms on the pointed truth in what they say. He himself knows where he stands: he is a man of property, he is a professional man, he is a voter and taxpayer, he is the husband of one of the caryatides of society, he is the father of four children, he is one of four men with plates who walk up the aisles of the church in frock coats on Sunday morning.

He acts from those positions. He acts only from them. His feeling is adequate to those positions. But he feels nothing more. So this is what is called "achieving a character." He has "achieved" nothing of the sort. This prison-house is not the edifice of his will; it was built about him by his destiny. It is nothing but his circumstances catching him in a trap. This character is a highwayman. It came up behind him, like a thief in the night. It cried "Halt! Stick 'em up!" And there he stopped; and delivered up his youth; and went no further. And that is why men know where he stands, and can count on him.

Yes: they can count on him—and so they don't count him any longer. If he speaks in public, his friends don't come out: they know well enough what he will say. If he publishes a book, no one buys it; they have the book that he wrote ten years ago. If he is absent from a committee, no one misses his counsel: any one of the members can easily present his "views." If a subscription list is circulating, they put him down for ten dollars without consulting him: he always gives ten dollars. If his own children conceive any enterprise, tainted with novelty, scandal, or promise of vivid interest, they first conspire with their mother to placate him, knowing for cei - tain that "Dad will oppose it." Yes: he can be counted on. He is no longer an incalculable force. He is an *homme rangé*. He is a character. He is fixed at forty—like a monument, like a gravestone, with one blank line waiting to mark the formal decease and burial of his body.

Isn't it true that when one begins to stop growing one begins to die? When did he begin to die? He looks backward to discover the point at which his vital force began to draw in from the branches to the trunk and gradually retire towards the earth. He looks backward thirty years—thirty-five years. There was a time, back there, very early in his life—say between his fifth and his tenth years—when every morning multiplied his budding interests, and the green young shoots of his curiosity pushed eagerly into "the blooming buzzing confusion" of the universe.

Between five and ten he was a Roosevelt for versatility—yet in that respect he was exactly like every normal child! There was not a dull page from table of contents to index in the whole of life's sweet scented manuscript. All arts, all sciences, all religions, all philosophies, all histories, all customs of life "intrigued" him.

He modeled in clay, he painted in water colors, he composed unrecorded melodies, he participated in the folk dancing called "London Bridge Is Falling Down"; he was an "out-of-door naturalist" and explorer of rivers, caves, and valleys; he was a collector and classifier of stamps, minerals, coins, curiosities from the Holy Land, insects, flowers, birds' eggs; he shuddered under the knife of Aztec sacrifice; he learned from the Koran that Paradise is under the shadow of the sword; he wrote to his grandfather for a copy of the Hebrew alphabet that he might study the Decalogue in God's own tongue; he dipped into "The Light of Asia"; he studied idolatry in the old Chinese quarter; he was interested in Jesus; he was knocked down by experimenting with the current in a trolley wire; he manufactured gunpowder, and cannon from brass shotgun shells; he molded bullets; he tanned squirrel skins; he attempted to stuff birds; he made maps of pulped brown butcher's paper; he prepared medicines from herbs; he distilled liquor and attempted to petrify wood; he built houses and trapezes and dams and attempted to build a lake; he raised pigeons, chickens, rabbits, and snakes; he drilled for oil; he examined openings in the fruit industry, lawnmowing, pickling, floriculture, printing, and the newspaper business; but most of all his heart was set on gold-mining, exploring Indian graves, and swinging a rawhide lariat from a saddle of Spanish leather while spurring a lean broncho after the mavericks scurrying through the sagebrush of a western mesa.

Suppressed desires? Not at all! He found time and means and energy for all this rich and various life by the time he was thirteen. He has squeezed all the juice from those oranges. But what has he done since? Soon after thirteen, a drouth descended upon the tropical exuberance of his experience. The lighter foliage of his life withered up. Education fell upon him like a blight, and the luxuriant quick blossoms of childhood were scattered. His sensuous contacts with the world diminished with amazing rapidity. He began to be concerned with words rather than with things; and things shrivelled and dried and disappeared under the labels that he was taught to attach to them. His education, he perceives, operated like the old-fashioned dentistry, by killing off and extracting the nerves, so that a man in middle life should find himself with a set of dead and, theoretically, untroublesome bones in his mouth. (Only, it seems, these dead things festered.) His education was designed to make out of a piece of living matter a substantial economic block, useful for home-building, useful in the fundamental structure of society. He had been taken, so to speak, out of his own hands by the race, and had been thrust, half alive, into a chink of the wall, and on him an inscription had been carved: "Here lies a solid character. *Requiescat in pace.*"

At just about this point one may predict with considerable assurance either that nothing at all will happen, or that something like a miracle will happen. Either Brown will quietly resign himself to being Brown for the rest of his days; or Brown will become that most dangerous type of rebel, a middle-aged rebel, and attempt to become something new and strange.

Let us assume first that at forty there is little rebellion left in this solid character. After a brief period of wistfulness, he surrenders to the indolence which men flatter with the name of destiny. He settles firmly down at the point of view to which his circumstances have driven him. In that case, there is a fair likelihood that in his leisure hours he will become a tedious utilitarian critic of his own upbringing. He will complain of the liberal education which unsettles youth and fills it with insatiable hungers by attempting to develop a general human personality instead of a sharp vocational instrument. He will turn around upon his Alma Mater and condemn her harshly for not having cut away, at an earlier age, all the young unprofitable shoots of his general human curiosity. He may declare that the fault of his education was its failure to make him an even keener, harder, sharper vocational instrument than he is.

"What good," he will say, "have history and literature and philosophy ever done to me? You teachers pumped me full of culture. You filled me up with stuff about the Middles Ages and the Renaissance and the Reformation and the Puritan Revolution. You wasted my youth in talk about the real and the ideal and the good and the beautiful. You lured me into listening to symphonies and looking at pictures and vibrating to the pity and terror of tragic drama. You peopled the greenwood of my imagination with poetic figures of knights and ladies on great adventures and romantic quests. And then I married a fairly good cook and you sent me into the world to serve as a chemist in a dye works or to write advertising for toothpowder and laundry soap. My education was not practical. It didn't prepare me for life. It was no good. I have no use for it."

To this complaint, it should be remarked in passing, there is a retort which all "liberal" educators should learn to make. It runs something like this: "You say that your education is 'no good.' We reply, O solid businesslike character, that your life is 'no good.' Your life is not good because you built it too small to hold the best of your possessions. The trouble with you is that you wasted the wealth that we gave you; you let it rust and mildew in cellar and attic. You lacked ingenuity to use your capital. You have not learned how to employ your culture in your life. You have made no outlets for your education. Don't blame us if you can't draw Niagara through a brass faucet into the kitchen sink. As occasion serves, we shall continue to 'pump' culture into you. Perhaps bye and bye you will burst. We rather hope that you will. Then possibly something more exhilarating than a solid businesslike character can be made of the ruins and fragments of you. Perhaps a personality can be made of the pieces. At any rate there will be no great loss if you burst. On the whole, go ahead and burst. You really aren't worth saving."

But now let us assume the more enlivening of the possibilities: let us assume that a miracle happens. As Brown looks dismally out from the barred small window of his character upon his life, and sees that it is finished, suddenly his past breaks away from him, as Sicily broke away from Italy, and a gulf yawns between. There is evidence that this thing does happen. His past is no longer his; it has become a part of human history. It has become a dramatic spectacle; sitting in the box of his character he regards it as it were across footlights, with spectatorial detachment. He can reexamine it now without shame or vanity or repentance. It interests him no longer as conduct waiting for the Judgment Day but as food for intellectual and aesthetic curiosity. He now finds a use for his culture in understanding, not judging, the whole of the human spectacle. He wheels a speculative eye upon his coevals— those dreary "substantial characters" who now for so many years have been giving one another, as Thoreau complained, the same old bite of the same musty old cheese that they are. They, too, have become dramatic spectacles, each one with its own individual savour! And his wife and the four children? The moment that he stops worrying about that abstract line which is the shortest distance between two points, he perceives at last the full colour and fragrance and taste of his relation to them.

What does all this mean? It means that at forty, when a man seems hermetically enclosed in his character, an angel may just possibly unbar the door, and, leaving his possessive, aggressive body sleeping there, let his spirit out for the recognition and appreciation of a new life. So long as he wished to possess and direct the world, the world erected barriers against him, and progressively shut him in. As soon as he exacts nothing of it, it gives him all—all its qualities for his discrimination and delectation. There is no way to return to his youth by retracing the caterpillar progress of the senses or by the renovation of cells that have become clogged with the hard deposit of years. But all those old interests which he had thought dead are now reborn with wings. He can return to his past, he can flit into his future, with the swift flight of a butterfly. While he seems to sleep in the barred prison-house of his character, and his old sweetheart weeps over the baldheaded, round-waisted man of property gently snoring there, he perchance has discovered that she can't be met at the old trysting place any more, and has pushed on up the highroad to the detour of pure poetic contemplation where all her fair qualities, her joy and blitheness and beauty, are recollected in tranquillity. Out of the death of the possessive passion, a rebirth of the mind and imagination!

If this miracle has happened, he feels, at forty, the possibility not merely of a new life but of a new kind of life opening before him. He sees the necessity of revising the "theory of education." At forty, instead of killing off the nerves, one should be occupied in reviving the spirits. Instead of closing old doors, one should be cutting new windows. Instead of sitting down and going to sleep at his own point of view, he should hunt for new ones, if he has to go to China or Alaska or Tierra del Fuego to find them. What a man of forty needs to do is to re-examine his metaphors. Let us try our hammer on this "solid character."

We spend our lives in a quarry of words. We immure our

selves behind a wall of images. We talk of characters; immediately the mallet and chisel are in our hands. We are sculptors, and our subjects are unhewn blocks of marble, and the form we seek is imposed from without. The chips fly. Chips of what? Is the imposition of marble qualities upon flesh and blood responsible for that grim and weary and hopeless look of the Old Man of the Mountain, which establishes itself at middle age upon faces once mobile and rosy? Has this entire theory of human sculpture a bearing upon the prevalence of ennui, rigor mortis, premature death, and petrification at forty? Is there a gleam of hope in a change of images?

"He built his house on a rock." Is that the best place for a house? Not if one cares for gardening. At forty, one is justified at least in enquiring whether what looked like a white rock was only a ribbon of foam. There is current an alternative set of images, which takes us out of the stone-quarry and the graveyard and away from the tedious refrain, *Requiescat in pace.*

Our lives are a bright-flowing mist of days and nights. Our blood is a swift-winding river. Our flesh is a changing flower. There is a season of buds and a season of fruit and a season of wine and perfume. And after the vintage, there are memories and dreams.

Is there no kinetic and flowing character—no form imposable upon wind and water: such form as the cloud takes in the West, such color; such shapes as life transiently rests in, rising from seed to blossom?

Come, let us make a new set of maxims, not for youths in their twenties with houses to build and children to educate, but for men of forty and upwards who are growing tired of one another and yet are not quite ready to die:

Unfold, leaf by leaf.

Become more and more intimate with life.

Ask no cold question of any joyous thing.

Go to all living things gently, listening for the wonder of the breath and the heartbeat.

Ask all successful and happy creatures for a clue.

Study all lovely things, with docility seeking their principle of beauty.

Consider whether it is better to change and be living than to be unchanged and dead.

Eschew pedantry and make much of fine art: it possesses a secret of eternal life.

Be your residence urban or rural, there is no provincialism so narrow as that developed by the inveterate maintenance of your own *point of view*.

Push on into untrodden forests, up unexplored valleys, seeking new springs of refreshment, crying at the foot of every mountain ridge, "Let us see what is on the other side."

Virginia Woolf

1882 · 1941

*Virginia Woolf was the daughter of Sir Leslie
Stephen, noted biographer, editor, and critic. She
and her husband, Leonard Woolf, established the
Hogarth Press and became central figures in a
group of writers which included Lytton Strachey,
E. M. Forster, the Sitwells, and J. M. Keynes.
Her novels reveal great concern with symbols and
with psychological processes, and her essays
contain some of the most discerning literary
criticism of her generation.*

MODERN FICTION

IN MAKING ANY SURVEY, even the freest and
loosest, of modern fiction it is difficult not to
take it for granted that the modern practice of the art is somehow an improvement upon the old. With their simple tools
and primitive materials, it might be said, Fielding did well and
Jane Austen even better, but compare their opportunities with
ours! Their masterpieces certainly have a strange air of simplicity. And yet the analogy between literature and the process, to choose an example, of making motor cars scarcely holds
good beyond the first glance. It is doubtful whether in the
course of the centuries, though we have learnt much about
making machines, we have learnt anything about making
literature. We do not come to write better; all that we can be
said to do is to keep moving, now a little in this direction, now
in that, but with a circular tendency should the whole course

of the track be viewed from a sufficiently lofty pinnacle. It need scarcely be said that we make no claim to stand, even momentarily, upon that vantage ground. On the flat, in the crowd, half blind with dust, we look back with envy to those happier warriors, whose battle is won and whose achievements wear so serene an air of accomplishment that we can scarcely refrain from whispering that the fight was not so fierce for them as for us. It is for the historian of literature to decide; for him to say if we are now beginning or ending or standing in the middle of a great period of prose fiction, for down in the plain little is visible. We only know that certain gratitudes and hostilities inspire us; that certain paths seem to lead to fertile land, others to the dust and the desert; and of this perhaps it may be worth while to attempt some account.

Our quarrel, then, is not with the classics, and if we speak of quarrelling with Mr. Wells, Mr. Bennett, and Mr. Galsworthy it is partly that by the mere fact of their existence in the flesh their work has a living, breathing, everyday imperfection which bids us take what liberties with it we choose. But it is also true that, while we thank them for a thousand gifts, we reserve our unconditional gratitude for Mr. Hardy, for Mr. Conrad, and in a much lesser degree for the Mr. Hudson, of *The Purple Land*, *Green Mansions*, and *Far Away and Long Ago*. Mr. Wells, Mr. Bennett, and Mr. Galsworthy have excited so many hopes and disappointed them so persistently that our gratitude largely takes the form of thanking them for having shown us what they might have done but have not done; what we certainly could not do, but as certainly, perhaps, do not wish to do. No single phrase will sum up the charge or grievance which we have to bring against a mass of work so large in its volume and embodying so many qualities, both admirable and the reverse. If we tried to formulate our meaning in one word we should say that these three writers are materialists. It is because they are concerned not with the spirit but with the body that they have disappointed us, and left us with the feeling that the sooner English fiction turns its back upon them, as politely as may be, and marches, if only into the desert, the better for its soul. Naturally, no single word reaches the centre of three separate targets. In the case of Mr. Wells it falls notably wide of the mark. And yet even with him it indicates to our thinking the fatal alloy in his genius, the great clod of clay that has got itself mixed up with the purity of his inspiration. But Mr. Bennett is perhaps the worst culprit of the three, inasmuch as he is by far the best workman. He can make a book so well constructed and solid in its craftsmanship that it is difficult for the most exacting of critics to see through what chink or crevice decay can creep in. There is not so much as a draught between the frames of the windows, or a crack in the boards. And yet—if life should refuse to live there? That is a risk which the creator of *The Old Wives' Tale*, George Cannon, Edwin Clayhanger, and hosts of other figures, may well claim to have surmounted. His characters live abundantly, even unexpectedly, but it remains to ask how do they live, and what do they live for? More and more they seem to us, deserting even the well-built villa in the Five Towns, to spend their time in some softly padded first-class railway carriage, pressing bells and buttons innumerable; and the destiny to which they travel so luxuriously becomes more and more unquestionably an eternity of bliss spent in the very best hotel in Brighton. It can scarcely be said of Mr. Wells that he is a materialist in the sense that he takes too much delight in the solidity of his fabric. His mind is too generous in its sympathies to allow him to spend much time in making things shipshape and substantial. He is a materialist from sheer goodness of heart, taking upon his shoulders the work that ought to have been discharged by Government officials, and in the plethora of his ideas and facts scarcely having leisure to realise, or forgetting to think important, the crudity and coarseness of his human beings. Yet what more damaging criticism can there be both of his earth and of his Heaven than that they are to be inhabited here and hereafter by his Joans and his Peters? Does not the inferiority of their natures tarnish whatever institutions and ideals may be provided for them by the generosity of their creator? Nor, profoundly though we respect the integrity and humanity of Mr. Galsworthy, shall we find what we seek in his pages.

If we fasten, then, one label on all these books, on which is one word, materialists, we mean by it that they write of unimportant things; that they spend immense skill and immense industry making the trivial and the transitory appear the true and the enduring.

We have to admit that we are exacting, and, further, that we find it difficult to justify our discontent by explaining what it is that we exact. We frame our question differently at different times. But it reappears most persistently as we drop the finished novel on the crest of a sigh—Is it worth while? What is the point of it all? Can it be that owing to one of those little deviations which the human spirit seems to make from time to time Mr. Bennett has come down with his magnificent apparatus for catching life just an inch or two on the wrong side? Life escapes; and perhaps without life nothing else is worth while. It is a confession of vagueness to have to make use of such a figure as this, but we scarcely better the matter by speaking, as critics are prone to do, of reality. Admitting the vagueness which afflicts all criticism of novels, let us hazard the opinion that for us at this moment the form of fiction most in vogue more often misses than secures the thing we seek. Whether we call it life or spirit, truth or reality, this, the essential thing, has moved off, or on, and refuses to be contained any longer in such ill-fitting vestments as we provide. Nevertheless, we go on perseveringly, conscientiously, constructing our two and thirty chapters after a design which more and more ceases to resemble the vision in our minds. So much of the enormous labour of proving the solidity, the likeness to life, of the story is not merely labour thrown away but labour misplaced to the extent of obscuring and blotting out the light of the conception. The writer seems constrained, not by his own free will but by some powerful and unscrupulous tyrant who has him in thrall to provide a plot, to provide comedy, tragedy, love, interest, and an air of probability embalming the whole so impeccable that if all his figures were to come to life they would find themselves dressed down to the last button of their coats in the fashion of the hour. The tyrant is obeyed; the novel is done to a turn. But sometimes, more and more often as time goes by, we suspect a momentary doubt, a spasm of rebellion, as the pages fill themselves in the customary way. Is life like this? Must novels be like this?

Look within and life, it seems, is very far from being "like this." Examine for a moment an ordinary mind on an ordinary day. The mind receives a myriad impressions—trivial, fantastic, evanescent, or engraved with the sharpness of steel. From all sides they come, an incessant shower of innumerable atoms; and as they fall, as they shape themselves into the life of Monday or Tuesday, the accent falls differently from of old; the moment of importance came not here but there; so that if a writer were a free man and not a slave, if he could write what he chose, not what he must, if he could base his work upon his own feeling and not upon convention, there would be no plot, no comedy, no tragedy, no love interest or catastrophe in the accepted style, and perhaps not a single button sewn on as the Bond Street tailors would have it. Life is not a series of gig lamps symmetrically arranged; but a luminous halo, a semi-transparent envelope surrounding us from the beginning of consciousness to the end. Is it not the task of the novelist to convey this varying, this unknown and uncircumscribed spirit, whatever aberration or complexity it may display, with as little mixture of the alien and external as possible? We are not pleading merely for courage and sincerity; we are suggesting that the proper stuff of fiction is a little other than custom would have us believe it.

It is, at any rate, in some such fashion as this that we seek to define the quality which distinguishes the work of several young writers, among whom Mr. James Joyce is the most notable, from that of their predecessors. They attempt to come closer to life, and to preserve more sincerely and exactly what interests and moves them, even if to do so they must discard most of the conventions which are commonly observed by the novelist. Let us record the atoms as they fall upon the mind in the order in which they fall, let us trace the pattern, however disconnected and incoherent in appearance, which each sight or incident scores upon the consciousness. Let us not take it for granted that life exists more fully in what is commonly thought big than in what is commonly thought small. Any one who has read *The Portrait of the Artist as a Young Man* or, what promises to be a far more interesting work, *Ulysses*,[1] now appearing in the *Little Review*, will have hazarded some theory of this nature as to Mr. Joyce's intention. On our part, with such a fragment before us, it is hazarded rather than affirmed; but whatever the intention of the whole there can be no question but that it is of the utmost sincerity and that the result, difficult or unpleasant as we may judge it, is undeniably important. In contrast with those whom we have called materialists Mr. Joyce is spiritual; he is concerned at all costs to reveal the flickerings of that innermost flame which flashes its messages through the brain, and in order to preserve it he disregards with complete courage whatever seems to him adventitious, whether it be probability, or coherence or any other of these signposts which for generations have served to support the imagination of a reader when called upon to imagine what he can neither touch nor see. The scene in the cemetery, for instance, with its brilliancy, its sordidity, its incoherence, its sudden lightning flashes of significance, does undoubtedly come so close to the quick of the mind that, on a first reading at any rate, it is difficult not to acclaim a masterpiece. If we want life itself here, surely we have it. Indeed, we find ourselves fumbling rather awkwardly if we try to say what else we wish, and for what reason a work of such originality yet fails to compare, for we must take high examples, with *Youth* or *The Mayor of Casterbridge*. It fails because of the comparative poverty of the writer's mind, we might say simply and have done with it. But it is possible to press a little further and wonder whether we may not refer our sense of being in a bright yet narrow room, confined and shut in, rather than enlarged and set free, to some limitation imposed by the method as well as by the mind. Is it the method that inhibits the creative power? Is it due to the method that we feel neither jovial nor magnanimous, but centred in a self which, in spite of its

[1] *Written April, 1919.*

tremor of susceptibility, never embraces or creates what is outside itself and beyond? Does the emphasis laid, perhaps didactically, upon indecency, contribute to the effect of something angular and isolated? Or is it merely that in any effort of such originality it is much easier, for contemporaries especially, to feel what it lacks than to name what it gives? In any case it is a mistake to stand outside examining "methods." Any method is right, every method is right, that expresses what we wish to express, if we are writers; that brings us closer to the novelist's intention if we are readers. This method has the merit of bringing us closer to what we were prepared to call life itself; did not the reading of *Ulysses* suggest how much of life is excluded or ignored, and did it not come with a shock to open *Tristram Shandy* or even *Pendennis* and be by them convinced that there are not only other aspects of life, but more important ones into the bargain.

However this may be, the problem before the novelist at present, as we suppose it to have been in the past, is to contrive means of being free to set down what he chooses. He has to have the courage to say that what interests him is no longer "this" but "that": out of "that" alone must he construct his work. For the moderns "that," the point of interest, lies very likely in the dark places of psychology. At once, therefore, the accent falls a little differently; the emphasis is upon something hitherto ignored; at once a different outline of form becomes necessary, difficult for us to grasp, incomprehensible to our predecessors. No one but a modern, perhaps no one but a Russian, would have felt the interest of the situation which Tchekov has made into the short story which he calls "Gusev." Some Russian soldiers lie ill on board a ship which is taking them back to Russia. We are given a few scraps of their talk and some of their thoughts; then one of them dies and is carried away; the talk goes on among the others for a time, until Gusev himself dies, and looking "like a carrot or a radish" is thrown overboard. The emphasis is laid upon such unexpected places that at first it seems as if there were no emphasis at all; and then, as the eyes accustom themselves to twilight and discern the shapes of things in a room we see how complete the story is, how profound, and how truly in obedience to his vision Tchekov has chosen this, that, and the other, and placed them together to compose something new. But it is impossible to say "this is comic," or "that is tragic," nor are we certain, since short stories, we have been taught, should be brief and conclusive, whether this, which is vague and inconclusive, should be called a short story at all.

The most elementary remarks upon modern English fiction can hardly avoid some mention of the Russian influence, and if the Russians are mentioned one runs the risk of feeling that to write of any fiction save theirs is waste of time. If we want understanding of the soul and heart where else shall we find it of comparable profundity? If we are sick of our own materialism the least considerable of their novelists has by right of birth a natural reverence for the human spirit. "Learn to make yourself akin to people. . . . But let this sympathy be not with the mind—for it is easy with the mind—but with the heart, with love towards them." In every great Russian writer we seem to discern the features of a saint, if sympathy for the sufferings of others, love towards them, endeavour to reach some goal worthy of the most exacting demands of the spirit constitute saintliness. It is the saint in them which confounds us with a feeling of our own irreligious triviality, and turns so many of our famous novels to tinsel and trickery. The conclusions of the Russian mind, thus comprehensive and compassionate, are inevitably, perhaps, of the utmost sadness. More accurately indeed we might speak of the inconclusiveness of the Russian mind. It is the sense that there is no answer, that if honestly examined life presents question after question which must be left to sound on and on after the story is over in hopeless interrogation that fills us with a deep, and finally it may be with a resentful, despair. They are right perhaps; unquestionably they see further than we do and without our gross impediments of vision. But perhaps we see something that escapes them, or why should this voice of protest mix itself with our gloom? The voice of protest is the voice of another and an ancient civilisation which seems to have bred in us the instinct to enjoy and fight rather than to suffer and understand. English fiction from Sterne to Meredith bears witness to our natural delight in humour and comedy, in the beauty of earth, in the activities of the intellect, and in the splendour of the body. But any deductions that we may draw from the comparison of two fictions so immeasurably far apart are futile save indeed as they flood us with a view of the infinite possibilities of the art and remind us that there is no limit to the horizon, and that nothing—no "method," no experiment, even of the wildest—is forbidden, but only falsity and pretence. "The proper stuff of fiction" does not exist; everything is the proper stuff of fiction, every feeling, every thought; every quality of brain and spirit is drawn upon; no perception comes amiss. And if we can imagine the art of fiction come alive and standing in our midst, she would undoubtedly bid us break her and bully her, as well as honour and love her, for so her youth is renewed and her sovereignty assured.

D. H. Lawrence

1885 · 1930

*David Herbert Lawrence was born in England and
lived in many parts of the world in search of peace
of mind, which he never found. He wrote
prodigiously in various forms—novels, short stories,
poems, plays, travel essays, literary criticism, and
psychological studies. Some of his books,
particularly* Lady Chatterley's Lover *(1928),
involved him in literary controversy and even
scandal. While the tranquillity he sought in such
varied regions as Italy, Mexico, Australia, and New
Mexico eluded him, he recorded his experiences in
each temporary home with vividness and beauty
that become increasingly apparent to new readers.*

THE SPIRIT OF PLACE

WE LIKE TO THINK of the old-fashioned
American classics as children's books. Just
childishness, on our part.

The old American art-speech contains an alien quality,
which belongs to the American continent and to nowhere else.
But, of course, so long as we insist on reading the books as
children's tales, we miss all that.

One wonders what the proper high-brow Romans of the
third and fourth or later centuries read into the strange utterances of Lucretius or Apuleius or Tertullian, Augustine or
Athanasius. The uncanny voice of Iberian Spain, the weird-
ness of old Carthage, the passion of Libya and North Africa;

you may bet the proper old Romans never heard these at all. They read old Latin inference over the top of it, as we read old European inference over the top of Poe or Hawthorne.

It is hard to hear a new voice, as hard as it is to listen to an unknown language. We just don't listen. There is a new voice in the old American classics. The world has declined to hear it, and has blabbed about children's stories.

Why?—Out of fear. The world fears a new experience more than it fears anything. Because a new experience displaces so many old experiences. And it is like trying to use muscles that have perhaps never been used, or that have been going stiff for ages. It hurts horribly.

The world doesn't fear a new idea. It can pigeon-hole any idea. But it can't pigeon-hole a real new experience. It can only dodge. The world is a great dodger, and the Americans the greatest. Because they dodge their own very selves. There is a new feeling in the old American books, far more than there is in the modern American books, which are pretty empty of any feeling, and proud of it. There is a "different" feeling in the old American classics. It is the shifting over from the old psyche to something new, a displacement. And displacements hurt. This hurts. So we try to tie it up, like a cut finger. Put a rag around it.

It is a cut, too. Cutting away the old emotions and consciousness. Don't ask what is left.

Art-speech is the only truth. An artist is usually a damned liar, but his art, if it be art, will tell you the truth of his day. And that is all that matters. Away with eternal truth. Truth lives from day to day, and the marvellous Plato of yesterday is chiefly bosh to-day.

The old American artists were hopeless liars. But they were artists, in spite of themselves. Which is more than you can say of most living practitioners.

And you can please yourself, when you read *The Scarlet Letter*, whether you accept what that sugary, blue-eyed little darling of a Hawthorne has to say for himself, false as all darlings are, or whether you read the impeccable truth of his art-speech.

The curious thing about art-speech is that it prevaricates so terribly, I mean it tells such lies. I suppose because we always all the time tell ourselves lies. And out of a pattern of lies art weaves the truth. Like Dostoevsky posing as a sort of Jesus, but most truthfully revealing himself all the while as a little horror.

Truly art is a sort of subterfuge. But thank God for it, we can see through the subterfuge if we choose. Art has two great functions. First, it provides an emotional experience. And then, if we have the courage of our own feelings, it becomes a mine of practical truth. We have had the feelings *ad nauseam*. But we've never dared dig the actual truth out of them, the truth that concerns us, whether it concerns our grandchildren or not.

The artist usually sets out—or used to—to point a moral and adorn a tale. The tale, however, points the other way, as a rule. Two blankly opposing morals, the artist's and the tale's. Never trust the artist. Trust the tale. The proper function of a critic is to save the tale from the artist who created it.

Now we know our business in these studies; saving the American tale from the American artist.

Let us look at this American artist first. How did he ever get to America, to start with? Why isn't he a European still, like his father before him?

Now listen to me, don't listen to him. He'll tell you the lie you expect. Which is partly your fault for expecting it.

He didn't come in search of freedom of worship. England had more freedom of worship in the year 1700 than America had. Won by Englishmen who wanted freedom, and so stopped at home and fought for it. And got it. Freedom of worship? Read the history of New England during the first century of its existence.

Freedom anyhow? The land of the free! This the land of the free! Why, if I say anything that displeases them, the free mob will lynch me, and that's my freedom. Free? Why I have never been in any country where the individual has such an abject fear of his fellow countrymen. Because, as

I say, they are free to lynch him the moment he shows he is not one of them.

No, no, if you're so fond of the truth about Queen Victoria, try a little about yourself.

Those Pilgrim Fathers and their successors never came here for freedom of worship. What did they set up when they got here? Freedom, would you call it?

They didn't come for freedom. Or if they did, they sadly went back on themselves.

All right then, what did they come for? For lots of reasons. Perhaps least of all in search of freedom of any sort: positive freedom, that is.

They came largely to get *away*—that most simple of motives. To get away. Away from what? In the long run, away from themselves. Away from everything. That's why most people have come to America, and still do come. To get away from everything they are and have been.

"Henceforth be masterless."

Which is all very well, but it isn't freedom. Rather the reverse. A hopeless sort of constraint. It is never freedom till you find something you really *positively want to be*. And people in America have always been shouting about the things they are *not*. Unless of course they are millionaires, made or in the making.

And after all there is a positive side to the movement. All that vast flood of human life that has flowed over the Atlantic in ships from Europe to America has not flowed over simply on a tide of revulsion from Europe and from the confinements of the European ways of life. This revulsion was, and still is, I believe, the prime motive in emigration. But there was some cause, even for the revulsion.

It seems as if at times man had a frenzy for getting away from any control of any sort. In Europe the old Christianity was the real master. The Church and the true aristocracy bore the responsibility for the working out of the Christian ideals; a little irregularly, maybe, but responsible nevertheless.

Mastery, kingship, fatherhood had their power destroyed at the time of the Renaissance.

And it was precisely at this moment that the great drift over the Atlantic started. What were men drifting away from? The old authority of Europe? Were they breaking the bonds of authority, and escaping to a new more absolute unrestrainedness? Maybe. But there was more to it.

Liberty is all very well, but men cannot live without masters. There is always a master. And men either live in glad obedience to the master they believe in, or they live in a frictional opposition to the master they wish to undermine. In America this frictional opposition has been the vital factor. It has given the Yankee his kick. Only the continual influx of more servile Europeans has provided America with an obedient labouring class. The true obedience never outlasting the first generation.

But there sits the old master, over in Europe. Like a parent. Somewhere deep in every American heart lies a rebellion against the old parenthood of Europe. Yet no American feels he has completely escaped its mastery. Hence the slow, smouldering patience of American opposition. The slow, smouldering, corrosive obedience to the old master Europe, the unwilling subject, the unremitting opposition.

Whatever else you are, be masterless.

> "Ca Ca Caliban
> Get a new master, be a new man."

Escaped slaves, we might say, people the republics of Liberia or Haiti. Liberia enough! Are we to look at America in the same way? A vast republic of escaped slaves. When you consider the hordes from eastern Europe, you might well say it: a vast republic of escaped slaves. But one dare not say this of the Pilgrim Fathers, and the great old body of idealist Americans, the modern Americans tortured with thought. A vast republic of escaped slaves. Look out, America! And a minority of earnest, self-tortured people.

The masterless.

> "Ca Ca Caliban
> Get a new master, be a new man."

What did the Pilgrim Fathers come for, then, when they came so gruesomely over the black sea? Oh, it was in a black spirit. A black revulsion from Europe, from the old authority of Europe, from kings and bishops and popes. And more. When you look into it, more. They were black, masterful men, they wanted something else. No kings, no bishops maybe. Even no God Almighty. But also, no more of this new "humanity" which followed the Renaissance. None of this new liberty which was to be so pretty in Europe. Something grimmer, by no means free-and-easy.

America has never been easy, and is not easy to-day. Americans have always been at a certain tension. Their liberty is a thing of sheer will, sheer tension: a liberty of THOU SHALT NOT. And it has been so from the first. The land of THOU SHALT NOT. Only the first commandment is: THOU SHALT NOT PRESUME TO BE A MASTER. Hence democracy.

"We are the masterless." That is what the American Eagle shrieks. It's a Hen-Eagle.

The Spaniards refused the post-Renaissance liberty of Europe. And the Spaniards filled most of America. The Yankees, too, refused, refused the post-Renaissance humanism of Europe. First and foremost, they hated masters. But under that, they hated the flowing ease of humour in Europe. At the bottom of the American soul was always a dark suspense, at the bottom of the Spanish-American soul the same. And this dark suspense hated and hates the old European spontaneity, watches it collapse with satisfaction.

Every continent has its own great spirit of place. Every people is polarized in some particular locality, which is home, the homeland. Different places on the face of the earth have different vital effluence, different vibration, different chemical exhalation, different polarity with different stars: call it what you like. But the spirit of place is a great reality. The Nile valley produced not only the corn, but the terrific religions of Egypt. China produces the Chinese, and will go on doing so. The Chinese in San Francisco will in time cease to be Chinese, for America is a great melting pot.

There was a tremendous polarity in Italy, in the city of Rome. And this seems to have died. For even places die. The Island of Great Britain had a wonderful terrestrial magnetism or polarity of its own, which made the British people. For the moment, this polarity seems to be breaking. Can England die? And what if England dies?

Men are less free than they imagine; ah, far less free. The freest are perhaps least free.

Men are free when they are in a living homeland, not when they are straying and breaking away. Men are free when they are obeying some deep, inward voice of religious belief. Obeying from within. Men are free when they belong to a living, organic, *believing* community, active in fulfilling some unfulfilled, perhaps unrealized purpose. Not when they are escaping to some wild west. The most unfree souls go west, and shout of freedom. Men are freest when they are most unconscious of freedom. The shout is a rattling of chains, always was.

Men are not free when they are doing just what they like. The moment you can do just what you like, there is nothing you care about doing. Men are only free when they are doing what the deepest self likes.

And there is getting down to the deepest self! It takes some diving.

Because the deepest self is way down, and the conscious self is an obstinate monkey. But of one thing we may be sure. If one wants to be free, one has to give up the illusion of doing what one likes, and seek what IT wishes done.

But before you can do what IT likes, you must first break the spell of the old mastery, the old IT.

Perhaps at the Renaissance, when kingship and fatherhood fell, Europe drifted into a very dangerous half-truth: of liberty and equality. Perhaps the men who went to America felt this, and so repudiated the old world altogether. Went one better than Europe. Liberty in America has meant so far the breaking away from *all* dominion. The true liberty will only begin when Americans discover IT, and proceed possibly to fulfil IT. IT being the deepest *whole* self of man, the self in its wholeness, not idealistic halfness.

That's why the Pilgrim Fathers came to America, then; and that's why we come. Driven by IT. We cannot see that invisible winds carry us, as they carry swarms of locusts, that invisible magnetism brings us as it brings the migrating birds to their unforeknown goal. But it is so. We are not the marvellous choosers and deciders we think we are. IT chooses for us, and decides for us. Unless of course we are just escaped slaves, vulgarly cocksure of our ready-made destiny. But if we are living people, in touch with the source, IT drives us and decides us. We are free only so long as we obey. When we run counter, and think we will do as we like, we just flee around like Orestes pursued by the Eumenides.

And still, when the great day begins, when Americans have at last discovered America and their own wholeness, still there will be the vast number of escaped slaves to reckon with, those who have no cocksure, ready-made destinies.

Which will win in America, the escaped slaves, or the new whole men?

The real American day hasn't begun yet. Or at least, not yet sunrise. So far it has been the false dawn. That is, in the progressive American consciousness there has been the one dominant desire, to do away with the old thing. Do away with masters, exalt the will of the people. The will of the people being nothing but a figment, the exalting doesn't count for much. So, in the name of the will of the people, get rid of masters. When you have got rid of masters, you are left with this mere phrase of the will of the people. Then you pause and bethink yourself, and try to recover your own wholeness.

So much for the conscious American motive, and for democracy over here. Democracy in America is just the tool with which the old mastery of Europe, the European spirit, is undermined. Europe destroyed, potentially, American democracy will evaporate. America will begin.

American consciousness has so far been a false dawn. The negative ideal of democracy. But underneath, and contrary to this open ideal, the first hints and revelations of IT. IT, the American whole soul.

You have got to pull the democratic and idealistic clothes off American utterance, and see what you can of the dusky body of IT underneath.

"Henceforth be masterless."

Henceforth be mastered.

Randolph Bourne

1886 · 1918

*Randolph Bourne, American essayist and journalist,
spent his short career working under great physical
handicaps. After graduating from Columbia
University in 1913, he went to Europe for a year of
study as holder of the Gilder Fellowship.
His liberal views on education, politics, and
society are brilliantly expressed in his* History of
a Literary Radical *(1920), from which
"One of Our Conquerors" is taken.*

ONE OF OUR CONQUERORS

WHEN DR. ALEXANDER MACKINTOSH BUTCHER was elected to the presidency of Pluribus University ten years ago, there was general agreement that in selecting a man who was not only a distinguished educator but an executive of marked business ability the trustees had done honor to themselves and their university as well as to the new president. For Dr. Butcher had that peculiar genius which would have made him as successful in Wall Street or in a governor's chair as in the classroom. Every alumnus of Pluribus knows the story told of the young Alexander Mackintosh Butcher, standing at the age of twenty-two at the threshold of a career. Eager, energetic, with a brilliant scholastic record behind him, it was difficult to decide into what profession he should throw his powerful talents. To his beloved and aged president the young man went for counsel. "My boy," said the good old man, "remember that no profession offers nobler opportunities for service to humanity than that of education." And what should he teach? "Philosophy is the noblest study of man." And a professor of philosophy the young Butcher speedily became.

Those who were so fortunate as to study philosophy under him at Pluribus will never forget how uncompromisingly he preached absolute idealism, the Good, the True and the Beautiful, or how witheringly he excoriated the mushroom philosophies which were springing up to challenge the eternal verities. I have heard his old students remark the secret anguish which must have been his when later, as president of the university, he was compelled to entertain the famous Swiss philosopher, Monsfilius, whose alluring empiricism was taking the philosophic world by storm.

Dr. Butcher's philosophic acuteness is only equaled by his political rectitude. Indeed, it is as philosopher-politician that he holds the unique place he does in our American life, injecting into the petty issues of the political arena the immutable principles of Truth. Early conscious of his duty as a man and a citizen, he joined the historic party which had earned the eternal allegiance of the nation by rescuing it from slavery. By faithful service to the chiefs of his state organization, first under the powerful Flatt, and later under the well-known Harnes, himself college-bred and a political philosopher of no mean merit, the young Dr. Butcher worked his way up through ward captain to the position of district leader. The practical example of Dr. Butcher, the scholar and educator, leaving the peace of his academic shades to carry the banner in the service of his party ideals of Prosperity and Protection has been an inspiration to thousands of educated men in these days of civic cowardice. When, three years ago, his long and faithful services were rewarded by the honor of second place on the Presidential ticket which swept the great states of Mormonia and Green Mountain, there were none of his friends and admirers who felt that the distinction was undeserved.

President Butcher is frequently called into the councils of the party whenever there are resolutions to be drawn up or statements of philosophic principle to be issued. He is in great demand also as chairman of state conventions, which his rare academic distinction lifts far above the usual level of such affairs. It was at one of these conventions that he made the memorable speech in which he drew the analogy between the immutability of Anglo-Saxon political institutions and the multiplication table. To the applause of the keen and hard-headed business men and lawyers who sat as delegates under him, he scored with matchless satire the idea of progress in politics, and demonstrated to their complete satisfaction that it was as absurd to tinker with the fundamentals of our political system as it would be to construct a new arithmetic. In such characteristic wisdom we have the intellectual caliber of the man.

This brilliant and profound address came only as the fruit of a lifetime of thought on political philosophy. President Butcher's treatise on "Why We Should Never Change Any Form of Government" has been worth more to thoughtful men than thousands of sermons on civic righteousness. No one who has ever heard President Butcher's rotund voice discuss in a public address "those ideas and practices which have been tried and tested by a thousand years of experience" will ever allow his mind to dwell again on the progressive and disintegrating tendencies of the day, nor will he have the heart again to challenge on any subject the "decent respect for the common opinions of mankind."

President Butcher's social philosophy is as sound as his political. The flexibility of his mind is shown in the fact that, although an immutabilist in politics, he is a staunch Darwinian in sociology. Himself triumphantly fit, he never wearies of expressing his robust contempt for the unfit who encumber the earth. His essay on "The Insurrection of the Maladjusted" is already a classic in American literature. The trenchant attack on modern social movements as the impudent revolt of the unfit against those who, by their personal merits and industry, have, like himself, achieved success, has been a grateful bulwark to thousands who might otherwise have been swept sentimentally from their moorings by those false guides who erect their own weakness and failure into a criticism of society.

Dr. Butcher's literary eminence has not only won him a chair in the American Academy of All the Arts, Sciences, and Philosophies, but has made him almost as well known abroad as at home. He has lectured before the learned societies of Lisbon on "The American at Home," and he has a wide circle of acquaintances in every capital in Europe. Most of the foreign universities have awarded him honorary degrees. In spite of his stout Americanism, Dr. Butcher has one of the most cosmopolitan of minds. His essay on "The Cosmopolitan Intellect" has been translated into every civilized language. With his admired friend, Owen Griffith, he has collaborated in the latter's endeavor to beat the swords of industrial exploitation into the ploughshares of universal peace. He has served in numerous capacities on Griffith's many peace boards and foundations, and has advised him widely and well how to distribute his millions so as to prevent the recurrence of war in future centuries.

Let it not be thought that, in recounting President Butcher's public life and services, I am minimizing his distinction as a university administrator. As executive of one of the largest universities in America, he has raised the position of college president to a dignity surpassed by scarcely any office except President of the United States. The splendid $125,000 mansion which President Butcher had the trustees of Pluribus build for him on the heights overlooking the city, where he entertains distinguished foreign guests with all the pomp worthy of his high office, is the precise measure both of the majesty with which he has endowed the hitherto relatively humble position, and the appreciation of a grateful university. The relations between President Butcher and the trustees of Pluribus have always been of the most beautiful nature. The warm and profound intellectual sympathy which he feels for the methods and practices of the financial and corporate world, and the extensive personal affiliations he has formed with its leaders, have made it possible to leave in his hands a large measure of absolute authority. Huge endowments have made Pluribus under President Butcher's rule one of the wealthiest of our higher institutions of learning. With a rare intuitive response to the spirit of the time, the President has labored to make it the biggest and most comprehensive of its kind. Already its schools are numbered by the dozens, its buildings by the scores, its instructors by the hundreds, its students by the thousands, its income by the millions, and its possessions by the tens of millions.

None who have seen President Butcher in the commencement exercises of Pluribus can ever forget the impressiveness of the spectacle. His resemblance to Henry VIII is more marked now that he has donned the crimson gown and flat hat of the famous English university which gave him the degree of LL.D. Seated in a high-backed chair—the historic chair of the first colonial president of Pluribus—surrounded by tier upon tier of his retinue of the thousand professors of the university, President Alexander Mackintosh Butcher presents the degrees, and in his emphatic voice warns the five thousand graduates before him against everything new, everything untried, everything untested.

Only one office could tempt President Butcher from his high estate. Yet even those enthusiastic alumni and those devoted professors who long to see him President of the United States have little hope of tempting him from his duties to his alma mater. Having set his hand to the plough, he must see Pluribus through her harvest season, and may God prosper the work! So, beloved of all, alumni and instructors alike, the idol of the undergraduates, a national oracle of Prosperity and Peace, President Butcher passes to a green old age, a truly Olympian figure of the time.

T. S. Eliot

1888 · ——

Thomas Stearns Eliot was born in St. Louis and educated at Harvard. After taking his master's degree in 1910, he traveled and studied abroad and soon took up residence in England. In 1927 he became a British citizen. The publication of The Waste Land *in 1922 made him the most conspicuous exponent of the poetry of intellectual defeatism and sterility, and the title of the poem has been used as a label for the period of the 1920's. His essays are characterized by the same excess of intellectuality and erudition that appears in his poems and deal with literary, critical, and social problems. They are always brilliant, crowded with allusion, and concentrated in style.*

TRADITION AND THE INDIVIDUAL TALENT

I

IN ENGLISH WRITING we seldom speak of tradition, though we occasionally apply its name in deploring its absence. We cannot refer to "the tradition" or to "a tradition"; at most, we employ the adjective in saying that the poetry of So-and-so is "traditional" or even "too traditional." Seldom, perhaps, does the word appear except in a phrase of censure. If otherwise, it is vaguely approbative, with the implication, as to the work approved, of some pleasing archaeological reconstruction. You can hardly make the word agreeable to English ears without this comfortable reference to the reassuring science of archaeology.

Reprinted from THE SACRED WOOD, by permission of the author and Methuen & Co., Ltd., London, England.

Certainly the word is not likely to appear in our appreciations of living or dead writers. Every nation, every race, has not only its own creative, but its own critical turn of mind; and is even more oblivious of the shortcomings and limitations of its critical habits than of those of its creative genius. We know, or think we know, from the enormous mass of critical writing that has appeared in the French language the critical method or habit of the French; we only conclude (we are such unconscious people) that the French are "more critical" than we, and sometimes even plume ourselves a little with the fact, as if the French were the less spontaneous. Perhaps they are; but we might remind ourselves that criticism is as inevitable as breathing, and that we should be none the worse for articulating what passes in our minds when we read a book and feel an emotion about it, for criticizing our own minds in their work of criticism. One of the facts that might come to light in this process is our tendency to insist, when we praise a poet, upon those aspects of his work in which he least resembles anyone else. In these aspects or parts of his work we pretend to find what is individual, what is the peculiar essence of the man. We dwell with satisfaction upon the poet's difference from his predecessors, especially his immediate predecessors; we endeavour to find something that can be isolated in order to be enjoyed. Whereas if we approach a poet without his prejudice we shall often find that not only the best, but the most individual parts of his work may be those in which the dead poets, his ancestors, assert their immortality most vigorously. And I do not mean the impressionable period of adolescence, but the period of full maturity.

Yet if the only form of tradition, of handing down, consisted in following the ways of the immediate generation before us in a blind or timid adherence to its successes, "tradition" should positively be discouraged. We have seen many such simple currents soon lost in the sand; and novelty is better than repetition. Tradition is a matter of much wider significance. It cannot be inherited, and if you want it you must obtain it by great labour. It involves, in the first place, the historical sense, which we may call nearly indispensable to anyone who would continue to be a poet beyond his twenty-fifth year; and the historical sense involves a perception, not only of the pastness of the past, but of its presence; the historical sense compels a man to write not merely with his own generation in his bones, but with a feeling that the whole of the literature of Europe from Homer and within it the whole of the literature of his own country has a simultaneous existence and composes a simultaneous order. This historical sense, which is a sense of the timeless as well as of the temporal and of the timeless and of the temporal together, is what makes a writer traditional. And it is at the same time what makes a writer most acutely conscious of his place in time, of his contemporaneity.

No poet, no artist of any art, has his complete meaning alone. His significance, his appreciation is the appreciation of his relation to the dead poets and artists. You cannot value him alone; you must set him, for contrast and comparison, among the dead. I mean this as a principle of aesthetic, not merely historical, criticism. The necessity that he shall conform, that he shall cohere, is not one-sided; what happens when a new work of art is created is something that happens simultaneously to all the works of art which preceded it. The existing monuments form an ideal order among themselves, which is modified by the introduction of the new (the really new) work of art among them. The existing order is complete before the new work arrives; for order to persist after the supervention of novelty, the *whole* existing order must be, if ever so slightly, altered; and so the relations, proportions, values of each work of art toward the whole are readjusted; and this is conformity between the old and the new. Whoever has approved this idea of order, of the form of European, of English literature, will not find it preposterous that the past should be altered by the present as much as the present is directed by the past. And the poet who is aware of this will be aware of great difficulties and responsibilities.

In a peculiar sense he will be aware also that he must inevitably be judged by the standards of the past. I say judged, not amputated, by them; not judged to be as good as, or worse or better than, the dead; and certainly not judged by the canons of dead critics. It is a judgment, a comparison, in which two things are measured by each other. To conform merely would be for the new work not really to conform at all; it would not be new, and would therefore not be a work of art. And we do not quite say that the new is more valuable because it fits in; but its fitting in is a test of its value—a test, it is true, which can only be slowly and cautiously applied, for we are none of us infallible judges of conformity. We say: it appears to conform, and is perhaps individual, or it appears individual, and may conform; but we are hardly likely to find that it is one and not the other.

To proceed to a more intelligible exposition of the relation of the poet to the past: he can neither take the past as a lump, an indiscriminate bolus, nor can he form himself wholly on one or two private admirations, nor can he form himself wholly upon one preferred period. The first course is inadmissible, the second is an important experience of youth, and the third is a pleasant and highly desirable supplement. The poet must be very conscious of the main current, which does not at all flow invariably through the most distinguished reputations. He must be quite aware of the obvious fact that art never improves, but that the material of art is never quite the same. He must be aware that the mind of Europe—the mind of his own country—a mind which he learns in time to be much more important than his own private mind—is a mind which changes, and that this change is a development which abandons nothing *en route*, which does not superannuate either Shakespeare, or Homer, or the rock drawing of the Magdalenian draughtsmen. That this development, refinement perhaps, complication certainly, is not, from the point of view of the artist, any improvement. Perhaps not even an improvement from the point of view of the psychologist or not to the extent which we imagine; perhaps only in the end based upon a complication in economics and machinery. But the difference between the present and the past is that the conscious present is an awareness of the past in a way and to an extent which the past's awareness of itself cannot show.

Some one said: "The dead writers are remote from us because we *know* so much more than they did." Precisely, and
they are that which we know.

I am alive to a usual objection to what is clearly part of my
programme for the *metier* of poetry. The objection is that the
doctrine requires a ridiculous amount of erudition (pedantry),
a claim which can be rejected by appeal to the lives of poets
in any pantheon. It will even be affirmed that much learning
deadens or perverts poetic sensibility. While, however, we
persist in believing that a poet ought to know as much as will
not encroach upon his necessary receptivity and necessary
laziness, it is not desirable to confine knowledge to whatever
can be put into a useful shape for examinations, drawing-
rooms, or the still more pretentious modes of publicity. Some
can absorb knowledge, the more tardy must sweat for it.
Shakespeare acquired more essential history from Plutarch
than most men could from the whole British Museum. What
is to be insisted upon is that the poet must develop or procure
the consciousness of the past and that he should continue to
develop this consciousness throughout his career.

What happens is a continual surrender of himself as he is at
the moment to something which is more valuable. The
progress of an artist is a continual self-sacrifice, a continual
extinction of personality.

There remains to define this process of depersonalization
and its relation to the sense of tradition. It is in this depersonalization that art may be said to approach the condition of
science. I shall, therefore, invite you to consider, as a suggestive analogy, the action which takes place when a bit of
finely filiated platinum is introduced into a chamber containing oxygen and sulphur dioxide.

II

Honest criticism and sensitive appreciation is directed not
upon the poet but upon the poetry. If we attend to the confused cries of the newspaper critics and the susurrus of
popular repetition that follows, we shall hear the names of

poets in great numbers; if we seek not Bluebook knowledge but the enjoyment of poetry, and ask for a poem, we shall seldom find it. In the last article I tried to point out the importance of the relation of the poem to other poems by other authors, and suggested the conception of poetry as a living whole of all the poetry that has ever been written. The other aspect of this Impersonal theory of poetry is the relation of the poem to its author. And I hinted, by an analogy, that the mind of the mature poet differs from that of the immature one not precisely in any valuation of "personality," not being necessarily more interesting, or having "more to say," but rather by being a more finely perfected medium in which special, or very varied, feelings are at liberty to enter into new combinations.

The analogy was that of the catalyst. When the two gases previously mentioned are mixed in the presence of a filament of platinum, they form sulphurous acid. This combination takes place only if the platinum is present; nevertheless the newly formed acid contains no trace of platinum, and the platinum itself is apparently unaffected; has remained inert, neutral, and unchanged. The mind of the poet is the shred of platinum. It may partly or exclusively operate upon the experience of the man himself; but, the more perfect the artist, the more completely separate in him will be the man who suffers and the mind which creates; the more perfectly will the mind digest and transmute the passions which are its material.

The experience, you will notice, the elements which enter the presence of the transforming catalyst, are of two kinds: emotions and feelings. The effect of a work of art upon the person who enjoys it is an experience different in kind from any experience not of art. It may be formed out of one emotion, or may be a combination of several; and various feelings, inhering for the writer in particular words or phrases or images, may be added to compose the final result. Or great poetry may be made without the direct use of any emotion whatever: composed out of feelings solely. Canto XV of the *Inferno* (Brunetto Latini) is a working up of the emotion evident in the situation; but the effect, though single as that of any work of art, is obtained by considerable complexity of detail. The last quatrain gives an image, a feeling attaching to an image, which "came," which did not develop simply out of what precedes, but which was probably in suspension in the poet's mind until the proper combination arrived for it to add itself to. The poet's mind is in fact a receptacle for seizing and storing up numberless feelings, phrases, images, which remain there until all the particles which can unite to form a new compound are present together.

If you compare several representative passages of the greatest poetry you see how great is the variety of types of combination, and also how completely any semi-ethical criterion of "sublimity" misses the mark. For it is not the "greatness," the intensity, of the emotions, the components, but the intensity of the artistic process, the pressure, so to speak, under which the fusion takes place, that counts. The episode of Paolo and Francesca employs a definite emotion, but the intensity of the poetry is something quite different from whatever intensity in the supposed experience it may give the impression of. It is no more intense, furthermore, than Canto XXVI, the voyage of Ulysses, which has not the direct dependence upon an emotion. Great variety is possible in the process of transmutation of emotion: the murder of Agamemnon, or the agony of Othello, gives an artistic effect apparently closer to a possible original than the scenes from Dante. In the *Agamemnon*, the artistic emotion approximates to the emotion of an actual spectator; in *Othello* to the emotion of the protagonist himself. But the difference between art and the event is always absolute; the combination which is the murder of Agamemnon is probably as complex as that which is the voyage of Ulysses. In either case there has been a fusion of elements. The ode of Keats contains a number of feelings which have nothing particular to do with the nightingale, but which the nightingale, partly, perhaps, because of its attractive name, and partly because of its reputation, served to bring together.

The point of view which I am struggling to attack is perhaps related to the metaphysical theory of the substantial unity of the soul: for my meaning is, that the poet has, not a "personality" to express, but a particular medium, which is only a medium and not a personality, in which impressions and experiences combine in peculiar and unexpected ways. Impressions and experiences which are important for the man may take no place in the poetry, and those which become important in the poetry may play quite a negligible part in the man, the personality.

I will quote a passage which is unfamiliar enough to be regarded with fresh attention in the light—or darkness—of these observations:

> And now bethinks I could e'en chide myself
> For doting on her beauty, though her death
> Shall be revenged after no common action.
> Does the silkworm expend her yellow labours
> For thee? For thee does she undo herself?
> Are lordships sold to maintain ladyships
> For the poor benefit of a bewildering minute?
> Why does yon fellow falsify highways,
> And put his life between the judge's lips,
> To refine such a thing—keeps horse and men
> To beat their valours for her? . . .

In this passage (as is evident if it is taken in its context) there is a combination of positive and negative emotions: an intensely strong attraction toward beauty and an equally intense fascination by the ugliness which is contrasted with it and which destroys it. This balance of contrasted emotion is in the dramatic situation to which the speech is pertinent, but that situation alone is inadequate to it. This is, so to speak, the structural emotion, provided by the drama. But the whole effect, the dominant tone, is due to the fact that a number of floating feelings, having an affinity to this emotion by no means superficially evident, have combined with it to give us a new art emotion.

It is not in his personal emotions, the emotions provoked by particular events in his life, that the poet is in any way remarkable or interesting. His particular emotions may be simple, or crude, or flat. The emotion in his poetry will be a very complex thing, but not with the complexity of the emotions of people who have very complex or unusual emotions in life. One error, in fact, of eccentricity in poetry is to seek for new human emotions to express; and in this search for novelty in the wrong place it discovers the perverse. The business of the poet is not to find new emotions, but to use the ordinary ones and, in working them up into poetry, to express feelings which are not in actual emotions at all. And emotions which he has never experienced will serve his turn as well as those familiar to him. Consequently, we must believe that "emotion recollected in tranquillity" is an inexact formula. For it is neither emotion, nor recollection, nor, without distortion of meaning, tranquillity. It is a concentration, and a new thing resulting from the concentration, of a very great number of experiences which to the practical and active person would not seem to be experiences at all; it is a concentration which does not happen consciously or of deliberation. These experiences are not "recollected," and they finally unite in an atmosphere which is "tranquil" only in that it is a passive attending upon the event. Of course this is not quite the whole story. There is a great deal, in the writing of poetry, which must be conscious and deliberate. In fact, the bad poet is usually unconscious where he ought to be conscious, and conscious where he ought to be unconscious. Both errors tend to make him "personal." Poetry is not a turning loose of emotion, but an escape from emotion; it is not the expression of personality, but an escape from personality. But, of course, only those who have personality and emotions know what it means to want to escape from these things.

III

ὁ δὲ νοῦς, ἴσως, θειότερόν τι χαὶ ἀπαθές ἐστιν

This essay proposes to halt at the frontier of metaphysics or mysticism, and confine itself to such practical conclusions as can be applied by the responsible person interested in poetry. To divert interest from the poet to the poetry is a laudable aim: for it would conduce to a juster estimation of actual poetry, good and bad. There are many people who appreciate the expression of sincere emotion in verse, and there is a smaller number of people who can appreciate technical excellence. But very few know when there is expression of *significant* emotion, emotion which has its life in the poem and not in the history of the poet. The emotion of art is impersonal. And the poet cannot reach this impersonality without surrendering himself wholly to the work to be done. And he is not likely to know what is to be done unless he lives in what is not merely the present, but the present moment of the past, unless he is conscious, not of what is dead, but of what is already living.

Aldous Huxley

1894 · ——

Aldous Huxley, grandson of Thomas Henry and
brother of Julian Huxley, was prevented by an
affliction of the eyes from following a scientific
career similar to theirs. He studied English
literature at Oxford and then went into journalism.
His novels, such as Antic Hay *(1923) and* Brave
New World *(1932), and many of his essays dissect*
modern civilization in an effort to examine the ideals
and morals—or lack of them—that shape the age we
live in. Ape and Essence *(1948) presents a*
degraded few survivors of an atomic war and their
worship of evil.

THE OLIVE TREE

THE TREE OF LIFE; the Bodhi Tree; Yggdrasil
and the Burning Bush:

Populus Alcidae gratissima, vitis Iaccho,
formosae myrtus Veneri, sua laurea Phoebo. . . .

Everywhere and, before the world was finally laicized, at
all times, trees have been worshipped. It is not to be wondered at. The tree is an intrinsically "numinous" being. Solidi-
fied, a great fountain of life rises in the trunk, spreads in the
branches, scatters in a spray of leaves and flowers and fruits.
With a slow, silent ferocity the roots go burrowing down into
the earth. Tender, yet irresistible, life battles with the unliving
stones and has the mastery. Half hidden in the darkness, half
displayed in the air of heaven, the tree stands there, magnifi-

cent, a manifest god. Even to-day we feel its majesty and beauty—feel in certain circumstances its rather fearful quality of otherness, strangeness, hostility. Trees in the mass can be almost terrible. There are devils in the great pine-woods of the North, in the swarming equatorial jungle. Alone in a forest one sometimes becomes aware of the silence—the thick, clotted, living silence of the trees; one realizes one's isolation in the midst of a vast concourse of alien presences. Herne the Hunter was something more than the ghost of a Windsor gamekeeper. He was probably a survival of Jupiter Cernunnus; a lineal descendant of the Cretan Zeus; a wood god who in some of his aspects was frightening and even malignant.

> He blasts the tree, and takes the cattle,
> And makes milch-kine yield blood, and shakes a chain
> In a most hideous and dreadful manner.

Even in a royal forest and only twenty miles from London, the serried trees can inspire terror. Alone or in small groups, trees are benignly numinous. The alienness of the forest is so much attenuated in the park or the orchard that it changes its emotional sign and from oppressively sinister becomes delightful. Tamed and isolated, those leaping fountains of non-human life bring only refreshment to spirits parched by the dusty commerce of the world. Poetry is full of groves and shrubberies. One thinks of Milton, landscape-gardening in Eden, of Pope, at Twickenham. One remembers Coleridge's sycamore and Marvel's green thought in a green shade. Chaucer's love of trees was so great that he had to compile a whole catalogue in order to express it.

> But, Lorde, so I was glad and wel begoon!
> For over al, where I myn eyen caste,
> Weren trees, claad with levys that ay shal laste,
> Eche in his kynde, with colours fressh and grene
> As emerawde, that joy was for to sene.
> The bylder oke, and eke the hardy asshe,
> The peler (pillar) elme, the cofre unto careyne,
> The box pipe tree, holme to whippes lasshe,

> The saylynge firre, the cipresse deth to pleyne,
> The sheter (shooter) ewe, the aspe for shaftes pleyne,
> The olyve of pes, and eke the drunken vyne
> The victor palme, the laurere, to, devyne.

I like them all, but especially the olive. For what it symbolizes, first of all—peace with its leaves and joy with its golden oil. True, the crown of olive was originally worn by Roman conquerors at ovation; the peace it proclaimed was the peace of victory, the peace which is too often only the tranquillity of exhaustion or complete annihilation. Rome and its customs have passed, and we remember of the olive only the fact that it stood for peace, not the circumstances in which it did so.

> Incertainties now crown themselves assur'd,
> And peace proclaims olives of endless age.

We are a long way from the imperator riding in triumph the streets of Rome.

The association of olive leaves with peace is like the association of the number seven with good luck, or the colour green with hope. It is an arbitrary and, so to say, metaphysical association. That is why it has survived in the popular imagination down to the present day. Even in countries where the olive tree does not grow, men understand what is meant by "the olive branch" and can recognize, in a political cartoon, its pointed leaves. The association of olive oil with joy had a pragmatic reason. Applied externally, oil was supposed to have medicinal properties. In the ancient world those who could afford it were in the habit of oiling themselves at every opportunity. A shiny and well lubricated face was thought to be beautiful; it was also a sign of prosperity. To the ancient Mediterranean peoples the association of oil with joy seemed inevitable and obvious. Our habits are not those of the Romans, Greeks and Hebrews. What to them was "natural" is to-day hardly even imaginable. Patterns of behaviour change, and ideas which are associated in virtue of the pattern existing at a given moment of history will cease to be associated when that pattern exists no more. But ideas which are associated arbitrarily, in virtue of some principle, or some absence of principle, unconnected with current behaviour patterns will remain associated through changing circumstances. One must be something of an archaeologist to remember the old and once thoroughly reasonable association between olive oil and joy; the equally old, but quite unreasonable and arbitrary association between olive leaves and peace has survived intact into the machine age.

It is surprising, I often think, that our Protestant bibliolaters should have paid so little attention to the oil which played such an important part in the daily lives of the ancient Hebrews. All that was greasy possessed for the Jews a profound religious, social and sensuous significance. Oil was used for anointing kings, priests and sacred edifices. On festal days men's cheeks and noses fairly shone with it; a matt-surfaced face was a sign of mourning. Then there were the animal fats. Fat meat was always a particularly welcome sacrifice. Unlike the modern child, Jehovah revelled in mutton fat. His worshippers shared this taste. "Eat ye that which is good," advises Isaiah, "and let your soul delight itself in fatness." As for the prosperously wicked, "they have more than their heart can wish" and the proof of it is that "their eyes stand out with fatness." The world of the Old Testament, it is evident, was one where fats were scarce and correspondingly esteemed. One of our chief sources of edible fat, the pig, was taboo to the Israelites. Butter and lard depend on a supply of grass long enough for cows to get their tongues round. But the pastures of Palestine are thin, short and precarious. Cows there had no milk to spare, and oxen were too valuable as draught animals to be used for suet. Only the sheep and the olive remained as sources of that physiologically necessary and therefore delicious fatness in which the Hebrew soul took such delight. How intense that delight was is proved by the way in which the Psalmist describes his religious experiences. "Because thy lovingkindness is better than life, my lips shall praise thee. . . . My soul shall be satisfied as with marrow and fatness; and my mouth shall praise thee with joyful lips." In this age of Danish bacon and unlimited margarine it would never occur to a religious writer to liken the mystical ecstasy to a good guzzle at the Savoy. If he wanted to describe it in terms of a sensuous experience, he would probably choose a sexual metaphor. Square meals are now too common to be ranked as epoch-making treats.

The "olyve of pes" is, then, a symbol and I love it for what it stands. I love it also for what it is in itself, aesthetically; for what it is in relation to the Mediterranean landscape in which it beautifully plays its part.

The English are Germans who have partially "gone Latin." But for William the Conqueror and the Angevins we should be just another nation of Teutons, speaking some uninteresting dialect of Dutch or Danish. The Normans gave us the English language, that beautifully compounded mixture of French and Saxon; and the English language moulded the English mind. By Latin out of German: such is our pedigree. We are essentially mongrels: that is the whole point of us. To be mongrels is our mission. If we would fulfil this mission adequately we must take pains to cultivate our mongrelism. Our Saxon and Celtic flesh requires to be constantly rewedded to the Latin spirit. For the most part the English have always realized this truth and acted upon it. From the time of Chaucer onwards almost all our writers have turned, by a kind of infallible instinct, like swallows, towards the South—towards the phantoms of Greece and Rome, towards the living realities of France and Italy. On the rare occasions when, losing their orientation, they have turned eastward and northward, the results have been deplorable. The works of Carlyle are there, an awful warning, to remind us of what happens when the English forget that their duty is to be mongrels and go whoring, within the bounds of consanguinity, after German gods.

The olive tree is an emblem of the Latinity towards which our migrant's instinct commands us perpetually to turn. As well as for peace and for joy, it stands for all that makes us specifically English rather than Teutonic; for those Mediterranean influences without which Chaucer and Shakespeare could never have become what they learned from France and Italy, from Rome and Greece, to be—the most essentially native of our poets. The olive tree is, so to speak, the complement of the oak; and the bright hard-edged landscapes in which it figures are the necessary correctives of those gauzy and indeterminate lovelinesses of the English scene. Under a polished sky the olives state their aesthetic case without the qualifications of mist, of shifting lights, of atmospheric perspective, which give to English landscapes their subtle and melancholy beauty. A perfect beauty in its way; but, as of all good things, one can have too much of it. The British Constitution is a most admirable invention; but it is good to come back occasionally to fixed first principles and the firm outline of syllogistic argument.

With clarity and definition is associated a certain physical spareness. Most of the great deciduous trees of England give one the impression, at any rate in summer, of being rather obese. In Scandinavian mythology Embla, the elm, was the first woman. Those who have lived much with old elm trees— and I spent a good part of my boyhood under their ponderous shade—will agree that the Scandinavians were men of insight. There is in effect something blowsily female about those vast trees that brood with all their bulging masses of foliage above the meadows of the home counties. In winter they are giant skeletons; and for a moment in the early spring a cloud of transparent emerald vapour floats in the air; but by June they have settled down to an enormous middle age.

By comparison the olive tree seems an athlete in training. It sits lightly on the earth and its foliage is never completely opaque. There is always air between the thin grey and silver leaves of the olive, always the flash of light within its shadows. By the end of summer the foliage of our northern trees is a great clot of dark unmitigated green. In the olive the lump is always leavened.

The landscape of the equator is, as the traveller discovers to his no small surprise, singularly like the landscape of the more luxuriant parts of southern England. He finds the same thick woods and, where man has cleared them, the same park-like expanses of luscious greenery. The whole is illumined by the same cloudy sky, alternately bright and dark, and wetted by precisely those showers of hot water which render yet more oppressive the sultriness of July days in the Thames valley or in Devonshire. The equator is England in summer, but raised, so to speak, to a higher power. Falmouth cubed equals Singapore. Between the equatorial and the temperate zone lies a belt of drought; even Provence is half a desert. The equator is dank, the tropics and the sub-tropics are predominantly dry. The Sahara and Arabia, the wastes of India and Central Asia and North America are a girdle round the earth of sand and naked rock. The Mediterranean lies on the fringes of this desert belt and the olive is its tree—the tree of a region of sunlit clarity separating the damps of the equator from the damps of the North. It is the symbol of a classicism enclosed between two romanticisms.

"And where," Sir George Beaumont inquired of Constable, "where do you put your brown tree?" The reply was disquieting: the eccentric fellow didn't put it anywhere. There are no brown trees in Constable's landscapes. Breaking the tradition of more than a century, he boldly insisted on painting his trees bright green. Sir George, who had been brought up to think of English landscape in terms of raw Sienna and ochre, was bewildered. So was Chantrey. His criticism of Constable's style took a practical form. When "Hadleigh Castle" was sent to the Academy he took a pot of bitumen and glazed the whole foreground with a coat of rich brown. Constable had to spend several hours patiently scratching it off again. To paint a bright green tree and make a successful picture of it requires genius of no uncommon order. Nature is embarrassingly brilliant and variegated; only the greatest colourists know how to deal with such a shining profusion. Doubtful of their powers, the more cautious prefer to transpose reality into another and simpler key. The key of brown, for example. The England of the eighteenth-century painters is chronically autumnal.

At all seasons of the year the olive achieves that sober neutrality of tone which the deciduous trees of the North put on only in autumn and winter. "Where do you put your grey tree?" If you are painting in Provence, or Tuscany, you put it everywhere. At every season of the year the landscape is full of grey trees. The olive is essentially a painter's tree. It does not need to be transposed into another key, and it can be rendered completely in terms of pigment that are as old as the art of painting.

Large expanses of the Mediterranean scene are by Nature herself conceived and executed in the earth colours. Your grey tree and its background of bare bone-like hills, red-brown earth and the all but black cypresses and pines are within the range of the most ascetic palette. Derain can render Provence with half a dozen tubes of colour. How instructive to compare his olives with those of Renoir! White, black, *terra verde*—Derain's rendering of the grey tree is complete. But it is not the only complete rendering. Renoir was a man with a passion for bright gay colours. To this passion he added an extraordinary virtuosity in combining them. It was not in his nature to be content with a black, white and earth-green olive. His grey trees have shadows of cadmium green, and where they look towards the sun, are suffused with a glow of pink. Now, no olive has ever shown a trace of any colour warmer than the faint ochre of withering leaves and summer dusts. Nevertheless these pink trees, which in Renoir's paintings of Cagnes recall the exuberant girls of his latest, rosiest manner, are somehow quite startlingly like the cold grey olives which they apparently misrepresent. The rendering, so different from Derain's, is equally complete and satisfying.

If I could paint and had the necessary time, I should devote myself for a few years to making pictures only of olive trees. What a wealth of variations upon a single theme! Above Pietrasanta, for example, the first slopes of the Apuan Alps rise steeply from the plain in a series of terraces built up, step after step, by generations of patient cultivators. The risers of this great staircase are retaining walls of unmortared limestone; the treads, of grass. And on every terrace grow the olives. They are ancient trees; their boles are gnarled, their branches strangely elbowed. Between the sharp narrow leaves one sees the sky; and beneath them in the thin softly tempered light there are sheep grazing. Far off, on a level with the eye, lies the sea. There is one picture, one series of pictures.

But olives will grow on the plain as well as on the hillside. Between Seville and Cordoba the rolling country is covered with what is almost a forest of olive trees. It is a woodland scene. Elsewhere they are planted more sparsely. I think, for example, of that plain at the foot of the Maures in Provence. In spring, beside the road from Toulon to Fréjus, the ploughed earth is a rich Pozzuoli red. Above it hang the olives, grey, with soft black shadows and their highest leaves flashing white against the sky; and, between the olives, peach trees in blossom—burning bushes of shell-pink flame in violent and irreconcilable conflict with the red earth. A problem, there, for the most accomplished painter.

In sunlight Renoir saw a flash of madder breaking out of the grey foliage. Under a clouded sky, with rain impending, the olives glitter with an equal but very different intensity. There is no warmth in them now; the leaves shine white, as though illumined from within by a kind of lunar radiance. The soft black of the shadows is deepened to the extreme of night. In every tree there is simultaneously moonlight and darkness. Under the approaching storm the olives take on another kind of being; they become more conspicuous in the landscape, more significant. Of what? Significant of what? But to that question, when we ask it, nature always stubbornly refuses to return a clear reply. At the sight of those mysterious lunar trees, at once so dark and so brilliant beneath the clouds, we ask, as Zechariah asked of the angel: "What are these two olive trees upon the right side of the candlestick and upon the left side thereof? What be these two olive branches which through the two golden pipes empty the golden oil out of themselves? And he answered me and said, Knowest thou not what these be? And I said, No, my lord. Then said he, These are the two anointed ones, that stand by the Lord of the whole earth." And that, I imagine, is about as explicit and comprehensible an answer as our Wordsworthian questionings are ever likely to receive.

Provence is a painter's paradise, and its tree, the olive, the painter's own tree. But there are disquieting signs of change. During the last few years there has been a steady destruction of olive orchards. Magnificent old trees are being cut, their wood sold for firing and the land they occupied planted with vines. Fifty years from now, it may be, the olive tree will almost have disappeared from southern France, and Provence will wear another aspect. It may be, I repeat; it is not certain. Nothing is certain nowadays except change. Even the majestic stability of agriculture has been shaken by the progress of technology. Thirty years ago, for example, the farmers of the Rhône valley grew rich on silkworms. Then came the invention of viscose. The caterpillars tried to compete with the machines and failed. The female form is now swathed in woodpulp, and between Lyons and Avignon the mulberry tree and its attendant worm are all but extinct. Vines were next planted. But North Africa was also planting vines. In a year of plenty *vin ordinaire* fetches about a penny a quart. The vines have been rooted up again, and to-day the prosperity of the Rhône valley depends on peach trees. A few years from now, no doubt, the Germans will be making synthetic peaches out of sawdust or coal tar. And then—what?

The enemy of the olive tree is the peanut. *Arachis hypogaea* grows like a weed all over the tropics and its seeds are fifty per cent. pure oil. The olive is slow-growing, capricious in its yield, requires much pruning, and the fruit must be hand picked. Peanut oil is half the price of olive oil. The Italians, who wish to keep their olive trees, have almost forbidden the use of peanut oil. The French, on the other hand, are the greatest importers of peanuts in Europe. Most of the oil they make is re-exported; but enough remains in France to imperil the olives of Provence. Will they go the way of the mulberry trees? Or will some new invention come rushing up in the nick of time with a reprieve? It seems that, suitably treated, olive oil makes an excellent lubricant, capable of standing up to high temperatures. Thirty years from now, mineral lubricants will be growing scarce. Along with the castor-oil plant, the olive tree may come again triumphantly into its own. Perhaps. Or perhaps not. The future of Provençal landscape is in the hands of the chemists. It is in their power to preserve it as it is, or to alter it out of all recognition.

It would not be the first time in the course of its history that the landscape of Provence has changed its face. The Provence that we know—terraced vineyard and olive orchard alternating with pine-woods and those deserts of limestone and prickly bushes which are locally called garrigues—is profoundly unlike the Provence of Roman and mediaeval times. It was a land, then, of great forests. The hills were covered with a splendid growth of ilex trees and Aleppo pines. The surviving Forêt du Dom allows us to guess what these woods —the last outposts towards the south of the forests of the temperate zone—were like. To-day the garrigues, those end products of a long degeneration, have taken their place. The story of Provençal vegetation is a decline and fall, that begins with the ilex wood and ends with the garrigue.

The process of destruction is a familiar one. The trees were cut for firewood and shipbuilding. (The naval arsenal at Toulon devoured the forest for miles around.) The glass industry ate its way from the plain into the mountains, carrying with it irreparable destruction. Meanwhile, the farmers and the shepherds were busy, cutting into the woods in search of more land for the plough, burning them in order to have more pasture for their beasts. The young trees sprouted again—only to be eaten by the sheep and goats. In the end they gave up the struggle and what had been forest turned at last to a blasted heath. The long process of degradation ends in the garrigue. And even this blasted heath is not quite the end. Beyond the true garrigue, with its cistus, its broom, its prickly dwarf oak, there lie a series of false garrigues, vegetably speaking worse than the true. On purpose or by accident, somebody sets fire to the scrub. In the following spring the new shoots are eaten down to the ground. A coarse grass—baouco in Provençal—is all that manages to spring up. The shepherd is happy; his beasts can feed, as they could not do on the garrigue. But sheep and goats are ravenous. The new pasture is soon overgrazed. The baouco is torn up by the roots and disappears, giving place to ferocious blue thistles and the poisonous asphodel. With the asphodel the process is complete. Degradation can go no further. The asphodel is sheep-proof and even, thanks to its deeply planted tubers, fire-proof. And it allows very little else to grow in its neighbourhood. If protected long enough from fire and animals, the garrigue will gradually build itself up again into a forest. But a desert of asphodels obstinately remains itself.

Efforts are now being made to reafforest the blasted heaths of Provence. In an age of cigarette-smoking tourists the task is difficult and the interruptions by fire frequent and disheartening. One can hardly doubt, however, of the ultimate success of the undertaking. The chemists may spare the olive trees; and yet the face of Provence may still be changed. For the proper background to the olive trees is the thinly fledged limestone of the hills—pinkish and white and pale blue in the distance, like Cézanne's Mont Sainte Victoire. Reafforested, these hills will be almost black with ilex and pine. Half the painter's paradise will have gone, if the desert is brought back to life. With the cutting of the olive trees the other half will follow.

Charles Morgan

1894 · ——

Charles Morgan, English novelist, essayist, and critic, is best known for such novels as The Fountain *(1932),* Sparkenbroke *(1936), and* The Voyage *(1940). He took his degree at Oxford in 1921, after serving for several years in the Royal Navy before and during the first World War. Because of his earlier naval experience, he served at the Admiralty during the second World War. Since 1926 he has been the leading dramatic critic for the London* Times.

THE CONSTANT THINGS

A FEW EVENINGS AGO, after supper, there emerged by chance from a conversation which had for the moment divided itself into pairs a remark that drew attention to itself. It came from a man in the late forties, a traveller in the old days, and was addressed to a lady, his junior by more than a quarter of a century, wearing the uniform of the Wrens. "The alarming thing is," he said, "that this time it isn't only the changeable things that are changing, but the unchangeable as well. Anyhow, that's the danger— even for me. Not only dress and manners and bank-balances and the social order, but the sea and the sky and—Westminster Abbey."

"Westminster Abbey?" the girl repeated.

"That and Gray's country churchyard," he answered. "The

sea, the sky, the idea of glory and the idea of mortality—I find myself taking a different view of them. And you?"

By the movement of her lips and her silence, she asked for notice of that question, and he continued: "Your new Thackeray, when he sits down thirty or forty years hence to write a 'Vanity Fair' about *our* war, will come a cropper if he supposes that only the changes in our changeable things concern him. He will have to take the sea and the sky into account."

At this point the dialogue became submerged, and not until a little later was it possible to move across the room and join the two speakers. By this time they were fairly plunged in Thackeray, and "Vanity Fair," to which the girl had lately given a first reading, had come down from its shelf to the traveller's knee.

The difficulty was to draw him away from the book itself to his notion that the sea and the sky and Westminster Abbey were changing. What did he mean by that? And how did it bear on Thackeray? The second question, he said, was easy to answer. He and she had been discussing "Vanity Fair" at dinner, she having raised the subject à propos of dress or, rather, of costume. How odd that Thackeray should have considered the dress of the First Empire so unbecoming that he was compelled, in his illustrations, to adapt it to the fashion of his own period! What, she had wondered, would a future Thackeray, looking back from the nineteen-seventies or -eighties, think of battle-dress or of the uniform she was wearing? A future Thackeray, the traveller had answered, would have much worse problems than that. He would have enough—oh! more than enough—records in which to study the changes in our habit of life, and, as for our clothes, he would, like all wise novelists, rummage (with a grain of salt ever at hand) in the infallible wardrobe of Mr. Punch. But who would tell him what it felt like to be inside our strange costumes? The real change in us was not in our behaviour, our outward way of life, our consideration of things that were always changing (and were expected to change) from generation to generation, but in our view of things which were expected to remain constant through all the fickleness of man.

This the traveller had said at supper. Now, to make his point, he opened "Vanity Fair."

It had been, he declared, all very well for Thackeray. No doubt he had had his little troubles about costume, and had been compelled, as he ironically confessed in an illustrated footnote to his sixth chapter, to engage "a model of rank dressed according to the present fashion." No doubt, too, he had been bothered or delighted by appearances of the world that had altered since Napoleon came out of Elba, but for him Russell Square had still been, in effect, Russell Square. "Listen," said the traveller, turning on to Chapter Eighteen, and showing the girl that initial-letter in which Napoleon appears, "listen. Here is a piece for you:

' "Napoleon has landed at Cannes." Such news might create a panic at Vienna, and cause Russia to drop his cards, and take Prussia into a corner, . . . but how was this intelligence to affect a young lady in Russell Square, before whose door the watchman sang the hours when she was asleep, . . . who was always cared for, dressed, put to bed, and watched over by ever so many guardian angels, with and without wages? *Bon Dieu*, I say, is it not hard that the fateful rush of the great imperial struggle can't take place without affecting a poor little harmless girl of eighteen——?' "

The reader looked up to see what effect this passage was having on his young listener. She smiled, but it was a grave, unscornful smile, which gave the impression that there was more of envy than of feminist contempt in her imagining of Miss Amelia Sedley. All she said was "Guardian angels!" but in so wistfully neutral a tone that you might take it how you would; and there was a little silence before she produced the cautious platitude: "Those times won't come again."

"No," said the traveller, "indeed they won't. In that sense, times never do come again. Our age isn't exceptional in that. But what has been disturbing me is the discovery that things which, by my reading of the poets and historians and philosophers, have not greatly changed their aspect in past ages are

changing it now. Of course, this 'discovery' may be personal to me. In that case, with luck, I shall get over it. But suppose it isn't personal to me? Suppose that you and I and the others in this room and all mankind, when we look up at a night-sky or down from a Cornish cliff, are seeing something which, in its relationship to human life, is fundamentally different from what poets and shepherds and seamen and labourers and lovers have seen since paradise was lost?

"If that were true, if mankind is really changing its view of the constant things, then the consequent revolution of the mind will be incalculably greater than any other revolution has ever been. It will strike to the roots of poetry, of religion, of the love of men and women, of human nature itself. What I speak of as the 'constants' have always been——" he hesitated for a moment. "I won't say they have always been the consolation of man's suffering—they have been as often the knife-edge of his brief, piercing delights—but they have always given, in joy and sorrow, a perspective to his mortality. What happens if *that* perspective changes? Horace at once becomes incomprehensible. So does Catullus. So does Gray. And the author of Ecclesiastes and the author of 'Vanity Fair.' If a new generation should arise which doesn't in the least see the stars or the waves or a monument of bronze as they did, that new generation won't know, won't even trouble to ask very persistently, what the old boys were talking about. And if they do ask there'll be no one capable of telling them. . . . But my so-called discovery, made in Cornwall during a couple of weeks' leave last autumn, is meaningless unless, in some sort, others are feeling as I do. People much younger than I am. You, for example," he said, looking at the girl. "Do you also feel that something very odd may be happening to the sea and the stars?"

She said tentatively, as if she were searching her own memory for an experience that might correspond with his, "Probably I don't agree with you. But I know what you're driving at. What exactly did happen in Cornwall?"

Thus encouraged, he closed Thackeray, and waited until he could make up his mind where to begin his Cornish tale.

Suddenly he interrupted his own silence to exclaim: "I said sky and sea. Don't think that what I had in mind was bombers and submarines. They come into it, I dare say, but they themselves are ephemeral. Except in moments of panic, or of utter weariness, they don't affect one's view of the sky and the sea. Besides, not only the sky and the sea are in question. The song of birds, firelight and sunlight, the woods, the turn of the seasons, the earth itself and the smell of it, the whole natural magic going on behind our little journey from the cradle to the grave—well," he said, "you have to choose. What are they? Are they still what they have always been: the perspective of our mortality and, for some of us, an emblem or at least an analogy of our immortality? Or have they become, as it were, infected by our impermanence? Are they little more than a stage-setting to our personal and social drama? It's a question of relationship and of our view of that relationship. Are we related to them at all, as mankind has always supposed? Is the earth that we touch a part of ourselves, or has it become just a thing we walk on, like a pavement? Are we becoming, in our consciousness, separated from the stars—as indifferent to them as we are to the electric chandeliers in the lounge of an hotel? Are we being driven, or driving ourselves, into exile from the unity of nature? It is a simple question. The horrible thing is that it should ever have entered into anyone's mind—into my mind—to ask it."

"Why horrible?" the girl asked. "Doesn't it depend on the way in which you ask it? What you call exile from the unity of nature might be a kind of emancipation—one more step away from fears and superstitions and natural taboos. I believe—at least I have heard it said—that people who live in modern cities think much less about death than people who live in remote country. Whether that's good or bad, I don't know. I suppose it's a kind of freedom."

"The freedom," he suggested, "of pretending that the sun won't set."

"But if the day is young and good," she replied, "you can't always be thinking about the sunset."

"No," he acknowledged, "you can't always be thinking

about the sunset, but, if you rule it out of your consciousness, you rule out the sunrise too. It brings us back, in fact, to the electric chandeliers."

"It brings us back," she said, "to what happened in Cornwall, which you haven't told us yet."

His hesitation made it clear that he wished he had not raised false expectations of a story. There was, he protested, no story to tell; what had happened had happened inside himself. One morning he went out from a remote house in which he was lodging to a cliff that overlooked the sea in the neighbourhood of Zennor. In the forenoon and the early afternoon there was still summer in the air. When evening fell, night would close in cold and sharp; he would be glad then to draw the curtains and settle down to oil lamps and a fire of logs; but while daylight lasted there was enough warmth in the sun to make him turn his face to it and stretch out hands and wrists, and say, jealously, "Not winter yet." So he lay down on the cliff in the lee of rising ground and marked with his eye ledges in the offshore rocks so that he might observe the tide. In earlier life he had been a professional seaman and had none of a landsman's romanticism of the waves—only a kind of respect for the sea, a loyalty to it, such as one might have for a great officer who knew his job better than one knew it oneself. It wasn't what is often meant by the beauty of the sea that drew him to it. He didn't come to it for its decorative qualities, but he liked to be near it and alone with it for many hours at a stretch. Why? . . . Because he had found, as a matter of experience, that it quieted him, purged him of trifling anxieties and petty cares, and, in some miraculous way, reconciled his memories, his hopes, his disappointments, so that he was able—and he was evidently reluctant to speak the word—to harmonize himself. But this time, on the cliff at Zennor, he was in a troubled, melancholy mood and the sea gave him no release; it didn't draw his poisons out as it always had in the past; and the reason he offered was that the fault was his—he had, for that afternoon at any rate, lost his relationship with the sea.

If that had been all, it wouldn't have been so bad. But

this experience of detachment, of separation, was not confined to that particular afternoon, nor to the sea alone, nor to himself alone. He found that the sky and the earth and the trees and the blackberries had "nothing more to say to him" or, rather, that he had become incapable of responding to them. He came gradually to feel that he was alien to the natural universe instead of being native of it—"alien," he added, "in the sense in which one might say of an inanimate thing—a chair or a machine—that it was alien to human life. What distinguishes the inanimate from the animate is that the inanimate can't communicate, and that was my trouble. I couldn't communicate. If that is personal to me—if it's temporary and if the cause of it is simply overwork or what you will—then, like all personal failures, it's my look-out. But is it personal to me? I have begun to wonder whether a great part of mankind isn't in the same trouble. If it were true, it wouldn't be astonishing. Our way of life depends more and more on our contacts with non-natural and inanimate things; so does our way of death. Once upon a time a man's work was conditioned by sunrise and sunset, by the direction of the wind or the state of the sea or the turn of the seasons. He was continuously in communication with them. He thought of his life, and of his love, in terms of their power or mercy.

> When I have seen the hungry ocean gain
> Advantage on the kingdom of the shore,
> And the firm soil win of the watery main,
> Increasing store with loss, and loss with store;
> When I have seen such interchange of state,
> Or state itself confounded to decay;
> Ruin hath taught me thus to ruminate,
> That Time will come and take my love away.

Now, more and more, machines are the condition of his life. As yet he is not born mechanically but he is nourished, transported, given news, killed and buried mechanically. In so far as Nature has a share in these processes, that share is elaborately concealed from him. How often does it enter his mind that something must grow and something die that he may eat? I am not," the traveller concluded, "drawing the familiar moral that men are the slaves of their machines. What troubles me is the opposite aspect of the matter. Is mankind transferring its alliance? Is it becoming, in its mind, one with non-natural things, and losing altogether its ancient sense of being one with the sea and the earth? If it is——"

He turned to the girl, for she had moved as if she wished to interrupt him. Now she looked at him steadily and shook her head. "You wouldn't fear that if you were young."

"Di magni!" he exclaimed. "That would be a comforting answer if I could be sure that it was true. I was more afraid for the young than for the old."

Her eyebrows went up. "You might have been five years ago," she admitted. "No so much now. We are becoming less and less interested in pavements and less and less inclined to look for our gods in machines. There is even some possibility of a romantic revival. Amelia's dress may, so to speak, have come full-circle. Still you mustn't swear at us in Latin."

"I wasn't swearing," he answered, "I was quoting:

'Di magni, facite ut vere promittere possit,
   atque id sincere dicat et ex animo.' "

"Still," said she, "why Latin?"

"Someone," he acknowledged, "once translated it:

'God, make it come true!
Bring her to swear it, knowing all her heart!'

A loose version, perhaps, but it will serve." *

* *The verses of Catullus and the quoted translation ("Sparkenbroke,"*
2, xviii) are:
Iucundum, mea vita, mihi proponis amorem
   hunc nostrum inter nos perpetuumque fore.
di magni, facite ut vere promittere possit,
   atque id sincere dicat et ex animo,
ut liceat nobis tota perducere vita
   aeternum hoc sanctae foedus amicitiae.
Thou dost propose, beloved, this our love
Joyful and deathless. God, make it come true!
Bring her to swear it, knowing all her heart!
So against Time may yet sufficient prove
This timeless pledge of loving constancy.

James Thurber

1894 · ——

James Thurber displayed interest in writing and drawing as a boy, and as a young man he achieved success on several newspapers before he joined the staff of The New Yorker. *His cartoons are perhaps best known, but his most enduring work is to be found in his satirical stories and essays and in his fantasies. With E. B. White he wrote a humorous book,* Is Sex Necessary? *(1929), and with Elliot Nugent he wrote* The Male Animal, *which made a hit on Broadway in 1940.*

COURTSHIP THROUGH THE AGES

SURELY NOTHING in the astonishing scheme of life can have nonplussed Nature so much as the fact that none of the females of any of the species she created really cared very much for the male, as such. For the past ten million years Nature has been busily inventing ways to make the male attractive to the female, but the whole business of courtship, from the marine annelids up to man, still lumbers heavily along, like a complicated musical comedy. I have been reading the sad and absorbing story in Volume 6 (Cole to Dama) of the Encyclopædia Britannica. In this volume you can learn all about cricket, cotton, costume designing, crocodiles, crown jewels, and Coleridge, but none of these subjects is so interesting as the Courtship of Animals, which recounts the sorrowful lengths to which all males must go to arouse the interest of a lady.

We all know, I think, that Nature gave man whiskers and a mustache with the quaint idea in mind that these would prove attractive to the female. We all know that, far from attracting her, whiskers and mustaches only made her nervous and gloomy, so that man had to go in for somersaults, tilting with lances, and performing feats of parlor magic to win her attention; he also had to bring her candy, flowers, and the furs of animals. It is common knowledge that in spite of all these "love displays" the male is constantly being turned down, insulted, or thrown out of the house. It is rather comforting, then, to discover that the peacock, for all his gorgeous plumage, does not have a particularly easy time in courtship; none of the males in the world do. The first peahen, it turned out, was only faintly stirred by her suitor's beautiful train. She would often go quietly to sleep while he was whisking it around. The Britannica tells us that the peacock actually had to learn a certain little trick to wake her up and revive her interest: he had to learn to vibrate his quills so as to make a rustling sound. In ancient times man himself, observing the ways of the peacock, probably tried vibrating his whiskers to make a rustling sound; if so, it didn't get him anywhere. He had to go in for something else; so, among other things, he went in for gifts. It is not unlikely that he got this idea from certain flies and birds who were making no headway at all with rustling sounds.

One of the flies of the family Empidae, who had tried everything, finally hit on something pretty special. He contrived to make a glistening transparent balloon which was even larger than himself. Into this he would put sweet-meats and tidbits and he would carry the whole elaborate envelope through the air to the lady of his choice. This amused her for a time, but she finally got bored with it. She demanded silly little colorful presents, something that you couldn't eat but that would look nice around the house. So the male Empis had to go around gathering flower petals and pieces of bright paper to put into his balloon. On a courtship flight a male Empis cuts quite a figure now, but he can hardly be said to be happy. He never knows how soon the female will demand heavier presents, such as Roman coins and gold collar buttons. It seems probable that one day the courtship of the Empidae will fall down, as man's occasionally does, of its own weight.

The bowerbird is another creature that spends so much time courting the female that he never gets any work done. If all the male bowerbirds became nervous wrecks within the next ten or fifteen years, it would not surprise me. The female bowerbird insists that a playground be built for her with a specially constructed bower at the entrance. This bower is much more elaborate than an ordinary nest and is harder to build; it costs a lot more, too. The female will not come to the playground until the male has filled it up with a great many gifts: silvery leaves, red leaves, rose petals, shells, beads, berries, bones, dice, buttons, cigar bands, Christmas seals, and the Lord knows what else. When the female finally condescends to visit the playground, she is in a coy and silly mood and has to be chased in and out of the bower and up and down the playground before she will quit giggling and stand still long enough even to shake hands. The male bird is, of course, pretty well done in before the chase starts, because he has worn himself out hunting for eye glass lenses and begonia blossoms. I imagine that many a bowerbird, after chasing a female for two or three hours, says the hell with it and goes home to bed. Next day, of course, he telephones someone else and the same trying ritual is gone through with again. A male bowerbird is as exhausted as a night-club habitué before he is out of his twenties.

The male fiddler crab has a somewhat easier time, but it can hardly be said that he is sitting pretty. He has one enormously large and powerful claw, usually brilliantly colored, and you might suppose that all he had to do was reach out and grab some passing cutie. The very earliest fiddler crabs may have tried this, but, if so, they got slapped for their pains. A female fiddler crab will not tolerate any cave-man stuff; she never has and she doesn't intend to start now. To attract a female, a fiddler crab has to stand on tiptoe and brandish his claw in the air. If any female in the neighborhood is interested—and you'd be surprised how many are not—she comes over and engages him in light badinage, for which he is not in the mood. As many as a hundred females may pass the time of day with him and go on about their business. By nightfall of an average courting day, a fiddler crab who has been standing on tiptoe for eight or ten hours waving a heavy claw in the air is in pretty sad shape. As in the case of the males of all species, however, he gets out of bed next morning, dashes some water on his face, and tries again.

The next time you encounter a male web-spinning spider, stop and reflect that he is too busy worrying about his love life to have any desire to bite you. Male web-spinning spiders have a tougher life than any other males in the animal kingdom. This is because the female web-spinning spiders have very poor eyesight. If a male lands on a female's web, she kills him before he has time to lay down his cane and gloves, mistaking him for a fly or a bumblebee who has stumbled into her trap. Before the species figured out what to do about this, millions of males were murdered by ladies they called on. It is the nature of spiders to perform a little dance in front of the female, but before a male spinner could get near enough for the female to see who he was and what he was up to, she would lash out at him with a flat-iron or a pair of garden shears. One night, nobody knows when, a very bright male spinner lay awake worrying about calling on a lady who had been killing suitors right and left. It came to him that this business of dancing as a love display wasn't getting anybody anywhere except the grave. He decided to go in for web-twitching, or strand-vibrating. The next day he tried it on one of the nearsighted girls. Instead of dropping in on her suddenly, he stayed outside the web and began monkeying with one of its strands. He twitched it up and down and in and out with such a lilting rhythm that the female was charmed. The serenade worked beautifully; the female let him live. The Britannica's spider-watchers, however, report that this system is not always successful. Once in a while, even now, a female will fire three bullets into a suitor or run him through with a kitchen knife. She keeps threatening him from the moment he strikes the first low notes on the outside strings, but usually by the time he has got up to the high notes played around the center of the web, he is going to town and she spares his life.

Even the butterfly, as handsome a fellow as he is, can't always win a mate merely by fluttering around and showing off. Many butterflies have to have scent scales on their wings. Hepialus carries a powder puff in a perfumed pouch. He throws perfume at the ladies when they pass. The male tree cricket, Oecanthus, goes Hepialus one better by carrying a tiny bottle of wine with him and giving drinks to such doxies as he has designs on. One of the male snails throws darts to entertain the girls. So it goes, through the long list of animals, from the bristle worm and his rudimentary dance steps to man and his gift of diamonds and sapphires. The golden-eye drake raises a jet of water with his feet as he flies over a lake; Hepialus has his powder puff, Oecanthus his wine bottle, man his etchings. It is a bright and melancholy story, the age-old desire of the male for the female, the age-old desire of the female to be amused and entertained. Of all the creatures on earth, the only males who could be figured as putting any irony into their courtship are the grebes and certain other diving birds. Every now and then a courting grebe slips quietly down to the bottom of a lake and then, with a mighty "Whoosh!," pops out suddenly a few feet from his girl friend, splashing water all over her. She seems to be persuaded that this is a purely loving display, but I like to think that the grebe always has a faint hope of drowning her or scaring her to death.

I will close this investigation into the mournful burdens of the male with the Britannica's story about a certain Argus pheasant. It appears that the Argus displays himself in front of a female who stands perfectly still without moving a feather. (If you saw "June Moon" some years ago and remember the scene in which the songwriter sang "Montana Moon" to his grim and motionless wife, you have some idea what the female Argus probably thinks of her mate's display.) The male Argus the Britannica tells about was confined in a cage with a female of another species, a female who kept moving around, emptying ashtrays and fussing with lampshades all the time the male was showing off his talents. Finally, in disgust, he stalked away and began displaying in front of his water trough. He reminds me of a certain male (Homo sapiens) of my acquaintance who one night after dinner asked his wife to put down her detective magazine so that he could read her a poem of which he was very fond. She sat quietly enough until he was well into the middle of the thing, intoning with great ardor and intensity. Then suddenly there came a sharp, disconcerting *slap!* It turned out that all during the male's display, the female had been intent on a circling mosquito and had finally trapped it between the palms of her hands. The male in this case did not stalk away and display in front of a water trough; he went over to Tim's and had a flock of drinks and recited the poem to the fellas. I am sure they all told bitter stories of their own about how their displays had been interrupted by females. I am also sure that they all ended up singing "Honey, Honey, Bless Your Heart."

John Mason Brown

1900 · ——

John Mason Brown, dramatic critic, essayist, and
humorist, was born in Louisville, Kentucky, and
educated at Harvard. He is known to many radio
listeners as a book reviewer and as a witty
participant in programs devoted to current affairs
and the arts. His books present a wide range
in subject matter—from dramatic criticism
to light humor to histories of the modern
theater and the Normandy Invasion.

THE FRUIT OF ENLIGHTENMENT

WE ARE A NATION OF JOINERS. Maturity does
not release us from the fraternity or soror-
ity habit. Each city, each hamlet, up and down the land is
inhabited by more clubs than citizens. Clubs for every purpose,
all interests, all ages. Clubs practical or Pickwickian. Clubs
that lunch, sew, dine, sing, read, fish, golf, sail, play cards,
hunt, spy on birds, or, more arduous still, just sit and listen together. Clubs which overcrowd the calendar by meeting
regularly for countless causes, remembered or forgotten, but
chief among which no doubt is loneliness.

Among all the orders with which the land teems, there
are many larger but none more devoted than that happily
unorganized band of men and women whose eyes brighten
at the merest mention of Edith Hamilton. Ours (let me
proudly confess that I am, and have long been, a member)

is a small club, far smaller than it should be. Even so, it has its virtues.

We do not meet except by chance, and then conversationally, in the most unlikely places. We pay no dues. We have no officers, no committees, and no known list of members. No good works are required of us since Miss Hamilton has performed them for us by writing them. Our membership is self-elected and open to all. We discriminate only against those undiscriminating enough not to have read Edith Hamilton's books. Upon such mortals we squander our pity. We realize they have been discriminating against themselves.

Let a reader of *The Greek Way*, for example, encounter anywhere, at any time, a person hitherto unmet, and let one of them admit his admiration for it, however casually, and, more than ceasing to be strangers, the two are certain to become friends. Why not? Between them there is a bond; a union of tastes; a confession of shared ideals. They sense this instantly and rejoice in it.

Whereupon, without more ado, they generally proceed to hold a typical meeting of an Edith Hamilton club. Her name is the only sorority pin, fraternal grip, or party card necessary. It can fall like a gavel on the oddest assembly, calling it to order at least in a distant corner of a noisy room. I know whereof I write. I have taken part in far too many such impromptu sessions in one American town after another not to discover how binding a fraternity the Hamiltonians are.

The reasons for this, though compelling, are simple enough. Moreover, they are again made clear in *Witness to the Truth*, Miss Hamilton's latest book, a study of Christ and His interpreters, completed in her eighty-first year. If what follows is more in the nature of a club bulletin (printed for once) than a review, it is not only because the announcement of a new volume by Miss Hamilton is good news. It is also because I, as a mere believer in Christ and no theologian, have neither the equipment nor the inclination to criticize *Witness to the Truth*. I am content to stammer my gratitude for the illumination it has brought me, the pleasure it has given me, and the qualities it possesses which are very much its author's and hers alone.

In any period Edith Hamilton would be exceptional; in ours she is unique. At all times those people are few and far between who can—indeed, who must—be described as having nobility of mind and spirit. It is to this slim fellowship that Miss Hamilton belongs. She is as uncorrupted by the vulgarities of the present as she is undowned by its pressures. The Acropolis does not soar with greater grandeur above Athens than she does above most of her contemporaries.

She is a popularizer but no vulgarizer; a liaison officer between the finest that has been and the finest that is. She speaks to the layman without condescension or cajolery. Her style is Doric in its simplicity, its strength, its beauty. Neither the curse of classroom dullness nor the arid snobbery of many of culture's rarefied custodians is hers. Although a scholar, she is not a pedant. She writes from the heart as well as the head. Her learning and her living are linked. Large as is her erudition, her wisdom is larger. The elevation of her thinking is equaled only by the altitude of her spirit.

In many respects she is one of the last Greeks of the Great Age. Their calm, their reason, their realism, their pure sense of perfection, their genius for brevity, their concern with the imponderables—all these are hers. This is why among the countless ambassadors sent out by the ancient Athenians, few have served Athens more persuasively than she. But Miss Hamilton is more than an emissary from one nation. She is a citizen of two worlds—the antique and the modern—and is equally at home with the best of both.

Contemporary education has to a large extent plowed under the classic past. More than being dead, Latin and Greek have become buried languages. Our educators have seen to that. They have wanted to make education "popular" and sought to have it practical. The classics may have been all right as tag-furnishers for English gentlemen of a vanished age. But not for Americans. Not today, at any rate. Not in this age of science and mass production. Ask the Chamber of Commerce. Ask the Rotary Club. Ask the student or his parents. It's too hard trying to keep up with our own appalling times to bother about the remote past.

Did a knowledge of Xenophon or Juvenal ever turn a soda-jerker into a tycoon? The point of modern education in America is usefulness, not culture. If it aids in gaining profitable employment, it can skip interior richness. The results must be of an immediate cash-and-carry kind. Moreover, everything must be made as easy as possible. The motto of the so-called progressives is, apparently, spare the whim and spoil the child. Hence no brambles along the path. No disciplined marching. No steep cliffs to climb. Just a level and fairly straight highway (macadamed, of course) leading to a job.

Fortunately, Miss Hamilton is one of those (they are not too numerous any more) for whom the classic past is not dead. It lives for her even as she makes it live for us. Her pages are constant reminders to us—the ignorant—of both the delights and the nourishment which indulgent, insufficient schooling has denied us. We thank her the more for the kindness of her sharing because of the unkindness done us in our youth in kindness's name.

A mind—a real mind—is as uncommon among women as it is among men. Miss Hamilton's intellect is of a high and muscular variety. Obviously it is not the product of an education made easy for little minds by lazy, timid, or untutored teachers.

The best—the enduring, indisputable best—is Miss Hamilton's concern. Greatness neither frightens her nor embarrasses her. She runs to it rather than away from it. With it she is as much at home as most of us are with the topical, the third-rate, or trash. Culture for her is no pretension. It is, as it should be among educated people, the assumption of her living. If (between detective stories) she feeds on the classics; if she turns to Pindar, the great Greek tragedians, Aristophanes, Cicero, Horace, or the Gospels as readily as most of us turn to today's best sellers, it is because she enjoys them. The pleasure they give her is undimmed by any sense of duty.

Miss Hamilton related in *The Greek Way* how, more than fifty-five years ago when she was the first woman student at a German university, she once heard a famous scholar lecture. He was talking about the passage in which the ghosts will not speak to Odysseus until he has given them blood to drink. At this point the professor added, "So, too, the dear ghosts of that departed world will not speak to us unless we give them of our heart's blood." This is what Miss Hamilton has done unstintingly. It explains, at least in part, why they have spoken to her and she has been able to speak ably for them.

When she began reading Greek, I do not know. But in *The Roman Way* Miss Hamilton tells us she has read Latin ever since her father, "who knew nothing about methods for softening the rigors of study," started her at seven on *Six Weeks' Preparation for Caesar*. Since then she has continued to read Latin for pleasure. She reads it precisely as she would read German or French. Or, for that matter, English. Furthermore, she has the gift to make her pleasure contagious.

Although Miss Hamilton is now eighty, and young, she is in her twenties as a writer. She did not turn author until about 1927 after she had completed a full and successful career as headmistress of the Bryn Mawr School. From this delayed start, her writing gains immensely. Unlike most Americans, she does not turn out books smelling as much of hasty homework as a newly decorated apartment smells of paint. She writes from a full reservoir. Her subject is part of her, she of it. This is the explanation of her mellowness, her serenity, her ease, and her authority.

Although she wrote illuminatingly about the Romans in *The Roman Way* (and with particular charm about Horace), she could not hide her dislike of Imperial Rome. Her real love has always been the Greeks. Her *Mythology*, so much better than Bulfinch's, makes this clear. So does her *Three Greek Plays*, translations which are wonderfully free of the Swinburnian flourishes of Gilbert Murray. So, above all, does *The Greek Way* (now amplified into *The Great Age of Greek Literature* and soon to be included on the Penguin list) which is her finest work.

But the Bible has also held its fascinations for Miss Hamilton. Although she grappled valiantly with a difficult subject in *The Prophets of Israel*, any reader of that book was bound to suspect her major interest was the New Testament. *Witness to the Truth* indicates that these suspicions were not groundless. It stands in the same relationship to *The Prophets of Israel* as *The Greek Way* does to *The Roman Way*.

In her admirable essay on tragedy in *The Greek Way*, Miss Hamilton pointed out, "It is not given to all to suffer alike. We differ in nothing more than in our power to feel. There are souls of little and of great degree, and upon that degree the dignity and significance of each life depend. . . . To [tragedy's] realm those alone are admitted who belong to the only true aristocracy, that of passionate souls. Tragedy's one essential is a soul that can feel greatly."

Since Miss Hamilton belongs beyond question to that aristocracy of her own memorable definition, it is not surprising that she writes with wisdom, insight, and beauty about Jesus. Like T. R. Glover before her, she performs a service few clergymen succeed in performing, and preaches a far better sermon than can be heard in most churches in a decade of Sundays.

Miss Hamilton places Christ's agony against the background of Socrates's trial and death. She tells the absorbing story of how the Gospels came to be written. She brings all her scholarship, her realism, and her rare human and literary insight to distinguishing between the styles and minds of each of the four writers. She is masterly in her sketch of St. Paul, and at her noblest in dealing with Christ.

The fine thing about *Witness to the Truth* is that in it Miss Hamilton sees beyond ritual, theology, and the temporal church into what was the great, simple challenge of Christ and His teaching. The tragedy of the world, as she points out with eloquence, is how far it has gone from Christ in spite of Christianity. She knows that Christ and Christianity all too often have little in common.

What the ministers and the theologians will think of *Witness to the Truth*, I cannot guess and do not greatly care. I can only confess that it taught me, a professed and believing

Christian, countless things I did not know and had neither suspected nor thought about. I put it down the wiser, the more awakened, the more curious, and the firmer in faith. I put it down, too, once again understanding why it is that eyes brighten and strangers become friends at the merest mention of Edith Hamilton's name.

E. B. White
1899 · ——

Elwyn Brooks White has achieved first rank as a writer of essays and light verse. His brilliant, short essays in The New Yorker *and in* Harper's Magazine *have set a new standard for excellence comparable to that established by Addison in the eighteenth century or Hazlitt in the nineteenth. His gentle satire is usually directed toward the foibles of modern American society, and his humor veils but does not obscure a deep sense of tragedy.*

WALDEN

Miss Nims, take a letter to Henry David Thoreau. Dear Henry: I thought of you the other afternoon as I was approaching Concord doing fifty on Route 62. That is a high speed at which to hold a philosopher in one's mind, but in this century we are a nimble bunch.

On one of the lawns in the outskirts of the village a woman was cutting the grass with a motorized lawn mower. What made me think of you was that the machine had rather got away from her, although she was game enough, and in the brief glimpse I had of the scene it appeared to me that the lawn was mowing the lady. She kept a tight grip on the handles, which throbbed violently with every explosion of the one-cylinder motor, and as she sheered around bushes and lurched along at a reluctant trot behind her impetuous servant, she looked like a puppy who had grabbed something that was too much for him. Concord hasn't changed much, Henry; the farm implements and the animals still have the upper hand.

I may as well admit that I was journeying to Concord with the deliberate intention of visiting your woods; for although I have never knelt at the grave of a philosopher nor placed wreaths on moldy poets, and have often gone a mile out of my way to avoid some place of historical interest, I have always wanted to see Walden Pond. The account which you left of your sojourn there is, you will be amused to learn, a document of increasing pertinence; each year it seems to gain a little headway, as the world loses ground. We may all be transcendental yet, whether we like it or not. As our common complexities increase, any tale of individual simplicity (and yours is the best written and the cockiest) acquires a new fascination; as our goods accumulate, but not our well-being, your report of an existence without material adornment takes on a certain awkward credibility.

My purpose in going to Walden Pond, like yours, was not to live cheaply or to live dearly there, but to transact some private business with the fewest obstacles. Approaching Concord, doing forty, doing forty-five, doing fifty, the steering wheel held snug in my palms, the highway held grimly in my vision, the crown of the road now serving me (on the righthand curves), now defeating me (on the lefthand curves), I began to rouse myself from the stupefaction which a day's motor journey induces. It was a delicious evening, Henry, when the whole body is one sense, and imbibes delight through every pore, if I may coin a phrase. Fields were richly brown where the harrow, drawn by the stripped Ford, had lately sunk its teeth; pastures were green; and overhead the sky had that same everlasting great look which you will find on Page 144 of the Oxford pocket edition. I could feel the road entering me, through tire, wheel, spring, and cushion; shall I have intelligence with earth too? Am I not partly leaves and vegetable mold myself?—a man of infinite horsepower, yet partly leaves.

Stay with me on 62 and it will take you into Concord. As I say, it was a delicious evening. The snake had come forth to die in a bloody S on the highway, the wheel upon its head, its bowels flat now and exposed. The turtle had come up too to cross the road and die in the attempt, its hard shell smashed under the rubber blow, its intestinal yearning (for the other side of the road) forever squashed. There was a sign by the wayside which announced that the road had a "cotton surface." You wouldn't know what that is, but neither, for that matter, did I. There is a cryptic ingredient in many of our modern improvements—we are awed and pleased without knowing quite what we are enjoying. It is something to be traveling on a road with a cotton surface.

The civilization round Concord to-day is an odd distillation of city, village, farm, and manor. The houses, yards, fields look not quite suburban, not quite rural. Under the bronze beech and the blue spruce of the departed baron grazes the milch goat of the heirs. Under the porte-cochère stands the reconditioned station wagon; under the grape arbor sit the puppies for sale. (But why do men degenerate ever? What makes families run out?)

It was June and everywhere June was publishing her immemorial stanza: in the lilacs, in the syringa, in the freshly edged paths and the sweetness of moist beloved gardens, and the little wire wickets that preserve the tulips' front. Farmers were already moving the fruits of their toil into their yards, arranging the rhubarb, the asparagus, the strictly fresh eggs on the painted stands under the little shed roofs with the patent shingles. And though it was almost a hundred years since you had taken your ax and started cutting out your home on Walden Pond, I was interested to observe that the philosophical spirit was still alive in Massachusetts: in the center of a vacant lot some boys were assembling the framework of a rude shelter, their whole mind and skill concentrated in the rather inauspicious helter-skeleton of studs and rafters. They too were escaping from town, to live naturally, in a rich blend of savagery and philosophy.

That evening, after supper at the inn, I strolled out into the twilight to dream my shapeless transcendental dreams and see that the car was locked up for the night (first open the right front door, then reach over, straining, and pull up the handles of the left rear and the left front till you hear the click, then the handle of the right rear, then shut the right front but open it again, remembering that the key is still in the ignition switch, remove the key, shut the right front again with a bang, push the tiny keyhole cover to one side, insert key, turn, and withdraw). It is what we all do, Henry. It is called locking the car. It is said to confuse thieves and keep them from making off with the laprobe. Four doors to lock behind one robe. The driver himself never uses a laprobe, the free movement of his legs being vital to the operation of the vehicle; so that when he locks the car it is a pure and unselfish act. I have in my life gained very little essential heat from laprobes, yet I have ever been at pains to lock them up.

The evening was full of sounds, some of which would have stirred your memory. The robins still love the elms of New England villages at sundown. There is enough of the thrush in them to make song inevitable at the end of day, and enough of the tramp to make them hang round the dwellings of men. A robin, like many another American, dearly loves a white house with green blinds. Concord is still full of them.

Your fellow-townsmen were stirring abroad—not many afoot, most of them in their cars; and the sound which they made in Concord at evening was a rustling and a whispering. The sound lacks steadfastness and is wholly unlike that of a train. A train, as you know who lived so near the Fitchburg line, whistles once or twice sadly and is gone, trailing a memory in smoke, soothing to ear and mind. Automobiles, skirting a village green, are like flies that have gained the inner ear—they buzz, cease, pause, start, shift, stop, halt, brake, and the whole effect is a nervous polytone curiously disturbing.

As I wandered along, the toc toc of ping pong balls drifted from an attic window. In front of the Reuben Brown house a Buick was drawn up. At the wheel, motionless, his hat upon his head, a man sat, listening to Amos and Andy on the radio (it is a drama of many scenes and without an end). The deep voice of Andrew Brown, emerging from the car, although it originated more than two hundred miles away, was unstrained by distance. When you used to sit on the shore of your pond on Sunday morning, listening to the church bells

of Acton and Concord, you were aware of the excellent filter
of the intervening atmosphere. Science has attended to that,
and sound now maintains its intensity without regard for distance. Properly sponsored, it goes on forever.

A fire engine, out for a trial spin, roared past Emerson's
house, hot with readiness for public duty. Over the barn roofs
the martins dipped and chittered. A swarthy daughter of an
asparagus grower, in culottes, shirt, and bandanna, pedalled
past on her bicycle. It was indeed a delicious evening, and I
returned to the inn (I believe it was your house once) to rock
with the old ladies on the concrete veranda.

Next morning early I started afoot for Walden, out Main
Street and down Thoreau, past the depot and the Minute-
man Chevrolet Company. The morning was fresh, and in a
bean field along the way I flushed an agriculturist, quietly
studying his beans. Thoreau Street soon joined Number 126,
an artery of the State. We number our highways nowadays,
our speed being so great we can remember little of their
quality or character and are lucky to remember their number. (Men have an indistinct notion that if they keep up this
activity long enough all will at length ride somewhere, in
next to no time.) Your pond is on 126.

I knew I must be nearing your woodland retreat when
the Golden Pheasant lunchroom came into view—Sealtest
ice cream, toasted sandwiches, hot frankfurters, waffles, tonics,
and lunches. Were I the proprietor, I should add rice, Indian
meal, and molasses—just for old time's sake. The Pheasant,
incidentally, is for sale: a chance for some nature lover who
wishes to set himself up beside a pond in the Concord atmosphere and live deliberately, fronting only the essential
facts of life on Number 126. Beyond the Pheasant was a place
called Walden Breezes, an oasis whose porch pillars were
made of old green shutters sawed into lengths. On the porch
was a distorting mirror, to give the traveler a comical image
of himself, who had miraculously learned to gaze in an ordinary glass without smiling. Behind the Breezes, in a sun-
parched clearing, dwelt your philosophical descendants in
their trailers, each trailer the size of your hut, but all grouped

together for the sake of congeniality. Trailer people leave the city, as you did, to discover solitude and in any weather, at any hour of the day or night, to improve the nick of time; but they soon collect in villages and get bogged deeper in the mud than ever. The camp behind Walden Breezes was just rousing itself to the morning. The ground was packed hard under the heel, and the sun came through the clearing to bake the soil and enlarge the wry smell of cramped housekeeping. Cushman's bakery truck had stopped to deliver an early basket of rolls. A camp dog, seeing me in the road, barked petulantly. A man emerged from one of the trailers and set forth with a bucket to draw water from some forest tap.

Leaving the highway I turned off into the woods toward the pond, which was apparent through the foliage. The floor of the forest was strewn with dried old oak leaves and *Transcripts*. From beneath the flattened popcorn wrapper (*granum explosum*) peeped the frail violet. I followed a footpath and descended to the water's edge. The pond lay clear and blue in the morning light, as you have seen it so many times. In the shallows a man's water-logged shirt undulated gently. A few flies came out to greet me and convoy me to your cove, past the No Bathing signs on which the fellows and the girls had scrawled their names. I felt strangely excited suddenly to be snooping around your premises, tiptoeing along watchfully, as though not to tread by mistake upon the intervening century. Before I got to the cove I heard something which seemed to me quite wonderful: I heard your frog, a full, clear *troonk*, guiding me, still hoarse and solemn, bridging the years as the robins had bridged them in the sweetness of the village evening. But he soon quit, and I came on a couple of young boys throwing stones at him.

Your front yard is marked by a bronze tablet set in a stone. Four small granite posts, a few feet away, show where the house was. On top of the tablet was a pair of faded blue bathing trunks with a white stripe. Back of it is a pile of stones, a sort of cairn, left by your visitors as a tribute, I suppose. It is a rather ugly little heap of stones, Henry. In fact the hillside itself seems faded, browbeaten; a few tall skinny pines, bare of lower limbs, a smattering of young maples in suitable green, some birches and oaks, and a number of trees felled by the last big wind. It was from the bole of one of these fallen pines, torn up by the roots, that I extracted the stone which I added to the cairn—a sentimental act in which I was interrupted by a small terrier from a nearby picnic group, who confronted me and wanted to know about the stone.

I sat down for a while on one of the posts of your house to listen to the bluebottles and the dragonflies. The invaded glade sprawled shabby and mean at my feet, but the flies were tuned to the old vibration. There were the remains of a fire in your ruins, but I doubt that it was yours; also two beer bottles trodden into the soil and become part of earth. A young oak had taken root in your house, and two or three ferns, unrolling like the ticklers at a banquet. The only other furnishings were a DuBarry pattern sheet, a page torn from a picture magazine, and some crusts in wax paper.

Before I quit I walked clear round the pond and found the place where you used to sit on the north-east side to get the sun in the fall, and the beach where you got sand for scrubbing your floor. On the eastern side of the pond, where the highway borders it, the State has built dressing rooms for swimmers, a float with diving towers, drinking fountains of porcelain, and rowboats for hire. The pond is in fact a State Preserve, and carries a twenty-dollar fine for picking wild flowers, a decree signed in all solemnity by your fellow-citizens Walter C. Wardwell, Erson B. Barlow, and Nathaniel I. Bowditch. There was a smell of creosote where they had been building a wide wooden stairway to the road and the parking area. Swimmers and boaters were arriving; bodies plunged vigorously into the water and emerged wet and beautiful in the bright air. As I left, a boatload of town boys were splashing about in mid-pond, kidding and fooling, the young fellows singing at the tops of their lungs in a wild chorus:

> *Amer-ica, Amer-i-ca, God shed his grace on thee,*
> *And crown thy good with brotherhood*
> *From sea to shi-ning sea!*

I walked back to town along the railroad, following your custom. The rails were expanding noisily in the hot sun, and on the slope of the roadbed the wild grape and the blackberry sent up their creepers to the track.

The expense of my brief sojourn in Concord was:

Canvas shoes	$1.95	
Baseball bat	.25	gifts to take
Left-handed fielder's glove	1.25	back to a boy
Hotel and meals	4.25	
In all	$7.70	

As you see, this amount was almost what you spent for food for eight months. I cannot defend the shoes or the expenditure for shelter and food: they reveal a meanness and grossness in my nature which you would find contemptible. The baseball equipment, however, is the kind of impediment with which you were never on even terms. You must remember that the house where you practiced the sort of economy which I respect was haunted only by mice and squirrels. You never had to cope with a shortstop.

POETRY

I WISH POETS COULD BE CLEARER," shouted my wife angrily from the next room.

Hers is a universal longing. We would all like it if the bards would make themselves plain, or we think we would. The poets, however, are not easily diverted from their high mysterious ways. A poet dares be just so clear and no clearer; he approaches lucid ground warily, like a mariner who is determined not to scrape his bottom on anything solid. A poet's pleasure is to withhold a little of his meaning, to intensify by mystification. He unzips the veil from beauty, but does not remove it. A poet utterly clear is a trifle glaring.

From ONE MAN'S MEAT by E. B. White. Copyright 1939 by E. B. White. Used by permission of the publishers, Harper & Brothers.

The subject is a fascinating one. I think poetry is the greatest of the arts. It combines music and painting and story-telling and prophecy and the dance. It is religious in tone, scientific in attitude. A true poem contains the seed of wonder; but a bad poem, egg-fashion, stinks. I think there is no such thing as a long poem. If it is long it isn't a poem; it is something else. A book like *John Brown's Body*, for instance, is not a poem—it is a series of poems tied together with cord. Poetry is intensity, and nothing is intense for long.

Some poets are naturally clearer than others. To achieve great popularity or great fame it is of some advantage to be either extremely clear (like Edgar Guest) or thoroughly opaque (like Gertrude Stein). The first poet in the land—if I may use the word poet loosely—is Edgar Guest. He is the singer who, more than any other, gives to Americans the enjoyment of rhyme and meter. Whether he gives also to any of his satisfied readers that blinding, aching emotion which I get from reading certain verses by other writers is a question which interests me very much. Being democratic, I am content to have the majority rule in everything, it would seem, but literature.

There are many types of poetical obscurity. There is the obscurity which results from the poet's being mad. This is rare. Madness in poets is as uncommon as madness in dogs. A discouraging number of reputable poets are sane beyond recall. There is also the obscurity which is the result of the poet's wishing to appear mad, even if only a little mad. This is rather common and rather dreadful. I know of nothing more distasteful than the work of a poet who has taken leave of his reason deliberately, as a commuter might of his wife.

Then there is the unintentional obscurity, or muddiness, which comes from the inability of some writers to express even a simple idea without stirring up the bottom. And there is the obscurity which results when a fairly large thought is crammed into a three- or four-foot line. The function of poetry is to concentrate; but sometimes over-concentration occurs, and there is no more comfort in such a poem than there is in the subway at the peak hour.

Sometimes a poet becomes so completely absorbed in the lyrical possibilities of certain combinations of sounds that he forgets what he started out to say, if anything, and here again a nasty tangle results. This type of obscurity is one which I have great sympathy for: I know that quite frequently in the course of delivering himself of a poem a poet will find himself in possession of a lyric bauble—a line as smooth as velvet to the ear, as pretty as a feather to the eye, yet a line definitely out of plumb with the frame of the poem. What to do with a trinket like this is always troubling to a poet, who is naturally grateful to his Muse for small favors. Usually he just drops the shining object into the body of the poem somewhere and hopes it won't look too giddy. (I sound as though I were contemptuous of poets; the fact is I am jealous of them. I would rather be one than anything.)

My quarrel with poets (who will be surprised to learn that a quarrel is going on) is not that they are unclear but that they are too diligent. Diligence in a poet is the same as dishonesty in a bookkeeper. There are rafts of bards who are writing too much, too diligently, and too slyly. Few poets are willing to wait out their pregnancy—they prefer to have a premature baby and allow it to incubate after being safely laid in Caslon Old Style.

I think Americans, perhaps more than other people, are impressed by what they don't understand, and the poets take advantage of this. Gertrude Stein has had an amazing amount of newspaper space, out of all proportion to the pleasure she has given people by her writings, it seems to me, although I am just guessing. Miss Stein is preoccupied with an experimental sort of writing which she finds diverting and exciting and which is all right by me. Her deep interest in the sound that words make is laudable; too little attention is paid by most writers to sound, and too many writers are completely tone-deaf. But on the other hand I am not ready to believe that any writer, except with dogged premeditation, would always work in so elegantly obscure and elliptical a fashion as the author of "A rose is a rose"—never in a more conventional manner. To be one hundred per cent roundabout one must be pure genius—and nobody is that good.

On the whole, I think my wife is right: the poets could be a little clearer and still not get over on to ground which is unsuitably solid. I am surprised that I have gone on this way about them. I too am cursed with diligence. I bite my pencil and stare at a marked calendar.

Index